Implementing, Managing, and Maintaining a Microsoft® Windows® Server 2003 Network Infrastructure

Exam 70-291

Implementing, Managing, and Maintaining a Microsoft® Windows® Server 2003 Network Infrastructure

Exam 70-291

First Edition

Kenneth C. Laudon, Series Designer
Kenneth Rosenblatt
Richard Watson, MCSE, MCSA

The Azimuth Interactive MCSE/MCSA Team

Carol G. Traver, Series Editor
Robin L. Pickering
Russell Polo
David Langley
Brian Hill, MCSE, MCSA
Stacey McBrine, MCSE, MCSA
Brien Posey, MCSE
Russell Jones, MCSE
Tim Oliwiak, MCSE, MCT
Simon Sykes-Wright, MCSE
Nigel Kay, MCSE
David Lundell, MCSE, MCT
L. Ward Ulmer, MCSE, MCT
Wale Soyinka, MCP
David W. Tschanz, MCSE

PEARSON
Prentice
Hall

Upper Saddle River, New Jersey, 07458

Senior Vice President/Publisher: Natalie Anderson
Executive Editor Certification: Steven Elliot
Senior Marketing Manager Certification: Steven Rutberg
Marketing Assistant: Barrie Reinhold
Associate Director IT Product Development: Melonie Salvati
Project Manager, Editorial: Laura Burgess
Editorial Assistant: Jasmine Slowick
Editorial Assistant: Jodi Bolognese
Media Project Manager: Joan Waxman
Senior Managing Editor: Gail Steier de Acevedo
Senior Project Manager, Production: Tim Tate
Manufacturing Buyer: Jessica Rivchin
Art Director: Pat Smythe
Design Manager: Maria Lange
Interior Design: Kim Buckley
Cover Designer: Pat Smythe
Cover Photo: Joseph DeSciose/Aurora Photos
Associate Director, Multimedia: Karen Goldsmith
Manager, Multimedia: Christy Mahon
Full Service Composition: Azimuth Interactive, Inc.
Quality Assurance: Digital Content Factory Ltd.
Printer/Binder: Courier Companies, Inc., Kendallville
Cover Printer: Phoenix Color Corporation

Credits and acknowledgments borrowed from other sources and reproduced, with permission, in this textbook appear on appropriate page within text.

Microsoft® and Windows® are registered trademarks of the Microsoft Corporation in the U.S.A. and other countries. Screen shots and icons reprinted with permission from the Microsoft Corporation. This book is not sponsored or endorsed by or affiliated with the Microsoft Corporation.

10 9 8 7 6 5 4 3 2 1
0-13-145600-8

*To our families,
for their love, patience,
and inspiration.*

Brief Contents

Contents

Welcome to the Prentice Hall Certification Series!

You are about to begin an exciting journey of learning and career skills building that will provide you with access to careers such as Network Administrator, Systems Engineer, Technical Support Engineer, Network Analyst, and Technical Consultant. What you learn in the Prentice Hall Certification Series will provide you with a strong set of networking skills and knowledge that you can use throughout your career as the Microsoft Windows operating system continues to evolve, as new information technology devices appear, and as business applications of computers continues to expand. The Prentice Hall Certification Series aims to provide you with the skills and knowledge that will endure, prepare you for your future career, and make the process of learning fun and enjoyable.

Microsoft Windows and the Networked World

We live in a computer-networked world—more so than many of us realize. The Internet, the world's largest network, now has more than 500 million people who connect to it through an estimated 171 million Internet hosts. The number of local area networks associated with these 171 million Internet hosts is not known. Arguably, the population of local area networks is in the millions. About 60% of local area networks in the United States are using a Windows network operating system. The other networks use Novell or some version of UNIX NetWare (Internet Software Consortium, 2003). About 95% of the one billion personal computers in the world use some form of Microsoft operating system, typically some version of Windows. A growing number of handheld personal digital assistants (PDAs) also use versions of the Microsoft operating system called Microsoft CE. Most businesses—large and small—use some kind of client/server local area network to connect their employees to one another, and to the Internet. In the United States, the vast majority of these business networks use a Microsoft network operating system—either an earlier version such as Windows NT or Windows 2000, or the current version, Windows Server 2003.

The Prentice Hall Certification Series prepares you to participate in this computer-networked world and, specifically, for the world of Microsoft Windows 2000 and XP Professional client operating systems, as well as Windows 2000 Server and Server 2003 operating systems.

Prentice Hall Certification Series Objectives

The first objective of the Prentice Hall Certification Series is to help you build a set of skills and a knowledge base that will prepare you for a career in the networking field. There is no doubt that in the next five years, Microsoft will issue several new versions of its network operating system, and new versions of Windows client operating system. In the next five years—and thereafter—there will be a steady stream of new digital devices that will require connecting to networks. Most of what you learn in the Prentice Hall Certification Series will provide a strong foundation for understanding future versions of the operating system.

The second objective of the Prentice Hall Certification Series is to prepare you to pass the MCSE/MCSA certification exams and to receive certification. Why get certified? As businesses increasingly rely on Microsoft networks to operate, employers want to make sure their networking staff has the skills needed to plan for, install, and operate these networks. While job experience is an important source of networking knowledge, employers increasingly rely on certification examinations to ensure their staff has the necessary skills. The MCSE/MCSA curriculum provides networking professionals with a well-balanced and comprehensive body of knowledge necessary to operate and administer Microsoft networks in a business setting.

There is clear evidence that having the MCSE/MCSA certification results in higher salaries and faster promotions for individual employees. Therefore, it is definitely in your interest to obtain certification, even if you have considerable job experience. If you are just starting out in the world of networking, certification can be very important for landing that first job.

The Prentice Hall Series teaches you real-world, job-related skills. About 90% of the work performed by MCSE/MCSAs falls into the following categories, according to a survey researcher (McKillip, 1999):

■ Analyzing the business requirements for a proposed system architecture.
■ Designing system architecture solutions that meet business requirements.

- Deploying, installing, and configuring the components of the system architecture.
- Managing the components of the system architecture on an ongoing basis.
- Monitoring and optimizing the components of the system architecture.
- Diagnosing and troubleshooting problems regarding the components of the system architecture.

These are precisely the skills we had in mind when we wrote this Series. As you work through the hands-on instructions in the text, perform the instructions in the simulated Windows environment on the CD-ROM, and complete the problem solving cases in the book, you will notice our emphasis on analyzing, designing, diagnosing, and implementing the Windows software. By completing the Prentice Hall Certification Series, you will be laying the foundation for a long-term career based on your specialized knowledge of networks and general problem solving skills.

Preparing you for a career involves more than satisfying the official MCSE/MCSA objectives. As you can see from the list of activities performed by MCSE/MCSAs, you will also need a strong set of management skills. The Prentice Hall Certification Series emphasizes management skills along with networking skills. As you advance in your career, you will be expected to participate in and lead teams of networking professionals in their efforts to support the needs of your organization. You will be expected to describe, plan, administer, and maintain computer networks, and to write about networks and give presentations to other business professionals. We make a particular point in this Series of developing managerial skills such as analyzing business requirements, writing reports, and making presentations to other members of your business team.

Who Is the Audience for This Book?

The student body for the Prentice Hall Certification Series is very diverse, and the Series is written with that in mind. For all students, regardless of background, the Series is designed to function as a *learning tool* first, and, second, as a compact reference book that can be readily accessed to refresh skills. Generally, there are two types of software books: books aimed at learning and understanding how a specific software tool works, and comprehensive reference books. This series emphasizes learning and explanation and is student-centered.

The Prentice Hall Certification Series is well suited to beginning students. Many students will just be starting out in the networking field, most in colleges and training institutes. The Series introduces these beginning students to the basic concepts of networking, operating systems, and network operating systems. We take special care in the introductory chapters of each book to provide the background skills and understanding necessary to proceed to more specific MCSE/MCSA skills. We cover many more learning objectives and skills in these introductory lessons than are specifically listed as MCSE/MCSA objectives. Throughout all Lessons, we take care to *explain why things are done*, rather than just list the steps necessary to do them. There is a vast difference between understanding how Windows works and why, versus rote memorization of procedures.

A second group of students will already have some experience working with networking systems and Windows operating systems. This group already has an understanding of the basics, but needs more systematic and in-depth coverage of MCSE/MCSA skills they lack. The Prentice Hall Certification Series is organized so that these more experienced students can quickly discover what they do not know, and can skip over introductory Lessons quickly. Nevertheless, this group will appreciate the emphasis on explanation and clear illustration that we emphasize throughout.

A third group of students will have considerable experience with previous Microsoft operating systems such as Windows NT. These students may be seeking to upgrade their skills and prepare for the Windows 2000/XP/2003 MCSE/MCSA examinations. They may be learning outside of formal training programs as self-paced learners, or in distance learning programs sponsored by their employers. The Prentice Hall Certification Series is designed to help these students quickly identify the new features of new versions of Windows, and to rapidly update their existing skills.

Prentice Hall Series Skills and MCSE/MCSA Objectives

In designing and writing the Prentice Hall Certification Series, we had a choice between organizing the book into lessons composed of MCSE/MCSA domains and objectives, or organizing the book into lessons composed of skills needed to pass the MCSE/MCSA certification examinations (a complete listing of the domains and objectives for the relevant exam will be found inside the front and back covers of the book). We chose to organize the book around skills, beginning with introductory basic skills, and building to more advanced skills. We believe this is a more orderly and effective way to teach students the MCSE/MCSA subject matter and the basic understanding of Windows network operating systems.

Yet we also wanted to make clear exactly how the skills related to the published MCSE/MCSA objectives. In the Prentice Hall Series, skills are organized into Lessons. At the beginning of each Lesson, there is an introduction to the set of skills covered in the Lesson, followed by a table that shows how the skills taught in the Lesson support specific MCSE/MCSA objectives. All MCSE/MCSA objectives for each of the examinations are covered; at the beginning of each skill discussion, the exact MCSE/MCSA objective relating to that skill is identified.

We also recognize that as students approach the certification examinations, they will want learning and preparation materials that are specifically focused on the examinations. Therefore, we have designed the MCSE/MCSA Interactive Series (on CD ROM) to follow the MCSE/MCSA domains and objectives more directly. Students can use these tools to practice answering MCSE/MCSA examination questions, and practice implementing these objectives in a realistic simulated Windows environment.

What's Different About the Prentice Hall Series—Main Features and Components

The Prentice Hall Certification Series has three distinguishing features that make it the most effective MCSE/MCSA learning tool available today. These three features are a graphical illustrated 2-page spread approach, a skills-based systematic approach to learning MCSE/MCSA, and an interactive *multi-channel pedagogy*.

Graphical illustrated approach. First, the Prentice Hall Series uses a graphical, illustrated approach in a convenient *two-page spread format* (see illustration below). This makes learning easy, effective and enjoyable.

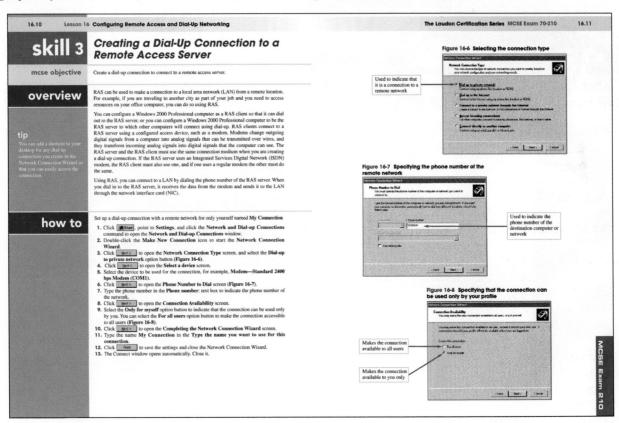

Each two-page spread is devoted to a single skill. On the left-hand side of the two-page spread, you will find a conceptual overview explaining what the skill is, why it is important, and how it is used. Immediately following the conceptual overview is a series of *How To Steps* showing how to execute the skill. On the right hand side of the two-page spread are screen shots that show you exactly how the screen should look as you execute the skills. The pedagogy is easy to follow and understand.

In addition to these main features, each two-page spread contains several *learning aids*:

- *More:* a brief section that explains more about how to use the skill, alternative ways to perform the skill, and common business applications of the skill.
- *Tips:* hints and suggestions to follow when performing the skill placed in the left margin.
- *Caution:* brief sections that tell you about the pitfalls and problems you may encounter when performing the skill placed in the left margin.

At the end of each Lesson, students can test and practice their skills using three End-of-Lesson features:

- *Test Yourself:* a multiple-choice examination that tests your comprehension and retention of the material in the Lesson.
- *Projects: On Your Own:* short projects that test your ability to perform tasks and skills in Windows without detailed step-by-step instructions.
- *Problem Solving Scenarios:* real-world business scenarios to help you analyze or diagnose a networking situation. The case generally requires you to write a report or prepare a presentation.

Skills-based systematic approach. A second distinguishing feature of the Prentice Hall Series is a *skills-based* systematic approach to MCSE/MCSA certification by using five integrated components:

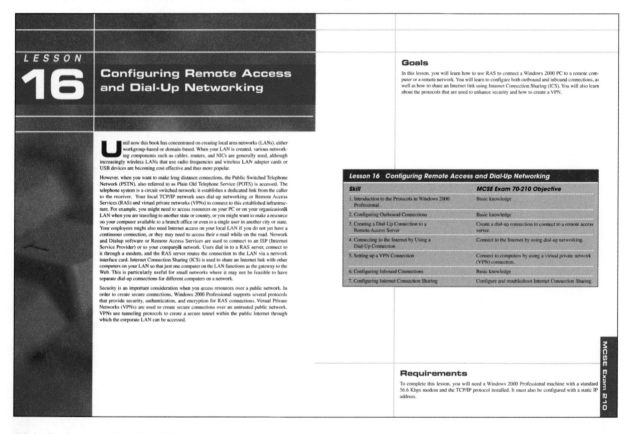

- Main Book—organized by skills.
- Project Lab Manual—for practicing skills in realistic settings.
- Examination Guide—organized by MCSE/MCSA domains and objectives to practice answering questions representative of questions you are likely to encounter in the actual MCSE/MCSA examination.
- Interactive multimedia CD ROM—organized by MCSE/MCSA domains and objectives—that allows students to practice performing MCSE/MCSA objectives in a simulated Windows environment.
- Powerful Website—provides additional questions, projects, and interactive training.

Within each component, the learning is organized by skills, beginning with the relatively simple skills and progressing rapidly through the more complex skills. Each skill is carefully explained in a series of steps and conceptual overviews describing why the skill is important.

The CD-ROM is especially useful to students who do not have access to a Windows network on which they can practice skills. It also is useful to all students who want to practice MCSE/MCSA skills efficiently without disturbing an existing network. Together, these five components make the Prentice Hall Certification Series an effective learning tool for students, increasing the speed of comprehension and the retention of knowledge.

Interactive media multi-channel learning. A third distinguishing feature of the Prentice Hall Certification Series is interactive media *multi-channel* learning. Multi-channel learning recognizes that students learn in different ways, and the more different channels used to teach students, the greater the comprehension and retention. Using the MCSE/MCSA Interactive Solutions CD-ROM, students can see, hear, read, and actually perform the skills needed in a simulated Windows environment on the CD-ROM. The CD-ROM is based directly on materials in the books, and therefore shares the same high quality and reliability. The CD-ROM and Website for the book provide high levels of real interactive learning—not just rote exam questions—and offer realistic opportunities to interact with the Windows operating system to practice skills in the software environment without having to install a new version of Windows or build a network.

Supplements Available for This Series:

1. Test Bank

The Test Bank is a Word document distributed with the Instructor's Manual (usually on a CD). It is distributed on the Internet to Instructors only. The purpose of the Test Bank is to provide instructors and students with a convenient way for testing comprehension of material presented in the book. The Test Bank contains forty multiple-choice questions and ten true/false questions per Lesson. The questions are based on material presented in the book and are not generic MCSE questions.

2. Instructor's Manual

The Instructor's Manual (IM) is a Word document (distributed to Instructors only) that provides instructional tips, answers to the Test Yourself questions and the Problem Solving Scenarios. The IM also includes an introduction to each Lesson, teaching objectives, and teaching suggestions.

3. PowerPoint Slides

The PowerPoint slides contain images of all the conceptual figures and screenshots in each book. The purpose of the slides is to provide the instructor with a convenient means of reviewing the content of the book in the classroom setting.

4. Companion Website

The Companion Website is a Pearson learning tool that provides students and instructors with online support. On the Prentice Hall Certification Series Companion Website, you will find the Interactive Study Guide, a Web-based interactive quiz composed of fifteen or more questions per Lesson. Written by the authors, there are more than 255 free interactive questions on the Companion Website. The purpose of the Interactive Study Guide is to provide students with a convenient online mechanism for self-testing their comprehension of the book material.

About This Book

Exam 70-291 Implementing, Managing, and Maintaining a Microsoft Windows Server 2003 Network Infrastructure

This book covers the subject matter of Microsoft's Exam 70-291. The focus in this book is on Windows Server 2003. You will learn about a variety of administrative tools that are used to implement, manage, and maintain the Windows Server 2003 operating system, such as the Microsoft Management Console, Control Panel, and the Registry. You will learn about network protocols, especially TCP/IP (Transmission Control Protocol/Internet Protocol). You will also learn to implement the Domain Name System (DNS), which is the hierarchical name service used on the Internet and by Microsoft's network operating system.

The following knowledge domains are discussed in this book:

- Implementing, Managing, and Maintaining IP Addressing.
- Implementing, Managing, and Maintaining Name Resolution.
- Implementing, Managing, and Maintaining Network Security.
- Implementing, Managing, and Maintaining Routing and Remote Access.
- Maintaining a Network Infrastructure.

How This Book Is Organized

This book is organized into a series of Lessons. Each Lesson focuses on a set of skills you will need to learn in order to master the knowledge domains required by the MCSE/MCSA examinations. The skills are organized in a logical progression from basic knowledge skills to more specific skills. Some skills—usually at the beginning of Lessons—give you the background knowledge you will need in order to understand basic operating system and networking concepts. Most skills, however, give you hands-on experience working with Windows Server 2003 and, in some cases, Windows 2000 Server and Windows XP Professional. You will follow step-by-step instructions to perform tasks using the software.

At the beginning of each Lesson, you will find a table that links the skills covered to specific exam objectives. For each skill presented on a 2-page spread, the MCSE/MCSA objective is listed.

The MCSE/MCSA Certification

The MCSE/MCSA certification is one of the most recognized certifications in the Information Technology world. By following a clear-cut strategy of preparation, you will be able to pass the certification exams. The first thing to remember is that there are no quick and easy routes to certification. No one can guarantee you will receive a certification—no matter what they promise. Real-world MCSE/MCSAs get certified by following a strategy involving self-study, on-the-job experience, and classroom learning, either in colleges or training institutes. Below are answers to frequently asked questions that should help you prepare for the certification exams.

What Is the MCP Program?

The MCP program refers to the Microsoft Certified Professional program that certifies individuals who have passed Microsoft certification examinations. Certification is desirable for both individuals and organizations. For individuals, an MCP certification signifies to employers your expertise and skills in implementing Microsoft software in organizations. For employers, MCP certification makes it easy to identify potential employees with the requisite skills to develop and administer Microsoft tools. In a recent survey reported by Microsoft, 89% of hiring managers said they recommend a Microsoft MCP certification for candidates seeking IT positions.

What Are the MCP Certifications?

Today there are seven different MCP certifications. Some certifications emphasize administrative as well as technical skills, while other certifications focus more on technical skills in developing software applications. Below is a listing of the MCP certifications. The Prentice Hall Certification Series focuses on the first two certifications.

- *MCSA:* Microsoft Certified Systems Administrators (MCSAs) administer network and systems environments based on the Microsoft Windows® platforms.
- *MCSE:* Microsoft Certified Systems Engineers (MCSEs) analyze business requirements to design and implement an infrastructure solution based on the Windows platform and Microsoft Server software.
- *MCDBA:* Microsoft Certified Database Administrators (MCDBAs) design, implement, and administer Microsoft SQL Server™ databases.
- *MCT:* Microsoft Certified Trainers (MCTs) are qualified instructors, certified by Microsoft, who deliver Microsoft training courses to IT professionals and developers.
- *MCAD:* Microsoft Certified Application Developers (MCADs) use Microsoft technologies to develop and maintain department-level applications, components, Web or desktop clients, or back-end data services.
- *MCSD:* Microsoft Certified Solution Developers (MCSDs) design and develop leading-edge enterprise-class applications with Microsoft development tools, technologies, platforms, and the Windows architecture.
- *Microsoft Office Specialist:* Microsoft Office Specialists (Office Specialists) are globally recognized for demonstrating advanced skills with Microsoft desktop software.
- *MCP:* Microsoft certified Professionals

What Is the Difference between MCSA and MCSE Certification?

There are two certifications that focus on the implementation and administration of the Microsoft operating systems and networking tools: MCSA and MCSE. The MCSA credential is designed to train IT professionals who are concerned with the management, support, and troubleshooting of existing systems and networks (see diagram below).

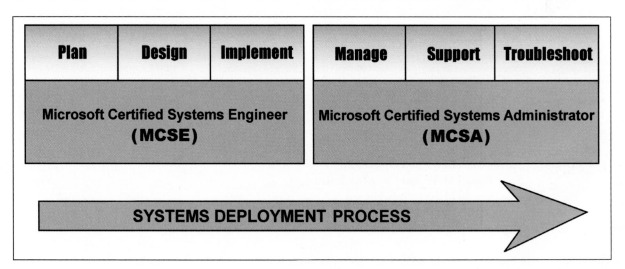

MCSA prepares you for jobs with titles such as Systems Administrator, Network Administrator, Information Systems Administrator, Network Operations Analyst, Network Technician, or Technical Support Specialist. Microsoft recommends that you have six to twelve months experience managing and supporting desktops, servers, and networks in an existing network infrastructure.

The MCSE certification is designed to train IT professionals who are concerned with the planning, designing, and implementation of new systems or major upgrades of existing systems. MCSE prepares you for jobs with titles such as Systems Engineer, Network Engineer, Systems Analyst, Network Analyst, or Technical Consultant. Microsoft recommends that you have at least one year of experience planning, designing, and implementing Microsoft products.

What Does the MCSA on Windows Server 2003 Require?

MCSA candidates are required to pass a total of four exams: three core exams and one elective exam. The list below shows examinations that are included in the MCSA track.

Core Exams (3 Exams Required)

(A) Networking System (2 Exams Required)

- *Exam 70-290:* Managing and Maintaining a Microsoft Windows Server 2003 Environment
  and
- *Exam 70-291:* Implementing, Managing, and Maintaining a Microsoft Windows Server 2003 Network Infrastructure

(B) Client Operating System (1 Exam Required)

- *Exam 70-270:* Installing, Configuring, and Administering Microsoft Windows XP Professional
  or
- *Exam 70-210:* Installing, Configuring, and Administering Microsoft Windows 2000 Professional

Elective Exams (1 Exam Required)

- *Exam 70-086:* Implementing and Supporting Microsoft Systems Management Server 2.0
- *Exam 70-227:* Installing, Configuring, and Administering Microsoft Internet Security and Acceleration (ISA) Server 2000, Enterprise Edition
- *Exam 70-228:* Installing, Configuring, and Administering Microsoft SQL Server 2000 Enterprise Edition
- *Exam 70-284:* Implementing and Managing Microsoft Exchange Server 2003
- *Exam 70-299:* Implementing and Administering Security in a Microsoft Windows Server 2003 Network

As an alternative to the electives listed above, you may substitute the following Microsoft certifications for an MCSA elective:

- MCSA on Microsoft Windows 2000
- MCSE on Microsoft Windows 2000
- MCSE on Microsoft Windows NT 4.0

You may also substitute the following third-party certification combinations for an MCSA elective:

CompTIA Exams: *CompTIA A+* and *CompTIA Network+*
CompTIA A+ and *CompTIA Server+*
CompTIA Security+

What Is the MCSE Curriculum for Windows Server 2003?

MCSE candidates are required to pass a total of seven exams: six core exams and one elective exam. The list below shows the examinations that are included in the MCSE track.

Core Exams (6 Exams Required)

(A) Networking System (4 exams required)

- *Exam 70-290:* Managing and Maintaining a Microsoft Windows Server 2003 Environment
- *Exam 70-291:* Implementing, Managing, and Maintaining a Microsoft Windows Server 2003 Network Infrastructure
- *Exam 70-293:* Planning and Maintaining a Microsoft Windows Server 2003 Network Infrastructure
  and
- *Exam 70-294:* Planning, Implementing, and Maintaining a Microsoft Windows Server 2003 Active Directory Infrastructure

(B) Client Operating System (1 Exam Required)

- *Exam 70-270:* Installing, Configuring, and Administering Microsoft Windows XP Professional
  or
- *Exam 70-210:* Installing, Configuring, and Administering Microsoft Windows 2000 Professional

(C) Design (1 Exam Required)

- *Exam 70-297:* Designing a Microsoft Windows Server 2003 Active Directory and Network Infrastructure
  or
- *Exam 70-298:* Designing Security for a Microsoft Windows Server 2003 Network

Elective Exams (1 Exam Required)

- *Exam 70-086:* Implementing and Supporting Microsoft Systems Management Server 2.0
- *Exam 70-227:* Installing, Configuring, and Administering Microsoft Internet Security and Acceleration (ISA) Server 2000 Enterprise Edition
- *Exam 70-228:* Installing, Configuring, and Administering Microsoft SQL Server™ 2000 Enterprise Edition
- *Exam 70-229:* Designing and Implementing Databases with Microsoft SQL Server™ 2000 Enterprise Edition
- *Exam 70-232:* Implementing and Maintaining Highly Available Web Solutions with Microsoft Windows 2000 Server Technologies and Microsoft Application Center 2000
- *Exam 70-282:* Designing, Deploying, and Managing a Network Solution for a Small- and Medium-Sized Business
- *Exam 70-284:* Implementing and Managing Microsoft Exchange Server 2003
- *Exam 70-297:* Designing a Microsoft Windows Server 2003 Active Directory and Network Infrastructure
- *Exam 70-298:* Designing Security for a Microsoft Windows Server 2003 Network
- *Exam 70-299:* Implementing and Administering Security in a Microsoft Windows Server 2003 Network

As an alternative to the electives listed above, you may substitute the following Microsoft certifications for an MCSE elective:

- MCSA on Microsoft Windows 2000
- MCSE on Microsoft Windows 2000
- MCSE on Microsoft Windows NT 4.0

You may also substitute the following third-party certification combinations for an MCSE elective:

- *CompTIA Security+*
- Unisys UN0-101: Implementing and Supporting Microsoft Windows Server 2003 Solutions in the Data Center

What About Upgrading From a Previous Certification?

Microsoft provides upgrade paths for MCSAs and MCSEs on Windows 2000 so that they can acquire credentials on Windows Server 2003 efficiently and economically. For details on upgrade requirements, visit the following Microsoft Web pages:

http://www.microsoft.com/learning/mcp/mcsa/windows2003/
http://www.microsoft.com/learning/mcp/mcse/windows2003/

Do You Need to Pursue Certification to Benefit from This Book?

No. The Prentice Hall Certification Series is designed to prepare you for the workplace by providing you with networking knowledge and skills regardless of certification programs. While it is desirable to obtain a certification, you can certainly benefit greatly by just reading these books, practicing your skills in the simulated Windows environment found on the MCSE/MCSA Interactive Series CD ROM, and using the online interactive study guide.

What Kinds of Questions Are on the Exam?

The MCSE/MCSA exams typically involve a variety of question formats.

(a) Select-and-Place Exam Items (Drag and Drop)

A select-and-place exam item asks candidates to understand a scenario and assemble a solution (graphically on screen) by picking up screen objects and moving them to their appropriate location to assemble the solution. For instance, you might be asked to place routers, clients, and servers on a network and illustrate how they would be connected to the Internet. This type of exam item can measure architectural, design, troubleshooting, and component recognition skills more accurately than traditional exam items can, because the solution—a graphical diagram—is presented in a form that is familiar to the computer professional.

(b) Case Study-Based Multiple-Choice Exam Items

The candidate is presented with a scenario based on typical Windows installations, and then is asked to answer several multiple-choice questions. To make the questions more challenging, several correct answers may be presented, and you will be asked to choose all that are correct. The Prentice Hall Certification Series Test Yourself questions at the end of each Lesson give you experience with these kinds of questions.

(c) Simulations

Simulations test your ability to perform tasks in a simulated Windows environment. A simulation imitates the functionality and interface of Windows operating systems. The simulation usually involves a scenario in which you will be asked to perform several tasks in the simulated environment, including working with dialog boxes and entering information. The Prentice Hall Certification Series Interactive Media CD-ROM gives you experience working in a simulated Windows environment.

(d) Computer Adaptive Testing

A computer adaptive test (CAT) attempts to adapt the level of question difficulty to the knowledge of each individual examinee. An adaptive exam starts with several easy questions. If you get these right, more difficult questions are pitched. If you fail a question, the next questions will be easier. Eventually the test will discover how much you know and what you can accomplish in a Windows environment.

You can find out more about the exam questions and take sample exams at the Microsoft Website:
http://www.microsoft.com/learning/mcp/default.asp.

How Long is the Exam?

Exams have fifty to seventy questions and last anywhere from 60 minutes to 240 minutes. The variation in exam length is due to variation in the requirements for specific exams (some exams have many more requirements than others), and because the adaptive exams take much less time than traditional exams. When you register for an exam, you will be told how much time you should expect to spend at the testing center. In some cases, the exams include timed sections that can help for apportioning your time.

What Is the Testing Experience Like?

You are required to bring two forms of identification that include your signature and one photo ID (such as a driver's license or company security ID). You will be required to sign a non-disclosure agreement that obligates you not to share the contents of the exam questions with others, and you will be asked to complete a survey. The rules and procedures of the exam will be explained to you by Testing Center administrators. You will be introduced to the testing equipment and you will be offered an exam tutorial intended to familiarize you with the testing equipment. This is a good idea. You will not be allowed to communicate with other examinees or with outsiders during the exam. You should definitely turn off your cell phone when taking the exam.

How Can You Best Prepare for the Exams?

Prepare for each exam by reading this book, and then practicing your skills in a simulated environment on the CD ROM that accompanies this series. If you do not have a real network to practice on (and if you do not build a small network), the next best thing is to work with the CD ROM. Alternatively, it is very helpful to build a small Windows Server 2003 network with a couple of unused computers. You will also require experience with a real-world Windows Server 2003 network. An MCSE/MCSA candidate should, at a minimum, have at least one year of experience implementing and administering a network operating system in environments with the following characteristics: a minimum of 200 users, five supported physical locations, typical network services and applications including file and print, database, messaging, proxy server or firewall, dial-in server, desktop management, and Web hosting, and connectivity needs, including connecting individual offices and users at remote locations to the corporate network and connecting corporate networks to the Internet.

In addition, an MCSE candidate should have at least one year of experience in the following areas: implementing and administering a desktop operating system, and designing a network infrastructure.

Where Can You Take the Exams?

All MCP exams are administered by Pearson VUE and Prometric. There are 3 convenient ways to schedule your exams with Pearson VUE:
- Online: **www.pearsonvue.com/ms/**
- Toll Free in the US and Canada: call (800) TEST-REG (800-837-8734). Or, find a call center in your part of the world at: **http://www.pearsonvue.com/contact/ms/**
- In person: at your local test center. Pearson VUE has over 3,000 test centers in 130 countries. To find a test center near you, visit: **www.pearsonvue.com**

To take exams at a Prometric testing center, call Prometric at (800) 755-EXAM (755-3926). Outside the United States and Canada, contact your local Prometric Registration Center. To register online with Prometric, visit the Prometric web site, **www.prometric.com**.

How Much Does It Cost to Take the Exams?

In the United States, exams cost $125 USD per exam as of January, 2002. Certification exam prices are subject to change. In some countries/regions, additional taxes may apply. Contact your test registration center for exact pricing.

Are There Any Discounts Available to Students?

Yes. In the US and Canada, as well as other select regions around the globe, full-time students can take a subset of the MCP exams for a significantly reduced fee at Authorized Academic Testing Centers (AATCs). For details on which countries and exams are included in the program, or to schedule your discounted exam, visit **www.pearsonvue.com/aatc**.

Can You Take the Exam More Than Once?

Yes. You may retake an exam at any time if you do not pass on the first attempt. But if you do not pass the second time, you must wait fourteen days. A 14-day waiting period will be imposed for all subsequent exam retakes. If you have passed an exam, you cannot take it again.

Where Can I Get More Information about the Exams?

Microsoft Websites are a good place to start:

MCP Program (general): **http://www.microsoft.com/learning/mcp/default.asp**

MCSE Certification: **http://www.microsoft.com/learning/mcp/mcse/**

MCSA Certification: **http://www.microsoft.com/learning/mcp/mcsa/**

There are literally thousands of other Web sites with helpful information that you can identify using any Web search engine. Many commercial sites will promise instant success, and some even guarantee you will pass the exams. Be a discriminating consumer. If it was that easy to become an MCP professional, the certification would be meaningless.

Acknowledgments

A great many people have contributed to the Prentice Hall Certification Series. We want to thank Steven Elliot, our editor at Prentice Hall, for his enthusiastic appreciation of the project, his personal support for the Azimuth team, and his deep commitment to the goal of creating a powerful, accurate, and enjoyable learning tool for students. We also want to thank David Alexander of Prentice Hall for his interim leadership and advice as the project developed at Prentice Hall, and Jerome Grant for supporting the development of high-quality certification training books and CDs for colleges and universities worldwide. Finally, we want to thank Susan Hartman Sullivan of Addison Wesley for believing in this project at an early stage and for encouraging us to fulfill our dreams.

The Azimuth Interactive MCSE/MCSA team is a dedicated group of technical experts, computer scientists, networking specialists, and writers with literally decades of experience in computer networking, information technology and systems, and computer technology. We want to thank the members of the team:

Kenneth C. Laudon is the Series Designer. He is Professor of Information Systems at New York University's Stern School of Business. He has written twelve books on information systems and technologies, e-commerce, and management information systems. He has designed, installed, and fixed computer networks since 1982.

Carol G. Traver is the Senior Series Editor. She is General Counsel and Vice President of Business Development at Azimuth Interactive, Inc. A graduate of Yale Law School, she has co-authored several best-selling books on information technology and e-commerce.

Kenneth Rosenblatt is a Senior Author for the Series. He is an experienced technical writer and editor who has co-authored or contributed to over two dozen books on computer and software instruction. In addition, Ken has over five years experience in designing, implementing, and managing Microsoft operating systems and networks. Ken is a co-author of the Prentice Hall Certification Series Exam 70-216, Exam 70-270, and Exam 70-291 textbooks.

Robin L. Pickering is a Senior Author for the Series. She is an experienced technical writer and editor who has co-authored or contributed to over a dozen books on computers and software instruction. Robin has extensive experience as a Network Administrator and consultant for a number of small to medium-sized firms. Robin is a co-author of the Prentice Hall Certification Series Exam 70-210, Exam 70-215, and Exam 70-290 textbooks.

Russell Polo is the Technical Advisor for the Series. He holds degrees in computer science and electrical engineering. He has designed, implemented, and managed Microsoft, UNIX, and Novell networks in a number of business firms since 1995. He currently is the Network Administrator at Azimuth Interactive.

David Langley is an Editor for the Series. David is an experienced technical writer and editor who has co-authored or contributed to over ten books on computers and software instruction. In addition, he has over fifteen years experience as a college professor, five of those in computer software training.

Brian Hill is a Technical Consultant and Editor for the Series. His industry certifications include MCSE 2000 and 2003, MCSA 2000 and 2003, MCSE+I (NT 4.0), CCNP, CCDP, MCT, MCP, Net+, and A+. Brian was formerly Lead Technology Architect and a Bootcamp instructor for Techtrain, Inc. His Windows 2000 experience spans back as far as the first Beta releases. Brian is a co-author of the Prentice Hall Certification Series Exam 70-217, Exam 70-290, and Exam 70-294 textbooks. In addition to the listed authors, Brian also contributed to this book. He is the author of Lesson 9, and provided invaluable review and comments on the rest of the lessons.

L. Ward Ulmer is a former Information Technology Director with eleven years of experience. He began teaching Computer Science in 1996 and has held teaching positions at Patrick Henry Academy and Trident Technical College. He became the Department Chair of Computer Technology Orangeburg-Calhoun Technical College, his current position, in 2000. Ward's certifications include MCSE, MCSA, CCNA, MCP+I, MCT, and CCAI. Ward is a co-author of the Prentice Hall Certification Series Exam 70-217 and Exam 70-294 Project Lab Manuals.

Acknowledgments (cont'd)

Richard Watson has worked in the industry for 10 years, first as a Checkpoint Certified Security Engineer (CCSE), and then as a Lead Engineer for a local Microsoft Certified Solution Provider. Among his many other industry certifications are MCSE on Windows 2000 and NT4, Microsoft Certified Trainer (MCT), Cisco Certified Network Associate (CCNA), and IBM Professional Server Expert (PSE). Richard is currently the President of Client Server Technologies Inc., which provides network installation and support, Web site design, and training in Beaverton, Oregon. Richard is a co-author of the Prentice Hall Certification Series Exam 70-220 and Exam 70-291 textbooks.

Stacey McBrine has spent more than 18 years configuring and supporting DOS and Windows-based personal computers and local area networks, along with several other operating systems. He is certified as an MCSE for Windows NT 4.0, and was one of the first 2000 persons in the world to achieve MCSE certification for Windows 2000. He has brought his real world experience to the classroom for the last 5 years as a Microsoft Certified Trainer. He holds several other certifications for Cisco, Linux, Solaris, and Security. Stacey is a co-author of the Prentice Hall Certification Series Exam 70-293 textbook and Exam 70-270 Lab Manual.

Mark Maxwell is a Technical Consultant and Editor for the Series. He has over fifteen years of industry experience in distributed network environments including TCP/IP, fault-tolerant NFS file service, Kerberos, Wide Area Networks, and Virtual Private Networks. In addition, Mark has published articles on network design, upgrades, and security, and he is a co-author of the Prentice Hall Certification Series Exam 70-216 Lab Manual.

Dr. Russell Jones is an Associate Processor and Area Coordinator of Decision Sciences at Arkansas State University and currently holds the Kathy White Endowed Fellowship in MIS. Dr. Jones received his PhD from the University of Texas-Arlington and has been on the ASU faculty for 16 years. He holds certifications from Microsoft, Novell, CompTIA, and Cisco, and is a co-author of the Prentice Hall Certification Series Exam 70-290 Project Lab Manual.

Nigel Kay, MCSE, is a technical writer from London, Ontario, Canada. He has contributed to several published IT certification guides, and is currently the documentation lead for a network security company. Previously, he worked for many years as a Network Administrator. Nigel is a co-author of the Prentice Hall Certification Series Exam 70-293 textbook and Project Lab Manual.

David W. Tschanz, MCSE, MCP+I, A+, iNET+, CIW, is an American who has been living in Saudi Arabia for the past 15 years. There he has worked on a variety of projects related to Web-based information management, training, and applications, as well as computer security issues. He writes extensively on computer topics and is a regular contributor to MCP Magazine. David is a co-author of the Prentice Hall Certification Series Exam 70-220 Lab Manual.

Brien M. Posey, MCSE, has been a freelance technical writer who has written for Microsoft, CNET, ZDNet, Tech Target, MSD2D, Relevant Technologies, and many other technology companies. Brien has also served as the CIO for a nationwide chain of hospitals and was once in charge of IT security for Fort Knox. Most recently, Brien has received Microsoft's MVP award for his work with Windows 2000 Server and IIS. Brien is a co-author of the Prentice Hall Certification Series Exam 70-218 textbook.

Tim Oliwiak, MCSE, MCT, is a network consultant for small- to medium-sized companies. He previously was an instructor at the Institute for Computer Studies, and a Network Engineer for the Success Network. Tim is a resident of Ontario, Canada. Tim is a co-author of the Prentice Hall Certification Series Exam 70-217 Project Lab Manual.

Simon Sykes-Wright, MCSE, has been a technical consultant to a number of leading firms, including NCR Canada Ltd. Simon is a co-author of the Prentice Hall Certification Series Exam 70-293 textbook.

David Lundell is a database administrator and Web developer for The Ryland Group in Scottsdale, Arizona. He holds MCSE, MCDBA, MCSD, MCT, CAN, and CCNA certifications, as well as an MBA from the University of Arizona. David is a co-author of the Prentice Hall Certification Series Exam 70-291 Project Lab Manual.

Wale Soyinka is a systems and network engineering consultant. He holds MCP, CCNA, and CCNP certification. He is the author of a series of lab manuals on Linux, and is a co-author of the Prentice Hall Certification Series Exam 70-218 Lab Manual.

Quality Assurance

The Prentice Hall Certification Series contains literally thousands of software instructions for working with Windows products. We have taken special steps to ensure the accuracy of the statements in this series. The books and CDs are initially written by teams composed of Azimuth Interactive Inc. MCSE/MCSA professionals and writers working directly with the software as they write. Each team then collectively walks through the software instructions and screen shots to ensure accuracy. The resulting manuscripts are then thoroughly tested by an independent quality assurance team of MCSE/MCSA professionals who also perform the software instructions and check to ensure the screen shots and conceptual graphics are correct. The result is a very accurate and comprehensive learning environment for understanding Windows products.

We would like to thank the primary member of the Quality Assurance Team for his critical feedback and unstinting efforts to make sure we got it right. The primary technical editor for this book is Jim Taylor. Jim Taylor is an independent consultant with over 30 years experience in the IT industry, including over 15 years experience with the Microsoft Windows operating systems, in addition to 14 years with the AIX and other Unix-like operating systems. Jim is an instructor and a consultant on various systems and platforms, and also serves as a technical editor of books on Microsoft, Linux, and Unix-related topics.

Other Books in the Prentice Hall Certification Series

Installing, Configuring, and Administering Microsoft® Windows® 2000 Professional Exam 70-210
   ISBN 0-13-142209-X

Installing, Configuring, and Administering Microsoft® Windows® 2000 Server Exam 70-215
   ISBN 0-13-142211-1

Implementing and Administering Microsoft® Windows® 2000 Network Infrastructure Exam 70-216
   ISBN 0-13-142210-3

Implementing and Administering a Microsoft® Windows® 2000 Directory Services
   Infrastructure Exam 70-217   ISBN 0-13-142208-1

Managing a Microsoft® Windows® 2000 Network Environment Exam 70-218
   ISBN 0-13-144744-0

Designing Security for a Microsoft® Windows® 2000 Network Exam 70-220   ISBN 0-13-144906-0

Managing and Maintaining a Microsoft® Windows® Server 2003 Environment Exam 70-290
   ISBN 0-13-144743-2

Planning and Maintaining a Microsoft® Windows® Server 2003 Network Infrastructure Exam 70-293
   ISBN 0-13-189306-8

Planning, Implementing, and Maintaining a Microsoft® Windows® Server 2003 Active Directory
   Infrastructure Exam 70-294   ISBN 0-13-189312-2

Designing a Microsoft® Windows® Server 2003 Active Directory and Network Infrastructure
   Exam 70-297   ISBN 0-13-189316-5

Designing Security for a Microsoft® Windows® Server 2003 Network Exam 70-298
   ISBN 0-13-117670-6

Introducing Microsoft Windows Server 2003 Network Infrastructure

A Windows Server 2003 network offers advanced features for maintaining your data, network resources, and network services. In addition to adding new security and management features, Windows Server 2003 includes enhanced versions of features from its predecessor, Windows 2000 Server. Overall, the Windows Server 2003 family provides more flexibility, operability, and reliability of network communications than any of Microsoft's previous network operating systems.

Windows Server 2003's network infrastructure consists of computers, devices, and the services through which the computers in a network communicate with each other. Before creating a network infrastructure, you need to develop a plan to use the features of Windows Server 2003 effectively. Network planning involves four phases: analysis, design, testing, and deployment.

To facilitate communication among the computers in your Windows Server 2003 network, the following supported protocols can be used:

◆ Transmission Control Protocol/Internet Protocol (TCP/IP)
◆ NWLink
◆ AppleTalk
◆ Infrared Data Association (IrDA)

Additionally, Windows Server 2003 provides various networking services for the network. These include:

◆ Dynamic Host Configuration Protocol (DHCP)
◆ Domain Name System (DNS)
◆ Windows Internet Naming Service (WINS)
◆ Routing and Remote Access Service (RRAS)
◆ Network Address Translation (NAT)
◆ Security services, such as Encrypting File System (EFS) and Microsoft Certificate Services

Goals

In this lesson, you will be introduced to the concepts of network infrastructure, the various phases involved in deploying a network plan, and the protocols used in Windows Server 2003 networks for communication. In addition, you will learn about Windows Server 2003 network services such as DNS, DHCP, WINS, NAT, RRAS, Security services, and Microsoft Certificate Services.

Lesson 1   Introducing Microsoft Windows Server 2003 Network Infrastructure

Skill	Exam 70-291 Objective
1. Introducing Network Infrastructure	Basic knowledge
2. Identifying the Phases in Setting Up a Windows Server 2003 Network	Basic knowledge
3. Introducing Windows Server 2003 Network Protocols	Basic knowledge
4. Introducing Windows Server 2003 Network Services	Basic knowledge

Requirements

There are no special requirements for this lesson.

skill 1

Introducing Network Infrastructure

exam objective

Basic knowledge

overview

Network infrastructure refers to a set of computers and network devices that are connected to each other, and the services that facilitate communication among them.

You can classify the components of a network infrastructure as either physical or logical (**Figure 1-1**). **Physical infrastructure** includes computers, cables, network interface cards, hubs, and routers. **Logical network infrastructure** includes the following software components:

◆ **Network protocols:** Network protocols are pre-defined sets of rules used by the networking components of a system to send information over a network. In Windows Server 2003, TCP/IP is the primary protocol used for communication between computers on a network.

◆ **IP addressing schemes:** An IP addressing scheme identifies each TCP/IP host computer on a network with an IP address. Each IP address is a 32-bit number, which is commonly divided into four binary octets, expressed as their decimal equivalents and separated by dots, such as 102.54.94.97.

◆ **Name resolution services:** IP addresses provide a unique address for each node on a TCP/IP network. The numerical form of IP addresses can make them difficult to remember. Name resolution services overcome this problem by assigning names to each host, and providing a means for determining and discovering the names assigned to hosts on the network. These names act as aliases for the IP addresses and you can use them to refer to a TCP/IP host. A connection is established between a source host and a destination host only after resolving the host name to an IP address. In Windows Server 2003, you can use various methods to resolve names to IP addresses, including DNS and WINS.

◆ **Remote Access Service (RAS):** You use RAS to connect remote clients working from remote locations to a network. The connection is made using a telephone connection or other Wide Area Network (WAN) link to the RAS server. The RAS server then provides access to the resources on the network. This effectively makes the RAS client behave as though it were connected inside the network.

◆ **Routing:** Routing is used to select the optimal path for transferring a data packet between networks. This helps minimize the time and cost associated with the delivery of data. If the optimal route fails, routers will attempt to use an alternate path to the destination if one exists. Many newer routing protocols also support load balancing across several paths to the same destination.

◆ **Network Address Translation (NAT):** The Network Address Translation protocol allows multiple computers on a network to connect to the Internet through a single connection.

◆ **Security services:** If your network is accessible to anyone outside the network, the chances of intruders tampering with your data (also referred to as hacking) increase. To secure networks from hackers, Windows Server 2003 supports security features, such as Kerberos authentication, IP security, Certificate Services, and Encrypting File System (EFS).

Figure 1-1 Logical and physical network infrastructure

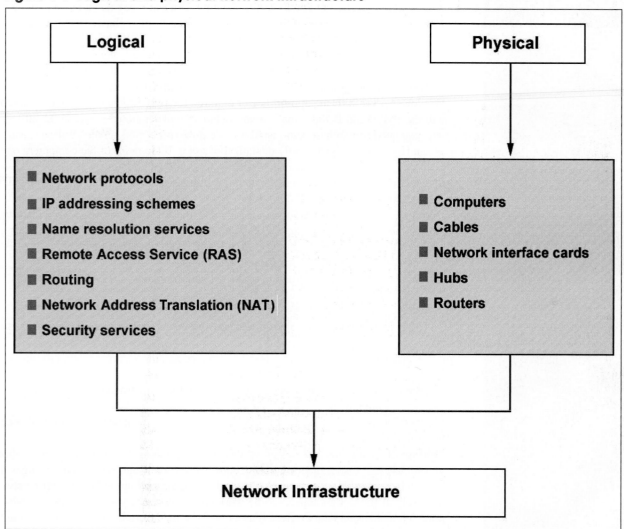

skill 2

Identifying the Phases in Setting Up a Windows Server 2003 Network

exam objective

Basic knowledge

overview

Setting up a Windows Server 2003 network infrastructure that is customized for the requirements of your organization requires careful planning. You can break down the deployment of Windows Server 2003 in an enterprise environment into five main phases (**Figure 1-2**):

◆ **Analysis:** In the analysis phase, you identify your organization's objectives in implementing a Windows Server 2003 network. In this phase, you must identify the areas of the network that need to be upgraded or modified before you deploy a Windows Server 2003 network. As you assess the network, you should determine which new features of Windows Server 2003 are appropriate or required for your implementation. For example, will the SMTP and POP3 e-mail server included with Windows Server 2003 suffice, or will you need to purchase and install a more powerful e-mail server? Will you want to assign IP addresses dynamically or statically, and to some or all of the computers on the network? Imagine how difficult it would be to assign and document IP addresses every time a client joined the network! Dynamic addressing can be implemented in Windows Server 2003 by using DHCP.

◆ **Design:** The design phase involves the planning and designing of the network infrastructure for the deployment of Windows Server 2003, based on the upgrade requirements that you identify in the analysis phase (**Figure 1-3**). The design phase involves:

    Step 1: Determining the hardware requirements.

    Step 2: Designing the structure of the network (domains, sites, WAN links, bandwidth needs, routing requirements, etc.)

    Step 3: Determining Active Directory requirements.

    Step 4: Determining the appropriate network resources and their placement in the network structure.

    Step 5: Identifying the services to be provided and the servers required to run those services.

    Step 6: Determining the need for security and the infrastructure required to implement it.

See the More section on page 1.8 for further information about tasks that you will need to perform in the design phase.

◆ **Testing:** To ensure that the design of your network meets its functional specifications, you should first test your design in a controlled environment, so that any changes that need to be made to the configuration and infrastructure will not affect the entire network adversely. If the design appears to be working successfully, you should then conduct a pilot deployment, in which selected users perform their normal business tasks using the new features. In this manner, you can reduce the risks involved in deploying a new design on your network. The phase may include:

    • Testing routing

    • Testing Windows Server 2003 services

    • Running bandwidth analyses

    • Running security tests

    • Testing applications for compatibility with Windows Server 2003.

    • Configuring client hardware.

    • Configuring client operating systems, applications, and desktop options, such as multilingual support or accessibility features for disabled users.

◆ **Deploying Windows Server 2003 on a network:** The actual deployment of Windows Server 2003 on a network should begin only after the success of the testing phase. The deployment phase involves the implementation of the Windows Server 2003 operating system on computers in the network. This could be a first-time installation if you are migrating from another platform, such as Novell NetWare, or an upgrade from earlier versions of Windows operating systems. Once you have installed Windows Server 2003

Figure 1-2 Phases in setting up a Windows Server 2003 network

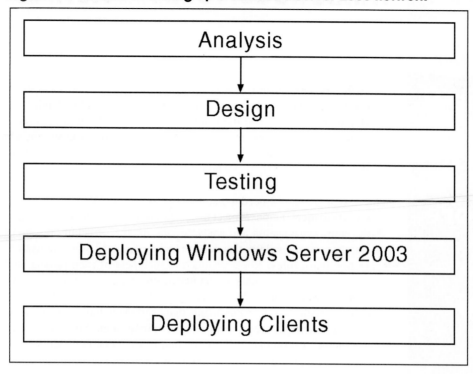

Figure 1-3 Design phase activities

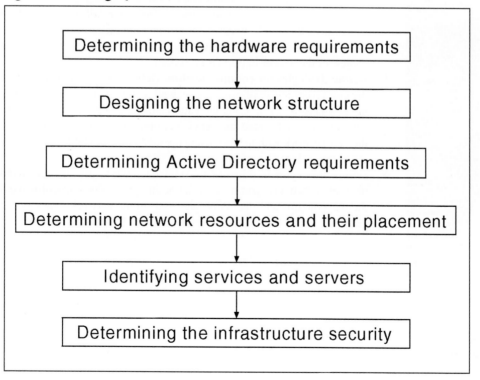

skill 2

Identifying the Phases in Setting Up a Windows Server 2003 Network *(cont'd)*

exam objective

Basic knowledge

overview

on the network, the next task is to implement the advanced management features decided upon in the planning stage to increase the reliability and scalability of your network.

◆ **Deploying clients:** The final step in setting up a Windows Server 2003 network is to allow client computers throughout your organization to access the services provided by the servers. In this phase, all problems encountered on client computers while deploying Windows Server 2003 that weren't addressed in the testing phase are resolved.

more

In the design phase, you need to perform the following tasks:

◆ **Create project teams:** Project teams will be responsible for studying the requirements of the entire organization and analyzing the internal structure, resources, users, locations, and the security policies that need to be implemented in the network.

◆ **Define team roles:** Roles assigned to members of each project team depend on their skills. Roles may include product management, program management, development, test, user experience, and release management **(Table 1-1)**. Working together, these teams come up with a set of requirements that need to be implemented in the new network.

◆ **Document the current computing environment:** Study and document the current computing environment and use the findings as input in the documentation of the design objectives for the future environment.

◆ **Document design objectives:** The objectives for the new design are based on the comparison between the current network and the future network environment, which itself is based on future project objectives. The gaps between the current and the future network environments, along with the Windows Server 2003 features that can fill the gaps, are documented for future reference.

◆ **Create a risk assessment document:** Document all of the risk factors related to the design to enable the Network Administrators to prepare for possible problems. This documentation might expose possible risks such as resource availability, merger of two companies, or the loss of important personnel.

◆ **Define strategies for communication:** Define the communications strategy for keeping the employees aware of progress, as well as for sharing information and feedback about the new network. Your communication strategies will include decisions about communication issues such as the frequency and mechanisms for sharing status of deployment of the new network with the users, and the method(s) available for users to provide feedback about the system.

◆ **Define strategies to educate users:** To be able to use the new Windows Server 2003 network effectively, you need to define the processes that will make the users aware of the technologies and methodologies used in the network. You can accomplish this task through formal training sessions and feedback from users.

Table 1-1   Team roles during design phase

Role	Goal	Focus During Planning
Product Management	Satisfied customers	• Conceptual design • Business requirements analysis • Communications plan
Program Management	Delivering the solution within project constraints	• Conceptual and logical design • Functional specification • Master project plan • Master project schedule • Budget
Development	Build to specification	• Technology evaluation • Logical and physical design • Development plan/schedule • Development estimates
Test	Ensure all product quality issues are identified and addressed	• Design evaluation • Testing requirements • Test plan/schedule
User Experience	Enhanced user effectiveness	• Usage scenarios/use cases • User requirements • Localization/accessibility requirements • User documentation/training • Plan/schedule for usability testing
Release Management	Smooth deployment and ongoing operations	• Design evaluation • Operations requirements • Pilot and deployment plan/schedule

skill 3

Introducing Windows Server 2003 Network Protocols

exam objective

Basic knowledge

overview

In a Windows Server 2003 network, computers use network protocols for communication with each other. Protocols are pre-defined rules for sending information over a network. When planning a Windows Server 2003 network, you also need to know the protocols that will be required to support the network. Windows Server 2003 supports the following protocols:

◆ **Transmission Control Protocol/Internet Protocol (TCP/IP):** TCP/IP is a set of protocols that allows computers to exchange data over a network and across networks **(Figure 1-4)**. TCP and IP are two of the many protocols commonly referred to as "TCP/IP." Applications use higher-level protocols such as TCP to send and receive data over a network. The higher-level protocols in turn call upon lower-level protocols such as IP to break up application data into packets, calculate routing information, transmit data packets across network media, receive the packets at the destination, and pass them back up to higher-level protocols. TCP is a higher-level protocol that ensures that packets that have been sent are correctly reassembled into the original messages and then passed up to the application. TCP/IP is the core set of protocols used by the Internet. TCP/IP has been implemented on nearly all platforms and is suitable for large and small networks.

◆ **NWLink:** The NWLink protocol provides connectivity between Microsoft Windows and Novell NetWare operating systems so that clients can access resources on NetWare servers. NWLink is Microsoft's 32-bit implementation of the Internetwork Packet Exchange/Sequence Packet Exchange (IPX/SPX) protocol, which is used for communication between computers in Novell NetWare networks. NWLink is the most commonly used protocol in a network environment in which Microsoft clients access client/server applications running on Novell NetWare servers and vice-versa.

◆ **AppleTalk:** AppleTalk is a protocol suite used for communication among Apple Macintosh computers. AppleTalk supports Apple's LocalTalk cabling scheme, as well as EtherTalk and TokenTalk networks, which can be assigned a network range so that the network can support more nodes. EtherTalk and TokenTalk networks can have as many as 253 nodes for every octet in the network range, for a maximum of 16.5 million nodes. AppleTalk can connect Macintosh computers and printers if they are equipped with proper hardware and software.

◆ **Infrared Data Association (IrDA):** This is a protocol designed to provide wireless line-of-sight connectivity between the infrared ports of connected devices, such as a wireless mouse or keyboard. The protocols of the IrDA suite provide services similar to those provided by TCP/IP. However, IrDA is not currently intended to provide networking connectivity on the scale that TCP/IP does. Rather, IrDA facilitates the use of short-range connectivity, such as that required by portable devices like PDAs and cell phones, as well as peripheral devices like printers and digital cameras. Using IrDA, applications on different computers can open multiple reliable connections to send and receive data simultaneously. The organization that creates, promotes, and standardizes IrDA technology is, itself, known as IrDA. IrDA supports the implementation of easy-to-use and zero-configuration wireless devices. You can visit the IrDA web site at **http://www.irda.org** to learn more about the types of products and applications that support IrDA.

Figure 1-4 TCP/IP

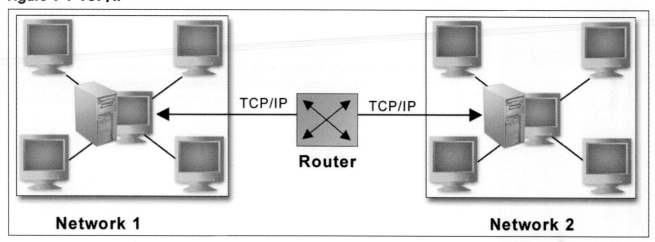

skill 3

Introducing Windows Server 2003 Network Protocols (cont'd)

exam objective

Basic knowledge

overview

◆ **Point-to-Point Tunneling Protocol (PPTP) and Layer Two Tunneling Protocol (L2TP):** PPTP is a tunneling protocol that is used to create secure connections to corporate networks over the Internet. L2TP is another tunneling protocol used to create virtual private networks (you can also use PPTP to create secure connections for VPNs). If you use L2PT, a "tunnel" will be created, but the data sent through it will not be encrypted. Therefore, you must use L2TP in conjunction with IPSec. Both of these protocols work over dial-up lines, public TCP/IP networks (the Internet), local network links, and WAN links. PPTP uses Microsoft Point-to-Point Encryption (MPPE) to provide encryption so that communications are secure.

◆ **Hypertext Transmission Protocol (HTTP):** HTTP is an Application layer protocol of TCP/IP and is used to transmit data across the Internet. When Web servers transmit Web pages to clients, HTTP compression compacts the Web pages to facilitate the transmission of the data.

All of the protocols supported by Windows Server 2003 have advantages and disadvantages. **Table 1-2** lists some of these advantages and disadvantages.

Table 1-2 Advantages and disadvantages of the protocols supported by Windows Server 2003

Protocol	Advantages	Disadvantages	Recommended Usage
TCP/IP	• Native protocol for Unix, Novell, and Windows networks • Not vendor specific • Flexible		Environments of all sizes that support Internet applications
NWLink	• Routable protocol • Easy-to-configure		Connection with NetWare resources
AppleTalk	• Inexpensive • Supports Apple's LocalTalk cabling scheme, as well as Ethernet and IBM Token Ring	Requires specific AppleTalk hardware and software	Connection with Macintosh computers and printers
IrDA	• Provides wireless, walk-up, line-of-sight connectivity between devices • Easy-to-use	• Complex to install because wireless devices require IrDA ports for networking • Line-of-sight and short range requirements can pose logistical problems	Wireless, point-to-point networking over very short distances such as in synchronizing a PDA with a PC
PPTP	• Secures connections with encryption • Works over a variety of network types		Connection to corporate networks over the Internet
L2TP	• Works over a variety of network types • Compresses message headers	Does not encrypt data	Virtual private networks

skill 4

Introducing Windows Server 2003 Network Services

exam objective

Basic knowledge

overview

Along with various protocols, Windows Server 2003 provides a number of network services to support a Windows Server 2003 network. These services facilitate address allocation, name resolution, and remote access, and also provide network security capabilities **(Figure 1-5)**. Some of the important network services available in Windows Server 2003 are described below:

◆ **Dynamic Host Configuration Protocol (DHCP):** The DHCP service runs on the network's DHCP servers. DHCP servers dynamically allocate IP addresses to DHCP-enabled clients on the network. Allocating IP addresses dynamically ensures that you assign a unique IP address to each computer and device on the network. It also eliminates the need to assign IP addresses manually, which would be time-consuming and prone to errors. Dynamic allocation is especially helpful when clients relocate to another segment of the network. DHCP provides configuration to clients running most versions of the Windows operating system. The Windows Server 2003 operating system is set to retrieve an IP address from the DHCP server by default. Automating the assignment of IP addresses to clients simplifies the administration of a network's TCP/IP configuration.

◆ **Domain Name System (DNS):** DNS is used to locate computers by host names rather than by IP addresses. The service of translating computer names to IP addresses and vice-versa is known as name resolution. With a name resolution service enacted, a user can enter the name of a target computer and establish a connection to that computer using the language that computers understand-numbers. DNS is a great improvement over the Hosts.txt file that was used in the past to store computer name-to-address mapping. Previously, an Administrator had to update the Hosts.txt file. DNS is the main name resolution service for Windows Server 2003. The distributed database used by DNS updates dynamically as hosts register and update their information. The Internet uses DNS to locate various Web servers and network hosts.

◆ **Windows Internet Naming Service (WINS):** The WINS naming service translates NetBIOS names into IP addresses so that users can locate a computer on a network. Many networks include computers running different operating systems such as Windows 95, 98, NT, and 2000. Prior to Windows 2000, NetBIOS was the default naming convention for Microsoft networks. Therefore, Microsoft networks still support the resolution of NetBIOS names to IP addresses. Many applications also rely on NetBIOS naming. When network users want to find a computer on the network using its NetBIOS name, there must be a method for assigning or mapping an IP address to the computer name. The main method is a WINS database on a WINS server, which functions as a lookup directory. The WINS database in Windows Server 2003 is updated dynamically so that, as the DHCP server assigns clients different IP addresses as they connect to different subnets, the database stays current. Without WINS, users can browse their own subnet using NetBIOS broadcasts, but they cannot establish connections to computers on other subnets unless they use the LMHOSTS file name resolution method (see Lesson 5).

◆ **Routing and Remote Access Service (RRAS):** This service connects remote or mobile workers to their organization's network so that they can work as if their computers were physically connected to the network. RRAS works with several network protocols, including TCP/IP and IPX. Workers can connect to a Local Area Network (LAN) with a modem by dialing the phone number of the RRAS server, or by using a virtual private network (VPN). The client computers connect to a RRAS server using a configured access device. When a remote client accesses a RRAS server, it receives the data from the modem or VPN and sends it to the network through a network interface card (NIC).

caution

Certain computers on your network should not be DHCP-enabled clients. For example, the DHCP server itself, DNS servers, and any other computers whose IP addresses should be static, should not be DHCP-enabled clients.

tip

NetBIOS names, unlike the DNS naming space, which is hierarchical, use a flat namespace. In flat namespaces, all of the names within the namespace should be unique.

Figure 1-5 Windows Server 2003 services

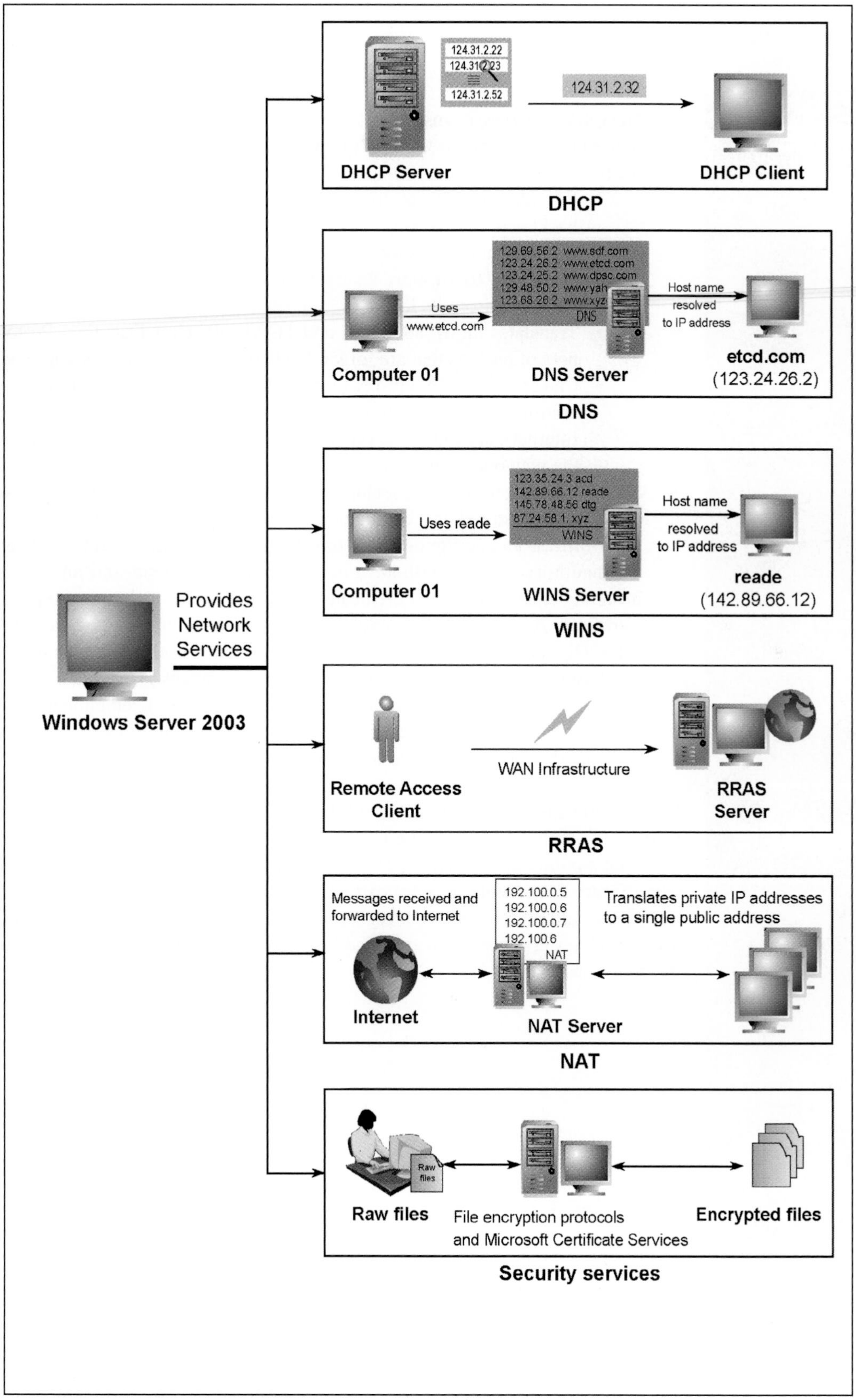

skill 4

Introducing Windows Server 2003 Network Services (cont'd)

exam objective

Basic knowledge

overview

◆ **Network Address Translation (NAT):** NAT is an Internet standard that enables a LAN to use one set of IP addresses for internal traffic and a second set of addresses for external traffic. NAT:

- Provides security by hiding internal IP addresses, making it more difficult for hackers to access them.
- Enables an organization to allocate as many intranet (internal) IP addresses as necessary to support its network clients without having to lease additional addresses from its ISP.
- Translates the IP addresses and TCP/UDP (User Datagram Protocol) port numbers of packets that are forwarded between the private network and the Internet.
- Can serve as a DNS proxy for the other computers on the network. When the NAT computer receives name resolution requests, it forwards the requests to the Internet-based DNS server for which it is configured and returns the responses to the network client.

◆ **Security services:** Provide techniques to ensure that only authorized users are able to access the data stored on a computer. Most security measures involve data encryption and passwords. Data encryption is the translation of data into a form that is unintelligible to an unauthorized user without a deciphering mechanism and an encryption key. By installing and configuring Certificate Services, Network Administrators can implement a Certificate Authority (CA) for issuing, renewing, managing, and revoking digital certificates. Digital certificates can be used to verify that a user sending a message is an authorized user, and can provide the recipient with the means to encode a reply or download a file from a Web site with assurances that the file has not been tampered with. Certificate Services contains a comprehensive public key infrastructure, a critical component in ensuring data security for services in e-commerce.

tip

You can easily administer Certificate Services using the Certification Authority snap-in in the Microsoft Management Console (MMC).

more

When a user needs to send encrypted data, the user applies for a digital certificate from a Certificate Authority (CA). The CA issues an encrypted digital certificate containing the applicant's public key, a private key, and other identification information required to access data **(Figure 1-6)**. Public Key Infrastructure (PKI) refers to the system of digital certificates, Certificate Authorities, and other registration authorities that are used to authenticate Internet users involved in transactions over the Internet. PKI is vital for ensuring security in e-commerce transactions.

Figure 1-6 Creating a Certificate

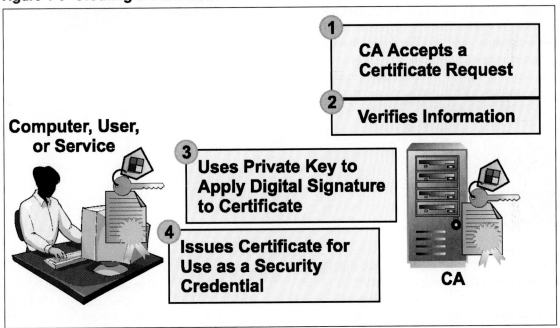

Summary

◆ Network infrastructure consists of logical infrastructure and physical infrastructure.

◆ Deployment of Windows Server 2003 in an enterprise environment can be broken down into the following phases:

- Analysis: Used to identify the areas of the network infrastructure, such as servers, routers, and network services that must be upgraded or modified before deploying Windows Server 2003.
- Design: Involves planning for and designing the network infrastructure for your deployment of Windows Server 2003.
- Testing: Involves verifying your network design before deploying it on a full-scale network.
- Windows Server 2003 deployment: Involves the installation of the Windows Server 2003 operating system on computers.
- Client deployment: Involves installation of client operating systems and configuration of client computers to access the Windows Server 2003 server.

◆ Protocols used in Windows Server 2003 include:

- Transmission Control Protocol/Internet Protocol (TCP/IP)
- NWLink
- AppleTalk
- Infrared Data Association (IrDA)
- Point-to-Point Tunneling Protocol (PPTP)
- Layer Two Tunneling Protocol (L2TP)
- Hypertext Transfer Protocol (HTTP)

◆ Network services are used to provide address allocation, naming resolution, remote access, and security capabilities in the network. Windows Server 2003 supports the following services:

- Dynamic Host Configuration Protocol (DHCP)
- Domain Name Service (DNS)
- Windows Internet Naming Service (WINS)
- Routing and Remote Access Services (RRAS)
- Network Address Translation (NAT)
- Security services, including Encrypting File System (EFS) and Microsoft Certificate Services

Key Terms

AppleTalk
Domain Name Service (DNS)
Dynamic Host Configuration Protocol (DHCP)
Infrared Data Association (IrDA)
Layer Two Tunneling Protocol (L2TP)
Logical infrastructure
Microsoft Certificate Services

Network Address Translation (NAT)
Network infrastructure
NWLink
Physical infrastructure
Point-to-Point Tunneling Protocol (PPTP)
Protocol

Routing and Remote Access Services (RRAS)
Transmission Control Protocol/ Internet Protocol (TCP/IP)
Virtual Private Network (VPN)
Windows Internet Naming Service (WINS)

Test Yourself

1. Which of the following are components of the logical infrastructure of a network? (Choose all that apply.)
a. Security services
b. Computers
c. Routers
d. Protocols
e. Name resolution services

2. The protocol preferred for communication between computers on a routed network is:
a. TCP/IP
b. NWLink

c. IrDA
d. AppleTalk

3. NWLink is: (Choose all that apply.)
a. Used to provide connectivity with Macintosh computers and printers.
b. A 32-bit implementation of the Microsoft-compatible IPX/SPX protocol.
c. A protocol suite that provides wireless connectivity between devices.
d. A non-routable protocol.
e. Used to provide connectivity only with Novell networks.

4. The server deployment phase of setting up a Windows Server 2003 network involves:
   a. Verifying the infrastructure design implementation of the network before deploying it on a full-scale network.
   b. Installation of the Windows Server 2003 operating system on computers.
   c. Allowing client computers throughout your organization to access Windows Server 2003 features.
   d. Planning the implementation of Active Directory for deployment.

5. In the _____ phase of planning a Windows Server 2003 network, you check for hardware and software requirements, network infrastructure, and file, print, and Web servers in your current network environment.
   a. Analysis
   b. Testing
   c. Deploying clients
   d. Design

6. The graphic artists at your company have recently received large, flat-panel monitors, which they would like to hang on their office walls in front of drafting tables. They would like to keep their computers at their desks with their standard input and output hardware (mouse, keyboard, standard monitor), and have only a wireless stylus and drawing tablet on their drafting tables. Which of the following protocols will enable you to support this technology?
   a. IrDA
   b. AppleTalk
   c. NWLink
   d. NetBIOS

7. You need to provide new computers to the employees who have recently joined your organization. These computers will be included in the network. Identify the service that will be used to assign IP addresses dynamically to the new computers on the network.
   a. RRAS
   b. DHCP
   c. NAT
   d. WINS

8. Which of the following network services is used to resolve NetBIOS names into IP addresses in order to locate a computer on a network?
   a. NAT
   b. DHCP
   c. RRAS
   d. WINS

Problem Solving Scenarios

1. You are a Network Administrator at a company that is planning to set up a Windows Server 2003 network. Your first responsibility is to plan the logical and physical infrastructure of the network. Then, you will actually deploy the network. Outline in a report what you will do in the design phase; how you will generate the required information; and the protocols that you will adopt for use on the network.

2. While creating the plan for your company's Windows Server 2003 network, you conclude that there is a real need to assign IP addresses dynamically so that the client computers on the network can communicate with each other and with the network servers. Prepare a report that identifies the services and protocols that will be required for achieving connectivity among the various resources on the network.

Understanding IP Addressing and TCP/IP

The Windows Server 2003 Transmission Control Protocol/Internet Protocol (TCP/IP) suite is a set of protocols (or rules) that facilitates communication among resources of varying configurations across a network. These rules manage the content, format, timing, sequencing, and error control of the messages that are exchanged by devices on a network. Overall, the protocol determines how clients and servers must package data in order to send it to other computers on the network, as well as how they should interpret data that they receive.

Each network resource that communicates through TCP/IP is identified with a unique IP address. An IP address is a 32-bit number assigned to the hosts on the network. Computers, printers, routers, and other devices that are identified with an IP address are all hosts. Each IP address consists of a network ID and a host ID. The network ID identifies the network to which the host belongs, and the host ID identifies the destination or source host on the network.

IP addresses belong to one of five classes: A, B, C, D, or E. These classes are designed to accommodate the increasing number of networks and to ensure that duplicate IP addresses do not exist across networks. A, B, and C are the most commonly used address classes. Class D addresses are used for multicast applications and Class E addresses are used for experimental purposes.

Before you implement TCP/IP on a network, you should take some time to plan the implementation. You must consider such factors as the network's size, as well as its physical and logical layout. After planning, the first step in assigning an IP address to a host on a network is to install TCP/IP on the host. Then, you need to configure TCP/IP by assigning addresses to the hosts, which can be done manually or dynamically. Once you have assigned addresses to the hosts on the network, different kinds of traffic can begin to flow into the network.

Verification of TCP/IP configuration ensures that your computer is able to connect to other TCP/IP hosts on the network. Troubleshooting TCP/IP problems can occupy a large portion of a Network Administrator's time. Diagnostic utilities such as Ping, Ipconfig, and Tracert enable you to troubleshoot problems associated with TCP/IP. The Ping utility verifies that one host can reach another across the network. If you cannot ping another host, error messages may reveal routing or other problems. Even receiving no response to the Ping utility can reveal information about network problems. The Ipconfig utility provides information about configuration, IP address, subnet mask, and default gateway of the host computer. The Tracert utility enables you to locate the route being used to transfer data between communicating devices.

Goals

In this lesson, you will learn about the TCP/IP protocol suite, the benefits of using TCP/IP, IP addressing, and TCP/IP address classes. You will also learn to install and configure TCP/IP on your computer, test the TCP/IP configuration, and troubleshoot TCP/IP addressing problems.

Lesson 2 Understanding IP Addressing and TCP/IP

Skill	Exam 70-291 Objective
1. Introducing TCP/IP	Basic knowledge
2. Introducing IP Addressing	Basic knowledge
3. Introducing Subnetting	Basic knowledge
4. Installing and Configuring TCP/IP	Configure TCP/IP addressing on a server computer. Manage Routing and Remote Access routing interfaces.
5. Configuring TCP/IP Manually	Configure TCP/IP addressing on a server computer.
6. Using Automatic Private IP Addressing (APIPA)	Configure TCP/IP addressing on a server computer. Diagnose and resolve issues related to Automatic Private IP Addressing (APIPA).
7. Testing the TCP/IP Configuration	Troubleshoot TCP/IP addressing. Diagnose and resolve issues related to incorrect TCP/IP configuration. Troubleshoot connectivity to the Internet.
8. Troubleshooting TCP/IP Addressing	Troubleshoot TCP/IP addressing. Diagnose and resolve issues related to incorrect TCP/IP configuration. Troubleshoot connectivity to the Internet.

Requirements

To complete this lesson, you must have administrative rights on a Windows Server 2003 computer that is connected to a network.

skill 1

Introducing TCP/IP

exam objective

Basic knowledge

overview

tip
The DoD was the government agency that funded the development of TCP/IP.

Transmission Control Protocol/Internet Protocol (TCP/IP) is a network protocol suite that is used to provide connectivity across operating systems and hardware platforms. TCP/IP is scalable, and therefore appropriate for implementation on the networks of both small businesses and large corporations. TCP/IP is also the core protocol of the Internet. It provides reliable and routable data transfer over LANs or WANs.

The TCP/IP suite is based on a conceptual model created by the Department of Defense (DoD) that consists of four layers. These layers are Network Interface, Internet, Transport, and Application **(Figure 2-1)**. The **Network Interface layer** sits at the bottom of the model. Its function is to send and receive IP datagrams to or from a physical network adapter, which then moves the data over network media such as coaxial, fiber-optic, or twisted-pair cables. The Network Interface layer is also known as the Network Access Layer. The **Internet layer** receives data from the Transport layer and sends data to the Network Interface layer. The Internet layer makes routing decisions so that it can forward packets toward the destination. The Internet layer supports:

◆ **Internet Protocol (IP)**, a connectionless protocol that is responsible for the delivery of packets. It is connectionless in that it does not establish and manage a session between two communicating devices to perform its function. IP is unreliable in that it does not always guarantee delivery and does not attempt to recover data if it is lost, duplicated, or delayed.

◆ **Address Resolution Protocol (ARP)**, which is responsible for resolving the IP address of a computer to its media access control (MAC) address. This ensures that packets reach the correct destination. Resolved addresses are maintained in a temporary cache so that they do not have to be resolved repeatedly.

◆ **Internet Control Message Protocol (ICMP)**, which supports packets containing error, control, and information messages. ICMP packets, as they are also known, are used by higher-level protocols to solve transmission problems, and by Network Administrators to pinpoint the source of network problems. Common ICMP messages appear in **Table 2-1**.

◆ **Internet Group Management Protocol (IGMP)**, which manages IP multicasting. In IP multicasting, an IP datagram is transmitted to a set of hosts called the IP multicast group that is identified by a single IP multicast address.

The **Transport layer** establishes connections between computers and transfers data using Transmission Control Protocol (TCP), User Datagram Protocol (UDP), or Pragmatic General Multicast (PGM). **TCP** provides a one-to-one, stream-oriented, and reliable delivery of data between computers. It is used for transferring large amounts of data in a managed session with error recovery. **UDP** provides a one-to-one or one-to-many connectionless method of communication. However, it is unreliable as there is no session management and therefore no guarantee of delivery. UDP is generally used by applications that transmit small amounts of data. **PGM** is Windows Server 2003's reliable multicast protocol.

Figure 2-1 The DoD model

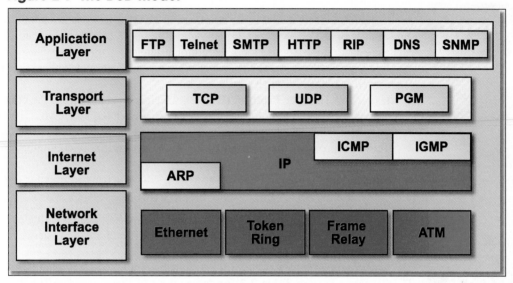

Table 2-1 Common ICMP messages	
ICMP Message	**Function**
Echo Request	A simple troubleshooting message used to check connectivity with the destination computer.
Echo Reply	A response message to an Echo Request message.
Redirect	A message sent by a router to inform a host that is sending a message that there is a better path to the destination computer.
Source Quench	A message sent by a router to inform a sending host that its IP datagrams are being removed due to congestion at the router. The sending host then lowers the transmission rate
Time Exceeded	A message used to inform the sender that the TTL (Time to Live) field in the IP packet has expired, and the packet was dropped. Each router along a path is required to decrement the TTL by at least 1. Since most IP packets have a TTL of 128, this means that most packets will cross no more than 128 routers en route to their destination. IP's maximum TTL is 255. This message is used by Tracert and Pathping to determine the path to a specific host.
Destination Unreachable	A message sent by a router to inform the sending host that a packet cannot be delivered.

skill 1

Introducing TCP/IP *(cont'd)*

exam objective

Basic knowledge

overview

At the top of the DoD model is the **Application layer**, which enables applications to access the services of the other layers. It also defines the protocols that applications must use to exchange data. These Application layer protocols include:

◆ **File Transfer Protocol (FTP)**, which allows a computer to download files from a server, as well as upload files to a server.

◆ **Hypertext Transfer Protocol (HTTP)**, which is used to transfer the contents of a Web page into a Web browser for viewing. Web browsers interpret HTML (Hypertext Markup Language), the main programming language used for Web pages.

◆ **Telnet**, a protocol that is used to log on to network host computers from a remote location.

◆ **Simple Mail Transfer Protocol (SMTP)**, which is used to transfer e-mail messages between computers.

Using TCP/IP, you can set up a robust and scalable client/server networking environment. You can easily add new nodes to a TCP/IP network as the need for a larger network arises.

more

The Application layer also provides services that are used to access and manage resources on TCP/IP networks. See **Table 2-2** for descriptions of these services. The Application layer enables applications to access the services offered by TCP/IP protocols through application programming interfaces (APIs). An API consists of a set of functions and commands that are called by an application code to perform network functions.

Table 2-2   Application layer services

Service	Function
Domain Name System (DNS)	A system for resolving host names to IP addresses.
Routing Information Protocol (RIP)	A routing protocol that routers use to exchange routing information on a network.
Simple Network Management Protocol (SNMP)	A protocol used to collect and exchange network management information such as that used by an enterprise network management application like Tivoli, System Patrol, or Netview.

skill 2

Introducing IP Addressing

Basic knowledge

overview

tip

A host is a computer, printer, router, or other device on a network.

IP addresses are 32-bit numbers used to logically locate a host. IP addresses are in binary for a very simple reason: Computers only natively understand binary. Anything else has to be translated into binary for the computer to properly understand it. While the actual IP address is a binary number, you normally see it converted into decimal. This is because humans typically have great difficulty in remembering large binary numbers. For instance, remembering **11000000.10101000.00001000.00101000** is rather difficult. However, remembering the same number, **192.168.8.40**, once converted to decimal, is fairly easy.

For this reason, one of the first things you'll have to understand about IP addressing is binary math. Binary math isn't very complex, it's just alien. Binary is base-2 numbering, which means each digit can only have 2 possible values: 0 or 1. Like decimal numbers, binary numbers have place values. In decimal, 768 is seven hundred sixty-eight because of the place values. Seven is in the hundreds place, meaning that you multiply 7 x 100 to get its value of 700. Six is in the tens place (6x10=60), and 8 is in the ones place. To get the final value for the number, you add the value of each digit to each other (700+60+8=768). Binary works the same way; the place values are just different. In binary, the place values advance by multiples of 2s instead of 10s. For example, consider the binary number 10110. The far right bit is the ones place, just like in decimal. Anything in this position you multiply by 1. This position has a special name—LSB (Least Significant Bit). To find the value of the next bit (second bit from the far right), you multiply the previous bit value by 2. Since our previous bit value was 1, and 1x2=2, the value for the second bit position is 2. Similarly, the next position is 4 (2x2), the next is 8, and the far left bit position (known as the MSB or Most Significant Bit) has a value of 16. This is shown in **Table 2-3**.

To convert this binary number into decimal, we simply multiply the value by the number in the same bit position, then add all of the final values to each other. In this example, this would work as follows (starting from the LSB): 0x1=0, 1x2=2, 1x4=4, 0x8=0, and 1x16=16. When you add them up, you get 16+0+4+2+0=22. This is shown in **Table 2-4**.

That takes care of converting from binary into decimal, but what about converting decimal into binary? That conversion is a little more difficult, but still fairly easy. The simplest way to do this is to subtract, one bit at a time, starting with the MSB. To do this, you first have to find the MSB for the number. You do this by finding the largest power of 2 that will fit in the number. Eventually, you'll know the powers of two, but for now, just begin with 1 and start doubling. For instance, if you wanted to convert 234 to binary, you first find the largest power of 2 that will fit in it. To do this, start at 1 and begin doubling: 1, 2, 4 ,8, 16, 32, 64, 128, 256. The largest power of 2 that will fit into 234 is 128. Therefore 128 is your MSB, and must be a 1, making our binary number at this juncture 10000000. However, that number is 128, so now we have to figure out which additional bits to set to create 234. The next bit position to the right of the 128-bit is 64. 128+64=192, which is less than the number we are looking for (234), so we can set that bit as well. This gives us 11000000 (192). The next bit position is 32. 128+64+32=224, so that bit can be set as well. This gives us 11100000. The next position is the 16's place. 128+64+32+16=240, which is too large, so we will leave the 16s place unset and move on to the 8s place. 128+64+32+0+8=232, which is smaller than 234, so the 8s place is set. At this point, it should be obvious that we only need 2 to make the final number, so our final binary number is as shown in **Table 2-5**.

Once you understand binary, IP addressing gets a lot easier. The next thing to understand is the structure of an IP address. IP addresses are structured into 4 **octets** of 8 bits each. Since each octet has 8 bits, that means the largest possible number in any given octet is 255. This means the total range of possible IP addresses is from 0.0.0.0 to 255.255.255.255. This

Table 2-3   Place values for a binary number

Bits	1	0	1	1	0
Value	16	8	4	2	1

Table 2-4   Converting binary into decimal

Bits	1		0		1		1		0	
Value	16		8		4		2		1	
Total	16	+	0	+	4	+	2	+	0	= 22

Table 2-5   Converting decimal into binary

Bits	1		1		1		0		1		0		1		0	
Value	128		64		32		16		8		4		2		1	
Total	128	+	64	+	32	+	0	+	8	+	0	+	2	+	0	= 234

skill 2

Introducing IP Addressing (cont'd)

exam objective   Basic knowledge

overview

address is then divided into at least two, and usually three sections: network, host, and subnet. All IP addresses have a network section and a host section, but not all have a subnet section (this is the topic of the next skill). The network section (sometimes referred to as the **network ID**) defines which logical network you are a member of. A logical network is the area that your host can issue a broadcast to unimpeded. A **broadcast** is a packet destined for all computers. This is in contrast to a **unicast**, which sends a packet to a specific computer. Broadcasts are useful in many cases. For instance, when trying to locate a specific computer on your logical network, your computer will broadcast a query for the destination computer's MAC address. Anytime the computer wants to get the entire segment's attention, it will use a broadcast packet.

However, broadcasts have their own problems. First, routers do not forward broadcasts. In fact, this is the whole purpose of a router—to stop broadcasts. Routing is simply a side-effect. Second, since broadcasts must be listened to by all computers, broadcasts can waste processor time on all hosts en-masse. Similarly, since broadcasts must be transmitted to all hosts on a segment, broadcasts can waste bandwidth.

The network section of an IP address tells the client which logical network it is on. Any other host with an identical network section should be able to receive this host's broadcasts. For example, if your IP address is 172.16.1.1, and the network section of that IP is 172.16, then you should be able to broadcast to any other host whose address begins with 172.16. This also means that in order to communicate with a host whose address does not start with 172.16, you would need to use a router.

Routers are devices that connect two or more network segments. Their job is simply to receive frames from their connected networks and send those messages to the correct destination network. If you need to reach an IP address that has a different network section than your own IP address, you need to use a router.

As for the host portion (sometimes referred to as a **host ID**), it is simply a unique number that defines your host on that network (**Figure 2-2**). For example, in the previous example (172.16.1.1), your host number is 1.1. You are therefore host 1.1 on network 172.16.

In order to define the section boundaries of an IP address, we need another 32-bit number, known as the subnet mask. The **subnet mask** is used to determine which section of the IP address is the host section, and which section is the network section. The part of the subnet mask that is binary 1s defines that section of the IP address as the network section, while the 0s represent the host section. For example, in the IP address 10.4.1.3 with a subnet mask of 255.0.0.0, 10 is the network portion, and 4.1.3 is the host portion. This is shown below:

IP	10.	4.	1.	3
Mask	255.	0.	0.	0

This works because the host will use a process known as **ANDing** (also referred to as the logical AND operation) to find the network address. ANDing is an operation that is performed by multiplying one binary number by the other binary number. Since ANDing is performed on the binary numbers, you obviously have to convert the IP address and subnet mask to binary in order to perform the process. After you do the conversions, you simply multiply the two numbers bit by bit to get a result. For example, to AND 192.168.23.2 with the subnet mask 255.255.255.0, you would perform the following:

```
      11000000.10101000.00010111.00000010    IP address (192.168.23.2)
  x   11111111.11111111.11111111.00000000    Subnet mask (255.255.255.0)
      11000000.10101000.00010111.00000000    Result (192.168.23.0)
```

Figure 2-2 Each resource on a network has a different host ID

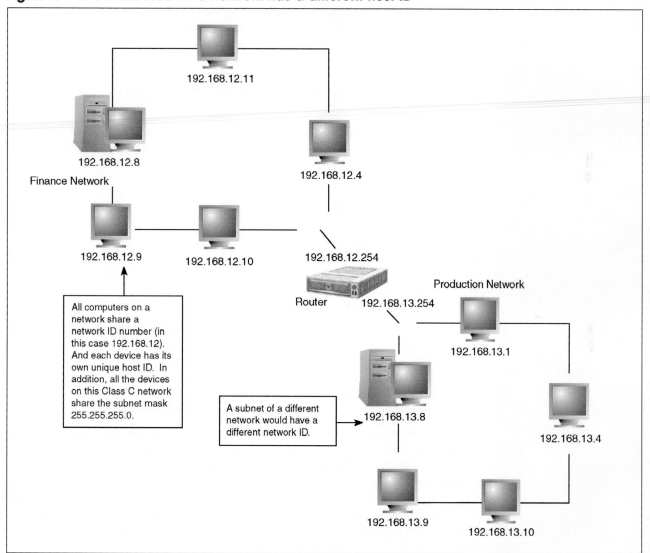

skill 2

Introducing IP Addressing (cont'd)

exam objective

Basic knowledge

overview

So what does ANDing really tell you? The result of your ANDing operation will be the network address for that IP address. The network address is used to determine if you can communicate with your destination without using a router. Here's how it works:

◆   You AND your IP address and your subnet mask to find your network address

◆   You AND your destination's IP address and subnet mask to find it's network address

◆   If the results (network addresses) are exactly the same, then you are on the same network, and should be able to receive each other's broadcasts. If not, then you need to use a router to communicate.

It is important to realize that subnet masks must be "running" binary 1s. In other words, the binary 1s and 0s in a subnet mask must be contiguous. This means each octet can only have 9 possible subnet values:

◆   0 (Binary: 00000000)

◆   128 (Binary: 10000000)

◆   192 (Binary: 11000000)

◆   224 (Binary: 11100000)

◆   240 (Binary: 11110000)

◆   248 (Binary: 11111000)

◆   252 (Binary: 11111100)

◆   254 (Binary: 11111110)

◆   255 (Binary: 11111111)

This also means that once you have a binary 0 in any octet, the rest of the octets will all be binary 0s. For example, the subnet mask 255.255.248.0 is valid, as the 0s and 1s are all contiguous (Binary: 11111111.11111111.11111000.00000000). However, the subnet mask 255.240.224.0 is not valid, as the 1s and 0s are not contiguous (Binary: 111111111.11110000.11100000.00000000). The rule that the 1s and 0s have to be contiguous does not simply apply to one octet; it applies to the entire subnet mask.

So how do you determine what the subnet mask should be? The class of IP address you are using determines the default subnet mask. IP addresses are divided into classes based on the number in the first octet (the far left octet) of an IP address. Classes were originally created to divide IP address ranges into different sizes for different-sized organizations. However, classful IP addressing is wasteful, and has therefore been mostly discarded. Still, you must be able to recognize classes, mostly because they define the default subnet mask when configuring TCP/IP. There are five classes of IP addresses, A through E. The details for these address classes are provided in **Table 2-6** and **Table 2-7**.

Classes A through C are useable for host addresses. Class D is used for multicasting purposes only (discussed further in Lesson 4), and Class E addresses are marked for experimental purposes.

Note that the class A addresses 0 and 127 are reserved and may not ever be used. The 0 network is reserved for computers that do not have an IP address, and the 127 address is used for loopback.

more

If you are trying to decide which IP address structure to use for your network, you should first decide if you need (or want) your clients to be directly connected to the Internet, or if you would like them to use a Network Address Translation (NAT) device. If you want each client to be directly connected, you will need a block of public IP addresses large enough to support all directly connected clients. You typically get these IP addresses from your provider (ISP). Due to the shortage of available public IP addresses, this is not recommended, however.

Table 2-6   Properties of TCP/IP address classes

Class	Value Range	Network ID	Host ID	Number of Networks	Number of Hosts
A	1–127 (127 reserved)	First octet	Last three octets	126	16,777,214
B	128–191	First two octets	Last two octets	16,384	65,534
C	192–223	First three octets	Last octet	2,097,152	254
D	224–239	N/A	N/A	N/A	N/A
E	240–254	N/A	N/A	N/A	N/A

Table 2-7   Default network masks for IP address classes

Class	Bits for network mask (binary notation)	Network mask (decimal notation)
A	11111111 00000000 00000000 00000000	255.0.0.0
B	11111111 11111111 00000000 00000000	255.255.0.0
C	11111111 11111111 11111111 00000000	255.255.255.0

skill 2

Introducing IP Addressing (cont'd)

exam objective

Basic knowledge

more

Usually, you will want to use private addressing with an internal NAT device. Private addresses are IP addresses that are specifically defined as being unroutable over the Internet. Since you cannot use these addresses to access the Internet, this means that multiple organizations can use the addresses internally without conflicting with each other. However, it also means that for any of these organizations to access the Internet, a NAT device must be used. The NAT device (which can be a router, server, or even a client with Internet Connection Sharing enabled) will translate your private IP addresses into public IP addresses so your clients can reach the Internet. Basically, the NAT device has a valid public IP address (or several public IP addresses, known as a pool) applied to its external interface, and a private IP address on its internal interface. When a client wants to access the Internet, it sends its packets to the NAT device's internal interface. The NAT device then replaces the private IP address in the packet with one of its public IP addresses, and forwards the packet to the Internet resource. When the response returns from the Internet, the NAT server reverses the operation to send the packet back to the client **(Figure 2-3)**.

Private address ranges that have been reserved for internal use are listed below:

Class A: 10.0.0.0
Class B: 172.16.0.0–172.32.0.0
Class C: 192.168.0.0–192.168.255.0

Figure 2-3 Network Address Translation

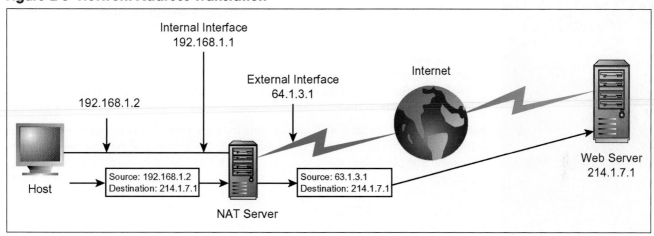

skill 3   *Introducing Subnetting*

exam objective

Basic knowledge

overview

Subnetting is a subject that strikes fear into the hearts of many MCSE students. Like binary, it's not that complex, just alien. In fact, once you have a good grasp on binary, subnetting is fairly easy. When you are subnetting, you are simply attempting to break a large network down into smaller, more manageable pieces. For example, a class B IP address has 65,534 total host addresses for a single logical segment. That would be an impossible number of computers to squeeze into a single segment. However, if you broke the larger network into 256 sub-networks, each sub-network could host 254 devices, which is a much more reasonable number (**Figure 2-4**).

Subnetting is accomplished by "stealing" bits from the host section to create a new subnet section. You do this by extending the default mask. For example, if you had the IP address 172.16.0.0 with the default mask, you could break it into 256 sub-networks by simply changing the mask from the default 255.255.0.0 to 255.255.255.0. This creates a new, 8-bit subnet section, as shown in **Figure 2-5**. Then, you would have 172.16.0.0, 172.16.1.0, 172.16.2.0, and so on, up to 172.16.255.0, each as its own sub-network. This means that a client with an IP address of 172.16.23.1 would need to use a router to communicate with 172.16.3.1.

When you are subnetting, there are five things you will need to be able to identify in an address:
◆   The network address
◆   The broadcast address
◆   The range of valid IP addresses
◆   The number of subnets
◆   The number of hosts per subnet

To determine the network address, you simply used ANDing after converting the address to binary. The result of the ANDing operation will be the network address.

While we have already discussed what the network address is, the broadcast address is new. The broadcast address is the address used to perform a broadcast to the subnet. The biggest reason you must know how to find the broadcast address, however, is because it is the last IP address in the subnet (while the network address is the first IP address in the subnet)

To determine the broadcast address, you must first find the network address. Then, turn all of the host bits into binary 1s. Finally, convert the final result into decimal. For example, if given the IP address 192.168.15.73, with the subnet mask, 255.255.255.224, first you must identify the network address:

	11000000.10101000.00001111.01001001	IP address (192.168.15.73)
x	11111111.11111111.11111111.11100000	Subnet mask (255.255.255.224)
	11000000.10101000.00001111.01000000	Network address: (192.168.15.64)

Next, you turn all of the bits in the host section of the result (identified by the section of the subnet mask that is all 0s) into binary 1s, and convert the binary to decimal (the bolded section is the host section):

11000000.10101000.00001111.010**00000**	Network address (192.168.15.64)
11111111.11111111.11111111.111**00000**	Subnet mask (255.255.255.224)
11000000.10101000.00001111.010**11111**	Broadcast address (192.168.15.127)

Figure 2-4 Subnetting

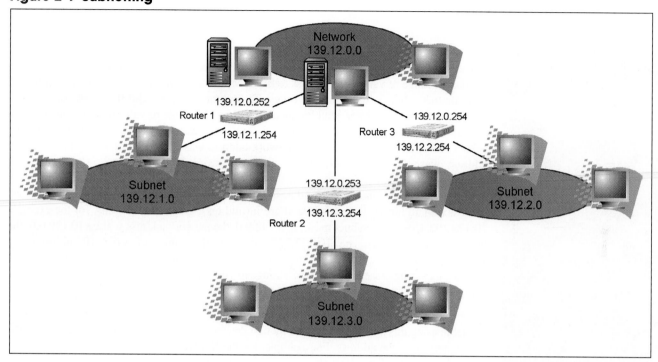

Figure 2-5 Creating a new, 8-bit subnet section

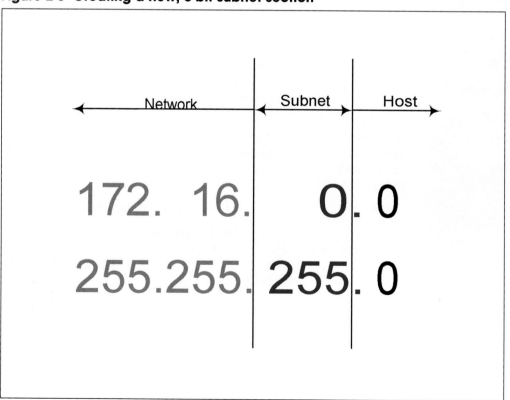

skill 3

Introducing Subnetting (cont'd)

exam objective

Basic knowledge

overview

The range of valid IP addresses tells you which IP addresses are valid on this subnet. In other words, the range of valid IP addresses tells you which addresses can communicate with each other on that subnet without using a router. To find the range of valid IP addresses, you simply find the network address and broadcast address. The range of valid IP addresses is every IP address between the two. For instance, in our previous example (192.168.15.73, with the subnet mask, 255.255.255.224), the network address was 192.168.15.64 and the broadcast address was 192.168.15.127, so the range of valid IP addresses is 192.168.16.65–192.168.15.126. All numbers *between* the network address and broadcast address are valid. This is because only the network address (the all binary 0s host address) and the broadcast address (the all binary 1s host address) are invalid on a given subnet. Thus, for the example 10.123.102.4, with the subnet mask, 255.248.0.0, the network address will be 10.120.0.0, the broadcast address will be 10.127.255.255, and the range of valid IP addresses is 10.120.0.1–10.127.255.254. All addresses between the network address and broadcast address, including those that may look strange to you such as 10.120.255.0 and 10.127.0.0 are valid.

After you find the range of valid IP addresses, you must determine the number of subnets available using this mask. This is done by first determining the number of bits available in the subnet section of the address. For example, for the IP address 10.123.102.4, with the subnet mask, 255.248.0.0, the subnet section is 5 bits long. This is because the address is a class A address, which means that the network section is the first 8 bits, and the host section would normally be the last 24 bits. However, we have changed the default mask and stolen 5 bits for the subnet section, making the subnet section 5 bits long, as shown in **Table 2-8**.

For another example, for the IP address, 192.168.122.45, with the subnet mask 255.255.255.252, the subnet section is 6 bits long, as shown in **Table 2-9**.

Once you have determined how many bits are in the subnet section, you can perform a simple formula using any scientific calculator to determine the number of subnets: 2^n, where N is the number of bits in the subnet section. For example, in the 10.123.102.4 (255.248.0.0) example, 5 bits are in the subnet section, and $2^5 = 32$, so we have 32 subnets.

Determining the number of host addresses in each subnet follows the same formula, with a slight twist. First, you must determine how many bits are in the host section of the IP address. This is done by simply finding parts of the subnet mask that are all binary 0s. For example, in 10.123.102.4 (255.248.0.0), the host section is 19 bits long, as shown below:

Custom Mask: **11111111.11111000.00000000.00000000**

Once you have determined how many bits are in the host section, use the following formula to determine the number of hosts: 2^n-2. You have to subtract 2 IP addresses from the calculation because you cannot use the first and last IP address of any subnet. So, in our example, there are $2^{19} = 524,288 - 2$ for 524,286 hosts per subnet.

more

VLSM (Variable Length Subnet Masking) changes subnetting by removing the requirement that all subnets be of equal size. For example, for the IP address 192.168.34.0, with the subnet mask, 255.255.255.224, you would typically have 8 subnets, with 30 hosts in each subnet. However, what if you want 1 subnet with 126 hosts, one subnet with 62 hosts, and 2 subnets with 30 hosts? This is what VLSM allows you to do. It really is easier than it sounds. The trick is to break the IP address into its largest subnets and then subnet the subnets. For example, in this case, you would first create two subnets by subnetting the address with a single bit. This would make the mask 255.255.255.128, which would create the 192.168.34.0 (255.255.255.128) and 192.168.34.128 (255.255.255.128) subnets, with each subnet contain-

Table 2-8   Custom mask with five stolen bits

IP address 10.123.102.4 with subnet mask 255.248.0.0

Custom Mask:	11111111.**11111**000.00000000.00000000
Default Mask (Class A):	11111111.00000000.00000000.00000000

Table 2-9   Custom mask with six stolen bits

IP address 192.168.122.45 with subnet mask 255.255.255.252

Custom Mask:	11111111.11111111.11111111.**111111**00
Default Mask (Class A):	11111111.11111111.11111111.00000000

skill 3

Introducing Subnetting (cont'd)

exam objective

Basic knowledge

more

ing 126 host addresses. Then you would take one of these subnets (we'll use the 192.168.34.128 subnet as an example, though it doesn't matter which one you use) and subnet it into 2 more subnets by adding another bit. This would give you the 192.168.34.128 and 192.168.34.192 subnets, each with the 255.255.255.192 mask, and 62 host addresses. You then take one of the 62 host subnets (again, it doesn't matter which one, but we'll use 192.168.34.192 as an example), and sub-subnet it by adding another bit to the mask. This will create your final two subnets, 192.168.34.192 and 192.168.34.224, each with the 255.255.255.224 mask and 30 hosts. In the end, you would have 4 subnets, one with 126 hosts, one with 62 hosts, and two with 30 hosts each, as shown in **Table 2-10**.

CIDR (Classless Inter-Domain Routing) works just like VLSM as far as subnetting is concerned, but CIDR makes one additional distinction: Classes don't matter. In other words, in CIDR, the class of address you are given does not necessarily denote the network section. This is useful for modern implementations with public IP addresses, as public IP addresses are now most commonly obtained from your ISP, which simply subnets you a section of their much larger address block. For example, your ISP may give you a block of 128 IP addresses in the following format 64.1.1.128 (255.255.255.128). Even though this is a class A address block, your organization does not have the entire class A IP block; the ISP owns that. You are simply being allowed to use one subnet of that block. So for your organization, the network section of the address would not be the first 8 bits, as in a typical class A, but rather, the first 25 bits (the part that was masked by the ISP, 11111111.11111111.11111111.10000000). You could subnet it further if you wanted (for instance, by changing the mask to 255.255.255.192), but you can't reduce the number of 1s in the mask.

Additionally, CIDR also provides a much easier way of notating subnet masks, known as CIDR notation. CIDR notation is simply a forward slash (/) following the IP address with the number of bits in the mask. For instance, the IP address 172.16.142.13 255.255.240.0 is represented as 172.16.142.13 / 20 in CIDR notation, as there are 20 binary 1s in the subnet mask (11111111.11111111.11110000.00000000).

Table 2-10	Variable Length Subnet Masking (VLSM)	
	192.168.34.0	255.255.255.128
	192.168.34.128	255.255.255.192
	192.168.34.192	255.255.255.224
	192.168.34.224	255.255.255.224

skill 4

Installing and Configuring TCP/IP

exam objective

Configure TCP/IP addressing on a server computer. Manage Routing and Remote Access routing interfaces.

overview

To enable communication between your Windows Server 2003 server and the various network components, you need to have TCP/IP installed and configured correctly. The installation of TCP/IP usually occurs by default when you install the Windows Server 2003 operating system. However, if the default installation process was not used, you can install TCP/IP manually.

how to

Install TCP/IP manually.

1. Click **Start** on the taskbar, point to **Control Panel**, point to **Network Connections**, and click **Local Area Connection**. This will open the **Local Area Connection Status** dialog box **(Figure 2-6)**.
2. Click **Properties** on the **General** tab to open the **Local Area Connection Properties** dialog box.
3. Click **Internet Protocol (TCP/IP)**, and then click **Install...** to open the **Select Network Component Type** dialog box.
4. Click **Protocol** in the **Click the type of network component you want to install** list box **(Figure 2-7)**.
5. Click **Add...** to open the **Select Network Protocol** dialog box.
6. Select the **Internet Protocol (TCP/IP)** option and click **OK**.
7. After the command completes, close the Local Area Connections Properties dialog box and the Local Area Connection Status dialog box.

tip

If Internet Protocol (TCP/IP) is not listed, the protocol is already installed.

more

The default installation of TCP/IP in Windows Server 2003 uses **Internet Protocol version 4 (IPv4)**, which is still the standard used on the Internet and other TCP/IP networks. Windows Server 2003 also enables you to install **Microsoft TCP/IP version 6**, which you will see listed in the Select Network Protocol dialog box. **Internet Protocol version 6 (IPv6)** has been developed to replace IPv4. With the dramatic rise in the number of IP addresses required in the last ten years, the IPv4 address space has run out of room. IPv6 offers 128-bit addresses, as opposed to the 32-bit addresses of IPv4. This will allow for a much greater pool of addresses. IPv6 will also improve over IPv4 in other areas such as encryption, routing, and automatic address assignment. Most corporate and home networks continue to use IPv4 internally. However, IPv6 implementation has begun on the networks that provide the backbone of the Internet.

Once TCP/IP is running, you will need to select an addressing scheme so that the devices on your network can communicate. A static IP addressing scheme requires that you manually assign an IP address to each host on your network. To assign IP addresses dynamically, you need a device performing as a DHCP (Dynamic Host Configuration Protocol) server. Many devices, including routers and a Windows 2003 Server computer, can perform this function. For more information on DHCP, see Lesson 4.

tip

Corporate networks typically reside behind firewalls and use IP addresses ranges that are reserved for internal networks that are not connected directly to the Internet.

Figure 2-6 Local Area Connection Status dialog box

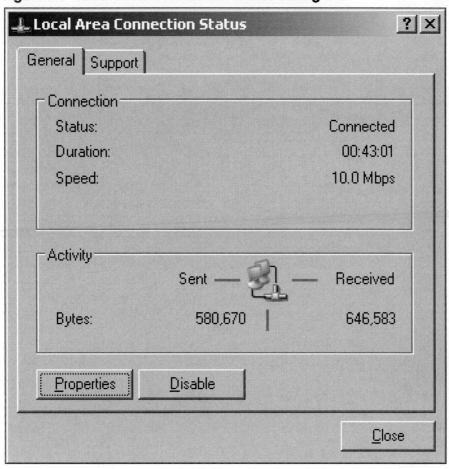

Figure 2-7 Select Network Component dialog box

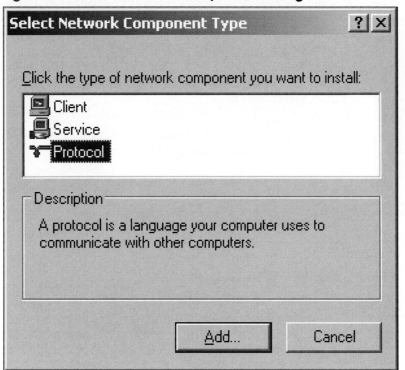

skill 5

Configuring TCP/IP Manually

exam objective

Configure TCP/IP addressing on a server computer.

overview

For an implementation of TCP/IP on your network to be successful, you need to configure TCP/IP by assigning IP addresses. You can configure TCP/IP on a Windows Server 2003 network in the following ways:

tip

Clients who receive address assignments dynamically from a DHCP server may receive a different IP address from the available pool of addresses each time that they boot.

◆ Dynamic configuration: You can assign IP addresses to clients dynamically with Windows Server 2003 by using the Dynamic Host Configuration Protocol (DHCP) server service. Using DHCP, you can easily and dynamically assign addresses to systems on the network instead of configuring each system manually.

◆ Manual configuration: You configure TCP/IP computers manually if your network does not include a DHCP server. Manual configuration involves assigning static IP addresses to the computers on your network. Typically, you assign static IP addresses to servers, such as a print server or a DHCP server, as opposed to client computers.

◆ Automatic Private IP Addressing (APIPA): You can assign addresses to hosts on the network using Automatic Private IP Addressing, which automatically assigns IP addresses within the range 169.254.0.1–169.254.255.254 and with the subnet mask 255.255.0.0. APIPA can stand in for the DHCP service until it is available. It also checks for the availability of a DHCP server periodically, yielding to a server automatically when one is found. See Skill 6 for more information about APIPA.

how to

Configure TCP/IP manually.

1. Click **🎔 Start** on the taskbar, point to **Control Panel**, point to **Network Connections**, and click **Local Area Connection**. This will open the **Local Area Connection Status** dialog box.
2. Click **Properties** on the **General** tab to open the **Local Area Connection Properties** dialog box.
3. On the **General** tab, select **Internet Protocol (TCP/IP)** in the **This connection uses the following items** list box (**Figure 2-8**).
4. Click **Properties** to open the **Internet Protocol (TCP/IP) Properties** dialog box.
5. For manual configuration, select the **Use the following IP address** option button. Then, type the IP address, subnet mask, and default gateway in their respective fields (**Figure 2-9**). You may also enter the IP address of the preferred DNS server and, if applicable, the alternate DNS server. To do this, click the **Use the following DNS server addresses** option button, which will enable the **Preferred DNS Server** and **Alternate DNS Server** entry fields.
6. Click **OK** to close the Internet Protocol (TCP/IP) Properties dialog box.
7. Click **Close** to close the Local Area Connection Properties dialog box.
8. Close the Local Area Connection Status dialog box.

Figure 2-8 Selecting Internet Protocol (TCP/IP)

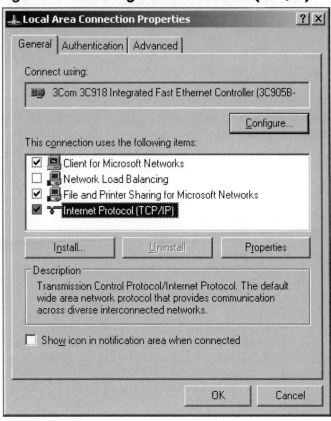

Figure 2-9 Configuring an IP address

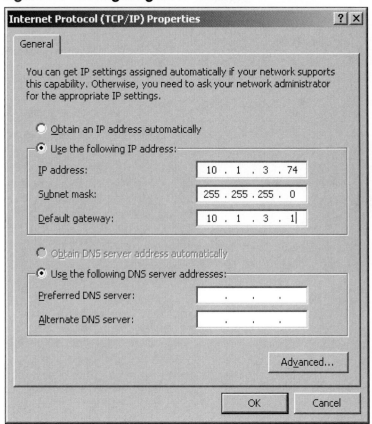

skill 5

Configuring TCP/IP Manually (cont'd)

exam objective

Configure TCP/IP addressing on a server computer.

more

A **default gateway** establishes a set route that communicating TCP/IP hosts must follow. A default gateway is the default router for your computer. It is the router your computer will use to get to any network that is not specifically defined in its routing table. TCP/IP hosts manage and maintain **routing tables**. These tables can provide specifications as simple as directing all non-local network traffic through the default gateway. The routing table can also provide specific paths to specific networks, if need be. This will be covered further in the next lesson.

You can use the Internet Protocol (TCP/IP) Properties dialog box to configure your computer to obtain an IP address automatically. To do this, simply click the **Obtain an IP address automatically** option button (refer to **Figure 2-9** on page 2.19). Selecting this option enables Windows 2003 Server to obtain its TCP/IP configuration from a DHCP server on the network as the default method of obtaining an IP address.

If your network has a DNS server, then you can configure your computer to search for the services provided by a DNS server automatically. Open the Internet Protocol (TCP/IP) Properties dialog box and click the **Obtain the DNS server address automaticall**y option button.

You can also specify advanced TCP/IP settings for your computer. Click the **Advanced** button on the General tab of the Internet Protocol (TCP/IP) Properties dialog box (refer to **Figure 2-9** on page 2.19) to open the **Advanced TCP/IP Settings** dialog box (**Figure 2-10**). The four tabs available in this dialog box are as follows:

◆ **IP Settings:** Lists additional IP addresses and subnet masks that can be assigned to the network connections.

◆ **DNS:** Lists the DNS servers, by IP address, that Windows Server 2003 TCP/IP queries to resolve DNS domain requests from the client.

◆ **WINS:** Lists the WINS server Windows Server 2003 queries to resolve NetBIOS names assigned to the computers on the network.

◆ **Options:** Lists optional TCP/IP configurations that are available for use by the client.

Figure 2-10 The Advanced TCP/IP Settings dialog box

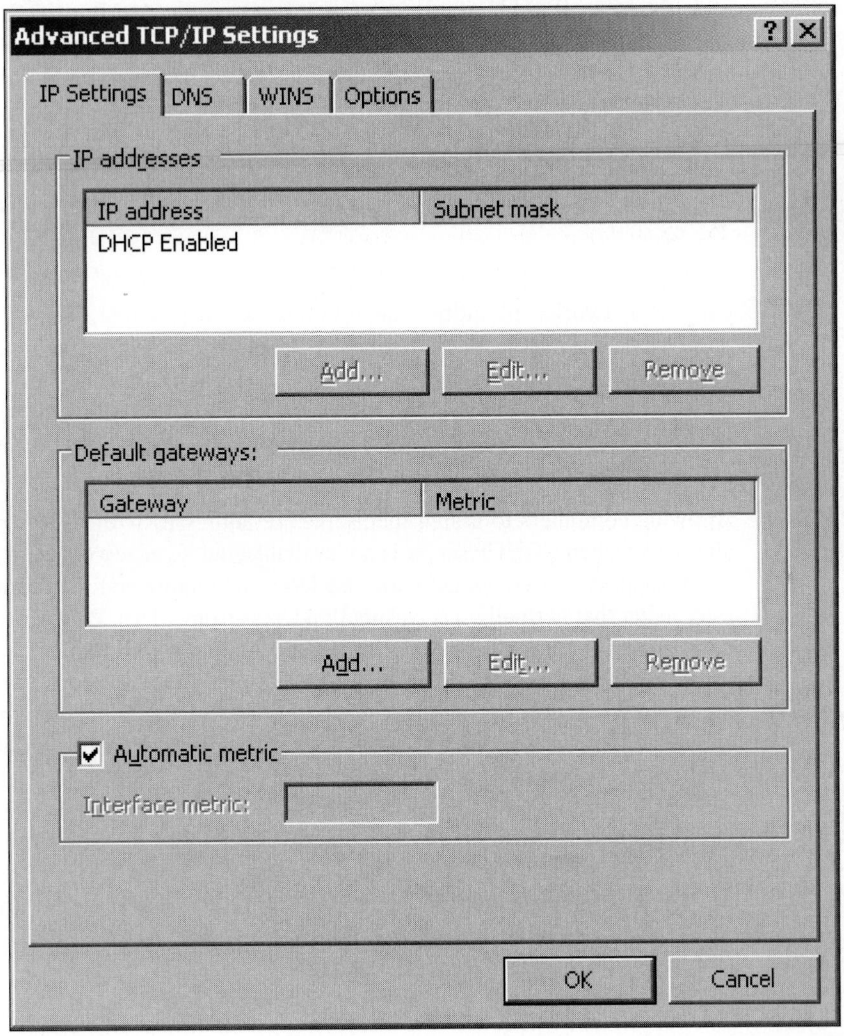

skill 6

Using Automatic Private IP Addressing (APIPA)

exam objective

Configure TCP/IP addressing on a server computer. Diagnose and resolve issues related to Automatic Private IP Addressing (APIPA).

overview

Ordinarily, Windows Server 2003 relies on the presence of a DHCP server to obtain an IP address automatically. However, in the absence of a DHCP server, the operating system can still obtain an IP address automatically through the **Automatic Private IP Addressing (APIPA)** feature. When no DHCP server is available, DHCP clients receive a randomly chosen IP address from a range of addresses that is reserved for APIPA. This range spans the addresses from 169.254.0.0 through 169.254.255.254. These addresses are not in use on the Internet. APIPA generates an address from the range and broadcasts it over the network. If no other computer responds to the address, the computer knows that it can take the address for itself. The address will always be in the format 169.254.x.x and have a subnet mask of 255.255.0.0.

APIPA cannot assign a default gateway, so remote access and any communication with external networks, including the Internet, is not possible. Therefore, using APIPA for computers that need to communicate with outside networks, such as Web servers, is not recommended. APIPA-addressed computers that have obtained their IP addresses with APIPA will generally only be able to communicate with other APIPA-enabled computers (which include Windows 2000, Windows XP, Windows 2003, Windows 98, and Macintosh computers) on the same subnet that have also acquired an IP address with APIPA.

Allowing computers to assign themselves IP addresses with APIPA may seem like a good alternative when a DHCP server is not available, but it can also cause problems, especially for large organizations whose networks use DNS and require communication across networks. If a computer that normally receives its IP address from a DHCP server assigns itself an APIPA address when the DHCP server fails, the APIPA address will remain in effect when the DHCP server resumes functionality. This will leave the computer isolated from the network and unable to communicate. To resolve this problem, the easiest solution is usually to run the command ipconfig /renew (or just reboot). However, you can also disable APIPA entirely by modifying the Registry.

how to

Disable automatic address configuration by using a Registry key. (You must be logged on as an Administrator.)

1. Click **Start** and then click **Run** on the Start menu to open the **Run** dialog box.
2. In the **Open** text box, type **regedt32** and click [OK]. The **Registry Editor** window opens.
3. Click the plus sign next to **HKEY_LOCAL_MACHINE** to expand the node in the left pane of the window (**Figure 2-11**). Continue expanding nodes until you have browsed to the following key: **HKEY_LOCAL_MACHINE\SYSTEM\CurrentControlSet\ Services\Tcpip\Parameters**.
4. Right-click the **Parameters** folder, point to **New**, and then click **DWORD Value** (**Figure 2-12**).
5. Rename the new DWORD Value, which is highlighted in the right pane, **IPAutoconfigurationEnabled**.
6. Double-click the new DWORD Value to open the **Edit DWORD Value** dialog box and make sure that the **Value data** text box is set to **0** (**Figure 2-13**). The **Hexadecimal** option button should be selected in the **Base** section by default. Click [OK].
7. Open the **File** menu and click **Exit** to close the Registry Editor.
8. Restart the computer.

caution

Do not make any changes to the Registry of a computer unless you have been given permission to do so. Editing the Registry improperly can result in significant malfunctions of the operating system.

more

To test whether a computer is using an IP address that it assigned to itself using APIPA, you can run the Ipconfig utility, which is discussed in detail later in this lesson.

Figure 2-11 The Registry Editor

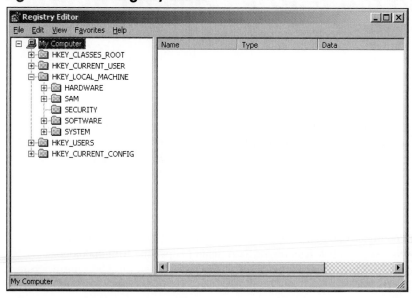

Figure 2-12 Creating a new DWORD Value

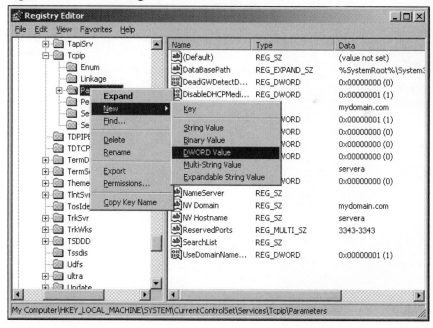

Figure 2-13 The Edit DWORD Value dialog box

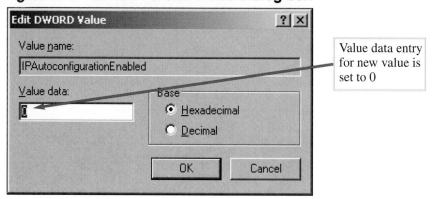

Value data entry
for new value is
set to 0

skill 7

Testing the TCP/IP Configuration

exam objective

Troubleshoot TCP/IP addressing. Diagnose and resolve issues related to incorrect TCP/IP configuration. Troubleshoot connectivity to the Internet.

overview

Once you have configured TCP/IP on your computer, either manually or automatically, you can verify its connectivity to ensure that TCP/IP is configured properly. To verify TCP/IP configuration, you can use the **Ipconfig** utility, which provides information about the host computer configuration, IP address, subnet mask, and default gateway. Ipconfig enables you to determine whether an IP address is assigned to your computer and confirms that the TCP/IP protocol is running.

how to

Test the TCP/IP configuration of a computer on which TCP/IP has been implemented.

1. Click [*Start*] and then click **Run** on the Start menu to open the **Run** dialog box.
2. Type **cmd** in the **Open** text box and press **[Enter]** to open the **Command Prompt** window (**Figure 2-14**).
3. Type **ipconfig** at the command prompt and press **[Enter]**. Configuration information such as IP address, subnet mask, and default gateway appears in the window (**Figure 2-15**). Ipconfig can also inform you if a duplicate address has been configured.
4. Close the Command Prompt window.

more

You can access a detailed report of a computer's TCP/IP configuration by typing **ipconfig /all** at the command prompt. You can also use **ipconfig /renew** to renew the IP address of your computer, and **ipconfig /release** to release your IP address manually. If you register a host with DNS using **ipconfig /registerdns**, this will also renew the IP address. It should be noted that Windows 95 does not support Ipconfig. Instead, it only supports the Winipcfg command, which is a graphical interface that provides all of the same functions (except dynamic DNS). Also note that Windows NT and Windows 9x operating systems do not support dynamic DNS.

Figure 2-14 The Command Prompt window

```
C:\WINDOWS\system32\cmd.exe                                    _ □ X
Microsoft Windows [Version 5.2.3790]
(C) Copyright 1985-2003 Microsoft Corp.

C:\Documents and Settings\Administrator>
```

Type ipconfig at
command prompt

Figure 2-15 Using ipconfig to test TCP/IP configuration

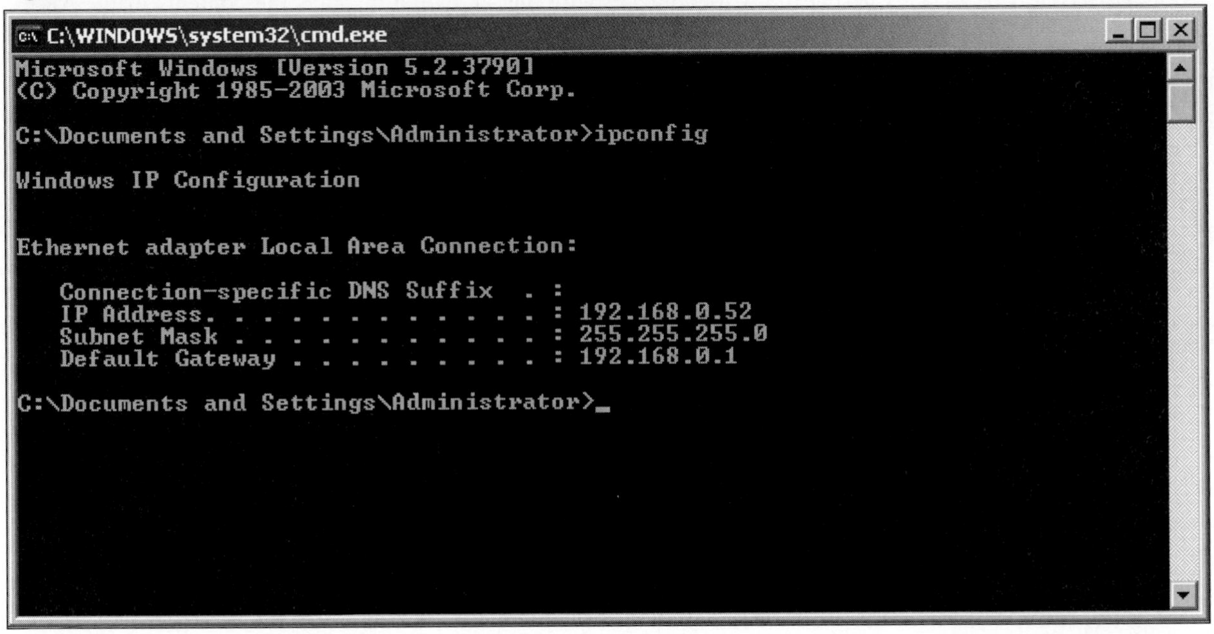

```
C:\WINDOWS\system32\cmd.exe                                    _ □ X
Microsoft Windows [Version 5.2.3790]
(C) Copyright 1985-2003 Microsoft Corp.

C:\Documents and Settings\Administrator>ipconfig

Windows IP Configuration


Ethernet adapter Local Area Connection:

    Connection-specific DNS Suffix  . :
    IP Address. . . . . . . . . . . . : 192.168.0.52
    Subnet Mask . . . . . . . . . . . : 255.255.255.0
    Default Gateway . . . . . . . . . : 192.168.0.1

C:\Documents and Settings\Administrator>_
```

skill 8 | *Troubleshooting TCP/IP Addressing*

exam objective

Troubleshooting TCP/IP addressing. Diagnose and resolve issues related to incorrect TCP/IP configuration. Troubleshoot connectivity to the Internet.

overview

As careful as you might be in implementing the TCP/IP protocol, communication problems may still arise. In addition to Ipconfig, Windows Server 2003 offers utilities such as Ping, Pathping, Tracert, Arp, Hostname, and Route to troubleshoot various potential problems. You can run these utilities from the command prompt and use them as follows:

◆ **Ping:** You use the **Packet Internet Groper (Ping)** utility to diagnose networking difficulties, including whether a host computer can connect to the TCP/IP network. Ping is a diagnostic tool that checks the TCP/IP connectivity between two IP hosts. To use Ping, you enter the IP address or host name of the computer to which you want to connect at the command prompt using the syntax **ping <IP address>**. When you press **[Enter]**, the Ping command sends an ICMP Echo Request message to the desired TCP/IP host. Ping sends the message four times by default, which results in four Echo Reply messages that include the size of the messages and their Round Trip Times (RTT). If a reply includes an **unknown host** or **host unreachable** message, you know that a connectivity problem exists. **Figure 2-16** displays a properly functioning TCP/IP connection, as confirmed by the Ping utility. You can test TCP/IP connectivity with various forms of the Ping command, which are described in **Table 2-11**. The Ping command also has various switches available so that you can fine-tune its usage. For example, to control how many ICMP echo messages Ping sends, use **ping -n (*x*) <IP address>**, where x is the number of echo requests you want to send. **Ping -t <IP address>** sends a continuous ping to the specified host. The -l (lowercase L) switch enables you to change the size of the ICMP Echo Request message, which is 32 bytes by default. For example, you could enter **ping –l 256 <IP address>**. Enter **ping /?** at the command prompt to view other Ping switches that you may use.

◆ **Hostname:** The Hostname utility is used to display the host name of the local computer.

◆ **ARP:** You use the **Arp** command to display and modify the IP address-to-physical address (MAC address) translation tables that are used by Address Resolution Protocol. Using the Arp command with the **–a** switch displays the contents of the ARP cache **(Figure 2-17)**, while using the **–d** switch resets the cache.

◆ **Tracert:** The Tracert utility allows you to follow the route that data takes when it is transferred between devices. Tracert enables you to pinpoint the location at which a data transfer failed because the utility provides the Fully Qualified Domain Name and IP address of every gateway through which the data passed on its route to the remote host.

◆ **Pathping:** The Pathping utility combines the services of Ping and Tracert, giving you a statistical analysis of connectivity over the period required to make each hop in the route at 25 seconds per hop. Pathping displays the computer name and IP address for each hop that a data transfer takes on its route and also calculates the percentage of sent packets that are lost at each router or link along the way.

Figure 2-16 Reply messages received through the ping utility

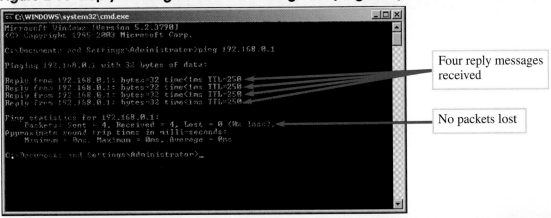

Four reply messages received

No packets lost

Table 2-11   Forms of the ping command

Command	Description
ping 127.0.0.1	127.0.0.1 is the loopback address. When you ping this IP address, you are attempting to connect back to your own computer through its internal TCP/IP protocol stack. If you do not receive a reply to this command, it indicates that TCP/IP is not installed or configured correctly on your computer.
ping <IP address of host computer>	Ping the address of your own host computer to verify that the computer has been added to the network correctly. If the routing table is correct, the command forwards the packet to the loopback address. A failure indicates that the network interface card is malfunctioning or that you have typed an incorrect IP address.
ping <IP address of default gateway>	Ping the address of the default gateway to determine whether you can reach it. If you cannot get a reply from the default gateway, either the network connection is not available or there is a hardware or software issue that is preventing you from reaching the gateway. Make sure that your network adapter's IP address is configured to be on the same subnet as your gateway.
ping <IP address of a remote host>	Ping the address of a remote host to confirm that you can communicate through a router. If you fail to receive a reply, one of the following is likely true:

a. You have entered an incorrect default gateway address.
b. The remote system is offline.
c. The routing table on the router is faulty.

d. The remote host does not have a route back to you.
e. Packets are discarded or lost due to congestion.
f. Your own firewall may be filtering Ping packets

Figure 2-17 Viewing the contents of the ARP cache

skill 8

Troubleshooting TCP/IP Addressing
(cont'd)

exam objective

Troubleshooting TCP/IP addressing. Diagnose and resolve issues related to incorrect TCP/IP configuration. Troubleshoot connectivity to the Internet.

overview

◆ **Route:** The Route command is used to display and edit the local routing table. You can use Route to specify the path that you want data packets to follow to a particular network, including the default gateway. Type **route print** at the command prompt to display the routing table on your computer (**Figure 2-18**). Use **route delete** to delete the default route from your computer.

how to

Troubleshoot TCP/IP connectivity using the tracert and pathping commands.

1. Log on to your computer as an Administrator and make sure that you have an active Internet connection.
2. Click **Start** and then click **Command Prompt** on the Start menu to open the **Command Prompt** window.
3. Type **tracert www.azimuth-interactive.com** at the command prompt and press **[Enter]**. Each hop to a router is recorded along with the time it took to reach the router, the FQDN (fully-qualified DNS host name) of the router, and the IP address of the router (**Figure 2-19**).
4. Type **tracert -h 5 www.azimuth-interactive.com**. The –h switch sets the number of hops to use to reach the specified host. When you press **[Enter]**, Tracert will attempt to trace the route to the destination host using a maximum of five hops.
5. Type **pathping www.azimuth-interactive.com** and press **[Enter]**. Pathping sends an ICMP echo request message to each router on the path from your computer to the destination host. The path of router hops is recorded as it is when you use Tracert. Then, Pathping calculates the percentage of packets lost out of packets sent (**Figure 2-20**).
6. Close the Command Prompt window.

tip

If Command Prompt does not appear on the Start menu, click Run instead, type cmd in the Open text box, and press [Enter].

more

You can access details about using many of these troubleshooting utilities by typing the command followed by /? at the command prompt and pressing [Enter].

Figure 2-18 Using route print to display the local routing table

```
C:\WINDOWS\system32\cmd.exe
C:\Documents and Settings\Administrator>route print

IPv4 Route Table
===========================================================================
Interface List
0x1 ........................... MS TCP Loopback interface
0x2 ...00 c0 4f 50 c3 ba ...... 3Com 3C918 Integrated Fast Ethernet Controller (
3C905B-TX Compatible)
===========================================================================
===========================================================================
Active Routes:
Network Destination        Netmask          Gateway       Interface  Metric
          0.0.0.0          0.0.0.0      192.168.0.1    192.168.0.52     20
        127.0.0.0        255.0.0.0        127.0.0.1       127.0.0.1      1
      192.168.0.0    255.255.255.0     192.168.0.52    192.168.0.52     20
     192.168.0.52  255.255.255.255        127.0.0.1       127.0.0.1     20
    192.168.0.255  255.255.255.255     192.168.0.52    192.168.0.52     20
        224.0.0.0        240.0.0.0     192.168.0.52    192.168.0.52     20
  255.255.255.255  255.255.255.255     192.168.0.52    192.168.0.52      1
Default Gateway:       192.168.0.1
===========================================================================
Persistent Routes:
  None

C:\Documents and Settings\Administrator>
```

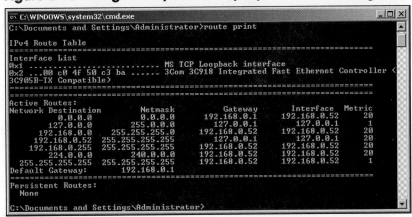

Figure 2-19 Results of the Tracert command

```
Command Prompt
Microsoft Windows [Version 5.2.3790]
(C) Copyright 1985-2003 Microsoft Corp.

C:\Documents and Settings\Administrator>tracert www.azimuth-interactive.com

Tracing route to azimuth-interactive.com [64.49.254.91]
over a maximum of 30 hops:

  1    <1 ms    <1 ms    <1 ms  192.168.0.1
  2     7 ms     9 ms     9 ms  10.135.0.1
  3     9 ms     8 ms    10 ms  dstswr1-vlan2.rh.osngny.cv.net [67.83.231.33]
  4     9 ms     9 ms     9 ms  67.83.231.1
  5     8 ms     9 ms    10 ms  r2-srp1-0.cr.whplny.cv.net [67.83.238.50]
  6     8 ms     9 ms     9 ms  r1.srp5-0.wan.whplny.cv.net [67.83.238.1]
  7    13 ms    13 ms    13 ms  r2-srp0-0.in.nycmny83.cv.net [65.19.96.84]
  8     *       14 ms    17 ms  sl-gw37-nyc-14-0.sprintlink.net [65.19.101.142]

  9    13 ms    14 ms    13 ms  sl-bb21-nyc-4-0.sprintlink.net [144.232.13.65]
 10    13 ms    14 ms    13 ms  sl-bb22-nyc-14-0.sprintlink.net [144.232.7.102]

 11    35 ms    35 ms    36 ms  sl-bb21-chi-9-0.sprintlink.net [144.232.9.149]
 12    54 ms    53 ms    54 ms  sl-bb21-fw-10-0.sprintlink.net [144.232.8.54]
 13    54 ms    53 ms    54 ms  sl-gw40-fw-8-0.sprintlink.net [144.232.8.246]
 14    65 ms    67 ms    66 ms  sl-racks-2-0.sprintlink.net [144.232.204.10]
 15    63 ms    62 ms    61 ms  vl130.core1.sat.rackspace.com [64.39.2.33]
 16    63 ms    64 ms    63 ms  vl905.aggr5.sat2.rackspace.com [64.39.2.82]
 17    61 ms    62 ms    66 ms  64.49.254.91

Trace complete.

C:\Documents and Settings\Administrator>
```

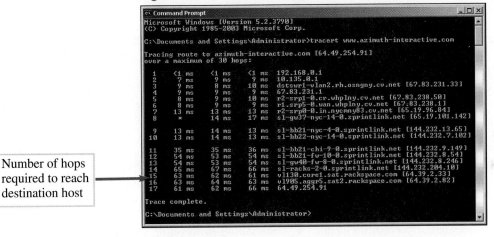

Number of hops required to reach destination host

Figure 2-20 Using the Pathping command

```
Command Prompt
 12  sl-bb21-fw-10-0.sprintlink.net [144.232.8.54]
 13  sl-gw40-fw-8-0.sprintlink.net [144.232.8.246]
 14  sl-racks-2-0.sprintlink.net [144.232.204.10]
 15  vl130.core1.sat.rackspace.com [64.39.2.33]
 16  vl905.aggr5.sat2.rackspace.com [64.39.2.82]
 17  64.49.254.91

Computing statistics for 425 seconds...
            Source to Here   This Node/Link
Hop  RTT    Lost/Sent = Pct  Lost/Sent = Pct  Address
  0                                           servera.mydomain.com [192.168.0.70
]
                                0/ 100 =  0%   |
  1    0ms     0/ 100 =  0%     0/ 100 =  0%  192.168.0.1
                                0/ 100 =  0%   |
  2   13ms     0/ 100 =  0%     0/ 100 =  0%  10.135.0.1
                                0/ 100 =  0%   |
  3   11ms     0/ 100 =  0%     0/ 100 =  0%  dstswr1-vlan2.rh.osngny.cv.net [67
.83.231.33]
                                0/ 100 =  0%   |
  4   ---    100/ 100 =100%   100/ 100 =100%  67.83.231.1
                                0/ 100 =  0%   |
  5   ---    100/ 100 =100%   100/ 100 =100%  r2-srp1-0.cr.whplny.cv.net [67.83.
238.50]
                                0/ 100 =  0%   |
  6   ---    100/ 100 =100%   100/ 100 =100%  r1.srp5-0.wan.whplny.cv.net [67.83
.238.1]
                                0/ 100 =  0%   |
  7   ---    100/ 100 =100%   100/ 100 =100%  r2-srp0-0.in.nycmny83.cv.net [65.1
9.96.84]
                                0/ 100 =  0%   |
  8   16ms     0/ 100 =  0%     0/ 100 =  0%  sl-gw37-nyc-14-0.sprintlink.net [6
5.19.101.142]
                                0/ 100 =  0%   |
  9   16ms     0/ 100 =  0%     0/ 100 =  0%  sl-bb21-nyc-4-0.sprintlink.net [14
4.232.13.65]
                                0/ 100 =  0%   |
 10   15ms     1/ 100 =  1%     1/ 100 =  1%  sl-bb22-nyc-14-0.sprintlink.net [1
44.232.7.102]
                                0/ 100 =  0%   |
 11   35ms     1/ 100 =  1%     1/ 100 =  1%  sl-bb21-chi-9-0.sprintlink.net [14
4.232.9.149]
                                0/ 100 =  0%   |
 12   57ms     0/ 100 =  0%     0/ 100 =  0%  sl-bb21-fw-10-0.sprintlink.net [14
4.232.8.54]
                                0/ 100 =  0%   |
 13   57ms     0/ 100 =  0%     0/ 100 =  0%  sl-gw40-fw-8-0.sprintlink.net [144
.232.8.246]
                                1/ 100 =  1%   |
 14   ---    100/ 100 =100%    99/ 100 = 99%  sl-racks-2-0.sprintlink.net [144.2
32.204.10]
                                0/ 100 =  0%   |
 15   ---    100/ 100 =100%    99/ 100 = 99%  vl130.core1.sat.rackspace.com [64.
39.2.33]
                                0/ 100 =  0%   |
 16   ---    100/ 100 =100%    99/ 100 = 99%  vl905.aggr5.sat2.rackspace.com [64
.39.2.82]
                                0/ 100 =  0%   |
 17   62ms     1/ 100 =  1%     0/ 100 =  0%  64.49.254.91

Trace complete.
```

Summary

◆ Transmission Control Protocol/Internet Protocol (TCP/IP) is a network protocol suite that is used to provide connectivity across operating systems and hardware platforms.

◆ TCP/IP is scalable, and therefore appropriate for implementation on the networks of both small businesses and large corporations.

◆ TCP/IP is the core protocol of the Internet.

◆ The TCP/IP suite is based on a conceptual model developed by the Department of Defense that consists of four layers. These layers are Network Interface, Internet, Transport, and Application.

◆ Computers that use the TCP/IP protocol must have an IP address that identifies them on the network. IP addressing is an addressing scheme used to identify each TCP/IP host—a device such as a computer, printer, or router on a network.

◆ Routers are devices that connect two or more network segments.

◆ An IP address is a 32-bit number that is displayed in four 8-bit sections called octets.

◆ You can express an IP address in decimal, hexadecimal, and binary notation.

◆ IP addresses have a uniform format that includes a network ID and a host ID.

◆ The network ID, also known as the network address, is identical for all hosts on the same network. It identifies the network, and is determined by the 1-bits in the network mask.

◆ The host ID, or host address, uniquely identifies each resource (workstation, server, router, etc.) on a network.

◆ The Internet community has defined five classes of addresses: A, B, C, D, and E. Each address class accommodates networks of different sizes. A, B, and C are the most commonly used classes.

◆ The address class to which an IP address belongs specifies the default for which bits of the address should be used for the network ID and which bits should be used for the host ID. You can use a subnet to customize your network mask.

◆ Subnetting is the process of breaking down a large network into smaller, more manageable pieces.

◆ A subnet mask is used to determine which section of an IP address is the host section, and which section is the network section.

◆ VLSM and CIDR change subnetting by removing the requirement that all subnets be of equal size.

◆ The installation of TCP/IP usually occurs by default when you install the Windows Server 2003 operating system.

◆ The default installation of TCP/IP in Windows Server 2003 uses Internet Protocol version 4 (IPv4), which is the standard used on the Internet and other TCP/IP networks.

◆ Internet Protocol version 6 (IPv6) has been developed to replace IPv4 to address the problem of exhausting the supply of unique IP addresses.

◆ You can configure TCP/IP on a Windows Server 2003 computer manually, dynamically, or by using Automatic Private IP Addressing (APIPA).

◆ You can use the Ipconfig utility, which provides information about the host computer configuration, to verify TCP/IP configuration.

◆ In addition to Ipconfig, Windows Server 2003 offers utilities such as Ping, Pathping, Tracert, Arp, Hostname, and Route to troubleshoot various potential problems.

Key Terms

Address Resolution Protocol (ARP)
ANDing
Application layer
Arp utility
Automatic Private IP Addressing (APIPA)
Broadcast
CIDR (Classless Inter-Domain Routing)
Default gateway
Host
Host ID
Hostname
Internet Control Message Protocol (ICMP)

Internet Group Management Protocol (IGMP)
Internet layer
Internet Protocol (IP)
Internet Protocol version 4 (IPv4)
Internet Protocol version 6 (IPv6)
IP address
Ipconfig
Network ID
Network Interface layer
Octet
Pathping
Ping (Packet Internet Groper)
Pragmatic General Multicast (PGM)

Route
Router
Routing table
Subnet mask
Subnetting
Tracert
Transmission Control Protocol (TCP)
Transmission Control Protocol/ Internet Protocol (TCP/IP)
Transport layer
Unicast
User Datagram Protocol (UDP)
VLSM (Variable Length Subnet Masking)

Test Yourself

1. To which address class does the network ID 120.0.0.0 belong?
a. Class A
b. Class B
c. Class C
d. Class D

2. Which of the following Application layer protocols enables you to transfer the contents of a Web page into a Web browser for viewing?
a. FTP
b. Telnet
c. SMTP
d. HTTP

3. Which of the following would you use to find out the IP address of the computer on which you are working?
a. Ping
b. Ipconfig
c. Advanced button
d. Ipv6

4. Which octet(s) represent the network ID in a Class C IP address?
a. First
b. First two
c. First three
d. All four

5. Which of the following addresses represents the default netmask for a Class B network?
a. 255.255.255.255
b. 255.255.255.0
c. 255.255.0.0
d. 255.0.0.0

6. The maximum number of hosts on a network that uses a Class A address is:
a. 16,777,214
b. 255
c. 254
d. 126

7. In the absence of a DHCP server, a Windows Server 2003 computer can assign itself an IP address automatically by using:
a. Loopback
b. ARP
c. Telnet
d. APIPA

8. The value of the octet 192 is expressed in binary notation as:
a. 10101000.
b. 11000000.
c. 00000011.
d. 00011000.

9. Which utility enables you to pinpoint the location at which a data transfer failed?
a. Ping
b. Route
c. Ping 127.0.0.1
d. Tracert

10. You can disable APIPA by using a:
a. Registry key
b. Multicast
c. Router
d. Control message

11. How many subnets are available for a class A address with a /22 mask?
a. 16,384
b. 8
c. 8096
d. 8094

12. What is the range of valid IP addresses for the 192.168.17.128/29 subnet?
a. 192.168.17.0–192.168.17.255
b. 192.168.1.0–192.168.255.255
c. 192.168.17.129–192.168.17.254
d. 192.168.17.1–192.168.17.254
e. 192.168.17.129–192.168.17.130

13. What is the network address for a host with the IP address of 172.16.49.219/25?
a. 172.16.0.0
b. 172.16.49.128
c. 172.16.49.0
d. 172.16.32.0

Problem Solving Scenarios

1. You work as a Network Administrator for a company that rents construction vehicles and provides services to other engineering and construction companies. Your company has purchased 3 new Windows Server 2003 computers. One of them will act as a secondary domain controller and the other two will act as file and print servers. A new HP network printer has also been purchased to be used by all of the clients on the new network. The network consists of 200 workstations. All of the hardware has been verified against the Windows Server Catalog. You have been asked to implement and test the TCP/IP suite of protocols on the new network. In doing so, you must decide between static and dynamic addressing and choose the range of addresses to use. Prepare a report for management explaining the rationale behind the IP addressing scheme you choose and the steps you will need to take in order to implement and test the new network configuration.

2. You are a Network Systems Administrator faced with the responsibility of implementing a new network. One of the file servers in the new network will also function as a Web server that allows access to and downloading of sensitive corporate documents over the company intranet. This Web server must not offer any other Web services except this high-security service. All of the other systems in your company must be configured to obtain an IP address and other configuration information using DHCP. Assume that the DHCP server is already in place. Prepare a document for management explaining the plan of action you will follow to implement such a network. Include as many details as you believe are relevant.

3 Understanding IP Routing

Routing refers to the process of selecting the path by which a source computer transfers packets of data across networks to a destination computer. When a host has to send data to another host, it uses the Internet Protocol (IP) address of the destination host to identify where to send the information. A source host can only send data to a computer on its own LAN segment. If the destination is on another LAN segment or another network, the source host sends its packet to a router on its own LAN. The router then will deliver the packet to its destination, or continue to forward the packet until it reaches a router that can deliver it. A packet has a header, which includes the IP address of the destination as well as the IP address of the source.

A host can transmit data directly to another computer on the same network. However, if the destination computer resides on a different network, a router, or gateway, acts as the interface between the two networks. When a packet arrives at a gateway, the network adapter sends the IP datagram to be inspected at the IP layer. IP reads the destination address on the packet and then looks for the address in a routing table. The router then forwards the packet on the appropriate path to the network based on the network's entry in the routing table. A router helps minimize communication costs and maximize communication efficiency by determining the best path for the packet to follow to the intended destination. Windows Server 2003 computers store defined routes in routing tables automatically. If the default route is not the best path for a packet (for instance, if a route to the specific destination is in the routing table), then the packet will be sent along the best possible path instead.

Demand-dial routing is a Windows Server 2003 feature that enables a server to detect when an alternative to the network path is required for a connection. For example, to connect to a low-traffic remote network, you might use dial-up telephone lines instead of leased dedicated lines. The server uses a dial-up connection to forward packets across a Point-to-Point Protocol (PPP) link, establishing a temporary link between the server and the destination path. Demand-dial connections sometimes charge based on the length of time that the connection is established, and are only active when demand necessitates, thus enabling organizations to reduce communication costs.

Goals

In this lesson, you will learn about the various types of IP routing, how to install and configure IP routing on Routing and Remote Access Service, how to use TCP/IP packet filtering to specify the type of incoming traffic on the network, how to install and configure static and demand-dial routing, and how to identify the remote administration tools provided by Windows Server 2003.

Lesson 3   Understanding IP Routing

Skill	Exam 70-291 Objective
1. Introducing IP Routing	Manage TCP/IP routing.
2. Introducing Routing Tables	Manage TCP/IP routing. Troubleshoot connectivity to the Internet.
3. Updating a Routing Table Manually	Manage TCP/IP routing. Manage routing tables. Troubleshoot connectivity to the Internet.
4. Configuring Static Routing	Manage TCP/IP routing.
5. Managing Routing Protocols	Manage routing protocols.
6. Installing and Configuring Demand-Dial Routing	Manage Routing and Remote Access routing interfaces. Troubleshoot Routing and Remote Access routing. Troubleshoot demand-dial routing.
7. Configuring TCP/IP Filtering	Manage routing ports. Manage packet filters. Manage Routing and Remote Access routing interfaces.

Requirements

To complete this lesson, you will need administrative rights on a Windows Server 2003 computer that is connected to a network.

skill 1

Introducing IP Routing

Manage TCP/IP routing.

overview

Routing refers to the process of selecting the path by which a source computer transfers packets of data across networks to a destination computer. In order to understand routing, you must first understand some basic details about packet formats. **Packets** (also known as frames, datagrams, and messages, depending on where in the DoD model we are discussing them) are individual units in a communications stream. Data to be sent is divided into small chunks and specific information is appended to the data to provide various identifying information.

Figure 3-1 illustrates the format of an IP header. Looking at this diagram, you can see that an IP header is composed of several components, only one of which is the actual data to be sent. However, what the diagram does not show you is that headers (and typically, a single trailer) exist both before and after the IP header. For example, a layer 2 header (Datalink layer of the OSI model) would come before the IP header. If the header were an Ethernet header, it would contain the source and destination MAC addresses, as well as the total frame length and an identifier denoting the next-layer protocol (IP in this case). In the data section of the IP header, there would be another header (most likely TCP or UDP), detailing specifics used for those protocols, and so on. Each protocol has its own information, which must be processed at the receiving end, and each protocol can be conceptualized as being "sandwiched" in the data section of the previous protocol. By splitting the responsibilities for different aspects of the protocol suite between the different protocols in this way, TCP/IP provides modularity.

Now, at this point, you are probably wondering why two types of source and destination addresses are needed. Why are both the MAC addresses in the Datalink header, and the IP addresses in the IP header, needed? The reason is to provide modularity. If each lower level device (such as a switch or network card) only supported IP, and even more specifically, only supported IP version 4, you would need to change all of the network components in order to upgrade to IP version 6 or use a different Network layer protocol (such as IPX). Therefore, the Datalink layer is specifically responsible for addressing between physical devices. In Ethernet, this is done using MAC addresses, which are 12-digit hexadecimal addresses identifying the manufacturer and serial number for the network card.

However, MAC addresses (and most other Datalink addresses) have no provision for a network section. This makes them ineffective for routing purposes. Thus, the IP address is used to determine the network you are on. In fact, network determination can be considered to be the primary purpose of an IP address. What network you are on is critical because, as we discussed previously, routers (which connect different networks) block all broadcasts. To understand the importance of this statement, let's walk through a simple scenario.

Imagine that you have two computers on the 192.168.1.0/24 network, using IP addresses 192.168.1.2 and 192.168.1.3. You have one computer on the 10.0.0.0/8 network, using the 10.0.0.2 IP address. Between the two networks, you have a router with two IP addresses. 192.168.1.1 is used on the 192.168.1.0/24 network, and 10.0.0.1 is used on the 10.0.0.0/8 network. When the 192.168.1.2 computer wishes to communicate with the 192.168.1.3 computer, it must first find the MAC address of that computer. To find the MAC address, it uses the ARP protocol to broadcast an ARP query to the entire network. This ARP broadcast will inform all hosts that the 192.168.1.2 PC is looking for the MAC address used by the computer using the 192.168.1.3 IP address. Most computers will notice that this is not their IP address, and simply discard the packet, but 192.168.1.3 will respond to the request, informing 192.168.1.2 of its MAC address. Once the 192.168.1.2 computer has received the MAC address for the destination, it can begin communication with that host.

tip

The MAC address is often called the "burned-in" address.

tip

In some cases, a router might not be able to transmit data because the router is unable to find a path to the destination network. In such a case, the router sends an error message to the source computer indicating that the data was not sent to the destination computer.

Figure 3-1 Contents of an IP packet

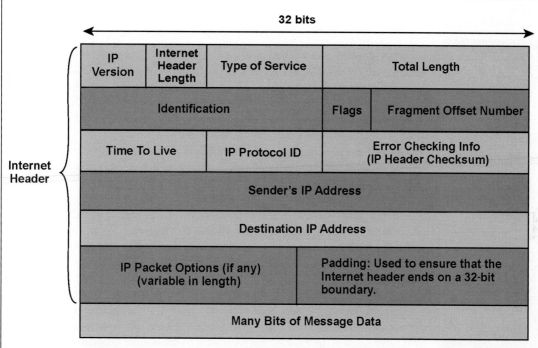

- **IP Version: (4 bits)** The IP Version field indicates the format of the Internet header, either IPv4 or IPv6
- **Internet Header Length: (4 bits)** The length of the Internet header in 32-bit words (x4 = length in bits). It points to the beginning of the data. The minimum value for a correct header is 5.
- **Type of Service: (8 bits)** Provides parameters for quality of service. In general there is a three way tradeoff between low-delay, high-reliability, and high-throughput.
- **Total Length: (16 bits)** The length of the datagram, including Internet header and data, measured in octets. A datagram can be up to 65,535 octets long; however, datagrams this long are impractical for most hosts and networks. All hosts must be prepared to accept datagrams of up to 576 octets either whole or in fragments.
- **Identification: (16 bits)** An identifying value assigned by the sender to aid in assembling the fragments of a datagram.
- **Flags: (3 bits)** Various control flags Bit 0: reserved, must be zero
  Bit 1: (DF) 0 = May Fragment, 1 = Don't Fragment. Bit 2: (MF) 0 = Last Fragment, 1 = More Fragments.
- **Fragment Offset: (13 bits)** Indicates where in the datagram this fragment belongs.
- **Time To Live: (8 bits)** The maximum time the datagram is allowed to remain in the Internet system. If this field contains the value zero, the datagram must be destroyed.
- **IP Protocol ID: (8 bits)** Indicates the next layer protocol used in the data portion of the IP datagram.
- **Header Checksum: (16 bits)** Checksum for the header only. Must be recomputed and verified each time the Internet header is processed because some header fields change (for example, Time To Live).

skill 1

Introducing IP Routing (cont'd)

exam objective

Manage TCP/IP routing.

overview

However, this presents a problem when attempting to communicate to a computer on another network. Since ARP uses broadcasts, the ARP protocol cannot be used to find MAC addresses for machines on the other side of a router. Therefore, the process changes a bit. Whenever a computer needs to communicate using IP, first it performs the ANDing process to determine whether it should use ARP or whether it needs to use a router. If the results in the ANDing process are exactly the same, the computer can use ARP directly. Otherwise, the computer will attempt to use a router, as different AND results indicate that the computer is on a remote network. To use a router, the computer first checks its route table for a listing for the destination network. If a matching entry is found, the computer will use ARP to find the MAC address for the router listed in the table. It will then send the packet to the router by inserting the router's MAC address in the packet. However, the destination IP address for the remote computer does not change. In other words, if 192.168.1.2 is trying to communicate with 10.0.0.2, it will send a packet to its router using the router's MAC address, but still containing the IP address (10.0.0.2 in this case) for the end destination. Upon receiving the packet, the router will examine the destination IP address and examine its route table. If no entry matching the network address is found, the packet is dropped, and an ICMP Destination Unreachable message is sent back to the source IP. If a matching entry is found, and it is local to the router, the router will use ARP to locate the MAC address of the destination, modify the MAC addresses in the packet, and forward it to the correct destination. If a matching entry is found that is remote to the router (through another router, for example), the router will use ARP to find the MAC address for the next router insert that address into the packet, and forward the packet to the next hop router. In this case, this process continues until the packet reaches a router that is local to the end destination, or until a router drops the packet due to lack of a valid route for the destination network.

Viewed in this manner, you can see that routing is a hop-by-hop process. In other words, neither the router nor the source defines the entire path that the packet will take. They simply forward it to the next hop, which performs the same process, forwarding it, hop by hop, until it reaches its final destination. The number of routers used to transmit the data to its destination is known as the **hop count**.

more

Routers communicate with each other using routing protocols (**Table 3-1**). There are two main types of routing protocols:

♦ **Interior routing protocols** connect two or more routers that are administered under a common administrative authority, which can be an administrator or a group of administrators with common administrative rights. Windows Server 2003 supports two interior routing protocols: **Routing Information Protocol (RIP)** and **Open Shortest Path First (OSPF)**. RIP is simpler and easier to configure than OSPF, but OSPF is the more efficient protocol.

♦ **Exterior routing protocols** are used to exchange information between networks that are administered under different administrative authorities. The first exterior routing protocol developed was Exterior Gateway Protocol (EGP). A more effective version developed later was **Border Gateway Protocol (BGP)**. The latest version is called BGP-4.

Routing protocols will be covered with further detail in Skill 5.

Table 3-1   Routing Protocols

Protocol	Description
Routing Information Protocol (RIP)	RIP is one of the two interior routing protocol used by Windows Server 2003. It is based on a simple distance vector-based algorithm. RIP broadcasts periodic updates that contain the entire routing table because there is no provision for advertising only changes. Bandwidth is wasted because the entire routing table is transmitted every thirty seconds, making it far less efficient than OSPF; however, it is easier to configure. One configuration problem with RIP is that the updates produce what is referred to as routing loops. Routes "loop," or pass through a single router multiple times because RIP relies on its neighboring routers to know the correct path. It does not keep track of the entire path. Another problem with RIP is that its only metric is hop count. RIP will choose a slower link as the "better" link, if it has a lower hop count even if the connection speed is faster for the path that requires more hops.
Open Shortest Path First	OSPF is the other interior routing protocol used by Windows Server 2003. It was developed for IP networks and is based on the SPF algorithm (sometimes called the Dijkstra Shortest Path First algorithm, after its creator). It is a much more complex and difficult protocol to configure than RIP. However, unlike RIP, OSPF calculates the entire path to each given destination. First, hello messages are sent every 5 seconds to the OSPF multicast address. These hello messages only contain a small amount of information, so bandwidth is kept to a minimum. OSPF routers become "acquainted" and keep track of each other's status. Link State Advertisements (LSAs) are sent to all of these "neighbors," informing them of their directly connected networks (links). The neighboring routers forward the unaltered LSA to all of their neighbors, which then forward it to their neighbors, and so on, until all routers have a copy of the LSA. As each LSA as received, it is added to a list of routers and their links, called the Link State Database. Thus, each OSPF router creates its own, highly accurate map of the network and the routing table is built from this map. This functionality ensures that OSPF does not suffer from the difficulties with routing loops that plague RIP.
Border Gateway Protocol (BGP)	BGP is an exterior routing protocol used to exchange routing information for the Internet. It is the protocol used between ISPs. Universities and corporations generally use an interior routing protocol such as RIP or OSPF, while ISPs use BGP4.

skill 2

Introducing Routing Tables

exam objective

Manage TCP/IP routing. Troubleshoot connectivity to the Internet.

overview

All IP hosts must maintain a route table. Routing tables are used to determine the next hop for a given network. Route tables contain several components, listed in **Table 3-2**.

Each route in the table will contain an entry for each of these components. The most important of these are the destination network and mask, because they define which network or networks the route will match. This matching process is performed in exactly the same way as when you are subnetting: By ANDing the mask with the entered destination in the table to determine the network addresses matched. The easiest way to understand this, however, is to simply think of it like this: If the bit in the mask is a binary 1, then that portion of the address in the route must match the destination address in the packet in order for it to be used. For example, the route destination **192.168.0.0** with a mask of **255.255.0.0** will match all packets destined for **192.168.0.0–192.168.255.255**. Similarly, the route **192.168.1.1** with a mask of **255.255.255.255** will only match packets with a destination address of **192.168.1.1**. This particular type of route is a special route, known as a host route, because it only matches one specific host (**Figure 3-2**).

Another special type of route is the default route, which is any destination with all 0s in the mask. Usually, you will see the default route listed as **0.0.0.0** with a **0.0.0.0** mask, but the route **172.16.2.1** with a **0.0.0.0** mask is also a default route. Since the mask is all 0s, the route entry will match all destinations. Default routes are typically found on client computers and on routers with only one path to the Internet.

However, just because a default route matches all destinations does not necessarily mean that it is used for all destinations. IP hosts use a best match philosophy regarding the routing table. The route that best matches the actual destination IP in the packet will be used. To help understand this, let's examine an example using the routing table entries listed below:

1. Destination: 192.0.0.0   Mask: 255.0.0.0
2. Destination: 192.168.0.0   Mask: 255.255.0.0
3. Destination: 192.168.1.0   Mask: 255.255.255.0
4. Destination: 192.168.1.2   Mask: 255.255.255.255
5. Destination: 0.0.0.0   Mask: 0.0.0.0

Using this table, if you send a packet to **192.168.1.2**, the packet will be sent using route number **4,** as it matches the destination IP the best. However, a packet destined for **192.168.3.1** would use route number **2**, and a packet destined for **172.16.1.1** would use route number **5** (the default route). The best match for any given IP packet will be used.

After the matching statements (destination and mask), you have the exit interface and the next hop. The exit interface simply defines which interface the host will forward the packet out of to reach the defined next hop. As such, it is normally automatically defined based on the next hop address. The next hop is the IP address of the local interface for the next hop router. In other words, this address is the IP address applied to the router interface that is on the same subnet as the host.

Finally, you have the metric. Metrics are typically used with dynamic routing to define the most preferred next hop router when there are multiple paths to a given destination. The value for the metric varies drastically depending on the dynamic routing protocol used, but in all cases, lower metrics signify preferred routes.

Table 3-2 Columns of a routing table

Column headings	Description
Network Destination	Lists the network IDs of the destination networks to which data is sent, including the local LAN. An ID of all zeros typically indicates the default gateway.
Netmask	The netmask is used in conjunction with the destination to define the destination addresses that this route will match.
Gateway	Lists the IP addresses of the adjacent routers, including your own host as a gateway to your directly-connected LAN, and your internal loopback (127.0.0.1).
Interface	Lists the IP addresses that correspond to the network interface used to forward the data packet to the destination computer or other routers. For most hosts, this will be either their own network adapter or their internal loopback interface.
Metric	Lists the cost of each route and enables you to select the best route when multiple routes to the same destination are available.

Figure 3-2 The ANDing process

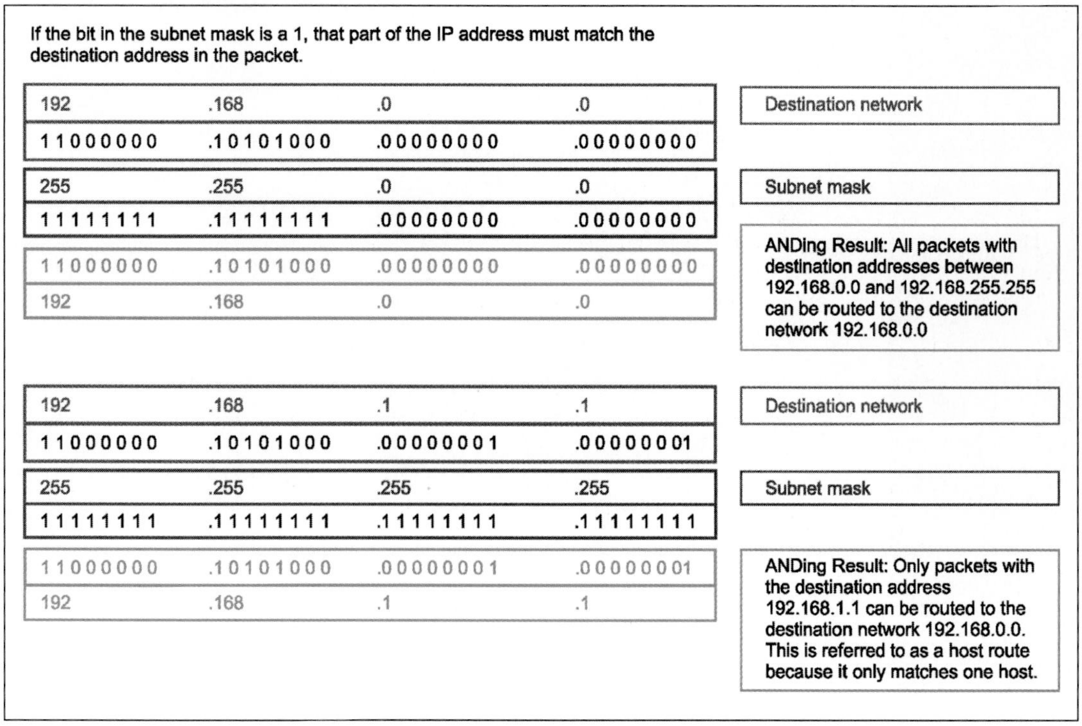

If the bit in the subnet mask is a 1, that part of the IP address must match the destination address in the packet.

192	.168	.0	.0	Destination network
11000000	.10101000	.00000000	.00000000	
255	.255	.0	.0	Subnet mask
11111111	.11111111	.00000000	.00000000	
11000000	.10101000	.00000000	.00000000	ANDing Result: All packets with destination addresses between 192.168.0.0 and 192.168.255.255 can be routed to the destination network 192.168.0.0
192	.168	.0	.0	

192	.168	.1	.1	Destination network
11000000	.10101000	.00000001	.00000001	
255	.255	.255	.255	Subnet mask
11111111	.11111111	.11111111	.11111111	
11000000	.10101000	.00000001	.00000001	ANDing Result: Only packets with the destination address 192.168.1.1 can be routed to the destination network 192.168.0.0. This is referred to as a host route because it only matches one host.
192	.168	.1	.1	

skill 2

Introducing Routing Tables (cont'd)

exam objective

Manage TCP/IP routing. Troubleshoot connectivity to the Internet.

overview

While all hosts will keep a routing table, that table can only contain the base routes required by IP. In this case, the host would not be able to reach any networks except those to which it is directly connected. By default, in Windows Server 2003, you will always have the following routes in your routing table:

- ◆ Destination: 127.0.0.0   Mask: 255.0.0.0
- ◆ Destination: Network address for each NIC   Mask: Same used for your IP
- ◆ Destination: IP address for each NIC   Mask: 255.255.255.255
- ◆ Destination: Broadcast address for each NIC   Mask: 255.255.255.255
- ◆ Destination: 224.0.0.0   Mask: 240.0.0.0
- ◆ Destination: 255.255.255.255   Mask: 255.255.255.255

These entries define routes for your loopback network (any IP beginning with 127), your locally connected networks, the multicast address range (224-239), and the all networks broadcast address (255.255.255.255/32). Any additional entries will need to be added either manually, using either the Route command or Routing and Remote Access, or dynamically, using a dynamic routing protocol. The only real exception to this is in the case of the default route. Any IP address that is configured for the default gateway under IP properties will become your default route. This occurs regardless of whether the address is entered manually or through DHCP.

You can view the routing table on your local machine by opening a command prompt and typing the command **route print (Figure 3-3)**.

Figure 3-3 Route print

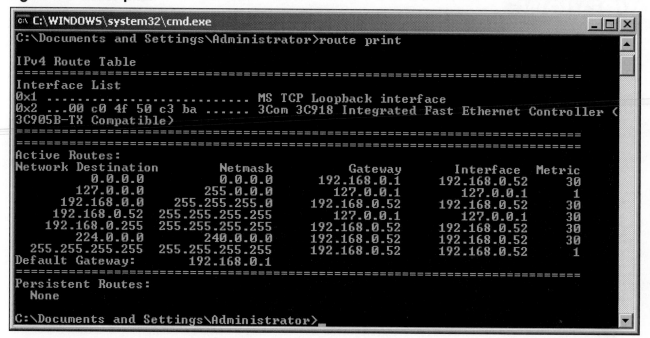

skill 3

Updating a Routing Table Manually

exam objective

Manage TCP/IP routing. Manage routing tables. Troubleshoot connectivity to the Internet.

overview

There will be times in which the base entries along with a default gateway do not suffice. In all but the simplest routing scenarios, you will need to add routes to the routers (and sometimes, on other hosts as well). For example, **Figure 3-4** illustrates a very simple routing scenario which requires you to add additional routes. The spoke routers simply need a default route back to the hub router. However, the hub router needs an entry in the routing table for each of the networks attached to each of the spoke routers (192.168.1.0/24, 192.168.2.0/24, and 192.168.3.0/24). If this step is neglected, the clients attached to the spoke routers will be able to get to 172.16.0.0/16, but their packets will not be returned, because the hub router will not have a path back.

As alluded to in the last skill, there are two methods of adding routes to your routing tables; statically, or dynamically. **Static routing** has a bad reputation with many Administrators, but if you do not have any redundant paths, you should almost always use static routing. Static routes are just that: static. They are entered, updated, and removed manually, using either the **Route** command (**Table 3-3**), or the **Routing and Remote Access** console. While this seems like a lot of work, it really isn't, normally. If you have no redundant paths in your network (for instance, in a hub and spoke layout), then there are no paths to update in the event of a failure. You simply enter your static routes once, and should only need to change them when the network is reconfigured.

The other method of updating the routing table is through **dynamic routing**. Dynamic routing protocols come in many different forms, but they all have one primary goal: They facilitate the exchange of routes between routers. Using a dynamic routing protocol, each router will learn of the paths available in the network and automatically enter, remove, and update those paths as necessary. In addition, some dynamic routing protocols are capable of load balancing across multiple paths to the same destination. However, be aware that dynamic routing comes with a price. Bandwidth will be consumed to some degree due to the propagation of route advertisements (though the specific amount varies, again, with the protocol), and all routing protocols will utilize processor and memory resources to some degree. However, if you have redundant paths in your network, a dynamic routing protocol is almost a necessity, as static routing cannot automatically detect changes in the environment (such as when a path is invalid).

tip

If you are using the Route command to enter routes you must make sure that you use the -p flag for all routes that you wish to make permanent. If you neglect to use this command, the routes will be removed at the next reboot.

how to

Update a Windows Server2003 routing table manually. (You will need to have an IP address on the 192.168.0.0/24 network in order to complete this exercise.)

1. Click **Start** and then click **Run** to open the **Run** dialog box.
2. In the Open text box, type **cmd**, and then click **OK**. The **Command Prompt** window opens.
3. At the command prompt, type **route add 135.45.1.15 mask 255.255.255.255 192.168.0.1**. This command enables communication with the host 135.45.1.15 from a gateway host 192.168.0.1.
4. Press the **[Enter]** key to update the routing table manually with the new route.
5. Type **route print** at the command prompt and press **[Enter]** to view the new route added to the routing table (**Figure 3-5**).

Figure 3-4 Simple routing scenario

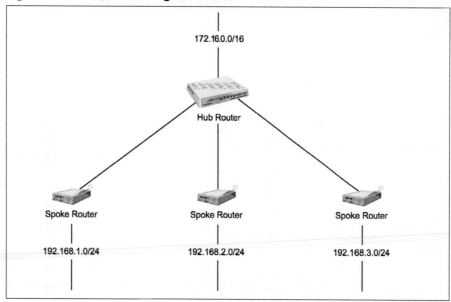

Table 3-3   Commands for adding or modifying static routes in a routing table

Task	Command
Add a route	route add [network] mask [netmask] [gateway]
Add a persistent route that remains preserved when a system restarts	route –p add [network] mask [netmask] [gateway]
Delete a route	route delete [network] [gateway]
Modify a route	route change [network] [gateway]
Display routing table	• route print • netstat –rn
Clear all routes (flushes the routing table with the exception of the base routes discussed earlier)	route –f

Figure 3-5 Updating a routing table manually

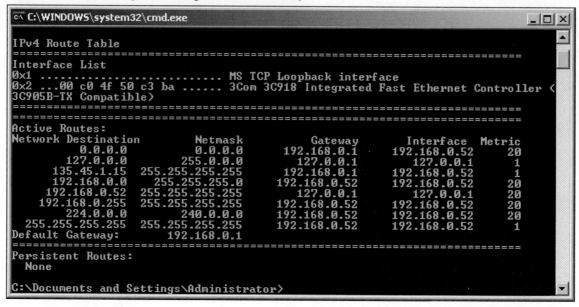

skill 4

Configuring Static Routing

exam objective

Manage TCP/IP routing.

overview

Generally speaking, a host has implicit routes, static (or explicit) routes, and dynamic routes. Implicit routes are configured automatically as a result of the fact that a host can deliver a packet directly to any other host on the same network segment. You configure static routing when your computer will only be exchanging data between specific remote hosts and networks. You configure static routing by adding static routes to or removing static routes from a routing table. The address class to which an IP address belongs specifies which bits of the address should be used for the network ID and which bits should be used for the host ID.

how to

Configure static routing in a routing table.

1. Click **Start**, point to **Administrative Tools**, and click **Routing and Remote Access**. The **Routing and Remote Access** console opens.
2. Right-click your server name in the left pane and choose **Configure and Enable Routing and Remote Access** to open the **Routing and Remote Access Server Setup Wizard**.
3. Click **Next >** to open the **Configuration** screen.
4. Choose the **Custom Configuration** option and click **Next >**.
5. Select only the **LAN routing** check box, and click **Next >**.
6. Click **Finish** to exit the wizard. A dialog box will appear asking if you wish to start the Routing and Remote Access service. Click **Yes** to start the service.
7. Click **IP Routing** in the left pane to view the options for IP Routing in the details pane.
8. Right-click **Static Routes** and select **New Static Route** to open the **Static Route** dialog box **(Figure 3-6)**.
9. Select **Local Area Connection** in the **Interface** list box.
10. Type **155.143.134.0** in the **Destination** text box to specify the destination for the route.
11. Type **255.255.255.0** in the **Network mask** text box to specify the network mask for the static route.
12. Type the router IP address, **192.168.0.1**, in the **Gateway** box to specify the forwarding IP address for the static route.
13. Type the metric associated with the static route in the **Metric** spin box. The default value is **1** **(Figure 3-7)**.
14. Click **OK** to close the Static Route dialog box.
15. Close the Routing and Remote Access console.

tip

Dynamic routes are created when the IP protocol receives ICMP redirect messages in a static routing environment. The ICMP messages, which are sent by routers, inform the IP protocol of better routes to a host or network.

tip

The destination can be a host address, subnet address, network address, or the destination for the default route (0.0.0.0).

Figure 3-6 Static Route dialog box

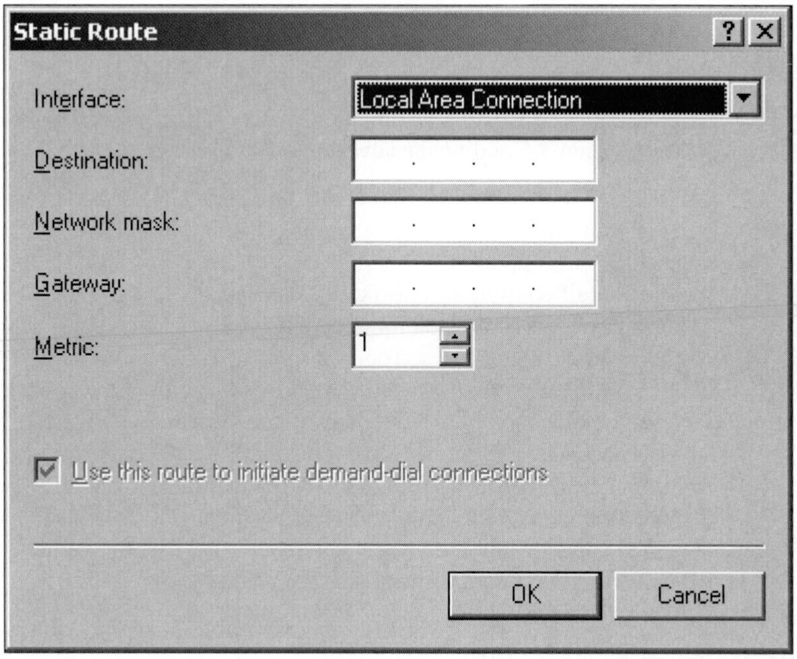

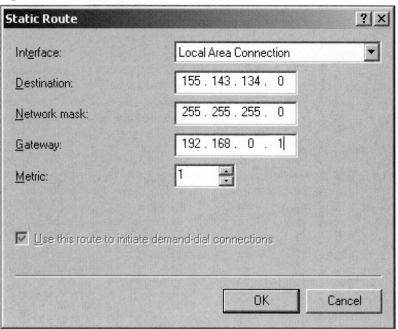

Figure 3-7 New static route

skill 5

Managing Routing Protocols

exam objective

Manage routing protocols.

overview

Dynamic routing in Windows Server 2003 is limited to two well known, vendor-independent routing protocols: Routing Information Protocol (RIP), and Open Shortest Path First (OSPF). **Tables 3-4** and **3-5** outline the advantages and disadvantages of the two protocols.

RIP is the simpler of the two protocols. It operates based on a very simple distance vector-based algorithm. In RIP, routers learn of paths to other networks through periodic advertisements, known as updates. By default, RIP routers broadcast these advertisements every 30 seconds on all configured interfaces. The updates in RIP contain the entire routing table, because there is no provision for advertising only changes. This functionality means that not only does every client and server connected to RIP-enabled segments receive the broadcast, but bandwidth is also excessively wasted by transmitting the entire routing table every thirty seconds. In order to enable RIP to advertise a network, you must also necessarily enable RIP advertisements across that network. This means that if you wish to advertise a client subnet that does not include any RIP routers, RIP will still send advertisements on that network, by default. To eliminate this problem, you must change the mode of the interface connected to the client subnet from periodic update mode to silent RIP mode. Silent RIP mode disables RIP advertisements on the given interface.

RIP updates, which include the entire routing table, also produce a much more complex problem: routing loops. RIP must include some additional complexity due to its propensity to create routes that "loop," or pass through a single router multiple times. This occurs because RIP doesn't keep track of the entire path. It simply relies on its neighboring routers to know the correct path. For example, a router may send an advertisement about network 1 to another router. The second router would then add the route to its table. Later, the original router may lose its path to the network. Without additional functionality, the second router might send an advertisement about network 1 back to the original router, even though its only path to that network was through the original router. This would cause a problem where any packet sent to network 1 would be endlessly passed between both routers until the TTL expired, creating a router-based game of hot potato. For this reason, split horizon is employed in RIP to reduce the possibility of routing loops. Split horizon stipulates that any route learned through a particular interface will never be advertised back out of that interface. So in this example, after enabling split horizon, the second router would never send an advertisement about network 1 back to the router from which it learned of that network.

tip

There are actually two forms of split horizon: Split horizon and split horizon with poison reverse. Split horizon with poison reverse differs in that it actually does send the advertised route back to the originating router, but it does so with an infinite metric. This ensures that if the route was previously entered incorrectly it will be properly removed.

However, split horizon still does not solve a great number of RIP's looping problems, so an additional timer was added to help resolve these problems. This timer, known on Windows routers as the route removal timer, can be thought of as a reality check for the router. Once a route has been determined to be invalid, RIP still retains it in the routing table until the route removal timer expires (120 seconds, by default). This helps ensure that an incorrect entry for the same path is not added to the table by allowing the timers on all neighboring routers to expire (forcing them to remove the route as well). However, this also causes a quite large time gap between the time a link is considered dead and the time convergence, or unity in the routing tables of all routers, is achieved. Each RIP router marks a route as dead (or expired) if an advertisement has not been heard for the route before the route expiration timer expires (180 seconds, by default). After the route has been marked expired, the route removal timer must still elapse before the route will actually be removed from the table. Therefore, the time differential between failure and removal of the route from the routing table on a RIP router, using the default timers, is 5 minutes (300 seconds). While you can modify the timers on a RIP router, this is not suggested, as poor timer choices can lead to serious routing loops.

However, you can reduce the time period required for convergence fairly significantly by using an additional feature of RIP known as triggered updates. Triggered updates, when

Table 3-4   RIP advantages and disadvantages

Advantages	Disadvantages
Easily installed and configured.	Only metric used to determine "best" route is hop count. Can lead to pinhole congestion.
Supports load balancing across redundant paths.	Maximum hop count is 15.
Supports route filters.	Maximum number of routing table entries per update packet is limited to 25.
Supports equal cost load balancing across redundant routes.	Substantial traffic increase on each subnet when routing tables for a large inter-network must be sent.
Supports IPX.	Wasted bandwidth because the entire routing table is broadcast every 30 seconds.
	No Area Border routing capabilities.
	Slow detection of downed routers. Time differential between route failure and route removal is 5 minutes. RIP waits for 3 minutes after not receiving an update before determining that the route must be expired; then 2 minutes more must pass before the route removal timer expires and the route is removed. (In RIP v2, triggered updates alleviate this problem.)

Table 3-5   OSPF advantages and disadvantages

Advantages	Disadvantages
Superior scaling capabilities compared to RIP on large inter-networks.	More difficult to configure.
Superior routing decisions compared to RIP because the routing table is not based only on hop count.	Calculating the routing database requires more processing by the router.
More rapid detection of downed routers; changes are more quickly propagated to other routers.	Memory intensive.
More control over the size of the routing table.	Does not support IPX.
Supports VLSM and authentication.	Does not support demand-dial routing.

skill 5

Managing Routing Protocols (cont'd)

exam objective

Manage routing protocols.

overview

tip

The maximum hop count allowed in RIP is 15. A network with a hop count of 16 or greater is considered unreachable for communication by other networks.

enabled, allow a RIP router to immediately inform neighbors of the failure of any of its directly connected networks, rather than waiting for the next update interval.

One other disadvantage of RIP is the simplicity of its metric. The only metric used by RIP is hop count. Therefore, if one path uses a 1.544 Mbps connection at 3 hops and another path to the same destination uses a 44 Mbps connection at 6 hops, RIP will choose the slower link as the "better" link, due to its exclusive use of hop count. When a RIP router advertises a route, it does so with a metric one hop higher, by default, than its local metric. This means that each router along the path will add one to the metric, until the metric reaches 16, at which point the destination is considered unreachable through that path.

RIP does have a few advantages. It is easy to install and configure and it supports load balancing across redundant paths. In addition, RIP supports the configuration of route filters. Route filters are filters to block or allow routes to specific networks. This is useful in certain cases to keep a RIP router from creating a routing loop in advanced scenarios. Furthermore, RIP is available for both IP and IPX. Finally, RIP also supports equal-cost load balancing across redundant routes. However, since RIP does not take bandwidth into account, this can lead to RIP refusing to send any data over the faster of two links when the slow one becomes congested, a problem known as pinhole congestion.

RIP in Windows Server 2003 is available in two versions: RIP version 1 and RIP version 2. When possible, RIPv2 is the better choice, as it supports features not available in RIPv1 such as multicasted updates, VLSM support, and plain-text authentication (**Table 3-6**).

OSPF, on the other hand, is a much more complex and difficult protocol to understand and configure. OSPF is based on the Dijkstra Shortest Path First algorithm, and unlike RIP, OSPF does calculate the entire path to a given destination. OSPF begins by sending out hello messages once every 5 seconds to the OSPF multicast address. This address is only watched by OSPF routers, and therefore does not cause difficulties with non-OSPF hosts. Additionally, the hellos only contain a small amount of information, so bandwidth usage is minimal. As routers hear hello messages, they begin to form a "neighborship" with the remote router. This means that the OSPF routers are now aware of each other, and will, from this point on, keep track of each other's status. After this occurs, OSPF will send Link State Advertisements (LSAs) to all of its neighbors, informing them only of their directly connected networks (known as links). The neighboring routers will then forward the unaltered LSA to all of their neighbors, which will then forward it to their neighbors, and so on, until all routers have a copy of the LSA. As each LSA as received, it is added to a list of routers and their links called the Link State Database. By playing "connect the dots" using this database and the SPF algorithm, each OSPF router creates its own, highly accurate map of the network. The routing table is then built from this map (**Table 3-7**). This functionality ensures that OSPF does not suffer from the difficulties with loops that plague RIP. Additionally, since OSPF only sends hellos at periodic intervals (LSAs are sent only at boot and when a change occurs), OSPF is very light on bandwidth usage. Also, OSPF uses bandwidth as its metric, meaning that it can give a much more accurate representation of the actual speed of a given path. OSPF also scales to absolutely enormous sizes, as it supports an infinite number of hops (IP, on the other hand, only support 255 hops). Finally, convergence in OSPF is extremely rapid, due to its nature.

However, OSPF also has its share of disadvantages. The largest of these is the fact that it can be both processor and memory intensive in large environments. Creating and maintaining a complete map of the network is an intensive process, thus low-end routers may suffer. Therefore, OSPF routing domains are often divided into separate areas. Each OSPF router is

Table 3-6   Features available in RIPv2

Feature	Description
Multicasted updates	Multicasting of updates is less processor intensive on machines that are not RIP-enabled. With a broadcast, all computers must spend some time processing the update packets, even if they do not run the RIP routing protocol. Multicasts are ignored by computers that are not running RIP.
VLSM support	RIPv1 does not include the subnet mask with each update, and therefore does not support subnets of differing sizes.
Plain-text authentication	You can configure a password in RIPv2. This allows the router to differentiate between authorized routers and rogue routers. Advertisements from routers without the correct password will be ignored.

Table 3-7   How OSPF builds a routing table

1. Hello messages are sent every 5 seconds to the OSPF multicast address.

2. When all of the OSPF-enabled routers in the "neighborhood" are aware of each other, they send out their routing table as a Link State Advertisement (LSA) to all neighboring routers.
   - When a router receives an LSA from another router, it adds the information to its own LSA.
   - In this way, information from all routers in the neighborhood is dispersed throughout the network.

3. The routers compile all of the LSAs for the entire network into the Link State Database.

4. Using the Link State Database and the Dijkstra SPF algorithm, each router calculates its own highly accurate map of the network (link-state tree).
   - Each router constructs a different link-state tree. The router itself is the root of the tree and the path to every other subnet in the organization is outlined.

5. The routing table is built from the link-state tree based on the cheapest cost route to each subnet.
   - OSPF uses bandwidth and availability to determine the cheapest cost or "best" route.
   - The router then uses this routing table to route packets through the network.

skill 5

Managing Routing Protocols (cont'd)

exam objective

Manage routing protocols.

overview

only responsible for maintaining a database of its own area. By separating a large network into several areas, you can exponentially reduce the load on each router. Connectivity between areas is accomplished through the use of Area Border Routers (ABRs), which are routers that connect the backbone area (area 0) to another area (**Figure 3-8**). Since ABRs are connected to two areas, and therefore must maintain a complete map of both, the routers in a given area can simply send information destined for another area to the ABR for delivery. Redundancy for the ABRs is accomplished by configuring multiple ABRs for each area. Moreover, all areas must be connected to the backbone area through at least one ABR. Furthermore, under normal circumstances, areas cannot connect to any other area except the backbone.

There may be cases in which a remote area may have no other connectivity except to a different, non-backbone area. In these cases, an advanced feature of OSPF, known as virtual links, can be used to connect two non-backbone areas. Virtual links are essentially tunnels through a non-backbone area to the backbone. By creating a virtual link, you can temporarily resolve this problem. However, you should be aware that virtual links are not recommended in most cases, and permanent virtual links are almost always a bad idea, due to the additional troubleshooting difficulty they can impose.

OSPF in Windows Server 2003 supports most of the features of RIPv2, including VLSM support, plain-text authentication, and multicasting of updates. However, OSPF does not support IPX or demand-dial routing (**Table 3-8**).

Figure 3-8 Area Border Routers (ABRs)

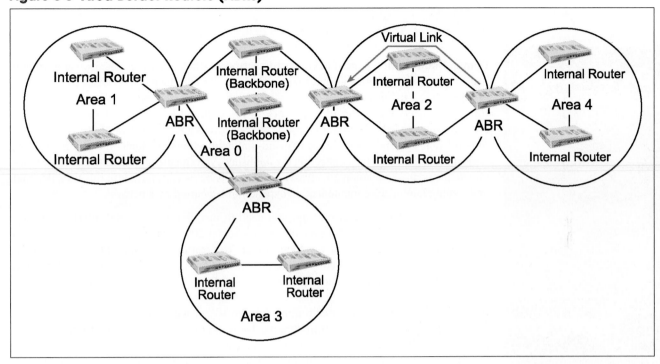

Table 3-8 Features supported by OSPF in Windows Server 2003	
Supported	**Not supported**
Multicasted updates	
VLSM support	
Plain-text authentication	
	IPX
	demand-dial routing

skill 6

Installing and Configuring Demand-Dial Routing

exam objective

Manage Routing and Remote Access routing interfaces. Troubleshoot Routing and Remote Access routing. Troubleshoot demand-dial routing.

overview

Demand-dial routing is used to connect to networks when the server detects that a network path is not available, when a router with a demand-dial interface detects that there is data to send, or to re-establish another connection such as a VPN that has been lost. Demand-dial routing connects the router of a network to the required host only for the time that the connection is needed. The server forwards packets across a Point-to-Point Protocol (PPP) link over the dial-up connection. Since demand-dial connections are sometimes charged on the basis of time for which the connection is established, you can use an idle time-out value to terminate the connection automatically when no data is being transferred. In this way, demand-dial routing minimizes communication expenditures incurred by a network.

In order to use demand-dial routing, you need to install a demand-dial interface on your router. A **demand-dial interface** on a Windows Server 2003-based router assists the router in establishing a connection with a remote router. You can use demand-dial filters to specify what types of traffic are allowed to create the connection. You install a demand-dial interface using the **Demand Dial Interface Wizard** on a valid port that is enabled for routing.

how to

Install and configure demand-dial routing through VPN connection.

1. Click **Start**, point to **Administrative Tools**, and click **Routing and Remote Access**. The **Routing and Remote Access** console opens.
2. If necessary, click the plus sign next to your server's name in the left pane of the window to expand the server node.
3. Right-click the server name and click **Properties**. On the **General** tab, click the **LAN and demand-dial routing** option button and then click **OK**. Click **Yes** to restart the router and make the configuration change.
4. Right-click **Network Interfaces** in the left pane of the window, and then click **New Demand-dial Interface** on the shortcut menu to start the **Demand-dial Interface Wizard**.
5. Click **Next >** to advance to the **Interface Name** screen of the Wizard.
6. Type **Demand VPN** in the **Interface name** text box to replace the suggested name for the demand-dial interface with a more descriptive name that suits the operation you are performing (**Figure 3-9**).
7. Click **Next >** to advance to the **Connection Type** screen of the Wizard.
8. Select the **Connect using virtual private networking (VPN)** option button.
9. Click **Next >** to advance to the **VPN Type** screen.
10. Leave the **Automatic selection** option button selected and click **Next >** to open the **Destination Address** screen.
11. Type the destination host's name or IP address in the **Host name or IP address** text box. Click **Next >** to advance to the **Protocols and Security** screen.
12. Make sure that the **Route IP packets on this interface** check box is selected (**Figure 3-10**) and click **Next >** to advance to the **Static Routes for Remote Networks** screen.
13. Click **Add** to open the **Static Route** dialog box. In the appropriate boxes, enter the address, network mask, and metric of the remote network with which this connection will communicate.
14. Click **OK** to confirm the new static route. Then click **Next >** to advance to the **Dial Out Credentials** screen.
15. Type a user name and the domain name in the **User name** and **Domain** text boxes, respectively.
16. Type a password in the **Password** text box, and then type the same password in the **Confirm password** text box (**Figure 3-11**). Click **Next >**.
17. Click **Finish** to complete the Demand-dial Interface Wizard.

Table 3-9 C

Port Type

Common TCP Port

Common UDP P

Common IP Prot

Select this check
box to activate
TCP/IP filtering

Lists the TCP po
numbers for TCI
that is allowed v
Permit Only is s
(WWW and SM
related traffic)

Lists the UPD
numbers for UI
that is allowed
Permit Only is
(SNMP, SMTP
and RIP-relate

Figure 3-9 Naming the new demand-dial interface

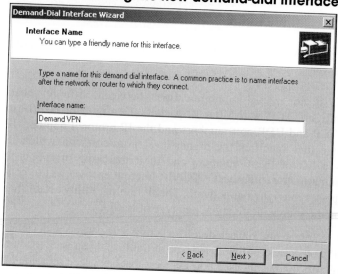

Figure 3-10 The Protocols and Security screen

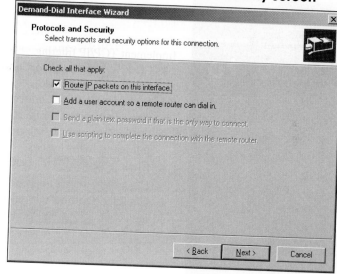

Figure 3-11 The Dial Out Credentials screen

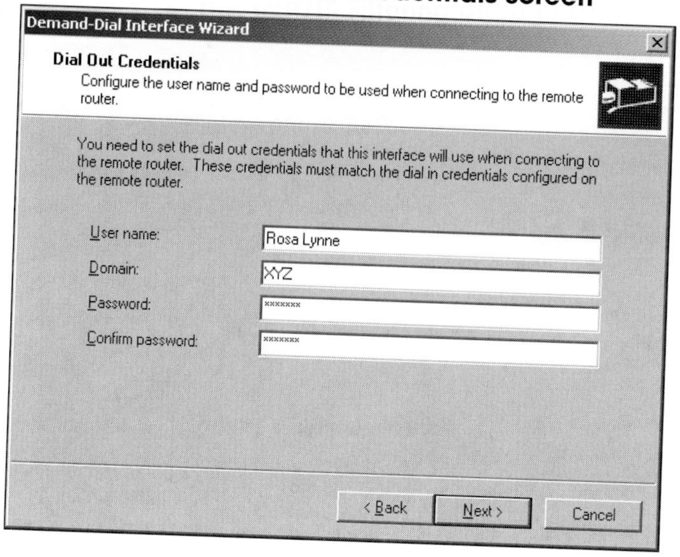

skill

skill 7

Configuring TCP/IP Filtering (cont'd)

exam objec

exam objective

Manage routing ports. Manage packet filters. Manage Routing and Remote Access routing interfaces.

overvie

how to

7. Click the **Enable TCP/IP Filtering (All adapters)** check box.
8. Click the first **Permit Only** option button, which enables [Add] and [Remove] under the **TCP Ports** section.
9. Click [Add] to open the **Add Filter** dialog box (**Figure 3-13**).
10. Type **23** in the **TCP Port** field to enable the TCP port for Telnet traffic only. (Note that we have chosen Telnet for example purposes only. Telnet is an insecure protocol, in that it transmits user ID and password in clear text, as well as the entire session in clear text. Many sites do not permit Telnet sessions on this basis.)
11. Click [OK] to close the Add Filter dialog box. The value 23 appears in the TCP Ports section (**Figure 3-14**). You can similarly enable filtering for the UDP and IP ports.
12. Click [OK] or [Close] to close the dialog boxes that remain open.

caution

Before configuring
TCP/IP filters, you
to plan for the kin
traffic that you wi
to enter your netw
specifying any arl
port number migh
prevent important
from reaching yor

how

Figure 3-13 The Add Filter dialog box

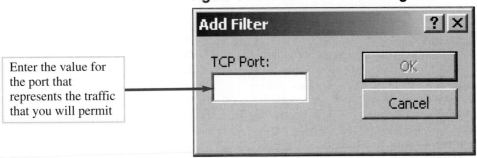

Enter the value for the port that represents the traffic that you will permit

Figure 3-14 Allowing only Telnet traffic through the TCP port

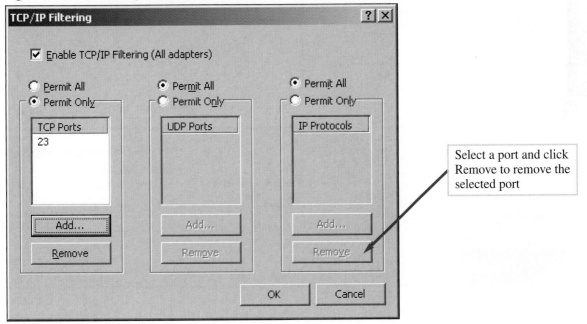

Select a port and click Remove to remove the selected port

Summary

- Routing refers to the process of selecting the path by which a source computer transfers packets of data across networks to a destination computer.
- Networks connect to each other through routers. Data that you send to a computer on another network is actually sent to the router that forwards it to the destination (or to another router and so on through the networks that ultimately lead to the final destination).
- Routers and hosts maintain routing tables to store entries of IP addresses of the local network and other connected networks.
- Routers serve to connect a source and a destination when they are on different network segments.
- Routing tables are used to determine the next hop for a given network.
- Routers use RIP to exchange routing information with other routers to update them about changes in the network layout. In RIP, routers learn of paths to other networks through periodic advertisements, known as updates.
- Routing is a hop-by-hop process, meaning that neither the router nor the source defines the entire path that the packet will take. They simply forward it to the next hop.
- OSPF is a link-state routing protocol that:
  - Enables routers to exchange routing table information.
  - Creates a map of the network that aids in the calculation of the best possible path to each network.
  - Maintains the status of routers in each path.
- Static routing enables routers to obtain their data packet transmission paths using a routing table that is built and updated manually.
- Dynamic routing provides routers with a method of sharing their routing information with other routers on the network.
- Metrics are typically used with dynamic routing to define the most preferred next hop router when there are multiple paths to a given destination.
- Static routing tables need to be reconfigured manually when there is a change in the existing network topology. You can update routing tables by adding or removing static routes from a routing table.
- You configure static routing when your computer will only be exchanging data between defined networks.
- Demand-dial routing minimizes the communication expenditure for a network. You run demand-dial routing on your server through a demand-dial interface.
- TCP/IP filtering enables you to control what type of information packets can pass through your network though TCP and UDP ports and IP protocols.

Key Terms

Border Gateway Protocol (BGP)
Demand-dial interface
Demand-dial routing
Dynamic routing
Exterior routing protocol

Hop count
Interior routing protocol
Open Shortest Path First (OSPF)
Packet
Routing

Routing Information Protocol (RIP)
Static routing
TCP/IP filtering

Test Yourself

1. Which of the following is an advantage of demand-dial routing?
   a. It establishes a connection using leased lines.
   b. It establishes a connection every 15 minutes in order to obtain route updates.
   c. It establishes a connection that is terminated when it is no longer required.
   d. It establishes a connection that only allows types of data packets that you specify.

2. In which of the following fields of the Static Route dialog box would you specify the forwarding IP address for a static route?
   a. Destination
   b. Network mask
   c. Gateway
   d. Metric

3. Which of the following would you use to control the flow of FTP traffic to and from your Windows Server 2003 computer?
   a. Telnet
   b. TCP/IP filtering
   c. Static routes
   d. Demand-dial routing

4. OSPF: (Choose all that apply.)
   a. Creates a map of the network.
   b. Calculates the best possible path to each network in a routing table.

c. Is a distance vector routing protocol.
d. Is a link-state protocol.

5. Hop count measures:
  a. The number of hosts on a network.
  b. The number of entries in a routing table.
  c. The amount of a time that a demand-dial connection remains open.
  d. The distance to a destination host in terms of routers.

6. Computers with different network IDs will send data to each other _____ in order to communicate.
  a. Directly
  b. Through a router
  c. Only on demand
  d. Using MAC addresses

7. When a router receives a data packet for which it doesn't have a defined route, the router:
  a. Forwards the packet to its default router.
  b. Delivers the packet using its header information.
  c. Creates an entry in its routing table.
  d. Closes the connection.

8. The command used to add a route to a routing table manually is:
  a. route print.
  b. route –p add [network] mask [netmask] [gateway].
  c. route add [network] mask [netmask] [gateway].
  d. route new [network] mask [netmask] [gateway].

Projects: On Your Own

1. Update a Windows Server 2003 static routing table manually.
  a. Open the **Command Prompt** window.
  b. Update the route table to enable communication with network **192.48.52.0** from a host with a host ID of **192.48.56.3** on a network with a network ID of **192.48.56.0**. The address of the gateway for the host is **192.48.56.1**.
  c. Run the command
  d. View the updated routing table.

2. Configure static routing with the **Destination**, **Network mask**, **Gateway**, and **Metric** options as **155.143.136.2**, **255.255.255.0**, **155.143.134.142**, and **1**, respectively.

  a. Open the **Routing and Remote Access** console.
  b. Open the **Static Route** dialog box.
  c. Specify the required details of the new route.
  d. Confirm the changes.

3. Implement **TCP/IP** filters.
  a. Open the **Local Area Connection Status** dialog box.
  b. Open the **Local Area Connection Properties** dialog box.
  c. Open the **Internet Protocol (TCP/IP) Properties** dialog box.
  d. Open the **Advanced TCP/IP Settings** dialog box.
  e. Enable TCP/IP filtering.
  f. Permit inbound traffic only through port **80**.

Problem Solving Scenarios

1. You are an Enterprise Network Administrator at a restaurant supply company. Each department at your company has its own network with an individual IP address range assigned to it. Accounts Receivable uses the IP range 192.168.1.x subnet mask 255.255.255.0, while Inventory uses the IP range 192.168.2.x subnet mask 255.255.255.0. However, due to recent changes in company policy, you are now required to establish connectivity between these two networks. The two networks do not need to connect to any other networks besides each other. Accounts Receivable has a server named INETServer with a static IP address of 192.168.1.104. Both departments will be connecting to the Internet though this server. Prepare a document explaining the steps you will follow in order to accomplish the required setup with minimum administrative effort and changes to the network.

2. As a Network Engineer, you have been asked to reconfigure your company's network to enable connectivity between the four subnets of the existing network. Although hosts on any subnet must be able to communicate with the hosts on all four subnets, all route information is of a sensitive nature and you must protect its security. Additionally, there is a network segment that is not physically connected to your company's network. However, occasionally employees on your company's network need to access data from that network segment. Create a PowerPoint (or other form of) presentation explaining the steps you will take in order to reconfigure the network to achieve the above objectives. Try to avoid making major changes to the network infrastructure.

4

Implementing and Managing DHCP

Dynamic Host Configuration Protocol (DHCP) is a service available in Windows that is used to assign IP addresses dynamically to clients on a network. If you configure TCP/IP manually on each client computer, the clients receive a fixed, or static, IP address. With this manual configuration, you run the risk of assigning duplicate IP addresses, which results in malfunctions on the network. If you do choose to assign IP addresses manually, thorough planning can reduce the likelihood of address conflicts. However, DHCP provides you with other options. By using the DHCP service on Windows Server 2003, you can assign IP addresses dynamically, eliminating the need to configure the IP address on each client manually.

In order to use the DHCP service, you must install a DHCP server on your network. Once you install the DHCP server, you need to authorize the server to assign valid IP addresses to clients. If an unauthorized server resides on the network, the unauthorized server might assign incorrect IP addresses to clients, acknowledge the DHCP client negatively, or provide some other type of invalid information, thus disrupting the network.

On the DHCP server, you create scopes (pools of valid IP addresses) to assign IP addresses to the clients on the network. In addition to scopes, you can create superscopes or multicast scopes depending on the requirements of your network.

When the IP addresses of clients are updated dynamically, the DNS service must be notified so that it can update the client name-to-IP address and IP address-to-name mapping on the DNS server. On a Windows Server 2003 network, you can integrate a DHCP server with the DNS service to enable dynamic updates of the DNS service.

Once you have installed and configured the DHCP Server service, you need to administer the DHCP server by performing tasks such as starting, stopping, and resuming the DHCP Server service. Additionally, you need to monitor the DHCP server's performance and troubleshoot it for problems that might occur on your network. For a thorough review of all matters concerning DHCP, visit http://www.ietf.org and search for RFC 2131.

Goals

In this lesson, you will learn about assigning IP addresses dynamically using the DHCP Server service in Windows Server 2003. You will learn to install and authorize the DHCP Server service and create scopes, superscopes, and multicast scopes. Additionally, you will learn to integrate the DHCP server with the DNS server, administer and monitor the DHCP server, and troubleshoot DHCP server problems.

Lesson 4 Implementing and Managing DHCP

Skill	Exam 70-291 Objective
1. Introducing the DHCP Server Service	Manage DHCP clients and leases.
2. Installing the DHCP Server Service	Manage DHCP clients and leases.
3. Configuring a DHCP Server	Manage DHCP.
4. Authorizing a DHCP Server	Manage DHCP. Diagnose and resolve issues related to DHCP authorization.
5. Introducing DHCP Scopes	Manage DHCP. Manage DHCP clients and leases.
6. Creating a DHCP Scope	Manage DHCP clients and leases. Manage DHCP scope options.
7. Using DHCP Reservations	Manage DHCP clients and leases. Manage reservations and reserved clients. Verify DHCP reservation configuration.
8. Managing DHCP Relay Agents	Manage DHCP Relay Agent. Verify that the DHCP Relay Agent is working correctly.
9. Integrating the DHCP and DNS Services	Manage DHCP.
10. Managing a DHCP Server	Manage DHCP. Manage DHCP databases.
11. Monitoring the DHCP Server Service	Examine the system event log and DHCP server audit log files to find related events. Diagnose and resolve issues related to DHCP authorization.
12. Troubleshooting DHCP Server Service Problems	Troubleshoot DHCP. Diagnose and resolve issues related to configuration of DHCP server and scope options. Verify database integrity.

Requirements

To complete this lesson, you will need administrative rights on a Windows Server 2003 computer configured as a domain controller and a minimum of four computers running a client operating system such as Windows 2000 Professional or Windows XP Professional.

skill 1

Introducing the DHCP Server Service

exam objective

Manage DHCP clients and leases.

overview

Dynamic Host Configuration Protocol (DHCP) manages TCP/IP configuration centrally by assigning IP addresses to computers that are configured to use the DHCP Server service **(Figure 4-1)**. A DHCP server has a database that stores the following information:

♦   A pool of IP addresses, also called a scope

♦   Configuration details, such as the address of a default gateway, a DNS server, and a WINS server

♦   The duration of a lease offered by the DHCP server for a particular scope. The lease sets the duration of time for which a client computer has permission to use the IP address that the DHCP server has assigned, and guarantees that the server will not give the address to any other client within that time.

Since DHCP can assign IP addresses dynamically, it provides the following benefits:

♦   Prevents the use of duplicate IP addresses on a network, thus minimizing network problems. When a Network Administrator configures IP addresses manually, the possibility of assigning duplicate addresses exists.

♦   Prevents the possibility of entering incorrect values for the subnet mask and default gateways by assigning these values to DHCP clients dynamically. You can specify these values while configuring the DHCP scope properties.

♦   Reduces administrative efforts. Assigning IP addresses manually simply requires a lot of time, especially on a large network. In addition, a DHCP server dynamically reassigns the IP address and the default gateway whenever a computer moves from one subnet to another.

You can configure a computer running Windows Server 2003 as a DHCP client by selecting the **Obtain an IP address automatically** option button in the **Internet Protocol (TCP/IP) Properties** dialog box. The process by which a client acquires an IP address is divided into the following four phases **(Figure 4-2)**:

IP lease discover: Whenever the lease of an existing client expires or a new client computer is introduced in a network, the client initiates the process of IP leasing. The client broadcasts a **DHCPDiscover** message to the network to search for a DHCP server. Since the client neither has an IP address nor knows the IP address of the DHCP server at this point, the client uses 0.0.0.0 as the source address and 255.255.255.255 as the destination address. The DHCPDiscover packet contains the MAC address and computer name of the client so that the DHCP server will have a record of the computer to which the IP address is assigned.

IP lease offer: When the DHCP server receives the DHCPDiscover packet, the server sends a **DHCPOffer** packet to the client. The DHCPOffer packet includes a possible IP address for the client. Additionally, the DHCPOffer packet contains the client MAC address, the subnet mask, the duration of the lease, and the IP address of the DHCP server. In situations where there is no DHCP server available, the client waits for one second for an offer of an IP address. If the client does not receive a response, it rebroadcasts the request three times. If the client does not receive an offer to any of these four requests, it will rebroadcast the request every five minutes and will continue to do so until it receives a response.

IP lease request: The client will respond to the first DHCPOffer it receives by sending a **DHCPRequest** message message to that server. Any subsequent DHCPOffer messages will be ignored.

tip

If a computer has multiple network adapters, separate DHCP processes will occur for each adapter and each adapter will receive a unique IP address.

Figure 4-1 Using DHCP to assign IP addresses

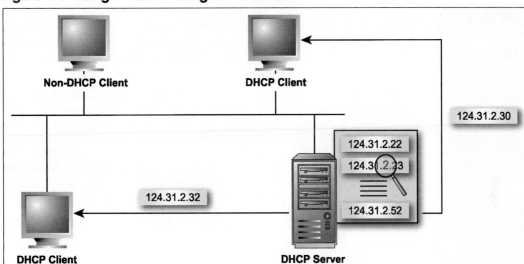

Figure 4-2 Four phases in acquiring an IP address through DHCP

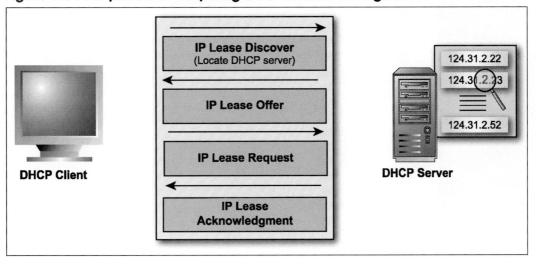

skill 1

Introducing the DHCP Server Service *(cont'd)*

exam objective

Manage DHCP clients and leases.

overview

IP lease acknowledgment: When the DHCP server receives the DHCPRequest packet, the server marks the IP address assigned to the client as leased in the IP address database. Additionally, the server sends a **DHCPAcknowledgment (DHCPAck)** packet to the client to verify that it can use the IP address.

A client leases an IP address for a specific period. However, a client will attempt to renew the IP address when half of the lease period has expired and every time the computer reboots. You can also use the ipconfig /renew command at the command prompt to renew an IP address **(Figure 4-3)**.

In the absence of a DHCP server, a computer can assign itself an IP address using Automatic Private IP Addressing (APIPA). See Lesson 2 for a detailed discussion of this process. When a DHCP server becomes available, the address that it assigns to the client replaces the APIPA address and netmask.

Figure 4-3 Renewing an IP address

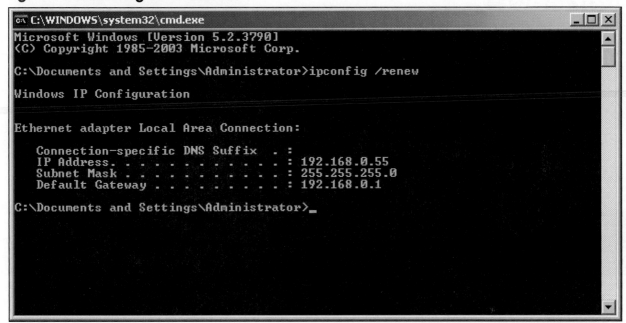

```
C:\WINDOWS\system32\cmd.exe                                          _ □ ×
Microsoft Windows [Version 5.2.3790]
(C) Copyright 1985-2003 Microsoft Corp.

C:\Documents and Settings\Administrator>ipconfig /renew

Windows IP Configuration


Ethernet adapter Local Area Connection:

   Connection-specific DNS Suffix   . :
   IP Address. . . . . . . . . . . : 192.168.0.55
   Subnet Mask . . . . . . . . . . : 255.255.255.0
   Default Gateway . . . . . . . . : 192.168.0.1

C:\Documents and Settings\Administrator>_
```

skill 2

Installing the DHCP Server Service

exam objective

Manage DHCP clients and leases.

overview

Before installing the DHCP Server service, you need to perform the following pre-installation tasks:

◆ Determine the hardware and storage requirements for the DHCP server

◆ Determine which computers you want to configure as DHCP clients with dynamic IP addresses and those that you want to configure manually using static TCP/IP configurations

◆ Determine the types of DHCP options and their values for the DHCP clients (range of IP addresses, netmasks, gateways, DNS server addresses, and so on)

To set up a Windows Server 2003 computer as DHCP server, you must add the role of DHCP server to the computer. Windows Server 2003 server computers do not acquire this role by default during the installation and setup of the operating system. You can add the DHCP Server role to your server through either the Manage Your Server window or the Control Panel.

how to

Install the DHCP Server service.

1. Click **Start**, point to **Control Panel**, and then click **Add or Remove Programs**. The **Add or Remove Programs** window opens.
2. Click the **Add/Remove Windows Components** button on the left side of the window to open the **Windows Components Wizard**.
3. On the **Windows Components** screen, double-click **Networking Services** in the **Components** scrolling list box to open the **Networking Services** dialog box (**Figure 4-4**).
4. Select the **Dynamic Host Configuration Protocol (DHCP)** check box, and then click **OK**.
5. Click **Next >** to advance to the **Configuring Components** screen, where Setup will configure the changes you selected (**Figure 4-5**).
6. If your server has been using a dynamically configured IP address, a message box will open prompting you to change the address to a static IP address (**Figure 4-6**). Click **OK** to open the **Local Area Connection Properties** dialog box and configure the static IP address (refer to Lesson 2, Skill 5 if necessary). When you have finished assigning this address and close the Local Area Connection Properties dialog box, the Wizard will complete the Configuring Components phase.
7. Click **Finish** on the **Completing the Windows Components Wizard** screen to close the Wizard (**Figure 4-7**).
8. Close the Add or Remove Programs window.

tip

To add the DHCP Server role from the Manage Your Server window, click Start and click Manage Your Server. Then, click Add or remove a role in the Manage Your Server window.

Figure 4-4 **The Networking Services dialog box**

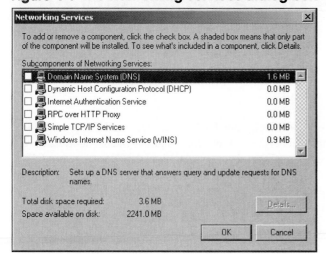

Figure 4-5 **The Configuring Components screen**

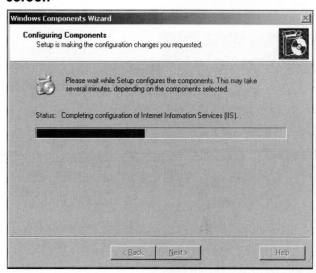

Figure 4-6 **Static IP message box**

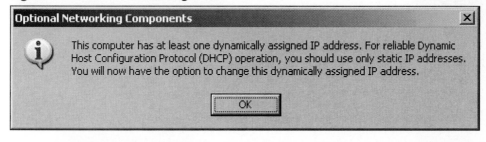

Figure 4-7 **Completing the Windows Components Wizard**

skill 2

Installing the DHCP Server Service
(cont'd)

exam objective

Manage DHCP clients and leases.

more

Since DHCP is a broadcast-based protocol, your DHCP messages will not pass through routers. This means that if multiple subnets in your network require dynamic addressing, you must either place a DHCP server on each segment, or relay the DHCP packets to a DHCP server. To relay the packets, you can use either a DHCP relay agent or an RFC 1542 compliant router. A relay agent is a server configured to relay DHCP packets to a DHCP server. Relaying is performed as shown in **Table 4-1**.

A relay agent can either be a router or a server; however, in most Microsoft materials, running a relay agent on a router is termed RFC 1542 compliance (also known as BOOTP Forwarding). However, the functionality for the DHCP relay agent is actually better defined in RFC 2131.

Table 4-1   DHCP relaying

- The relay agent listens on the subnet for DHCP broadcasts.

- When a DHCPDiscover broadcast is heard, the relay agent takes the DHCP information in the broadcast and creates a unicast packet with this information, with the addition of the relay agent's IP address.

- The unicast packet is sent directly to the DHCP server listed in the relay agent's configuration.

- The DHCP server responds to the unicast packet, sending the DHCPOffer information directly to the relay agent in a unicast packet.

- The relay agent broadcasts the DHCPOffer packet to the client's subnet.

- The client broadcasts the DHCPRequest message.

- The relay agent takes the information from the client's DHCPRequest message and creates a unicast with the same information, again, adding its IP address to the packet.

- The unicast DHCPRequest is sent directly to the DHCP server.

- The DHCP server sends a unicasted DHCPAck to the relay agent.

- The relay agent creates a broadcast DHCPAck from the information in the unicast packet and broadcasts the message on the client's subnet.

skill 4

Authorizing a DHCP Server

exam objective

Manage DHCP. Diagnose and resolve issues related to DHCP authorization.

overview

Windows Server 2003 DHCP servers in a domain environment must be authorized before they will function. Authorization is a feature originally added to the Windows 2000 DHCP Server service in an attempt to eliminate rogue DHCP servers. Since DHCP is a broadcast-based protocol, an improperly configured DHCP server could potentially cause IP address conflicts or incorrect IP addresses to be leased. For instance, if you have a DHCP server on your network issuing leases for the 172.16.1.0/24 subnet, and a user enables Internet Connection Sharing (ICS) on his or her computer, you will eventually have connectivity problems. This is because ICS has an IP address allocator, and automatically leases addresses in the 192.168.0.0/24 range to any DHCP client. Therefore, you will begin to see some clients lease the wrong addresses shortly after the user enables ICS. Clients with the 192.160.0.0/24 addresses will not be able to communicate with clients and servers using the correct 172.16.1.0/24 addresses.

DHCP authorization works by requiring the DHCP server to "ask for permission" from Active Directory before enabling. Essentially, the DHCP server will ask a domain controller for a DHCPInform packet when the service starts. The DHCPInform packet contains a list of up to 25 DHCP servers that are authorized to operate in the environment. If the DHCP server is not listed in the DHCPInform packet, the DHCP Server service will shut down on that server.

This functionality keeps unauthorized Windows 2000 and Windows Server 2003 DHCP servers from being functional in the forest; however, you should be aware that it does not prevent non-Windows 2000 and Server 2003 devices from enabling. For instance, DHCP allocators used by ICS (available in Windows 98 and later), the DHCP Server service in Windows NT, DHCP allocators enabled on routers, and DHCP servers running non-Microsoft operating systems do not require authorization and therefore are not affected by this prevention tactic.

tip

You must be the Enterprise Administrator to modify the list of authorized servers.

how to

Authorize a DHCP server.

1. Click [Start], point to **Administrative Tools**, and click **DHCP** to open the **DHCP** console.
2. Right-click **DHCP** in the console tree (left pane), and then click **Manage Authorized Servers** to open the **Manage Authorized Servers** dialog box.
3. Click [Authorize...] to open the Authorize DHCP Server dialog box (**Figure 4-10**).
4. Type the name or IP address of the DHCP server you wish to authorize in the **Name or IP address** text box and click .
5. The **Confirm Authorization** dialog box opens displaying the name and IP address of the server you have selected (**Figure 4-11**). Click [OK].
6. Click [Close] to close the Manage Authorized Servers dialog box.
7. Close the DHCP console.

more

You need to unauthorize a server in situations where you do not want a DHCP server to assign addresses to DHCP clients. You can unauthorize a server through the Manage Authorized Servers dialog box or by right-clicking the server in the DHCP console and clicking **Unauthorize** on the shortcut menu.

Figure 4-10 The Authorize DHCP Server dialog box

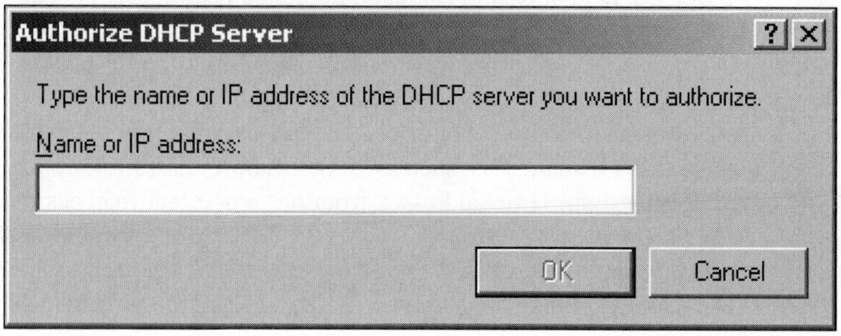

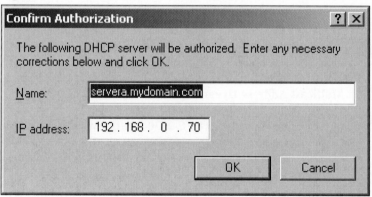

Figure 4-11 Confirm the authorization of a DHCP server

skill 5

Introducing DHCP Scopes

exam objective

Manage DHCP. Manage DHCP clients and leases.

overview

In order for a DHCP server to lease IP addresses to clients, you need to create DHCP scopes. A **scope** is a pool of IP address and other related configuration parameters from which DHCP offers leases to its clients. In order to understand how DHCP functions when you create and activate a scope, you first need to understand how DHCP allocates addresses from scopes. When a DHCP server hears a broadcast on an interface, the server will issue an address for that host from the scope that matches the primary IP address of that interface. For instance, if you have two IP addresses (such as 10.0.0.1 and 192.168.1.1) applied to a single interface, the DHCP server will issue addresses from the scope that matches the primary IP address (the first IP address listed). So in this case, the DHCP server would issue an IP address from the 10.0.0.0 scope. If the DHCP server receives a unicast, such as when relay agents are being used, it uses the relay agent's IP address (listed in the unicast) to determine which scope to issue an address from. The relay agent always lists the IP address associated with the interface from which it originally heard the client broadcast.

The way DHCP allocates IP addresses works well in most cases, but in some cases, such as in some phased network upgrades when you may have two logical networks running over the same physical network (known as mulitnetting), it can create problems. Since DHCP will never hand out two separate IP address ranges for the same physical segment if it is responding to broadcasts, you will need to use a special type of scope, called a superscope, to allow DHCP to issue addresses from all necessary IP address ranges. A **superscope** is simply two or more scopes (known as **member scopes**) included in a single superscope (**Figure 4-12**). By combining scopes into a superscope, you allow the DHCP server to issue addresses from all ranges in the superscope to clients, regardless of the DHCP server's primary IP address.

tip

The use of multinetting requires that an IP address for the additional logical networks be added to the router, and may also require additional routing table entries on other routers.

more

In addition to scopes and superscopes, you can also use multicast scopes. A **multicast scope** is a group of Class D IP addresses that is used by a DHCP server to lease IP addresses to the multicast DHCP clients. Multicast scopes are based on the process of multicasting (**Figure 4-13**). **Multicasting** is the process of transmitting a message to a select group of recipients. **Multicast Address Dynamic Client Protocol (MADCAP)**, a standard introduced by the Internet Engineering Task Force (IETF) and originally based on DHCP, defines the allocation of multicast addresses (see **RFC 2730** at **http://www.ietf.org/rfc.html**). Multicasting is used to address the need for delivering data packets from one point to multiple points. The three mechanisms used for point-to-multipoint delivery of information are dependent on the types of addresses provided:

- Unicasting enables the sending of data packets to each endpoint. However, this results in increased network traffic and needs a list of unicast recipient addresses to be maintained.
- Broadcasting enables the sending of data packets in a single packet. This is advantageous because by using a single packet, information can be sent to multiple recipients and there is no need to maintain a list of recipients. However, the broadcast packets used in broadcasting disturb the nodes on the network. Also, routers do not forward the broadcasts.
- Multicasting enables you to send data packets in a single packet to a select group of recipients. This method is advantageous as a single packet is used for information transfer and there is no need to maintain a list of recipients. The multicast addresses are assigned from the multicast range, **224.0.0.0** to **239.255.255.255**. The multicast clients need to have an IP address. A multicast client has two IP addresses: a unicast IP address and the multicast IP address. The DHCP server leases the unicast IP address and MADCAP leases the multicast IP address. The MADCAP clients request a multicast address when they participate in a multicast. The DHCP server can assign options while leasing the IP addresses, whereas MADCAP assigns multicast addresses to client applications that are configured to accept dynamically assigned multicast addresses. In order to participate in multicasting, the client application needs to know the multicast address for the content they want to receive.

Figure 4-12 Scopes and superscopes

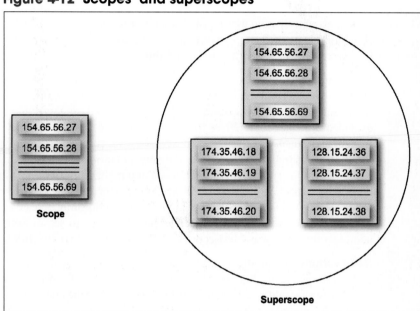

Figure 4-13 Multicasting

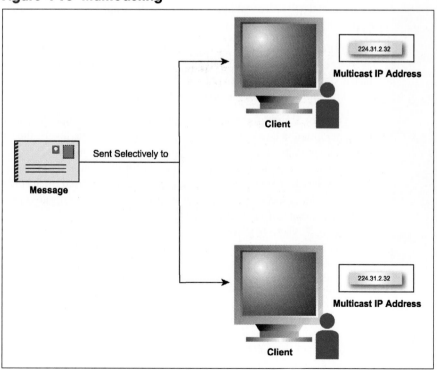

skill 6

Creating a DHCP Scope

exam objective

Manage DHCP clients and leases. Manage DHCP scope options.

overview

Scopes are simply little more than IP address ranges used by the DHCP server when issuing IP address leases. However, there are several aspects of a scope that you should consider before creating the scope, as shown in **Table 4-2**.

For current and future clients, you need to ensure that the address space and scope are large enough to not only take care of current needs, but also large enough to support future growth. Make sure to take into account static clients as well, as these addresses will need to be excluded from the scope. When you exclude an address (a process known as **exclusions**), you make it unavailable for leasing. In most cases, your routers and server will take up a block of the address space at the beginning of the range. In this case you don't actually need to exclude addresses, you can simply begin the scope at a higher number. For instance, if your address range is **192.168.1.1– 192.168.1.254**, and your servers and routers are statically configured to use the first 10 addresses of that range, then you would simply create a DHCP scope with the beginning address set to **192.168.1.11**. You only need to set an exclusion range for static addresses that are not at the start or end of the range, such as **192.168.1.50–192.168.1.70**.

Reservations, on the other hand, are configured when you want a client to obtain its IP address automatically, but you want it to receive the same IP address each time. When configuring a reserved address, you enter the MAC address of the client. This way, when the DHCP server gets a request from that MAC address, it knows to lease the reserved address to that client.

Options are additional IP configuration information you want to be applied to the client. By default, a client will only receive an IP address and subnet mask from a DHCP server. In order for the client to receive additional configuration options, such as default gateway and DNS server addresses, you need to configure DHCP options.

Options can be divided into four categories: server options, scope options, class options, and reserved options. Server options apply to the entire DHCP server, meaning that all scopes on that server will have the same options. Options which are commonly set at the server level are shown in **Table 4-3** (with the option code in parenthesis):

Scope options are settings that only apply to the specific scope they are configured for. When the same option is configured at both the server and scope levels, the scope level option will apply (the most specific level wins). Common scope options are:

◆ Router (03): Defines the default gateway for the clients.
◆ DNS Servers (06): Specifies the list of DNS servers used by the client. This is more commonly set at the server level, but is also sometimes configured per subnet, especially in organizations with widely dispersed physical locations.
◆ NetBIOS Name Servers (44): Specifies a list of WINS servers to be used by the client. This is more commonly set at the server level, but is also sometimes configured per subnet, especially in organizations with widely dispersed physical locations.

Class options are options that apply to a portion of a scope. Class options come in two forms, vendor classes and user classes. Vendor classes are defined by the operating system, and describe the operating system version. Vendor classes can be useful when you wish to assign options based on operating system version, for example, to specify more WINS servers for Windows 2000, XP, and Server 2003 computers (all of which support up to 12 WINS servers), but only specify 2 WINS servers for other computers. User options, on the other hand, are administrator-defined, and can be used to specify different options for any administrative purpose. For example, you may configure a user class of "Portable" and apply the class to all of your laptop computers. Then you would configure option 51 (Lease time) to be shorter in

tip

Reservations have to be part of the normal scope. If you exclude a reserved address, it will never be leased.

Table 4-2   Creating DHCP scopes

Aspects to consider:

◆ The number of current DHCP clients that will be serviced by the scope

◆ The expected number of future DHCP clients

◆ The number of non-DHCP clients, servers, and other hosts (including routers and in some cases, network printers) that will be using addresses on the target subnet

◆ Any necessary reservations

◆ The server, scope, class, and reservation options you wish to set

◆ Will you provide for scope redundancy?

Table 4-3   Options commonly set at the server level

◆ DNS Servers (06): Specifies the list of DNS servers used by the client.

◆ DNS Domain Name (15): Specifies the DNS domain suffix used by the client.

◆ NetBIOS Name Servers (44): Specifies a list of WINS servers to be used by the client.

◆ NetBIOS Node Type (46): Specific the NetBIOS node type for NetBIOS name resolution. This field is entered in hexidecimal as follows: 0x1 for B node, 0x2 for P node, 0x4 for M node, and 0x8 for H node.

skill 6

Creating a DHCP Scope (cont'd)

exam objective

Manage DHCP clients and leases. Manage DHCP scope options.

overview

duration for the laptop computers. In either case, the DHCP server knows which class to apply, based on optional fields describing the classes the computer is a member of in the DHCPDiscover packet. For user classes, you configure each computer to send the appropriate class code by issuing the command **ipconfig /setclassid [Adapter name] [class ID]**. If an option is set at both the class level and at the scope or server level, the class option takes precedence. Some common options set at the class level are shown in **Table 4-4**.

Finally, reserved options are options set for a specific reserved client. This is useful when you want a highly important client computer to use different servers or routers than everyone else to access resources (typically for performance reasons). Reserved options take precedence over all other levels, but only for one specific client.

After you make a decision on the options you wish to set, you should consider DHCP redundancy. Redundancy can be achieved by creating the same scope on two or more DHCP servers. However, since the DHCP servers do not keep up with addresses issued by other servers, you need to insure that the DHCP servers have no overlap in their available address ranges. To do this, you simply exclude a portion of the addresses on one server, and exclude the opposite portion on the other server. For instance, if you had two DHCP servers on a single subnet, and you were using the IP address range 192.168.1.1–192.168.1.254, you would create a scope on both servers for that range, and then exclude 50% of the addresses from each scope, as follows:

◆   Server 1: 192.168.1.1–192.168.1.254, excluded: 192.168.1.1–192.168.1.127
◆   Server 2: 192.168.1.1–192.168.1.254, excluded: 192.168.1.128–192.168.1.254

Alternately, an easier method of accomplishing this same feat is to simply enter in half of the range for each server. This would keep you from needing to create any exclusions, as follows:

◆   Server 1: 192.168.1.1–192.168.1.127
◆   Server 2: 192.168.1.128–192.168.1.254

The 50/50 split is typically used when you have a single subnet serviced by two servers. In situations where you have more than one subnet, you will typically want to use a 70/30 split, with the higher percentage of the addresses given to the server that is physically on the subnet in question. For instance, if Server 1 is on the 192.168.1.0/24 network, while server 2 is on the 192.168.2.0/24 network, you would set up two scopes for each server, as follows:

◆   Server 1
   •   192.168.1.1 - 192.168.1.178
   •   192.168.2.179 - 192.168.2.254
◆   Server 2
   •   192.168.1.179 - 192.168.1.254
   •   192.168.2.1 - 192.168.2.178

Finally, once you have created and configured your scopes, ensure that you activate them! Deactivated scopes will not lease any addresses.

how to

Create a DHCP scope.

1. Click [Start], point to **Administrative Tools**, and click **DHCP** to open the **DHCP** console.
2. Click the name of your DHCP server in the console tree on the left side of the window.
3. Click **Action** on the Menu bar, and then click **New Scope** to open the **New Scope Wizard (Figure 4-14)**.

Table 4-4　Options commonly set at the class level

◆ NetBIOS Name Servers (44): Specifies a list of WINS servers to be used by the client. This is commonly set to allow Windows 2000 and later operating systems to use a larger pool of WINS servers.

◆ IP Address Lease Time (51): Specifies the lease duration for the IP address. This is commonly used to give a shorter lease duration for portable computers. This option is entered in hexadecimal, in seconds. For instance, a lease period of 4 hours (14,400 seconds) would be 0x3840.

Figure 4-14 Opening the New Scope Wizard

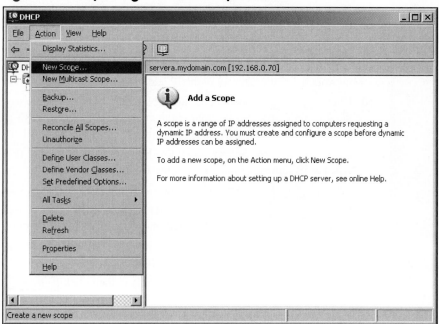

skill 6

Creating a DHCP Scope (cont'd)

exam objective

Manage DHCP clients and leases. Manage DHCP scope options.

how to

4. Click [Next>] to open the **Scope Name** screen. Type a name in the **Name** text box that will help you identify the scope easily. Type a description of the scope in the **Description** text box.

5. Click [Next>] to open the **IP Address Range** screen. Type the first address in your DHCP scope in the **Start IP address** text box (**Figure 4-15**). Type the last address in the range in the **End IP address** text box.

6. The subnet mask should be set automatically in the bottom half of the IP Address Range screen. If you need to change the subnet mask, you can specify it in terms of length (number of bits, for example, 24) or as an IP address (for example, 255.255.255.0).

7. Click [Next>] to open the **Add Exclusions** screen. On this screen, you can exclude addresses in the specified range from the scope. Exclusions allow you to maintain static addresses within the scope, such as the address of the DHCP server and other servers.

8. In the **Start IP address** text box, type the first address in the address range that you want to exclude from the scope. In the **End IP address** text box, type the last address in the range that you want to exclude from the scope (**Figure 4-16**). If you want to exclude only one address, type that address in the Start IP address text box only.

9. Click [Add] to add the range to the **Excluded address range** list box.

10. Click [Next>] to open the **Lease Duration** screen. The default lease duration is 8 days. You can reduce the duration for networks that consist mainly of portable computers and dial-up connections, and increase it for networks that use desktop computers with stable connections.

11. Click [Next>] to accept the default duration and open the **Configure DHCP Options** screen. If necessary, select the **Yes, I want to configure these options now** option button to configure the IP addresses for default gateways, DNS servers, and WINS servers.

12. Click [Next>] to open the **Router (Default Gateway)** screen. Type the address of your network's default gateway in the IP address text box (**Figure 4-17**) and click [Add].

13. Click [Next>] to open the **Domain Name and DNS Servers** screen. Type the name of the domain that you want your client computers to use for DNS name resolution in the **Parent domain** text box. Type the name of the DNS server that you want your scope clients to use in the **Server name** text box and click [Resolve] (**Figure 4-18**), or simply type the IP address of the server in the **IP address** text box.

14. Click [Add] to add the server address to the **IP address** list box.

15. Click [Next>] to open the **WINS Servers** screen. If you are on a network that is using older Windows clients and NetBIOS name-to-IP address resolution is required, type the name of a WINS server for this scope in the **Server name** text box and click [Resolve]. Alternatively, type the address in the **IP address** text box.

16. Click [Add] to add the WINS server, and then click [Next>] to open the **Activate Scope** screen.

17. Select the **Yes, I want to activate this scope now** option button, if necessary, or click [Cancel] if you are doing this as an exercise only and do not want to create the scope.

tip

You can press the period key (.) to begin a new octet in the Start IP address and End IP address text boxes.

caution

Do not proceed with the process of activating scopes if you already have another server running DHCP on the same network segment. You can check for the presence of other DHCP servers by running ipconfig /all or by running the Dhcploc.exe program from the Windows Support Tools folder.

Figure 4-15 The IP Address Range screen

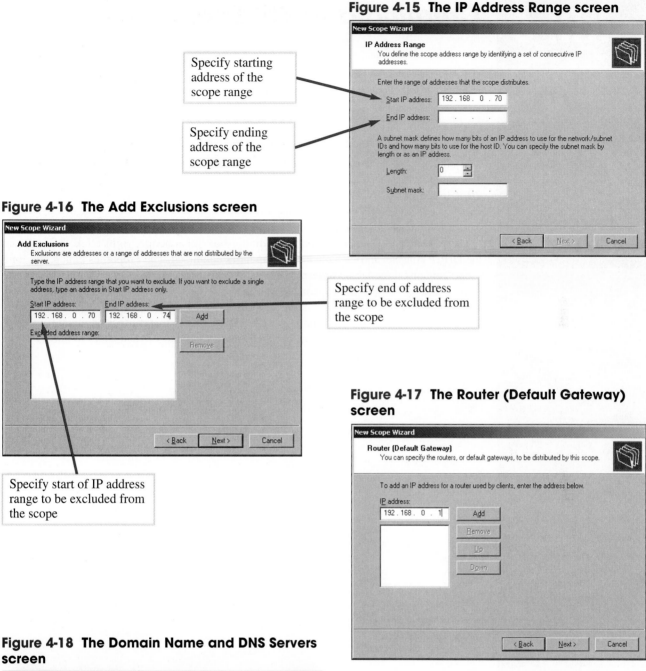

Specify starting address of the scope range

Specify ending address of the scope range

Figure 4-16 The Add Exclusions screen

Specify end of address range to be excluded from the scope

Specify start of IP address range to be excluded from the scope

Figure 4-17 The Router (Default Gateway) screen

Figure 4-18 The Domain Name and DNS Servers screen

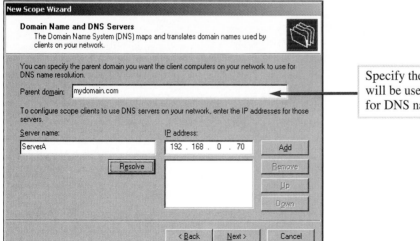

Specify the domain name that will be used by client computers for DNS name resolution

skill 6

Creating a DHCP Scope (cont'd)

exam objective

Manage DHCP clients and leases. Manage DHCP scope options.

overview

18. Click [Next >] to open the **Completing the New Scope Wizard** screen.
19. Click [Finish] to complete the creation of the new scope. The new scope is now listed in the DHCP console **(Figure 4-19)**.
20. Close the DHCP console.

more

You can change the configuration of an existing scope using its **Properties** dialog box **(Figure 4-20)**. To open the Properties dialog box for a scope, right-click the scope in the DHCP console, and then click the **Properties** command. The Properties dialog box for a scope contains three tabs: **General**, **DNS**, and **Advanced**. The General tab enables you to change settings such as the scope name, starting IP address, ending IP address, lease duration, and description. The DNS tab contains options for setting the DHCP server to update name and address information automatically on DNS servers that support dynamic updates. The Advanced tab provides options for assigning IP addresses dynamically to clients of the DHCP server, the BOOTP server, or both servers.

Figure 4-19 New Scope in the DHCP console

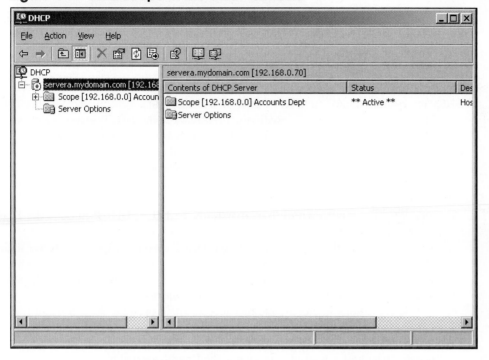

Figure 4-20 Scope Properties dialog box

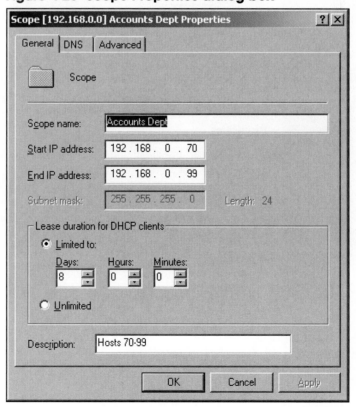

skill 7

Using DHCP Reservations

exam objective

Manage DHCP clients and leases. Manage reservations and reserved clients. Verify DHCP reservation configuration.

overview

DHCP reservations allow you to set aside an IP address so that a specific host will be able to lease the address exclusively. To configure a reservation, the DHCP server matches an IP address within an active scope with the hardware address of the network adapter for which you are creating the reservation. When the computer that contains this adapter boots, the DHCP server detects the network adapter's MAC address and leases the reserved IP address.

how to

Create a DHCP reservation.

1. Click **Start**, point to **Administrative Tools**, and click **DHCP** to open the **DHCP** console.
2. Click the plus sign next to the name of your DHCP server to expand the server node in the console tree.
3. Click the name of the scope in which you want to create the reservation to display the contents of the scope's folder in the details pane **(Figure 4-21)**.
4. Click **Reservations** in either pane to select it. Then, open the **Action** menu from the Menu bar and click **New Reservation** to open the **New Reservation** dialog box.
5. Type a name for the reservation in the **Reservation name** text box.
6. Type the IP address you want to reserve in the **IP address** text box.
7. Type the MAC address of the network adapter from the host for whom you want to reserve this address in the **MAC address** text box.
8. If desired, type a description in the **Description** text box **(Figure 4-22)**.
9. Click ⌗ Add ⌗ to create the reservation.
10. Click ⌗ Close ⌗ to close the New Reservation dialog box. The new reservation is now listed in the **Reservations** folder for the scope **(Figure 4-23)**.
11. Close the DHCP console.

tip

You can determine the MAC address of a client by running ipconfig /all from the command prompt on the client and looking at the line item labeled Physical address.

more

You can configure options for a reservation or verify its configuration by right-clicking it in the DHCP console and then clicking **Configure Options** on the shortcut menu. You can also change the general properties of an existing reservation by right-clicking it and then clicking **Properties**.

Although reserving an IP address is an effective way to maintain a constant IP address, a reservation is not a good substitute for configuring a static IP address. You should not allow critical servers like DNS, DHCP, and WINS to have their IP addresses configured automatically, even by reservation. Servers with less critical importance to the functioning of a network, such as print servers, however, can benefit both from a reserved IP address and the ease of management provided by a DHCP server.

Figure 4-21 Selecting a scope in the DHCP console

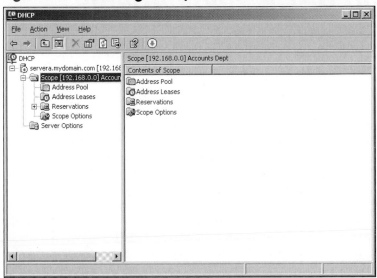

Figure 4-22 The New Reservation dialog box

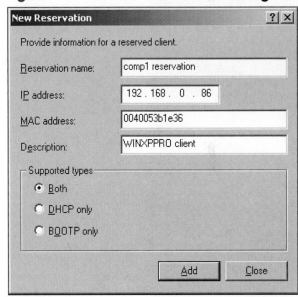

Figure 4-23 Working with a DHCP reservation

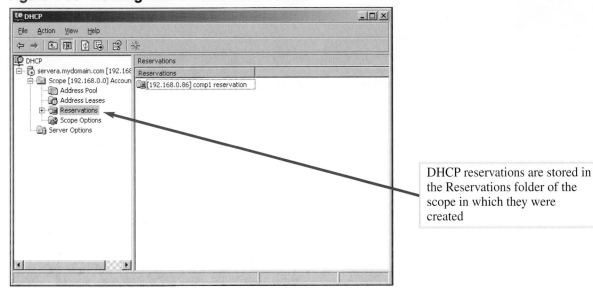

DHCP reservations are stored in the Reservations folder of the scope in which they were created

skill 8

Managing DHCP Relay Agents

exam objective

Manage DHCP Relay Agent. Verify that the DHCP Relay Agent is working correctly.

overview

caution

A Windows Server 2003 computer should not act as both a DHCP server and a DHCP relay agent.

When a DHCP client requests an IP address lease, it does so by broadcasting a DHCPDiscover packet. Broadcast packets, however, cannot pass through routers under normal circumstances. Therefore, clients generally receive their IP addresses from a DHCP server that is located on the same subnet as they are. This restriction can present a problem on larger networks, especially if you prefer to have DHCP clients serviced by only one DHCP server. **DHCP Relay Agent** is a routing protocol that makes it possible for DHCP clients to request an IP address from a DHCP server that is located on a remote subnet by converting the client's broadcasts into unicasts and forwarding them directly to the DHCP server. You can set up a Windows Server 2003 computer as DHCP relay agent by installing the DHCP Relay Agent protocol. The relay agent is able to redirect DHCPDiscover packets across routers to a remote DHCP server.

how to

tip

If you do not see DHCP Relay Agent listed under IP Routing, then you need to install the protocol. Right-click General, then click New Routing Protocol. Select DHCP Relay Agent in the New Routing Protocol dialog box, and click OK.

Configure DHCP Relay Agent on Windows Server 2003.

1. Log on to a Windows Server 2003 computer that is not your DHCP server as an **Administrator**.
2. Click **Start**, point to **Administrative Tools**, and click **Routing and Remote Access** to open the **Routing and Remote Access** console.
3. Double-click the name of the server to expand it in the console tree, if necessary, and then similarly expand the **IP Routing** node.
4. Right-click **DHCP Relay Agent** under the IP Routing node, and click **Properties** on the shortcut menu to open the **DHCP Relay Agent Properties** dialog box **(Figure 4-24)**.
5. Type the IP address of the DHCP server to which you want the relay agent to forward messages in the **Server address** text box.
6. Click **Add** to add the address to the Server address list box (you can add additional servers if desired), and then click **OK** to close the dialog box.
7. In the Routing and Remote Access console, right-click **DHCP Relay Agent** again, and this time click **New Interface** on the shortcut menu. The **New Interface for DHCP Relay Agent** dialog box opens **(Figure 4-25)**.
8. Select the interface through which you want the relay agent to be enabled, in this example the **Local Area Connection**, and click **OK**.
9. Close the Routing and Remote Access console.

more

You can also use the Routing and Remote Access console to verify that the DHCP Relay Agent is operating correctly. To do this, select **DHCP Relay Agent** under the IP Routing node in the console tree. Then, consult the statistics that the details pane displays to the right. These details summarize the activity in which the relay agent has been involved. If the DHCP Relay Agent is performing correctly, the details pane will show that the agent has received both requests and replies **(Figure 4-26)**. If you see only that requests or replies have been discarded, you should review the configuration of the relay agent.

Figure 4-24 The DHCP Relay Agent Properties dialog box

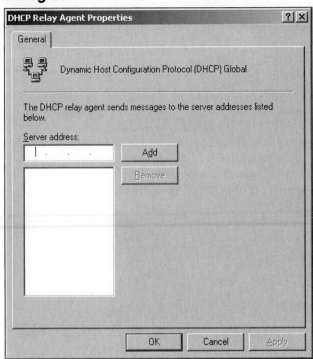

Figure 4-25 The New Interface for DHCP Relay Agent dialog box

Figure 4-26 Verifying the functionality of the DHCP Relay Agent

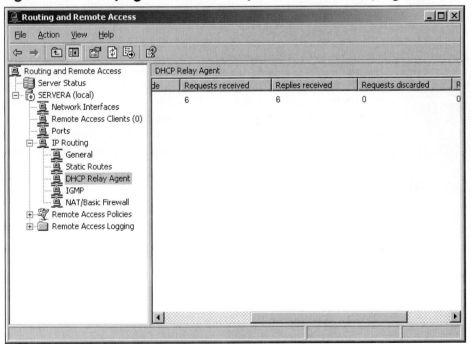

skill 9

Integrating the DHCP and DNS Services

exam objective

Manage DHCP.

overview

Part of the process of configuring a DHCP server, in addition to creating scopes and authorizing the server, is integrating DHCP with DNS. Whenever a client computer moves from one location to another, an IP address is assigned dynamically to the client in its new location. In a Windows Server 2003 network, you use the DNS service to resolve client host names to IP addresses, which other client computers on the network use to access resources such as files or services. To maintain information in the DNS database correctly, it is necessary to update the client host name-to-IP address and IP address-to-host name mapping. If the DHCP server cannot interact with DNS, then information maintained by the DNS server regarding a DHCP client, whose location may change, could be inaccurate.

To overcome such problems, you can configure your DHCP servers to register and update the Pointer (PTR) and Address (A) resource records of the clients that have been dynamically configured by the DHCP server in the DNS database. A **Pointer (PTR) record** associates an IP address to a host name. The **Address (A) record** associates a host name to its IP address. If configured to do so, registration and updating of resource records in the Windows Server 2003 DNS database by the DHCP server can occur dynamically because DNS service in Windows Server 2003 supports dynamic updates.

how to

Integrate the DHCP and DNS services.
1. Click **Start**, point to **Administrative Tools**, and click **DHCP** to open the **DHCP** console.
2. Right-click the DHCP server that you want to integrate with DNS, and click **Properties** on the shortcut menu to open the **Properties** dialog box for the DHCP server.
3. Click the **DNS** tab and make sure that the **Enable DNS dynamic updates according to the settings below** check box is selected (**Figure 4-27**).
4. You then have the choice of selecting whether to allow clients to determine when their records are updated (by request), or to update all DHCP client records automatically.
5. Select the appropriate option button, and then click **OK** to close the Properties dialog box.
6. Close the DHCP console.

more

The DNS tab of the Properties dialog box also offers options that allow you to purge the DNS database of A and PTR records for clients whose leases have been deleted, and dynamically update the A and PTR records of clients who are unable to request dynamic updates themselves, such as Windows NT 4.0 clients.

Figure 4-27 The DHCP server Properties dialog box

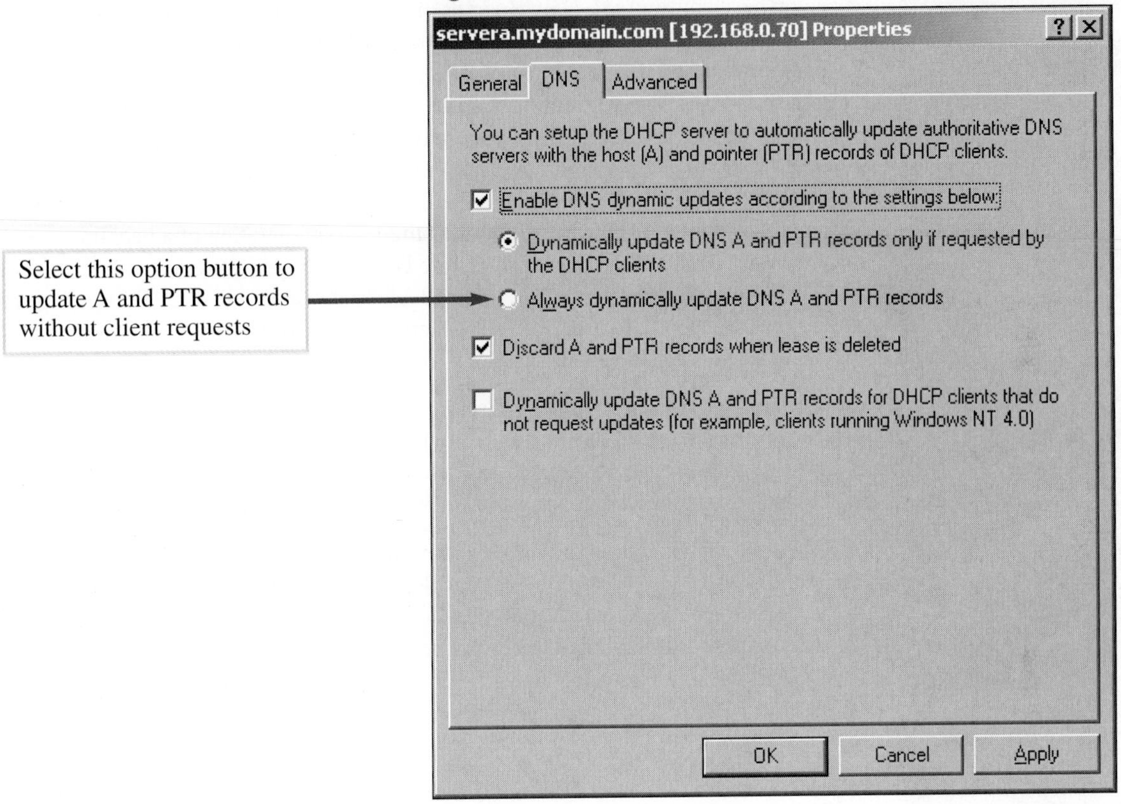

Select this option button to update A and PTR records without client requests

skill10   *Managing a DHCP Server*

exam objective   Manage DHCP. Manage DHCP databases.

overview

Once you have configured a DHCP server on your network, you can perform a variety of tasks to administer the DHCP server. Managing a DHCP server properly enables you to improve the performance of the server, as well as adapt the server to changes on your network. Examples of DHCP server administration include starting, stopping, pausing, resuming, or restarting the server, backing up the DHCP server database, migrating a DHCP server database to another server, and compacting the DHCP server database.

how to

Change the status of a DHCP server, for example, in preparation of a backup.
1. Open the **DHCP** console and select the DHCP server in the console tree.
2. Click **Action** on the Menu bar, point to **All Tasks**, and then click **Pause (Figure 4-28)**.
3. To resume the DHCP service, click Action, point to All Tasks, and then click **Resume**. You can also use the All Tasks menu to start, stop, and restart DHCP service.

You can create a backup of a DHCP server database either automatically or manually. If the DHCP service discovers corruption in its database, an automatic backup, created every 60 minutes by default, can be used to restore the database. However, if you want to restore a DHCP database manually, you must use a manually-backed-up database to do so.

Perform a manual backup of a DHCP server database.
1. In the console tree of the DHCP console, right-click the server whose database you want to back up and click **Backup** on the shortcut menu.
2. The **Browse for Folder** dialog box opens **(Figure 4-29)**. The default folder for saving a DHCP database during backup is **%systemroot%\WINDOWS\system32\dhcp\backup**. You may change this location, but the backup must be saved to a local folder.
3. Click ▭ OK ▭ to save the backup to the specified location. To verify that you have created a backup successfully, navigate to the folder in which you saved the database in **Windows Explorer** and find the file named **DhcpCfg**, which stores the backup copy of the database. Look at the **Date Modified** data in the details pane of Windows Explorer to verify that the file has just been changed.

Migrate the DHCP service from one server to another by moving the DHCP server database.
1. Create a manual backup of the current DHCP server database as you did above.
2. Stop the DHCP server service as described above. Stopping the DHCP server at this point ensures that the server will not grant any new IP address leases to clients or change any other data while you are moving the database.
3. Click ▭ Start ▭, point to **Administrative Tools**, and then click **Services** to open the **Services** console **(Figure 4-30)**.
4. Double-click **DHCP Server** in the details pane to open the **DHCP Server Properties (Local Computer)** dialog box.
5. On the **General** tab, click the down arrow in the **Startup type** list box, and then click **Disabled** on the drop-down list **(Figure 4-31)**.
6. Click ▭ OK ▭ to close the dialog box and to prevent this DHCP server from starting up again.
7. Copy the folder in which you saved the DHCP server database backup to the computer that will become the DHCP server.
8. Log on to the computer that will be the new DHCP server as an **Administrator**, make sure that the DHCP Server role is installed, and open the DHCP console.
9. Select the DHCP server in the console tree.

tip

A DHCP database backup saves scopes, reservations, server, scope, class, and reservation options, as well as leases.

Figure 4-28 Pausing the DHCP service

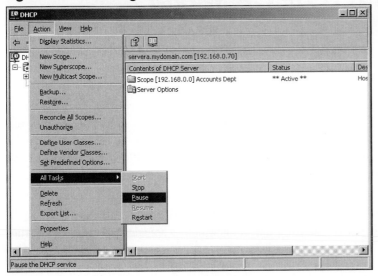

Figure 4-29 Choosing a location for the database backup

Figure 4-30 The Services console

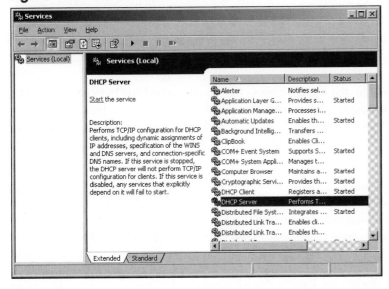

Figure 4-31 Disabling a DHCP server

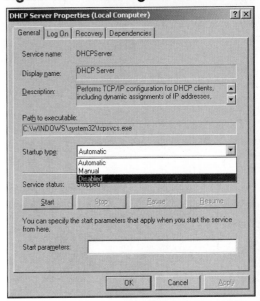

skill10

Managing a DHCP Server (cont'd)

exam objective

Manage DHCP. Manage DHCP databases.

how to

10. Open the Action menu, and then click **Restore** to open the Browse for Folder dialog box (**Figure 4-32**).
11. Select the folder to which you copied the backup of the DHCP database, and then click
    [OK]. If you are asked if you want to stop and then restart the DHCP service, click **Yes**.

DHCP, similar to WINS, runs off of a Microsoft Jet database engine. Like most databases, the DHCP database will expand in size over time, as new entries are added to it. However, when an entry is removed from the database, the database does not automatically reduce in size. Instead, the database size remains the same, but the removed records are now simply considered free space within the database. In order to actually reduce the size of the database, you need to perform what is known as an offline defrag, also called compacting the database. Microsoft recommends that you compact the DHCP database when it surpasses 30 MB in size. You can compact the database while the DHCP service is running, but taking the service offline first yields better results. You use the **Jetpack** program to compact the database, which is stored in **%systemroot%\WINDOWS\system32\dhcp\dhcp.mdb**.

Manually compact the DHCP database.
1. Stop the DHCP Server service.
2. Open a command prompt and navigate to the **%systemroot%\WINDOWS\system32\dhcp** directory by typing **cd \Windows\system32\dhcp** and pressing [**Enter**].
3. Type **jetpack dhcp.mdb compactdhcp.mdb** (**Figure 4-33**) and press [**Enter**]. In this command, **compactdhcp.mdb** is an arbitrary temporary name that you assign to the database.
4. Close the Command Prompt window.
5. Start the DHCP Server service.

more

If you are comfortable working in the Command Prompt window, Windows Server 2003 enables you to run many server administration tasks there through the **Netshell** command-line environment. To begin working in the Netshell environment, make sure you are logged in as an Administrator and run the **netsh** command at the command prompt. This command gives you access to the **netsh>** prompt. Run the **dhcp** command at the netsh> prompt to administer your DHCP server. This action results in a **netsh dhcp>** prompt. At any point along the way, you can enter Help, List, or ? to see what commands are available to you and how to use them. See **Figure 4-34** for an example of how to start managing the local DHCP server using Netshell commands. Using Netshell commands, you can add and delete servers, modify scopes, and so on.

Figure 4-32 Restoring a DHCP database

Figure 4-33 Compacting a database with Jetpack

Figure 4-34 Managing a server with Netshell commands

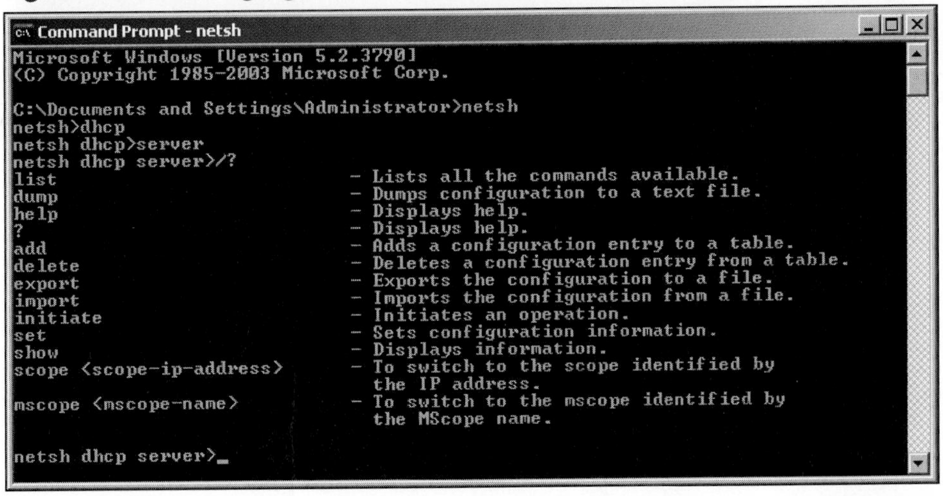

skill11 *Monitoring the DHCP Server Service*

exam objective

Examine the system event log and DHCP server audit log files to find related events. Diagnose and resolve issues related to DHCP authorization.

overview

Since the DHCP Server service is critical to assigning IP addresses to clients and configuring TCP/IP, monitoring the DHCP server is a high priority. Monitoring the performance of the DHCP server helps both in troubleshooting problems proactively and diagnosing problems after they have occurred. You can monitor the performance of the DHCP Server service using the following tools:

♦ **DHCP console**: In the DHCP console, you can check the basic statistics of the server by selecting the server in the console tree, clicking **Action** on the Menu bar, and then clicking **Display Statistics**. The **Server Statistics** dialog box (**Figure 4-35**) displays statistics such as server uptime, total number of addresses, number of available and leased addresses, and number of scopes.

♦ **Audit logging**: The DHCP Server service maintains logs of its activities on a daily basis in text files that it stores in the **%systemroot%\WINDOWS\system32\dhcp** folder. Each log file covers the 24 hours of a single day of the week, and the files are named accordingly, for example, **DhcpSrvLog-Wed.log**. Named as such, each day's log file is maintained for only a week until it is overwritten with the new log for that day of the week. A log file begins with a list of the event IDs that can be logged and their explanations followed by the events log itself (**Figure 4-36**). This list, however, only includes event IDs between 0 and 49. You will need to learn or keep a reference of event IDs 50 and over in order to identify the events to which they refer. For example, event IDs 51-57 relate to DHCP authorization events (**Table 4-5**). For a complete record of event IDs, from the DHCP console click **Help**, click **Help Topics**, and then search for the help topic titled **Analyzing server log events** on the **Search** tab.

An entry in the log file includes the event ID, the date of the event, the time of the event, a description of the event, as well as the IP address, host name, and MAC address of the client computer involved (or the network adapter of the client computer in the case of the MAC address). A comma separates each of these fields. Consecutive commas in a log entry signify an empty field or fields for that entry.

Figure 4-35 The Server Statistics dialog box

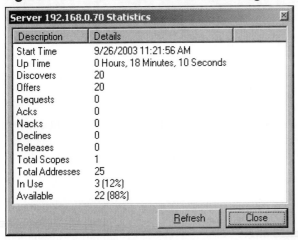

Figure 4-36 DHCP audit log file

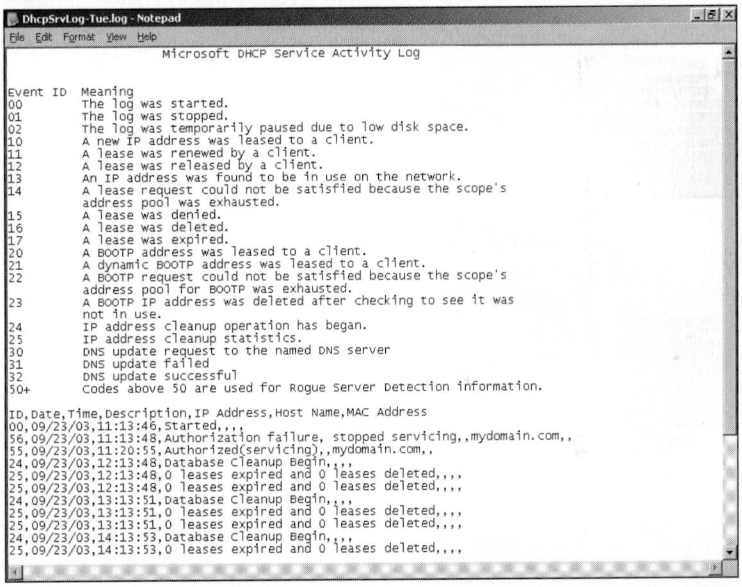

Table 4-5	Sampling of event ID codes	
Event ID	**Event**	**Details**
51	Authorization succeeded	DHCP server authorized to start on the network.
52	Upgraded to a Windows Server 2003 operating system	The unauthorized DHCP server detection feature was disabled due to a recent upgrade of the server to Windows Server 2003.
53	Cached authorization	DHCP server was authorized to start on the network using cached information because Active Directory was not available when the server started.
54	Authorization failed	DHCP was not authorized to start on the network.
55	Authorization (servicing)	DHCP server was successfully authorized to start.
56	Authorization failure, stopped servicing	DHCP server was not authorized to start and was shut down by the operating system. Server must be authorized again in Active Directory before you can start it again.
57	Server found in domain	Another DHCP server that is authorized in the same Active Directory domain has been detected.

skill11

Monitoring the DHCP Server Service
(cont'd)

exam objective

Examine the system event log and DHCP server audit log files to find related events. Diagnose and resolve issues related to DHCP authorization.

overview

You can control parameters of audit logging from the DHCP console by right-clicking the server name, and then clicking **Properties** on the shortcut menu to open the **Properties** dialog box for the server. For example, on the **General** tab, you can enable or disable audit logging **(Figure 4-37)**, and on the **Advanced** tab, you can change the location where the log files are stored **(Figure 4-38)**.

◆ **Event Viewer**: The Event Viewer in Windows Server 2003 provides a **System log**, which logs Information, Warning, and Error messages related to system events. You can use the System log to investigate problems with your DHCP server, or to gain further insight into an event that you have discovered in the DHCP audit logs. For example, suppose that you find an entry in the DHCP audit log for your DHCP server that begins as follows:

56, 09/23/03, 11:13:48, Authorization failure, stopped servicing…

tip

In the System log, errors related to the DHCP server are listed in the Source column as DHCPServer, while errors related to DHCP clients have a Source description of DHCP.

how to

Find this event in the Event Viewer's System log as follows:

1. Click [*Start*], point to **Administrative Tools**, and then click **Event Viewer**.
2. Double-click **System** in the details pane of the Event Viewer window to display the System log.
3. Use the information you have from the DHCP audit log, such as the date and time, and the column headings in the System log to locate the related event in the System log **(Figure 4-39)**.
4. Double-click the event in the details pane to open the **Event Properties** dialog box **(Figure 4-40)**. The **Description** text box displays a full description of the event and reasons why the event occurred.
5. Click [OK] to close the Event Properties dialog box.
6. Close the Event Viewer window.

Figure 4-37 Enabling/disabling audit logging

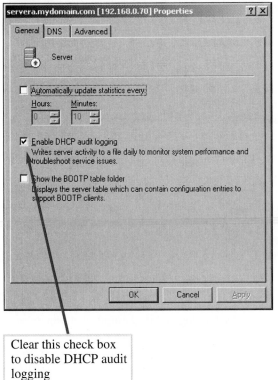

Clear this check box to disable DHCP audit logging

Figure 4-38 Changing the location of the log file

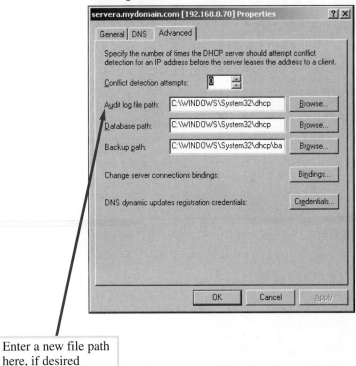

Enter a new file path here, if desired

Figure 4-39 The System log

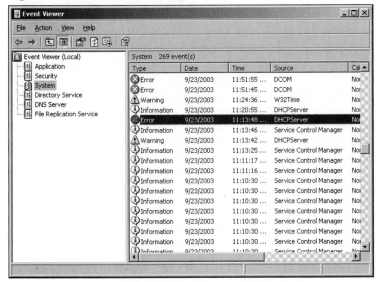

Figure 4-40 The Event Properties dialog box

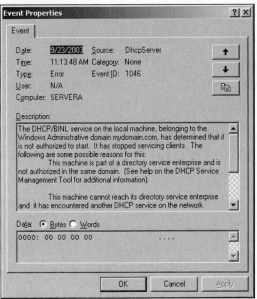

skill12 *Troubleshooting DHCP Server Service Problems*

exam objective

Troubleshoot DHCP. Diagnose and resolve issues related to configuration of DHCP server and scope options. Verify database integrity.

overview

Just as important as knowing how to monitor DHCP problems is knowing how to resolve them when they do surface. Major areas of DHCP troubleshooting include client configuration, server configuration, and database corruption.

Client configuration

◆ If a client is unable to connect to resources on the network, you can start troubleshooting with basic measures such as using the **ipconfig /all** command to help you determine the source of the connectivity problem. This will show whether the client's IP address was assigned by DHCP or configured automatically by another process such as APIPA. You can also check the origin of the client's address by opening the **Local Area Connection Status** dialog box to the **Support** tab, which indicates whether the IP address was assigned by DHCP (**Figure 4-41**).

◆ If you have determined that the client obtained its IP address appropriately, you might next want to check for address conflicts with other computers on the network. Evidence of address conflicts can appear both in the System log and in warnings that pop up from the client's system tray (notification area in Windows XP). Address conflicts can result from having multiple DHCP servers that are configured to assign addresses from the same pool, or from scopes being redeployed. You can search for superfluous DHCP servers, known as rogues, by running the **Dhcploc.exe** program from the **Windows Support Tools** folder on the server. If the conflict was the result of a scope redeployment, you can renew client leases by using either the **ipconfig /renew** command, or by clicking the **Repair** button on the Support tab of the Local Area Connection Status dialog box (**Table 4-6**).

◆ If a client is unable to obtain a DHCP address at all, as evidenced, for example, by an APIPA address, you can again begin by using ipconfig /renew or the Repair button. If those tools do not solve the problem, you should verify that a DHCP server is indeed deployed on the network, or, if the DHCP server resides on another subnet, that a relay agent is present and functioning. Next, check the physical connections between these devices. Finally, move on to the DHCP server itself. Here, you should verify that the DHCP Server role is installed and configured, and that the server is authorized. Also verify that the scope is active and that it has not exhausted the addresses in its range.

◆ Clients can also obtain their IP addresses from the wrong scope. This can occur when a rogue server is present, when authorized servers have scopes whose ranges intersect, or when a relay agent or router has been addressed incorrectly.

Server configuration

◆ The DHCP server itself must, of course, be addressed correctly. Its network ID must be the same as that of the subnet to which it pertains. If a DHCP server is not on the same subnet as the client, then there must be a DHCP relay agent on the client's subnet. In addition, the DHCP server must be bound to the connection that it uses for the subnet. You can view the network bindings of a DHCP server by opening its **Properties** dialog box to the **Advanced** tab and clicking the **Bindings** button. Finally, make certain that the server is authorized in Active Directory. You can verify this easily in the DHCP console. A green arrow pointing upward inside a white circle on the server icon indicates that the server is authorized.

◆ If the server is configured correctly, narrow in on the scope configuration and verify that:
  • The scope has been activated, indicated by the same arrow icon that indicates an authorized server.
  • The address range is correct, including a network ID that matches that of the DHCP server.

Figure 4-41 The Support tab of the Local Area Connection Status dialog box

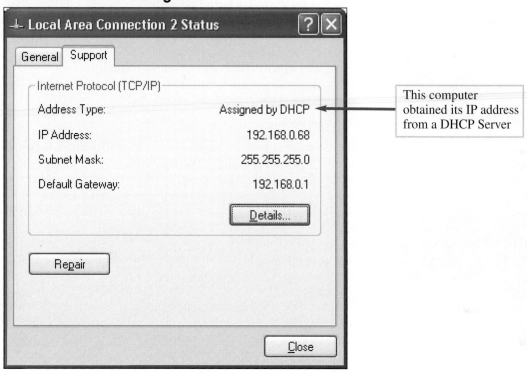

This computer obtained its IP address from a DHCP Server

Table 4-6 Steps completed by clicking the Repair button	
Command description	*Equivalent at command prompt*
1. Broadcasts a DHCPRequest message to renew lease	
2. Flushes the ARP cache	arp -d *
3. Flushes the NetBIOS cache	nbtstat -R
4. Flushes the DNS cache	ipconfig /flushdns
5. Reregisters client's IP address and NetBIOS name with WINS server	nbtstat -RR
6. Reregisters the client's name and IP address with DNS	ipconfig /registerdns

skill 12

Troubleshooting DHCP Server Service Problems *(cont'd)*

exam objective

Troubleshoot DHCP. Diagnose and resolve issues related to configuration of DHCP server and scope options. Verify database integrity.

overview

- The address range has not run out of available addresses. Even the most careful planning can fall victim to unexpected growth, resulting in address ranges that are inadequate for the demand. If address availability is a problem, you can decrease the lease duration setting so that clients do not occupy the address space unnecessarily when they do not require a lease.
- Address exclusions are configured properly.
- Reservations are configured properly, including that there are no conflicts between reservations and exclusions.

Database corruption

The DHCP database stores information about scope IP address leases in two forms: detailed and summary. If information in the DHCP console is not displaying correctly, it may be because these two records of the scope IP address lease information are in conflict. To rectify the inconsistencies between the detailed information and the summary information, you need to reconcile the DHCP database. You can also reconcile an individual scope.

how to

Reconcile the DHCP database.

1. Click **Start**, point to **Administrative Tools**, and then click **DHCP** to open the DHCP console.
2. Click the name of your DHCP server in the console tree to select the server.
3. Click **Action** on the Menu bar, and then click **Reconcile All Scopes (Figure 4-42)**.
4. The **Reconcile All Scopes** dialog box opens **(Figure 4-43)**. Click Verify .
5. If no data needs to be reconciled, click OK to close the dialog box.
6. If you do need to reconcile a scope, it will appear in the dialog box. Select the scope you want to reconcile **(Figure 4-44)** and click Reconcile to fix the discrepancies in the database.
7. Click OK to close the Reconcile All Scopes dialog box.
8. Close the DHCP console.

Figure 4-42 Reconciling the DHCP database

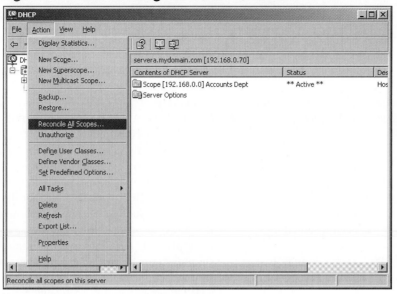

Figure 4-43 The Reconcile All Scopes dialog box

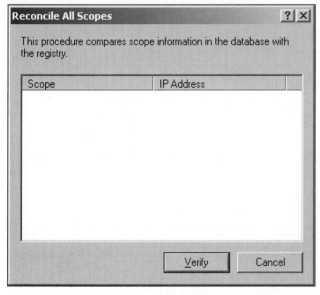

Figure 4-44 Reconciling a scope that has inconsistencies

Summary

◆ Dynamic Host Configuration Protocol (DHCP) manages TCP/IP configuration centrally by assigning IP addresses to computers that are configured to use the DHCP service.

◆ On the DHCP server, you create scopes (pools of valid IP addresses) to assign IP addresses to the clients on the network.

◆ The process of IP address assignment involves the following steps: IP lease discover, IP lease offer, IP lease request, and IP lease acknowledgment.

◆ In the absence of a DHCP server, a computer can assign itself an IP address using Automatic Private IP Addressing (APIPA), unless it has been disabled by a registry edit.

◆ To set up a Windows Server 2003 computer as DHCP server, you must add the role of DHCP server to the computer.

◆ The steps that you need to follow to configure a DHCP server include:
  • Creating scopes.
  • Authorizing the DHCP server in Active Directory.
  • Integrating the DHCP server with the DNS server.

◆ After installing the DHCP Server service, you must authorize the DHCP server in Active Directory.

◆ In order for a DHCP server to lease IP addresses to clients, you need to create DHCP scopes. A scope is a pool of IP addresses and other related configuration parameters from which a DHCP offers leases to its clients.

◆ Exclusions allow you to maintain static addresses within the scope, such as the address of the DHCP server.

◆ DHCP reservations allow you to set aside an IP address so that a specific host will be able to lease the address exclusively.

◆ DHCP Relay Agent is a routing protocol that makes it possible for DHCP clients to request an IP address from a DHCP server that is located on a remote subnet.

◆ Part of the process of configuring a DHCP server, in addition to creating scopes and authorizing the server, is integrating DHCP with DNS so that the DNS database stays up-to-date on client host name-to-IP address and IP address-to-host name mapping.

◆ Examples of DHCP server administration include starting, stopping, pausing, resuming, or restarting the server, backing up the DHCP server database, migrating a DHCP server database to another server, and compacting the DHCP server database.

◆ Monitoring the performance of the DHCP server helps both in troubleshooting problems proactively and diagnosing problems after they have occurred.

◆ Audit logging and the System log in the Event Viewer can help you learn specifics about problems you may encounter with the DHCP service.

◆ Major areas of DHCP troubleshooting include client configuration, server configuration, and database corruption.

◆ You can repair inconsistencies in the DHCP database by reconciling scopes.

Key Terms

Address (A) record
Bootstrap Protocol (BOOTP)
DHCP Relay Agent
DHCPAcknowledgment (DHCPAck)
DHCPDiscover
DHCPOffer
DHCPRequest

Dynamic Host Configuration Protocol (DHCP)
Exclusion
Member scope
Multicast Address Dynamic Client Protocol (MADCAP)
Multicast scope

Multicasting
Netshell
Pointer (PTR) record
Reservation
Scope
Superscope

Test Yourself

1. To ease administration, multiple scopes can be combined into:
   a. Multicast scopes
   b. Superscopes
   c. Multicast addresses
   d. Broadcast addresses

2. Which of the following defines the allocation of multicast addresses?
   a. APIPA
   b. TTL
   c. BOOTP
   d. MADCAP

3. Which of the following commands is used to view the DHCP configuration information on a Windows NT client computer?
   a. WINIPCFG
   b. ipconfig /all
   c. Jetpack
   d. net start dhcp server

4. Before migrating the DHCP service from one server to another, you should _____ the DHCP server to ensure that the server will not grant any new IP address leases to clients after you have already backed up the database.
   a. Pause
   b. Restart
   c. Stop
   d. Compact

5. Which of the following message packets does the DHCP server use to inform a client that an IP address is available to be leased?
   a. DHCPAcknowledgment
   b. DHCPDiscover
   c. DHCPRequest
   d. DHCPOffer

6. Which of the following commands is used to compact a DHCP database?
   a. netsh
   b. WINIPCFG
   c. ipconfig /all
   d. jetpack

7. Which of the following defines a range of IP addresses that can be leased to DHCP clients?
   a. DHCP Relay Agent
   b. Scope
   c. APIPA
   d. MADCAP

8. Registering and updating the Pointer (PTR) and Address (A) resource records of clients that have been dynamically configured by the DHCP server allows you to:
   a. Integrate DHCP with WINS.
   b. Redirect DHCPDiscover packets across routers.
   c. Integrate DHCP with DNS.
   d. Exclude an IP address from being leased.

9. A DHCP server leases a reserved IP address based on the client's:
   a. Network adapter MAC address
   b. APIPA-designated address
   c. NetBIOS name
   d. DHCPRequest message

10. In order to allow DHCP clients to request IP addresses from a DHCP server on a remote subnet, you must configure a:
    a. Superscope
    b. DHCP Relay Agent
    c. Multicast address
    d. Reservation

11. Which pair of tools will allow you to troubleshoot DHCP server problems most effectively?
    a. Event Viewer and Jetpack
    b. Event Viewer and DNS
    c. System log and WINIPCFG
    d. Audit logging and System log

12. Which of the following is an example of a DHCP audit log file name?
    a. DhcpSrvLog-Fri.log
    b. Dhcploc.exe
    c. RFC 2730
    d. %systemroot%\WINDOWS\system32\dhcp

Projects: On Your Own

1. View the basic statistics of a DHCP server.
   a. Open the **DHCP** console.
   b. Select the name of the server in the console tree.
   c. Open the **Action** menu and select the **Display Statistics** command.
   d. View the statistics provided by the **Server Statistics** dialog box, and then close the dialog box.
2. Stop the DHCP service.
   a. In the DHCP console, select the DHCP server.
   b. Open the **Action** menu, point to **All Tasks**, and click **Stop**.
   c. Start the service again.
3. View a DHCP audit log file.
   a. Open **Windows Explorer**.
   b. Navigate to **%systemroot%\WINDOWS\system32\dhcp**.
   c. Open the DHCP log file for today.
   d. Find the entry that corresponds to when you stopped the DHCP server in the previous question.
   e. Close the log file and Windows Explorer.
4. Reconcile a DHCP scope.
   a. Open the DHCP console, if necessary.
   b. Select an active scope.
   c. Open the **Action** menu and select **Reconcile**.
   d. Verify the scope.
   e. If necessary, reconcile the scope.
   f. Close the **Reconcile** dialog box and the DHCP console.

Problem Solving Scenarios

1. You are a Network Administrator at a rapidly growing independent retailer. As the company has grown, there have been more and more problems with manual IP addressing. Currently the LAN is based on Windows Server 2003 and uses DNS. Every time a client obtains an IP address, the related information has to be updated on the DNS server. The company has decided to move to dynamic IP addressing. Prepare a document describing the actions you will take to implement dynamic IP addressing while ensuring that the Web server on your LAN retains a static IP address.

2. You administer your company's DHCP server. Lately, you have been receiving feedback saying that the Windows NT 4 clients in your domain cannot access other computers using their computer names. Users have also begun to complain that they no longer can obtain IP addresses from the DHCP server. Moreover, existing clients are not able to renew their leases. After some investigation, you find out that the domain controller has failed and there is no other domain controller available. How will you handle the above scenario? Prepare a PowerPoint presentation that explains the plan you will follow to correct the situation.

On a Windows Server 2003 TCP/IP network, hosts (computers and other devices) use IP addresses to connect and communicate with each other. It is difficult to commit IP addresses to memory due to their numerical format. On a large network, it would be virtually impossible, not to mention inconvenient, to recall the IP address of a particular host without looking it up in a reference table of some sort. You can overcome this problem by using plain-language names for hosts instead of IP addresses. These names are valid when you use them to refer to a TCP/IP host on a network, and are likely to remain stable, unlike IP addresses, if a network is restructured.

Since hosts on a TCP/IP network use IP addresses to connect and communicate with each other, the names that you use to identify the hosts must be resolved to their associated IP addresses in order for a source host to establish a connection with the destination host. In Windows Server 2003, you can use various methods to resolve names to IP addresses, including broadcast, LMHOSTS file, NetBIOS name cache, NetBIOS name server, HOSTS file, and Domain Name System (DNS).

Of all the methods used for resolving host names, DNS is the most popular. Aside from its technical features, the main reason for its popularity is that DNS is the naming standard for the Internet. DNS is also an integral part of the Windows Server 2003 operating system. In addition to using DNS to resolve names, Windows uses it to locate different services on the network. Active Directory and many other system functions of Windows Server 2003 depend heavily on the DNS model.

To manage the DNS model effectively, you can divide the implementation of the service into small administrative units called zones, which store information about the host name-to-IP address and IP address-to-host name mappings for a particular DNS namespace in a separate zone database file. The zone file also contains references to other DNS name servers outside the zone so that name resolution requests can be forwarded up and down the hierarchical namespace. The hierarchical namespace in which a DNS server participates can be as simple as an individual corporate intranet or as widespread and complex as the entire Internet. In order for DNS to resolve host names effectively on your network, a thorough analysis of the factors that determine and influence the design of DNS is required.

Once you have designed your DNS infrastructure, you can start implementing DNS servers on your network. You designate a Windows Server 2003 computer as a DNS server by installing the Microsoft DNS Server service, also known as adding the DNS Server role.

Goals

In this lesson, you will learn about the various naming systems used for naming hosts on a network, as well as the methods used for resolving names to IP addresses. You will also learn about the functionality and structure of DNS and the important factors you need to consider while designing a DNS infrastructure. Finally, you will install a DNS server on a Windows Server 2003 computer.

Lesson 5   Understanding Name Resolution and DNS

Skill	Exam 70-291 Objective
1. Introducing Naming Systems	Basic knowledge
2. Introducing Host Name Resolution	Basic knowledge
3. Introducing NetBIOS Name Resolution	Basic knowledge
4. Using Multiple Name Resolution Methods	Basic knowledge
5. Introducing DNS	Basic knowledge
6. Introducing DNS Zones and DNS Server Roles	Basic knowledge
7. Examining Factors Affecting DNS Infrastructure	Basic knowledge
8. Installing the DNS Server Service	Install and configure the DNS Server service.

Requirements

To complete this lesson, you will need administrative rights on a Windows Server 2003 computer on a network.

skill 1

Introducing Naming Systems

exam objective

Basic knowledge

overview

To resolve host names to IP addresses on a network, you need to use a naming system. Windows Server 2003 supports two naming systems: the host naming system and the NetBIOS naming system. In the host naming system, you name network hosts using host names, and in the NetBIOS naming system, you name network hosts using NetBIOS names.

A **host name** is a name given to a host on a TCP/IP network in addition to its IP address. Host names make it easier for you to refer to hosts on a TCP/IP network. For example, it is easier to remember a client computer as computer01 or a print server as PrintServer than it is to remember their IP addresses (**Figure 5-1**).

A host name can be up to 255 characters long and can contain letters, numbers, and special characters such as "_" and "-". A single host in a TCP/IP network can have more than one referenced name in the DNS namespace. For example, a computer that has a host name **computer01** may also be referred to by the alias **FTP** in DNS to specify a function supported by computer01; you could use either of these names to refer to this computer.

A DNS host's name can be stored in two forms: Address Record (A) and fully qualified domain name (FQDN) (**Figure 5-2**). An Address Record is used to map a host name to an IP address. A **fully qualified domain name** defines a host by using Internet naming conventions. For example, **computer01** might be the alias for a computer, whereas **computer01.cosmo.com** might be the fully qualified domain name of the same computer in the **cosmo.com** domain. DNS host names are hierarchical, and they use the dot character to separate levels of the hierarchy.

NetBIOS allows applications using the NetBIOS API (application programming interface) to communicate over a single LAN segment. If a LAN is divided into smaller segments, then NetBIOS does not allow communication between the segments. Each network resource that uses NetBIOS should have a unique 16-byte name called a **NetBIOS name**. Unlike DNS's hierarchical naming scheme, NetBIOS uses a flat naming scheme, which requires that all NetBIOS resources on a network have unique NetBIOS names. Windows Server 2003 supports host names primarily, but it maintains support for NetBIOS names as well because computers running earlier versions of the Windows operating system and some legacy applications require NetBIOS names. NetBIOS names have a maximum length of 15 characters, as Microsoft uses the 16th character for a NetBIOS suffix.

more

A Windows Server 2003 computer has both a host name and a NetBIOS name. Applications running on a Windows Server 2003 computer use these names to refer to other network hosts. The type of name programs use depends on the API of the program. An API is a set of components and tools used within a software program to allow for communication within the TCP/IP network environment. Programs that use the Windows Sockets (WinSock) API, such as Web browsers, use host names, while network programs and services that use the NetBIOS API, such as File and Print Sharing for Microsoft Networks, use NetBIOS names to refer to network hosts.

Figure 5-1 Using IP addresses and names to access network resources

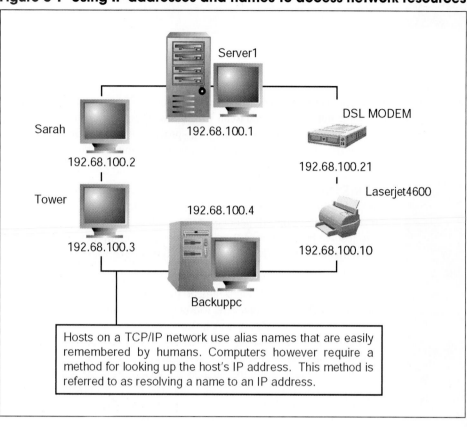

Server1

192.68.100.1

Sarah

192.68.100.2

Tower

192.68.100.3

192.68.100.4

Backuppc

DSL MODEM

192.68.100.21

Laserjet4600

192.68.100.10

Hosts on a TCP/IP network use alias names that are easily
remembered by humans. Computers however require a
method for looking up the host's IP address. This method is
referred to as resolving a name to an IP address.

Figure 5-2 Forms of host names

HOST NAME	FULLY QUALIFIED DOMAIN NAME (FQDN)	IP ADDRESS
Server1	Server1.bcg.com	192.68.100.1
Sarah	Sarah.bcg.com	192.68.100.2
Tower	Tower.bcg.com	192.68.100.3
Backuppc	Backuppc.bcg.com	192.68.100.4
Laserjet4600	Laserjet4600.bcg.com	192.68.100.10
Dslmodem	Dslmodem.bcg.com	192.68.100.21

skill 2 *Introducing Host Name Resolution*

exam objective

Basic knowledge

overview

When you use a host name to connect or communicate with other hosts on the network, the host name must be resolved to an IP address. This is because hosts on a TCP/IP network use IP addresses to identify each other. The process of determining the IP address of a host over the TCP/IP network by using a host name is known as host name resolution. To perform host name resolution, you can use the HOSTS file or a DNS server.

A **HOSTS file** is a text file that contains the static mappings of host names to IP addresses and is available on the local computer. The HOSTS file can contain multiple entries, with a single entry consisting of one IP address corresponding to one host name. TCP/IP utilities use this file to resolve host names to IP addresses on your computer. The HOSTS file is stored in the **%systemroot%\WINDOWS\system32\drivers\etc** folder on your Windows Server 2003 computer.

In a Windows Server 2003 environment, the process of resolving a host name to its IP address using the HOSTS file involves the following steps **(Figure 5-3)**:

1. A WinSock application uses a host name to reference a resource on the network.
2. If the host name is the same as the host name of your local computer, the name is resolved and the process of host name resolution ends.
3. If the host name is not the same as the local host name, the host name is searched for in the HOSTS file on the local computer. The file is read from top to bottom, and if an entry for the desired host name exists, the host name is resolved to the IP address.
4. After the host name is resolved to an IP address, the IP address is resolved to the hardware address of the host by processes going down the TCP/IP protocol stack.
5. If the HOSTS file does not have any entry for the desired host name and no other method of name resolution is configured on your computer, the process of name resolution ends and an error message displays.

Years ago, using the HOSTS file was the only method of host name resolution. However, with the growth of networking and the emergence of the Internet, managing host name resolution using the HOSTS file became difficult because the file is stored locally and must be updated manually. The **Domain Name System (DNS)** was designed to improve the process of resolving host names.

DNS is a hierarchical, distributed, and scalable database that contains mappings of host names to IP addresses. A source host used the information in the DNS database to resolve the host name of the destination host to its IP address in order to establish communication.

An important advantage of using DNS over a HOSTS file in Windows Server 2003 is that the implementation of DNS supports dynamic updates of host name-to-IP address mappings. Dynamic updates allow hosts on a network to register with the DNS database and update any changes in their configurations dynamically.

In a Windows Server 2003 environment, the process of resolving a host name to an IP address using DNS involves the following steps **(Figure 5-4)**.

1. When a user refers to a host by its host name, the resolver tries to resolve this name to its associated IP address. If the host name resolution is unsuccessful using the HOSTS file, a request is sent to the host's configured DNS sever for name resolution.
2. The DNS server database is queried for the requested host name, and if found, resolves the host name to an IP address.

tip

It is possible for an IP address to map to more than one host name in the HOSTS file when a host name has aliases. In this case, the first name listed for the IP address will be used.

tip

Some implementations of DNS provide for a search precedence to resolve host names. For example, you could specify that the resolver query DNS first, and then look in the HOSTS file. The risk of using the HOSTS file first is that it may become outdated and return incorrect data.

Figure 5-3 Resolving a host name to its IP address using the HOSTS file

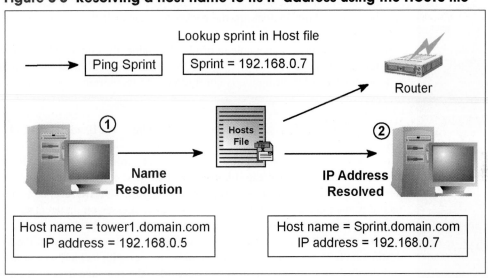

Figure 5-4 Resolving a host name to its IP address using the DNS server

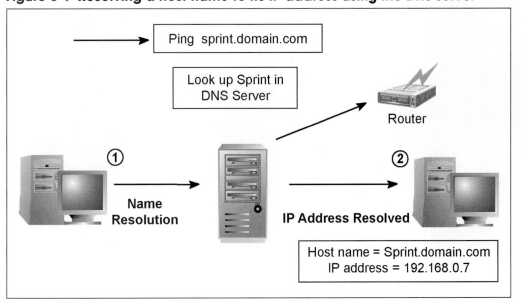

skill 2

Introducing Host Name Resolution
(cont'd)

exam objective   Basic knowledge

overview

3. After DNS resolves the host name to an IP address, the client passes the IP address down the protocol stack so that IP can call ARP to resolve the hardware address of the destination host, or forward the packet to a router if the destination host is on another subnet.
4. If the DNS server is not able to resolve the name, the client makes additional requests at intervals of 1, 2, 2, and 4 seconds. If the DNS server still does not respond and there are no other resolution methods configured, the resolution process stops and an error is reported.

more

Once the host name has been resolved to an IP address, the IP address must be resolved to the hardware address because the actual communication between two hosts occurs at the hardware level. The IP protocol uses the Address Resolution Protocol (ARP) to resolve an IP address to a hardware address (**Figure 5-5**). ARP first consults the source's local ARP cache to obtain the hardware address of the destination host. The ARP cache maintains a temporary record of mappings of IP addresses to hardware addresses on the local subnet. If ARP is not able to obtain the hardware address from the source's local cache, it sends a message containing the IP address of the destination host to all other hosts on the local subnet. The destination host, upon receipt of the message, replies with its hardware address. If the source and destination hosts are on different networks, the message is passed on to the router by determination of IP. The router then determines if it can communicate with the destination host, or if the packet must be sent to yet another router in order for the hardware address to be resolved. Upon receiving the hardware address of the destination host (or router if the destination host is on a different subnet), the source host can send the packet.

Figure 5-5 Address Resolution Protocol

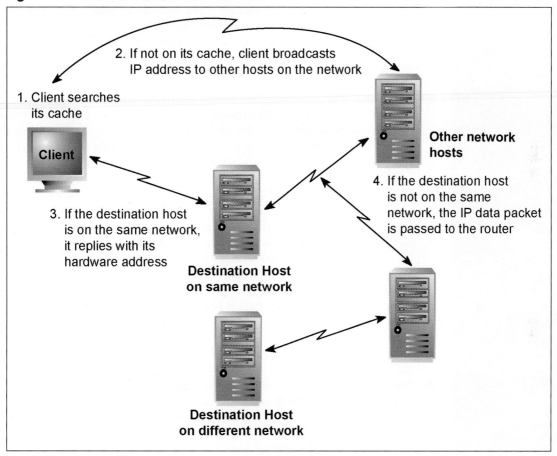

2. If not on its cache, client broadcasts
IP address to other hosts on the network

1. Client searches
its cache

Client

Other network
hosts

3. If the destination host
is on the same network,
it replies with its
hardware address

4. If the destination host
is not on the same
network, the IP data packet
is passed to the router

**Destination Host
on same network**

**Destination Host
on different network**

skill 3

Introducing NetBIOS Name Resolution

exam objective

Basic knowledge

overview

Another common system of naming hosts is the NetBIOS naming system. In the NetBIOS naming system, you use NetBIOS names to identify NetBIOS resources on a network. To enable TCP/IP hosts to communicate on a TCP/IP network with a NetBIOS resource, the NetBIOS name of the resource needs to be resolved to an IP address. The process of resolving a NetBIOS name to an IP address is known as **NetBIOS name resolution**.

Below are the various methods of NetBIOS name resolution supported by Windows Server 2003:

♦ **Broadcast:** The most basic method of NetBIOS name resolution, broadcast sends requests simultaneously to all network hosts. In this method, the NetBIOS name of the destination host is sent to all other hosts on the local subnet. Upon receiving the broadcast, the destination replies with its IP address directly to the source host (**Figure 5-6**). This method is only useful for small networks because large networks are made up of smaller networks connected by routers, which generally block broadcasts.

♦ **LMHOSTS file:** An LMHOSTS file is a text file, available on the local computer, that contains the static mappings of NetBIOS names to IP addresses of computers on remote networks only. NetBIOS name-to-IP address mappings of resources on the local network are not required in the LMHOSTS file because the name resolution of local resources is performed with the broadcast method. To resolve NetBIOS names using an LMHOSTS file, the file is read from top to bottom. If the entry for the destination NetBIOS resource is present, the NetBIOS name is resolved to its IP address (**Figure 5-7**). Therefore, it is good practice to place the names of frequently accessed resources at the top of the list of entries in the LMHOSTS file, provided that this does not raise administrative costs. The LMHOSTS file is stored in the **%systemroot%\WINDOWS\system32\drivers\etc** folder on your Windows Server 2003 computer.

♦ **NetBIOS name cache:** The NetBIOS name cache stores information about the most recently resolved NetBIOS names and is maintained in client memory. When resolving a NetBIOS name, the client first refers to the NetBIOS name cache and, if a mapping for the destination NetBIOS name is available in the cache, the NetBIOS name is resolved to its associated IP address. If the NetBIOS name cache cannot resolve the name, the client tries other available methods of NetBIOS name resolution.

♦ **NetBIOS Name Server (NBNS):** NetBIOS Name Server is an application that is responsible for mapping NetBIOS names to IP addresses. You do not need to manually enter mappings of NetBIOS names to IP addresses in an NBNS database because NetBIOS clients from different segments dynamically register their names with NBNS. When a host refers to a destination host using a NetBIOS name, the source host queries the NBNS database for the mapping of the destination NetBIOS name to its associated IP address. The NBNS queries its database, and upon finding the entry for the destination NetBIOS host, resolves its name to the associated IP address.

Microsoft's implementation of an NBNS is Windows Internet Naming Service (WINS). WINS allows clients on a network to register their NetBIOS name-to-IP address mappings dynamically in a database called the WINS database. The computer that is running WINS is called the WINS server.

Figure 5-6 Resolving a NetBIOS name to its IP address using a NetBIOS broadcast

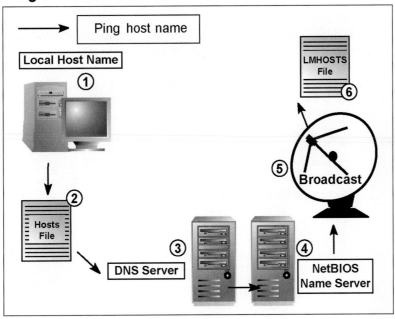

Figure 5-7 Resolving a NetBIOS name to its IP address using the LMHOSTS file

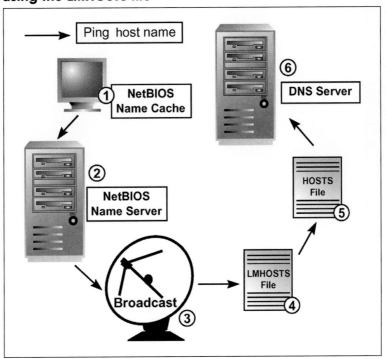

skill 3

Introducing NetBIOS Name Resolution (cont'd)

exam objective

Basic knowledge

more

In a Windows Server 2003 environment, the process of resolving a NetBIOS name to an IP address using WINS involves the following steps (**Figure 5-8**).

1. A user application enters a request for network service. The client first will check its NetBIOS name cache for the IP address. If a name is found the IP address is returned.

2. If the name is not resolved from the cache, a name query is sent to the client's primary WINS server. If this fails after two tries, the request is sent to the secondary WINS server, if available.

3. If neither WINS server can resolve the name, the client reverts to sending a broadcast message.

4. If the name remains unresolved, the client will check the LMHOSTS and HOSTS files, and finally DNS. If these actions fail to resolve the name, the command fails.

Figure 5-8 Resolving a NetBIOS name to its IP address using WINS

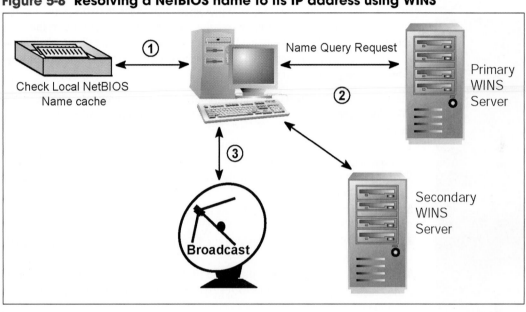

skill 4

Using Multiple Name Resolution Methods

Basic knowledge

overview

You use either the HOSTS file or DNS to resolve host names to IP addresses, and broadcast, the LMHOSTS file, NetBIOS name cache, and NetBIOS Name Server to resolve NetBIOS names to their IP addresses. On a Windows Server 2003 network, you can use any one of these methods for successful name resolution. You can also configure the TCP/IP network client to use all of the above-named resolution methods so that if one method fails to resolve the requested resource name, another method will be used in the attempt to resolve the resource name to its associated IP address.

When you configure the TCP/IP network client to use all name resolution methods available in Windows Server 2003, the process of host name resolution will involve the following steps **(Figure 5-9)**:

1. The process of host name resolution starts when a resource on a TCP/IP network is requested by its host name.
2. If the host name is the same as the local host name, the name is resolved and the process of host name resolution ends.
3. If the host name is not the same as the local host name, the host name is searched for in the HOSTS file.
4. If the HOSTS file cannot resolve the host name, a request is sent to the DNS server for host name resolution.
5. The DNS server looks for the name in its database and resolves it to an IP address. If the DNS server is not able to resolve the name, the client makes additional attempts at intervals of 1, 2, 3, and 4 seconds. The DNS server may not have the host name in its own zone file, and will therefore forward the name request up the DNS hierarchy to higher-level DNS servers until the requests reaches a DNS server that does contain the host name. Once the name is resolved, the local DNS server keeps the name in its DNS cache enabling the next resolution of the same name to occur quickly.
6. If, after the additional attempts, the DNS server is not able to resolve the host name, the NetBIOS name cache of the source host is queried for the name of the destination host.
7. If the name of the destination host is not found in the NetBIOS name cache, three attempts are made to contact the client's configured WINS server.
8. If, after the third attempt, the WINS server is unable to resolve the NetBIOS name of the destination host, the source host resorts to the broadcast method. The source generates three broadcast messages on the local network.
9. If the broadcast messages cannot resolve the NetBIOS name of the destination host, the LMHOSTS file of the source is queried for the NetBIOS name of the destination host.
10. If the LMHOSTS file cannot resolve the NetBIOS name of the destination host, the process of host name resolution ends and an error message is displayed.

Note that at any stage in the above process, if any method resolves the host name successfully, the process of host name resolution ends. If none of the methods is successful in resolving the host name, you cannot use a host name to connect and communicate with the destination host. In such a situation, the IP address of the destination host must be used to connect and communicate with the destination host.

Figure 5-9 Windows Server 2003 methods of resolving host names

Ping www.ussenate.org

1. Client request.
2. Check local host name.
3. Check local HOSTS file.
4. Check DNS Server.
5. Repeat requests at 1,2,3 and 4 seconds.
6. Check NetBIOS name cache.
7. Check client WINS server (3 times).
8. Broadcast on the network to other hosts.
9. Query LMHOSTS file of the source host for NetBIOS name of the destination host.
10. If NetBIOS name of the destination host cannot be resolved, process ends and error message is displayed.

Name resolution request may be forwarded up the DNS hierarchy

skill 5

Introducing DNS

exam objective

Basic knowledge

overview

Domain Name System (DNS) is the primary naming system of Windows Server 2003. In order to understand the workings of DNS and how DNS performs all its functions, you first need to understand the structure of DNS.

The structure of DNS is defined by the **DNS namespace**. The DNS namespace is a hierarchical arrangement of domains in DNS. Each top-level domain has a name, and each name is classified into a domain type (**Table 5-1**). In the DNS namespace, as you move down the hierarchy, the reference to a resource becomes more specific. As you add more sub-domains to the DNS hierarchy, the name of the parent domain is added to the child domain, or sub-domain. For example, in the domain name **city.state.us**, **city** represents a sub-domain of the **state.us** domain, and **state** is a sub-domain of the **us** top-level domain. **Domain names** are not case-sensitive and can be up to 63 characters in length.

The domain at the top of the DNS namespace is called the **root domain** and is represented by a period (.). The child domain of the root domain is called a **top-level domain**, and the child domain of a top-level domain is called a **second-level domain**. On the Internet, the commonly used top-level domains include com, edu, net, gov, org, tv, mil, info, and the various country codes such as uk and ca (United Kingdom and Canada). Second-level domains have two parts: a top-level name and a second-level name. You can use second-level domains to create a distinct place for your organization in the domain namespace and a distinct identity on the Internet. Some common examples of second-level domains are army.mil, whitehouse.gov, and google.com. Second-level domains can contain **sub-domains**. For example, in sales.google.com, sales is a sub-domain of the google.com second-level domain (**Figure 5-10**). A host name can also be at the bottom of the DNS hierarchy to designate a particular computer on the Internet or on a private network.

To identify a host completely in the DNS hierarchy, you use a fully qualified domain name (FQDN), which is a dotted name that uses a host name together with its domain names. You also use a FQDN to completely identify a host on a TCP/IP network, such as the Internet. For example, **computer01.intergalaxy.com** is a FQDN that identifies a host, **computer01**, on a TCP/IP network. It indicates that **computer01** is under the second-level domain, **intergalaxy**, which is under the top-level domain, **com**.

Understanding the DNS hierarchy makes it easy to understand the way DNS works to resolve host names to IP addresses and also to resolve IP addresses to host names. To accomplish this in a Windows Server 2003 network, DNS requires two main components: a resolver and a name server.

A **resolver** is application code that provides address information about other network hosts to the client. During the process of name resolution, if the client is unable to resolve the destination host name on its own, the resolver sends a query to DNS servers, including root servers, to look up DNS records on behalf of the client. The DNS server uses two types of queries, recursive and iterative, to contact other DNS servers in an attempt to resolve the host name if the DNS server cannot resolve the name by itself.

◆ A DNS server uses a **recursive query** to call a name server that assumes the full workload and responsibility for providing a complete answer to the query. If the DNS server cannot resolve the request from its database, it will then perform separate iterative queries to other servers (on behalf of the client) to assist in answering the recursive query. If the name server is not able to find the requested data or the specified domain name, the name server replies with an error message.

tip

A FQDN can have up to 255 characters from the set A-Z, a-z, 0-9, and -. To ease administration, it is wise to limit FQDNs to three or four levels.

Table 5-1   The DNS namespace

Domain hierarchy	Description
Root domain	The primary domain in the DNS namespace. The root domain is represented by a period (.).
Top-level domain	These domains are located below the root domain in the DNS namespace. They define the organization type or geographic location. On the Internet, top-level domains are the two and three character codes such as com, used for commercial organizations; gov, used for government entities; net, used for networking organizations; or org, used for non-profit organizations. You can see a list of the current top-level domains and the organizations that operate them at **http://www.iana.org/gtld/gtld.htm**.
Second-level domains	These are placed below the top-level domains in the DNS namespace. For example, the .com top-level domain assigns and registers second-level domains to individuals and organizations such as Microsoft, Yahoo, Apple, etc.
Host names	The host name is the leftmost portion of a FQDN and is located below the second-level domains and sub-domains, sometimes several layers down in the naming hierarchy. The host name designates a particular computer, either on the Internet or a private network.

Figure 5-10 DNS namespace hierarchy

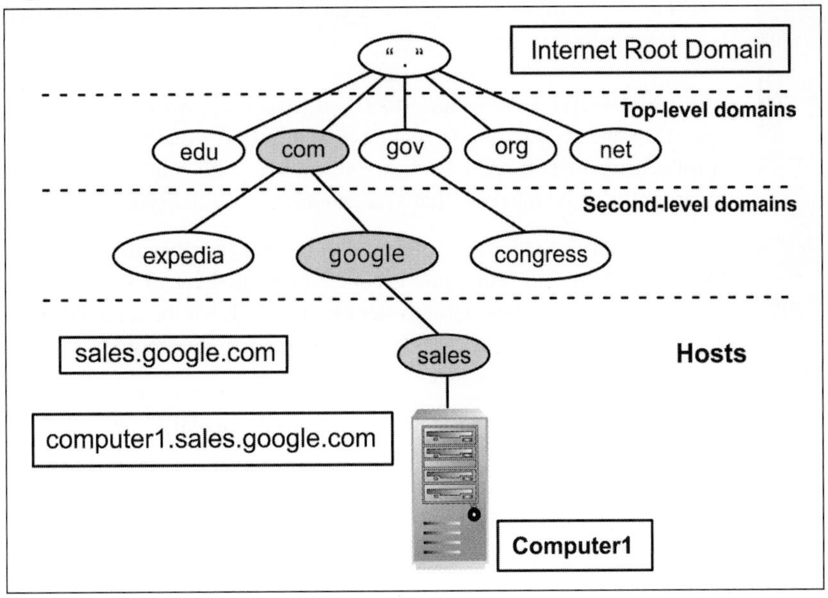

skill 5

Introducing DNS *(cont'd)*

exam objective

Basic knowledge

overview

◆ A DNS server uses an **iterative query** to call a name server to reply with the requested data or provide a reference to another name server that might be able to answer the request.

The **name server** contains address information about network hosts. During the process of DNS name resolution, when the resolver passes the client request to the DNS name server, the name server resolves the destination host name and responds with the IP address of the destination host. However, if a name server is unsuccessful in resolving the client request, it can forward the request to other name servers on the network.

Let's look at an example to understand the roles of resolver and name server in the process of DNS name resolution. Suppose you are on an intranet and want to access the Web site, **www.intergalaxy.com**, on the Internet. In order to connect to the desired site, you need to resolve the name of the Web site to its IP address. Using DNS, the name of the Web site will be resolved as follows (**Figure 5-11**):

1. The resolver on the client computer sends a recursive query to its designated name server on the local network asking to resolve **www.interagalaxy.com** to its IP address.
2. The local name server checks its database. If the local name server is unable to find any information for the requested domain, it sends an iterative query to a root server, which responds with the name of the top-level domain name server on the Internet.
3. In this case, the local name server sends an iterative query to the com name server for www.intergalaxy.com.
4. The com name server replies with the IP address of the name server for the intergalaxy.com domain.
5. The local name server sends an iterative query to the intergalaxy.com name server for www.intergalaxy.com.
6. The intergalaxy.com name server replies with the IP address of www.intergalaxy.com.
7. The local name server sends the IP address of www.intergalaxy.com to the client computer.

more

The name server's host name-to-IP address mappings are collected during the process of receiving and responding to recursive and iterative queries. The name servers use this stored information to resolve host names quickly. This method for storing frequently needed information in memory so that you can access it quickly when required is called caching.

The name servers store this information in their memory for a limited period of time specified by the returned data. This time is called **Time-to-Live (TTL)**. The Administrator of the name server to which the data belongs decides the TTL for the data. For example, you can make the TTL period long if changes in the data do not happen frequently and you do not want the data in the cache to be updated frequently.

On the other hand, if data changes take place regularly, you can keep the TTL short so that data in the cache is updated frequently. However, this would increase the load on the name server due to the frequent updates. Apart from the name server, client resolver service also stores information about recently resolved host name-to-IP address mappings in its memory for the time specified by its own TTL values.

Figure 5-11 Using DNS names to resolve a domain name to an IP address

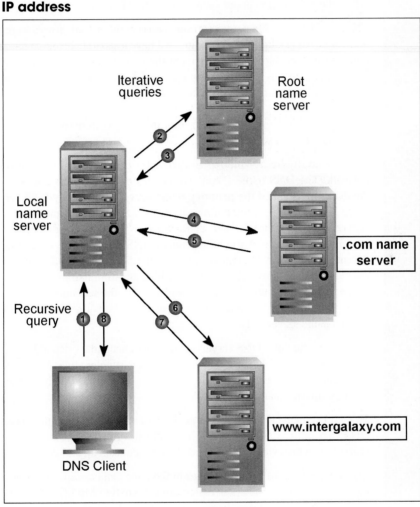

skill 6

Introducing DNS Zones and DNS Server Roles

exam objective

Basic knowledge

overview

In order to manage DNS effectively on larger networks, you can divide the DNS structure into units called zones. A **zone** is the scope of names that are served by a particular DNS name server. The part of the DNS namespace for which a zone is responsible is known as the **zone of authority**. A zone must contain at least one domain, called the root domain of that zone. All of the information about each zone is stored in a separate file called a **zone database file**.

The zone database file contains **resource records** that DNS uses to resolve host names to IP addresses. All resources in a domain must have a separate resource record in their domain zone database file, giving information about the type of resource and its role. A zone database file can contain various types of resource records; the most commonly used is the address (A) record, also known as the host record. **Table 5-2** provides a brief description of some of the different types of resource records that a zone database file can contain. The zone database files are stored with the file extension **.dns** in the **%systemroot%\WINDOWS\system32\dns** folder on the DNS server.

You can configure a Windows Server 2003 DNS server to perform different roles on the network. The DNS name server that creates or modifies its zones on a locally stored zone database file is called the **primary name server** or **primary DNS server**. This makes a primary DNS server the main authority for its zones. You can also have a **secondary name server** or **secondary DNS server** for a zone. This server maintains a copy of the zone database file that it receives from the primary DNS server of the zone (**Figure 5-12**). It can serve domain information for that zone across the network. Primary and secondary name servers exist in a master-slave relationship in which an Administrator only has to update the primary (master) server and the changes are replicated to the secondary servers. This relationship provides DNS with redundancy and a measure of backup, enabling name service to continue when a name server fails.

The designation of a DNS server as primary or secondary depends on which server stores and maintains the writable zone database file of a particular zone. The DNS server from which the secondary name server receives the copy of the zone database file is also known as the primary (master) name server.

To facilitate name resolution, a large domain may delegate name service to sub-domains in its DNS hierarchy. Each sub-domain would have its own name servers, both primary and secondary, which would also forward name requests up and down the hierarchy as required.

The process of transferring changes in the zone database file from the primary DNS server to the secondary DNS server is called **zone transfer**. Modifications and updates can only be made to the primary zone database file. The updated zone database file is then transferred to the secondary DNS servers.

caution

The data kept in a caching-only server is temporary, and the TTL values determine when a temporary record expires and is dropped.

You can also configure a DNS server as a **caching-only name server**. These DNS servers do not have their own local zone database files and therefore have no authority for any zone. They do not participate in zone transfers. Caching-only name servers primarily query, cache, and return the results of the name resolution process. They are used when you need to provide DNS services locally, but do not want to create a separate zone for the particular location. This scenario can arise when the number of hosts that require DNS service at a location is small, or when you do not want to increase administrative overhead by maintaining another zone.

When you implement a caching-only DNS server on your network for the first time, the cache is empty. As the server starts to service client requests, information is cached and builds. Thus, during the initial phase of service, more requests must be forwarded to other DNS servers.

Table 5-2   Types of resource records in a zone database file

Record type	Represented in file as	Description
Start of authority	SOA	First record in the DNS database file. Defines the general parameters for the DNS zone, including the name of the primary DNS server for the zone.
Name server	NS	Lists the additional name server in the zone.
Address (host name)	A	Associates a host name to its IP address.
IPv6 address	AAAA	Associates the host name with the corresponding 128-bit IPv6 address.
Canonical name (Alias)	CNAME	States the host name or the server name as a reference name, or alias, that can be referred to in place of the corresponding A record.
Pointer record	PTR	Associates an IP address to a host name.
Mail exchange	MX	Gives message routing to a mail exchanger host for mail sent to the domain name that you have specified.
Service record	SRV	Associates the location of a Windows Server 2003 with information about how to contact the service.

Figure 5-12   Master name server concept

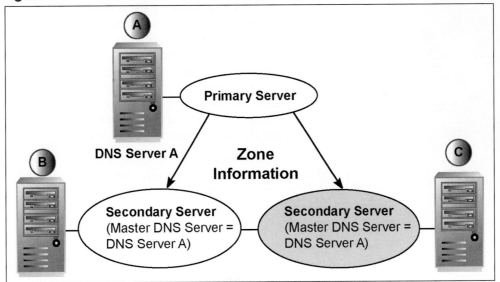

skill 7

Examining Factors Affecting DNS Infrastructure

exam objective Basic knowledge

overview

You can implement multiple DNS servers in your Windows Server 2003 network, but before you start to install and configure them, you need to plan and design your DNS infrastructure. There are various factors that you need to consider when designing your DNS infrastructure, including the size of the network, the geography of the network, security, bandwidth, and fault tolerance.

The size of your network is an important consideration when designing your DNS infrastructure. The factors that you need to consider in implementing DNS are different for small, mid-sized, and large networks. In a small network, you need to consider the number of users, administrative units, and sites, although the overall resiliency is most critical. When implementing DNS in a mid-sized or large network, in addition to the factors affecting a small network, you need to take into account the quality of connectivity between different locations, available bandwidth, and future network modifications. Based on these factors, you need to answer questions such as how many DNS domains and sub-domains you require, how many zones you need, and how many primary and secondary name servers and DNS caching-only servers you need to configure. For example, a single company would likely require just one domain, possibly divided into sub-domains. A multinational or multipurpose corporation would likely begin its DNS hierarchy with multiple domains.

Another important factor that you should consider when implementing DNS in your Windows Server 2003 network is whether you need to use DNS to resolve names of resources on an intranet or the Internet, or both. If you plan to use your DNS to serve both the intranet and Internet requirements of your organization, then you need to decide whether you want to use the same domain name on your intranet as well as the Internet. If you implement the same domain name, users should be able to access resources on both the intranet and the Internet by using a single domain name (**Figure 5-13**).

The major problem with using the same domain name is security, because in this situation your internal resources will be accessible from the Internet. To implement a secure setup for this situation, you need to create two separate DNS zones. One zone will allow Internet clients to access public resources and will not be configured to resolve the internal resources of the organization, thus securing internal resources. Since the DNS zone is not configured to resolve internal resources, the internal clients will not be able to access publicly available resources. You can overcome this problem by duplicating the zone you created for Internet clients and using it for internal clients. You can then configure hosts on your network to use this zone so that the internal clients can resolve external resources.

This will solve the problem of security, but it will lead to more administrative overhead because you need to manage two database files separately. So, if you want DNS to serve both the intranet and Internet resources, then it is better to use different domain names for the intranet and the Internet.

Additionally, you need to plan for the number of DNS servers that you require and their roles in order to ensure quick DNS name resolution and to make your DNS implementation reliable and fault-tolerant. It is recommended that you implement at least one primary DNS server *and* one secondary DNS server on you network, or two Active Directory-integrated servers. This will enhance reliability because if any one DNS server is not available, the other DNS server can handle the client requests. If the servers are integrated with Active Directory, all Active Directory-integrated DNS servers can make modifications to the database. However, the more DNS servers there are on the network, the more zone transfer traffic there will be. Therefore, you need to schedule zone transfers in such a way that both the primary and secondary DNS servers have the latest data, and the load on the name servers and the network is minimized.

Figure 5-13 Same internal and external DNS names

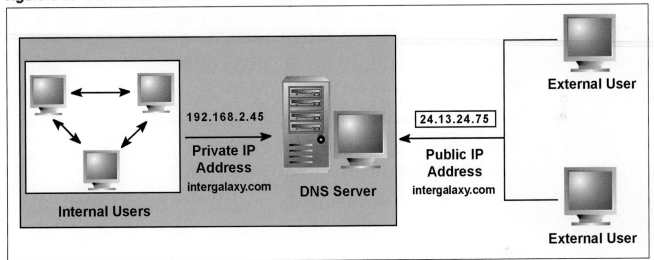

skill 7

Examining Factors Affecting DNS Infrastructure (cont'd)

exam objective   Basic knowledge

more   If you plan to have a presence on the Internet, then you need to register your domain name with an Internet naming authority such as Network Solutions. The domain name that you register is generally a second-level domain under a top-level domain (in the United States). You have the authority to maintain the domains that you register. However, various administrative bodies are assigned the task of managing the Internet root and top-level domains (visit **http://www.iana.org/gtld/gtld.htm** for details). For example, the Internet Assigned Numbers Authority (IANA) manages the root domain and a variety of organizations have been assigned the responsibility of managing the growing pool of top-level domains, such as .com, .net, .edu, .gov, and .org **(Figure 5-14)**.

If you plan to implement DNS only for your intranet, you are not required to register the domain name with any naming authority. However, you might come across a situation where the internal name you have chosen has already been registered by another organization. In this case, the internal clients will not be able to distinguish between the internal name and the publicly registered DNS name. To avoid this situation, it is preferred that you register the internal DNS name as well.

Figure 5-14 Management of the DNS infrastructure

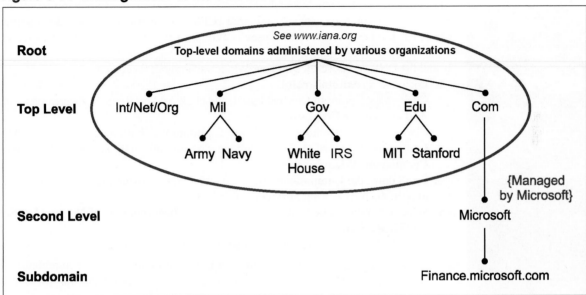

skill 8

Installing the DNS Server Service

exam objective

Install and configure the DNS Server service.

overview

You can implement a **DNS server** on a computer running Windows Server 2003 by installing the Microsoft DNS Server service. You can install the DNS Server service either by opening the **Control Panel** and running the **Window Components Wizard**, or by opening the **Manage Your Server** window and adding the **DNS Server role**. Before you install the DNS Server service, you need to have configured TCP/IP's properties on the Windows Server 2003 computer. The DNS Server service uses TCP/IP properties to configure the DNS server.

how to

Install the DNS Server service on your Windows Server 2003 computer.

1. Log on as an **Administrator**.
2. Click **Start**, point to **Control Panel**, and click **Add or Remove Programs** to open the **Add or Remove Programs** window.
3. Click the **Add/Remove Windows Components** button to open the **Windows Components Wizard**. A **Please wait** message appears on the screen while the **Windows Components Wizard** is loaded.
4. Scroll down the **Components** list and double-click **Networking Services (Figure 5-15)** to open the **Networking Services** dialog box.
5. Select **Domain Name System (DNS)** on the **Subcomponents of Networking Services** list **(Figure 5-16)**.
6. Click **OK** to close the **Networking Services** dialog box.
7. Click **Next >** to open the **Configuring Components** screen. Setup configures the components. This might take a few minutes. If you are prompted, insert the Windows Server 2003 installation CD-ROM, and click **OK**.
8. After the components are configured, the **Completing the Windows Components Wizard** screen opens. Click **Finish**.
9. Close the Add or Remove Programs window.

more

Once DNS is installed on a Windows Server 2003 computer, the command for launching the DNS management console is added to the Administrative Tools folder. To open the DNS console, click **Start**, point to **Administrative Tools**, and then click **DNS**. However, you cannot use DNS for name resolution until you have configured the DNS Server service (see Lesson 6).

Figure 5-15 The Components list

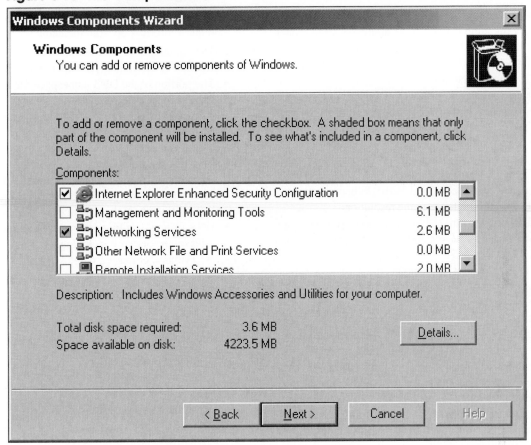

Figure 5-16 The Networking Services dialog box

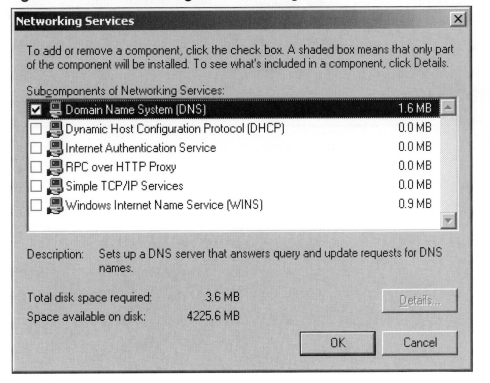

Summary

- A naming system is used to resolve the host names chosen by the administrator to IP addresses so that data packets can be transferred over a network.
- Windows Server 2003 supports both the host naming and NetBIOS naming systems.
- Host name resolution is the process of determining the IP address of a host that has been referred to by its host name. The HOSTS file and DNS are methods used for host name resolution.
- NetBIOS name resolution is the process of mapping a NetBIOS name to an IP address. Broadcast, LMHOSTS file, NetBIOS name cache, and NetBIOS name server are methods used for NetBIOS name resolution.
- Domain Name System (DNS) is a server role you can install on Windows Server 2003. The main task of DNS in a Windows Server 2003 environment is resolving host names to IP addresses, but clients on a Windows Server 2003 network can also use DNS to locate different services on the network:
  - The DNS structure is defined by the DNS namespace, which is a hierarchical grouping of names representing the arrangement of domains in the Internet.
  - The topmost domain in the DNS namespace hierarchy is called the root domain, and it is followed by the top-level domains and the second-level domains. Second-level domains can contain hosts and sub-domains.
  - A fully qualified domain name (FQDN) completely identifies a TCP/IP host using a combination of the domain name together with the host name.
  - The dynamics of DNS name resolution in Windows Server 2003 involve a resolver that makes a request and the name server that answers that request.
  - The resolver can use recursive or iterative queries to request information from the name server.
- A DNS database is divided into zones that contain information about domains and their resources.
  - The portion of the DNS namespace for which a DNS server is responsible is known as its zone of authority. A zone of authority of a DNS server represents at least one domain, which is known as the root domain of that zone.
  - The information about each zone is stored in a separate file called a zone database file. A zone database file consists of resource records that contain information about the resources in a DNS domain.
  - DNS servers can be configured to support different roles on the network including:
    - Primary, or master, name server
    - Secondary, or slave, name server
    - Caching-only name server
  - Zone transfer is the process of transferring changes to the zone database file from the primary DNS server to the secondary DNS server.
- Some of the factors that require consideration when designing the DNS infrastructure include:
  - Size of the network
  - Geography of the network
  - Security
  - Fault tolerance
  - Bandwidth
- You can implement a DNS server on a computer running Windows Server 2003 by installing the Microsoft DNS Server service either by running the Windows Components Wizard or by adding the DNS Server role in the Manage Your Server window.

Key Terms

Broadcast
Caching
Caching-only name server
DNS namespace
DNS server
Domain name
Domain Name System (DNS)
Fully qualified domain name (FQDN)
Host name
Host name resolution
HOSTS file
Iterative query

LMHOSTS file
Name server
NetBIOS
NetBIOS name
NetBIOS name cache
NetBIOS name resolution
NetBIOS Name Server (NBNS)
Primary DNS server (Primary name
   server)
Recursive query
Resolver
Resource record

Root domain
Secondary DNS server (Secondary
   name server)
Second-level domain
Sub-domain
Time-to-Live (TTL)
Top-level domain
Zone
Zone database file
Zone of authority
Zone transfer

Test Yourself

1. Applications using the Windows Sockets (WinSock) API use NetBIOS names to refer to network hosts.
   a. True
   b. False

2. Host names are:
   a. Nicknames for domain names.
   b. Unique, 16-byte names.
   c. Part of a flat naming scheme.
   d. Names given to nodes on a TCP/IP network in addition to IP addresses.

3. You can resolve NetBIOS names to IP addresses by using which of the following methods? (Choose all that apply.)
   a. HOSTS file
   b. LMHOSTS file
   c. DNS
   d. Broadcast

4. The Microsoft implementation of a NetBIOS name server is:
   a. DHCP
   b. DNS
   c. WINS
   d. NAT

5. You can configure Windows Server 2003 to use WINS to resolve host names to IP addresses.
   a. True
   b. False

6. Which of the following are the two main components of DNS?
   a. Zone database
   b. ARP cache
   c. Name server
   d. HOSTS file

7. The host name in the FQDN mailserver.newyork.cosmo.net is:
   a. newyork
   b. cosmo
   c. net
   d. mailserver

8. The resolver sends a recursive query to a name server requesting a reply with the required data or a reference to another name server.
   a. True
   b. False

9. The DNS server from which another DNS server gets its copy of the zone database is called the:
   a. Slave name server
   b. Caching-only name server
   c. Secondary name server
   d. Master name server

10. Which of the following record types is used to associate an IP address to a host name?
   a. Pointer
   b. Start of authority
   c. Name server
   d. Host

11. The Internet Assigned Numbers Authority (IANA) manages the _____ level of Internet accessible domains.
   a. Root
   b. Top
   c. Second
   d. Sub-domain

12. When configuring the DNS server, the DNS Server service uses the properties of:
   a. TCP/IP
   b. DHCP
   c. WINS
   d. ARP

13. Which of the following is an example of second-level domain?
   a. .
   b. .net
   c. cornell.edu
   d. .com

Projects: On Your Own

1. Install the DNS Server service.
   a. Open the **Control Panel**.
   b. Open the **Add or Remove Programs** window.
   c. Start the **Windows Components Wizard**.
   d. Open the **Networking Services** window.
   e. Install the **Domain Name System (DNS)**.
   f. Close the Windows Components Wizard and the Add or Remove Programs window.

Problem Solving Scenarios

1. Your LAN uses NetBIOS for name resolution and access to network shares and resources. Recently, the organization upgraded the network to Windows Server 2003. Until now, an external name server handled the organization's domain name and related details. Now, you must use that domain name on the new Windows Server 2003 network and configure DNS support to replace NetBIOS name resolution. Prepare a document explaining how you will proceed.

2. Your company's network is spread over five cities. The branches are connected via WAN links that are robust enough to handle name resolution traffic. Until now, all of the clients on the five branches have used only one DNS server, which is located at the company's main campus. Lately, however, the performance of the WAN has fallen dramatically. You must develop a plan of action that will resolve this problem. You can use, at most, one server computer at each branch office. The WAN link operates at 1 mbps (megabits per second) and may not be increased. Prepare a document describing the steps you would take with regard to DNS to bring the WAN back to an acceptable performance level.

Configuring and Managing a DNS Server

The presence of a DNS server on a Windows Server 2003 network is critical because DNS is the primary naming system of Windows Server 2003. Therefore, you need to install at least one DNS server on a Windows Server 2003 network. Before you can begin using the DNS server you have installed on your network to map host names to IP addresses, you need to configure the DNS server. The tool that Windows Server 2003 provides for managing and configuring a DNS server is the DNS console.

Configuring DNS mainly involves creating and configuring zones. After you create zones, you can configure them by setting properties in the DNS console. To ease the management of your DNS infrastructure, you can delegate the administration for parts of a zone to different authorities. You can also configure dynamic updates for zones so that you do not have to update information about resource records manually, making the administration and management of DNS much easier. In addition to configuring the DNS server, you need to configure DNS clients to refer to a specific DNS server. Otherwise, the DNS clients will not be able to use the services of DNS to resolve host names to IP addresses and vice versa.

Once you have configured the DNS server, you will be able to monitor the services that it provides for functionality and performance. You can perform tests to check the DNS server service by using options provided in the DNS console. Results from these tests will show whether your DNS server is able to handle name resolution requests successfully. After you are sure that your DNS server is functioning, you should start to monitor its performance. Various tools, such as the Performance console and the DNS console, exist for this purpose. Analysis of data provided by these tools gives you valuable information about the performance of your DNS server. You can use this information to diagnose and eliminate bottlenecks and other issues that are affecting the performance of the server.

Goals

In this lesson, you will learn about the DNS console and use its options to create zones and resource records. You will also configure DNS clients, configure zones for dynamic updates, and implement zone delegation. Finally, you will learn to manage and monitor a DNS server in a Windows Server 2003 network.

Lesson 6 Configuring and Managing a DNS Server

Skill	Exam 70-291 Objective
1. Describing the DNS Console	Manage DNS server options. Manage DNS record settings.
2. Configuring a Primary DNS Zone	Configure DNS server options. Configure DNS zone options. Manage DNS record settings.
3. Configuring Reverse Lookup Zones	Configure DNS zone options. Manage DNS zone settings.
4. Configuring a Caching-Only DNS Server	Configure DNS server options.
5. Configuring a DNS Client	Install and configure the DNS Server service.
6. Implementing Delegated DNS Zones	Configure DNS zone options.
7. Enabling Dynamic Updates for DNS Zones	Configure DNS zone options.
8. Configuring DNS Forwarding	Configure DNS forwarding.
9. Testing DNS Setup	Monitor DNS. Tools might include System Monitor, Event Viewer, Replication Monitor, and DNS debug logs.
10. Monitoring DNS Server Performance	Monitor DNS. Tools might include System Monitor, Event Viewer, Replication Monitor, and DNS debug logs.

Requirements

To complete this lesson, you will need administrative rights on a Windows Server 2003 computer with DNS installed and a client computer running an operating system such as Windows XP Professional or Windows 2000 Professional. You will also need administrative rights on a Windows Server 2003 computer that is not a root server.

Describing the DNS Console

Manage DNS server options. Manage DNS record settings.

overview

Once you install a DNS server, you need to manage and monitor it to ensure that it is able to handle client requests for name resolution efficiently. The first managing task after the installation of a DNS server involves configuration, which should be done before introducing the DNS server into the network. Methods that you can use to configure a Windows Server 2003 DNS server include:

◆ Manually editing the DNS files available in the **%systemroot%\WINDOWS\system 32\dns** folder. This folder is created on the hard disk of your server when you install DNS.

◆ Using the DNS console (which you can access from the Administrative Tools menu after installing DNS) to perform basic DNS tasks, including:

• Creation and maintenance of DNS databases
• Creation and management of DNS zones
• Creation of resource records in the DNS database
• Configuration of zone transfers
• Viewing of DNS server statistics

In addition to using the DNS console or manually editing DNS files, you can use a command-line utility, **Dnscmd**, to manage a DNS server. This utility is not available with the default installation of Windows Server 2003. In order to use Dnscmd, you must install the **Windows Support Tools** from your Windows Server 2003 installation CD-ROM. Browse to the **\support\tools** folder on the CD and double-click **suptools.msi**.

Of all the methods mentioned above, the DNS console is the preferred method of managing DNS because it provides a user-friendly interface and features. To open the DNS console window, click **Start**, point to **Administrative Tools**, and then click the **DNS** command. You can also open the DNS console by opening the **Run** dialog box from the **Start** menu, typing **dnsmgmt.msc** in the **Open** text box, and pressing **[Enter]**. The Dsnmgmt.msc file is the **Microsoft Management Console (MMC)** file for the DNS console and is available in the **%systemroot%\WINDOWS\system32** folder.

more

The DNS console contains several menu commands that can help you manage DNS configuration, including the creation of zones and resource records. You can access these commands from the Action menu in the DNS console when you have selected a DNS server. Some of the specialized commands include: **Set Aging/Scavenging for All Zones, Scavenge Stale Resource Records, Update Server Data Files**, and **Clear Cache**. The Action menu also contains general commands such as **All Tasks, Delete, Refresh, Export List**, and **Properties. Table 6-1** summarizes the commands of the Action menu. The Properties command is key because it opens the **Properties** dialog box, which you use to set the parameters for the DNS server. The DNS server Properties dialog box offers the following tabs: **Interfaces, Forwarders, Advanced, Root Hints, Debug Logging, Event Logging, Monitoring**, and **Security. Table 6-2** explains how you can use these tabs to help you manage your DNS server effectively.

Table 6-1 Action menu commands

Command	Description
Set Aging/Scavenging	Opens the Set Aging/Scavenging dialog box. You can use the options for All Zones available in this dialog box to automatically remove stale records from the selected DNS server and keep the DNS database clean of such records.
Scavenge Stale Resource Records	Removes all stale records, manually.
Update Server Data Files	Writes the in-memory changes of the DNS server to the hard disk, manually.
Clear Cache	Clears the DNS server's cache of resource record information, manually.
All Tasks	Provides commands to start, stop, pause, and restart the DNS service.
Delete	Deletes the selected DNS server.
Refresh	Refreshes the status information displayed for the DNS server in the DNS console.
Export List	Exports the DNS server information to a tab-delimited, comma-delimited, or Unicode text format.
Properties	Opens the Properties dialog box. The options in the Properties dialog box allow you to control the functionality of the selected DNS server.

Table 6-2 DNS Properties dialog box tabs

Tab	Description
Interfaces	Allows you to specify the IP addresses of the local computer that the DNS server should listen on for DNS requests. Using this tab, you can configure a multihomed server to resolve name requests that come over an internal network connection while stopping the server from resolving requests from the Internet.
Forwarders	Allows you to configure a list of IP addresses of other DNS servers to which the server you are configuring can forward name resolution requests.
Advanced	Allows you to configure various server options, such as Disable recursion, BIND secondaries, Fail on load if bad zone data, Enable round robin, Enable netmask ordering, and Secure cache against pollution. It also allows you to set the type of names that DNS can contain and to set the location from which the zone information will be initially loaded. You can use the Enable automatic scavenging of stale records option to allow automatic removal of stale records from the selected DNS server after a specified number of days.
Root Hints	Allows you to view a list of the top-level name servers from www.root-servers.org, which the DNS server uses to resolve requests for host names on the Internet. In the case of a private intranet that is isolated from the Internet, you can configure a DNS server as a root server in the local DNS namespace and the Root Hints tab will be disabled.
Debug Logging	Allows you to keep a log of the packets that a DNS server sends and receives for the purpose of troubleshooting. You can filter which packets are logged by criteria such as transport protocol and source address in order to conserve system resources.
Event Logging	Allows you to filter which events are included in the DNS Events log or disable DNS event logging.
Monitoring	Allows you to test your DNS server manually or automatically.
Security	Allows you to set permissions for the selected DNS server.

skill 2

Configuring a Primary DNS Zone

exam objective

Configure DNS server options. Configure DNS zone options. Manage DNS record settings.

overview

An important step in the configuration of a DNS server is the creation and configuration of zones. Zones are administrative units of DNS that help simplify the management of DNS. Each zone is responsible for a portion of the DNS namespace and contains information about all domains in that portion. The type of zone that you create determines the role of your DNS server (primary name server or secondary name server). Before you implement any DNS server, it is important that you know the different types of zones that you can create and which zone is required for the role that your DNS server will maintain on the network.

DNS supports the following categories of zones:
- **Forward lookup zones**: Used to resolve host names to IP addresses
- **Reverse lookup zones**: Used to resolve IP addresses to host names

The forward and reverse lookup zone categories support three zone types (**Table 6-3**):
- **Standard primary**: This zone maintains information about the part of the DNS namespace for which it is responsible in a text file and stores it locally on the hard disk of the DNS server. The DNS name server that maintains the standard primary zone is called the primary DNS server or the primary name server. All changes in information related to the part of the DNS namespace for which the primary name server is responsible should be made in its standard primary zone; the standard primary zone maintains the original copy of all information related to that part of the DNS namespace, which is then replicated to other dependent, or secondary, DNS servers during the process of zone transfer.
- **Standard secondary**: A primary name server needs to have one or more redundant backup servers. These backup servers are called secondary DNS servers or secondary name servers. Secondary name servers check the primary name server regularly for updates to the zone files. The secondary name servers then download these updates from the primary server as required so that they can answer client requests in the event that the primary server is not available on the network. When configuring a standard secondary zone, you need to specify the IP address of the primary name server for the secondary server.
- **Stub**: This zone is an abridged copy of a zone, in that its purpose is simply to maintain name server (NS) records for the name servers that do resolve requests that are made in the master zone. A stub zone is used on a server that will not respond to DNS requests itself, but instead will pass them to one of the name servers in the master zone for which the stub zone has an NS record. The server on which a stub zone resides is not authoritative in that zone.

The zone information for a standard primary and standard secondary zone is stored in a text file. When you create an Active Directory-integrated zone, information about the zone is stored in Active Directory. Since an **Active Directory-integrated zone** is a part of Active Directory, the zone inherits all of the security features of Active Directory; this allows for secure storage and transfer of zone information. One of the advantages of creating and maintaining an Active Directory-integrated zone, as opposed to a standard DNS zone, is the management of zone transfers. With a standard DNS zone, zone transfers result in all or part of the zone file being transferred between DNS servers. In the case of an Active Directory-integrated zone, the information is updated and replicated automatically across domains as part of the Active Directory replication cycle. An Active Directory-integrated zone appears as an object in Active Directory. You can create an Active Directory-integrated zone only if the DNS server holds the role of domain controller.

tip

The primary name server from which a secondary server downloads updates is also known as the master name server.

Table 6-3   Configuring a DNS server

Zone types	Server name	Function
Standard primary	Primary DNS server	Maintains the original copy of all information related to this part of the DNS namespace.
Standard secondary	Secondary DNS server	Provides redundancy when the primary DNS server is not available, and proximity options so that clients can order their list of name servers and increase response time to name requests.
Active Directory-integrated	Active Directory-integrated	Stores all of the information about zones and inherits all of the features of Active Directory.

Figure 6-1   The Select Configuration Action screen

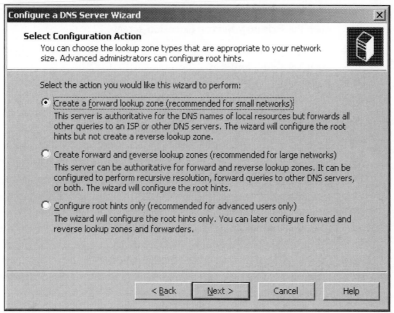

Figure 6-2   The Zone Name screen

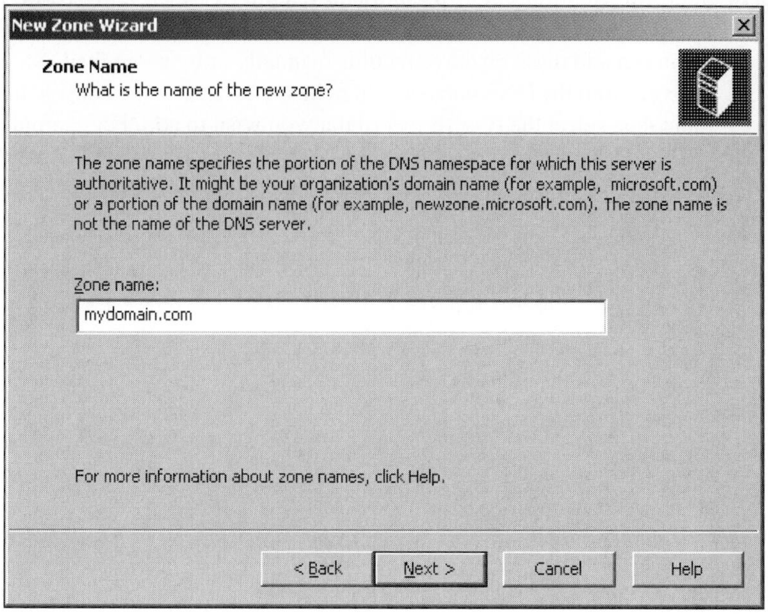

skill 2

Configuring a Primary DNS Zone
(cont'd)

Configure DNS server options. Configure DNS zone options. Manage DNS record settings.

how to

Configure a DNS server as a primary name server and configure a forward lookup zone as a standard primary DNS zone.

1. Click **Start**, point to **Administrative Tools**, and click **DNS** to open the **DNS console**.
2. Click the name of the DNS server in the console tree to select the server.
3. Click **Action** on the Menu bar, and then click the **Configure a DNS Server** command. The **Welcome** screen of the **Configure a DNS Server Wizard** opens.
4. Click [Next >] to open the **Select Configuration Action** screen (**Figure 6-1**).
5. Leave the **Create a forward lookup zone** option button selected and click [Next >] to open the **Primary Server Location** screen.
6. Leave the **This server maintains the zone** option button selected and click [Next >] to open the **Zone Name** screen.
7. In the **Zone name** text box, type **mydomain.com** as the name of the zone (**Figure 6-2**).
8. Click [Next >] to open the **Dynamic Update** screen.
9. Leave the **Allow only secure dynamic updates** option button selected and click [Next >] to open the **Forwarders** screen.
10. Select the **No, it should not forward queries** option button (**Figure 6-3**) and click [Next >] to open the **Completing the Configure a DNS Server Wizard** screen.
11. Click [Finish] to close the Wizard. The contents of the newly configured DNS server now appear in the details pane of the DNS console (**Figure 6-4**).
12. If necessary, click the plus symbol next to the name of the DNS server in the console tree to expand the server name. Then, click the **Forward Lookup Zones** folder in the console tree to display its contents in the details pane. The zone that you created appears.
13. Double-click the zone in the details pane to display its contents. The zone contains the resource records that were added by default during zone creation (**Figure 6-5**).
14. Click **File**, and then click Exit to close the DNS console.

more

If you need to add zones to your DNS server after configuring it, you use the **New Zone** command, which starts the **New Zone Wizard**. After you create and configure zones, you can add information about the domain resources by creating resource records. A zone must contain the resource records for all resources in a domain for which the zone is responsible. You can add these resource records manually or by using the DNS console. To add a resource record from the DNS console, click the zone name in the console tree, open the **Action** menu, and then select the type of record that you wish to add. For example, to add a resource record of the **Host** type, you would select **New Host (A)**. The **New Host** dialog box would open, in which you would enter the name of the host and its IP address in the fields provided.

Figure 6-3 The Forwarders screen

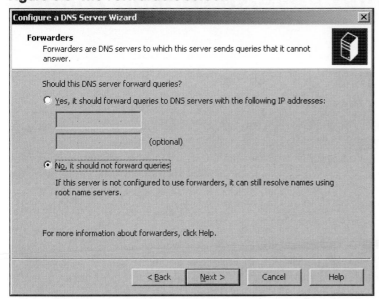

Figure 6-4 Configured DNS server

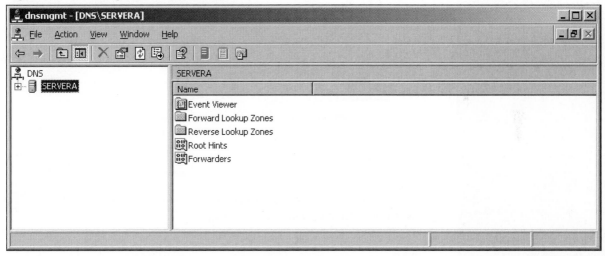

Figure 6-5 Resource records in the root zone

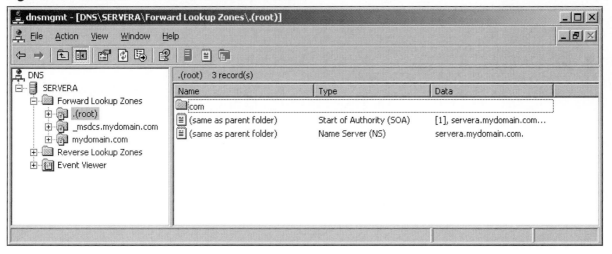

skill 3

Configuring Reverse Lookup Zones

exam objective

Configure DNS zone options. Manage DNS zone settings.

overview

In DNS, you use forward lookup zones to resolve host names to IP addresses and reverse lookup zones to resolve IP addresses to host names. A reverse lookup zone, also known as an **in-addr.arpa zone**, is the zone that is authoritative for the in-addr.arpa domain. The **in-addr.arpa domain** is a special domain that supports reverse lookups. In the in-addr.arpa domain, hosts are named with their IP addresses in the reverse sequence. For example, information about a host with an IP address of **123.78.100.10** is stored as **10.100.78.123.in-addr.arpa** in the in-addr.arpa domain.

The information about these in-addr.arpa hosts is added to the zone database file of the reverse lookup zone, called the **reverse lookup file**, by creating a Pointer (PTR) resource record. A PTR record is a resource record that associates an IP address with a host name in the in-addr.arpa domain. When resolving an IP address to the corresponding host name, the client queries the DNS server for a PTR record for that IP address. When this record is found, the IP address of a host is resolved to its host name.

how to

Configure a reverse lookup zone on a DNS server.
1. Open the DNS console.
2. Click the name of the DNS server in the console tree to select the server.
3. Click **Action** on the Menu bar, and then click the **New Zone** command. The Welcome screen of the **New Zone Wizard** opens.
4. Click ▮ Next > ▮ to open the **Zone Type** screen.
5. Select the **Primary zone** option button, if necessary, and click ▮ Next > ▮ to open the **Active Directory Zone Replication Scope** screen (**Figure 6-6**).
6. Select the **To all the domain controllers in the Active Directory domain <domain name>** option button, if necessary, and click ▮ Next > ▮ to open the **Forward or Reverse Lookup Zone** screen.
7. Select the **Reverse lookup zone** option button (**Figure 6-7**), and click ▮ Next > ▮ to open the **Reverse Lookup Zone** Name screen.
8. The **Network ID** option button is selected by default. Click in the Network ID field and type the network ID pertaining to the DNS clients whose IP addresses you need to resolve to host names (**Figure 6-8**). As you type, the name of the zone is entered automatically in the **Reverse lookup zone name** text box.
9. Click ▮ Next > ▮ to open the **Dynamic Update** screen.
10. Click the **Allow only secure dynamic updates** option button, if necessary, and then click to open the **Completing the New Zone Wizard** screen.
11. Click ▮ Finish ▮ to close the Wizard.
12. Double-click the **Reverse Lookup Zones** folder in the details pane of the DNS console to view the reverse lookup zone that you created.
13. Double-click the reverse lookup zone to view the resource records that it contains.
14. Click **File**, and then click **Exit** to close the DNS console.

Figure 6-6 The Active Directory Zone Replication Scope screen

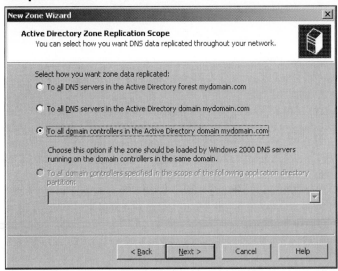

Figure 6-7 The Forward or Reverse Lookup Zone screen

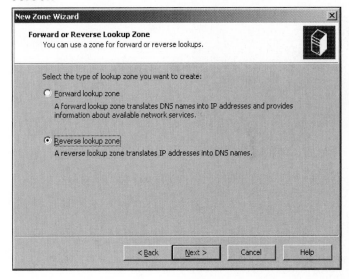

Figure 6-8 The Reverse Lookup Zone Name screen

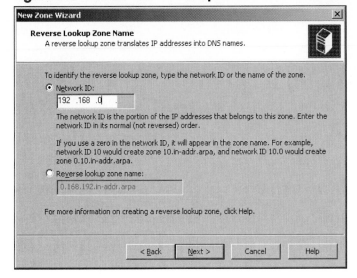

skill 3

Configuring Reverse Lookup Zones
(cont'd)

exam objective

Configure DNS zone options. Manage DNS zone settings.

more

Once you have created a reverse lookup zone, you can add pointer records for all of the required resources. To add a pointer record, right-click the reverse lookup zone name in the DNS console, and then click the **New Pointer (PTR)** command on the shortcut menu. The **New Resource Record** dialog box opens. In the **Host IP** number field, type the host ID of the network host for whom you are creating the record. In the **Host name** text box, type the name of the host (**Figure 6-9**). The host name and IP address should already exist in one of the forward lookup zones of your DNS structure. You can select the desired host from a list of existing hosts by clicking the **Browse** button in the New Resource Record dialog box, which opens the **Browse** dialog box (**Figure 6-10**).

Figure 6-9 The New Resource Record dialog box

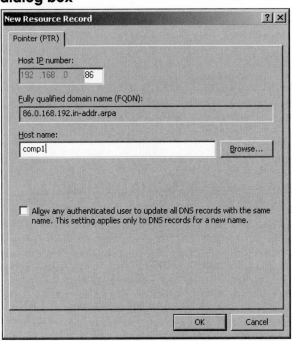

Figure 6-10 The Browse dialog box

skill 4

Configuring a Caching-Only DNS Server

exam objective

Configure DNS server options.

overview

Besides implementing a DNS server as a primary or secondary server, you can implement a DNS server as a caching-only name server. You generally install a **caching-only name server** in a location where you need to provide DNS services locally, but do not want to create separate zones. Such a scenario may arise when the number of hosts that require DNS services at a location is small, or when you do not want to increase the administrative overhead by maintaining another zone.

Another reason for considering the implementation of caching-only name servers, as opposed to primary or secondary, is zone transfer traffic. Caching-only name servers do not participate in zone transfers, unlike primary and secondary name servers. This could be a critical design consideration when deciding to implement DNS at remote locations connected to a central location by slow WAN links. In this situation, if you plan to implement a primary DNS server at the central location and a secondary DNS server at the remote location, the design could result in the generation of high zone transfer traffic. However, if you implement caching-only name servers at remote locations, you will be able to provide DNS services without generating zone transfer traffic.

Caching-only name servers store information collected during the process of resolving client queries. **Caching** is a method of storing frequently-requested information in memory so that clients can access it quickly, when required. If the caching-only server is unable to answer client requests, it forwards the request to a designated DNS server for name resolution and caches the resolved result. Cached records are still subject to Time-to-Live (TTL) values. Once the TTL of a record expires, the record must be resolved and cached again

how to

Implement a DNS server as a caching-only DNS server.
1. Open the DNS console.
2. Right-click the server name in the console tree, and then click **Properties** on the shortcut menu to open the **Properties** dialog box for the server.
3. Click the **Root Hints** tab (**Figure 6-11**). This tab contains entries for the root DNS servers. If the selected DNS server is a root DNS server on the network, then the options on this tab are disabled. The DNS server needs these root hints, which are stored in the root hints file (Cache.dns) to help locate root DNS servers. In order to allow a DNS server to act as a caching-only DNS server, you need to remove the default entries on the Root Hints tab and add the names and IP addresses of the name servers or hosts that the caching-only name server will use to resolve names.
4. Click [Remove] to remove the selected entry from the list on the Root Hints tab. Repeat this step for all other entries on the tab. The caching-only name server replaces the servers that you have deleted in the Root.hints file with the servers in the domain that it will call for name resolution. The primary and secondary name servers for the domain will continue to use, and occasionally update, the Root.hints file.
5. Click [Add...] to open the **New Resource Record** dialog box (**Figure 6-12**). This dialog box provides a space for you to type the fully qualified domain name (FQDN) of a host computer to be designated as an authoritative name server for this zone. In the **Server name** text box, type the name of the resource from which name server information will be cached. The name that you enter must match a valid Host (A) resource record in the DNS domain namespace. You can also click the **Browse** button to open the **Browse** dialog box and browse the hierarchy of your DNS to select the desired resource.
6. In the IP address box, type the IP address of the resource whose name you entered in the Server name text box. If you do not know the IP address of the desired resource, you can click [Resolve] to resolve the server name to its IP address.

caution

This exercise requires the use of a Windows Server 2003 computer with DNS installed that has not been configured as a root server.

tip

Clicking the Resolve button is a good idea because it enables you to test the DNS mechanism to ensure it can resolve the IP address of the host name of the server you've selected.

Figure 6-11 The Root Hints tab

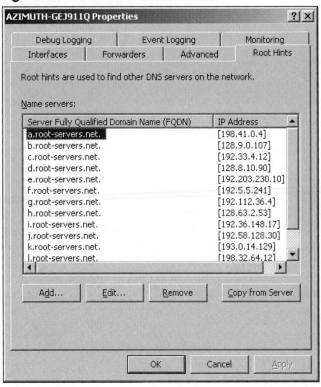

Figure 6-12 The New Resource Record dialog box

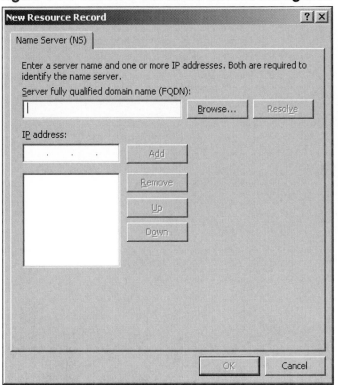

skill 4

Configuring a Caching-Only DNS Server *(cont'd)*

exam objective

Configure DNS server options.

how to

7. Click [Add...] to add the IP address of the selected resource to the IP address list (**Figure 6-13**). You have now designated the information that you wish to add to the Root Hints tab.
8. Click [OK] to create the new resource record and close the New Resource Record dialog box. You can now view the newly created resource record on the Root Hints tab of the Properties dialog box (**Figure 6-14**).
9. Click [OK] to close the Properties dialog box for the caching-only name server.
10. Close the DNS console.

more

When you implement the caching-only DNS server on your network for the first time, the cache is empty. As the server starts to service client requests, the information is cached and builds with time. Therefore, during the initial phase of service, the caching-only server must forward more requests to other DNS servers. As more requests are cached, the caching-only server can resolve the more frequently requested resources from its cache rather than forwarding the requests to other DNS servers for resolution.

Figure 6-13 Designating a name server for name resolution

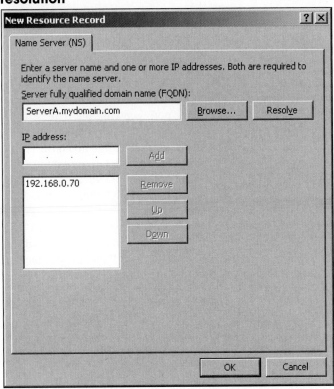

Figure 6-14 New resource record added for the caching-only name server

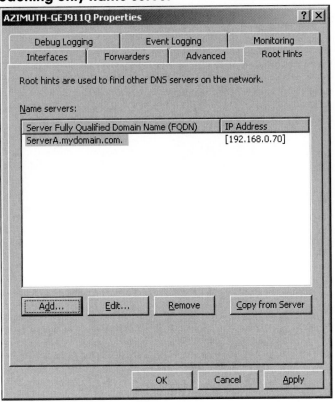

skill 5

Configuring a DNS Client

exam objective

Install and configure the DNS Server service.

overview

In a DNS environment, the client sends a request to a DNS name server to resolve a host name to its associated IP address. Upon receiving the request from the client, the DNS server resolves the destination host name to its corresponding IP address and responds back to the DNS client with the IP address of the IP destination host. Therefore, to complete the setup of DNS on your Windows Server 2003 network (once you have completed the configuration of the DNS server), you need to configure DNS clients running operating systems such as Window 2000 Professional and Windows XP Professional.

how to

Configure a Windows XP Professional client computer as a DNS client.
1. Log on to the Windows XP Professional client as an **Administrator**.
2. Click ![Start], and then click **Control Panel** to open the **Control Panel** window.
3. Double-click the **Network Connections** icon to open the **Network Connections** window.
4. Right-click the **Local Area Connection** icon and then click **Properties** on the shortcut menu to open the **Local Area Connection Properties** dialog box.
5. On the General tab, select **Internet Protocol (TCP/IP)** in the **This connection uses the following items** list box (**Figure 6-15**). Then, click ![Properties] to open the **Internet Protocol (TCP/IP) Properties** dialog box.
6. Click the **Use the following DNS server addresses** option button. In this section of the dialog box, you enter information about the preferred (primary) and alternate (secondary) DNS servers. Note that you must provide information for at least the preferred DNS server. In the Preferred DNS server box, type the IP address of the primary DNS server for this client (**Figure 6-16**).
7. Click ![OK] to close the Internet Protocol (TCP/IP) Properties dialog box.
8. Click ![OK] to close the Local Area Connection dialog box.
9. Click **File**, and then click **Close** to close the Network Connections window.

tip

A Windows Server 2003 computer without the DNS service installed can still act as a DNS client.

more

If you click the **Advanced** button in the Internet Protocol (TCP/IP) Properties dialog box to open the **Advanced TCP/IP Settings** dialog box, you can access additional options for configuring a DNS client. On the **DNS** tab (**Figure 6-17**), you can alter the order in which designated DNS servers are queried, configure settings for resolving unqualified domains, and set options for dynamic updates.

Figure 6-15 The Local Area Connection dialog box

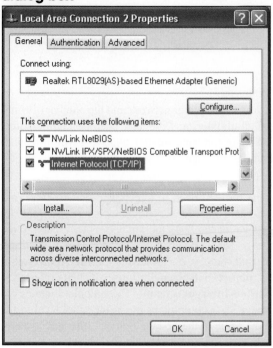

Figure 6-16 Designating a primary DNS server

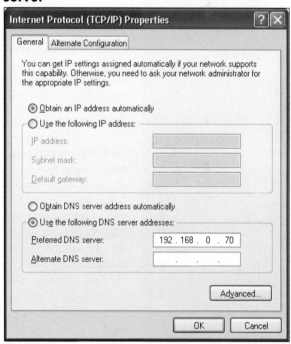

Figure 6-17 The DNS tab of the Advanced TCP/IP Settings dialog box

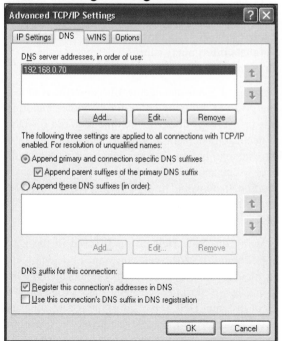

skill 6 | *Implementing Delegated DNS Zones*

Configure DNS zone options.

overview

Depending on the number of DNS servers you have on your network and the number of zones that each DNS server hosts, the task of administering DNS can become cumbersome. One way to avoid this problem is to divide a large zone into smaller zones that will be responsible for a portion of the domain for which the original zone was responsible. This is also known as **zone delegation**.

Before choosing to implement zone delegation, you need to understand the structure of a zone. A zone contains information about domains that have contiguous names. The domain represents a hierarchical design with each level of the DNS hierarchy directly related to the level above it and to the level below it; therefore, all sub-domains of a domain also use contiguous names. For example, assume that there is one zone for the **intergalaxy.com** domain. This domain has two sub-domains, **planets** and **constellations**, which are referred to as **planets.intergalaxy.com** and **constellations.intergalaxy.com**. These domain names are contiguous and use contiguous names because the sub-domains are at the same level in the domain hierarchy. These sub-domains use the name of their parent domain, **intergalaxy.com**, along with their names to form complete names. The same is true for the sub-domains of planets and constellations. For example, if **planets.intergalaxy.com** has a sub-domain named **inner**, then the full name of this sub-domain will be **inner.planets.intergalaxy.com**.

Taking the above example of **intergalaxy.com** to explain zone delegation, a single zone is responsible for all domains using the contiguous name **intergalaxy.com**, such as **planets.intergalaxy.com**, **constellations.intergalaxy.com**, and **inner.planets.intergalaxy.com**. However, for better management of such a zone, you can divide the chain of domains using contiguous names into parts and create separate zones for each part. For example, instead of having a single zone take care of all domains using the contiguous name **intergalaxy.com**, you can create separate zones for the sub-domains, **planets.intergalaxy.com** and **constellations.intergalaxy.com**. In doing so, the zone responsible for **intergalaxy.com** would be responsible for all sub-domains except for **planets.intergalaxy.com** and **constellations.intergalaxy.com**. The zone responsible for **inner.planets.intergalaxy.com** would be responsible only for this domain and its sub-domains. These separate zones, created for managing parts of the chain of domains using contiguous names, are called **delegated zones (Table 6-4)**. In the above example, the separate zone that you create for the sub-domain **planets.intergalaxy.com** is a delegated zone of the parent zone, which manages the **intergalaxy.com** domain **(Figure 6-18)**.

Implementing zone delegation helps in distributed zones management because the responsibility for managing different zones can be given to different authorities. Another important benefit of implementing zone delegation is that it helps decrease the time required for DNS servers to resolve DNS queries. You will need to implement a primary and secondary DNS server in each delegated sub-domain. For example, before creating delegated zones for the **intergalaxy.com** domain, there would be only one zone handling DNS queries for the entire **intergalaxy.com** domain. After zone delegation, there would be separate zones handling DNS queries for their respective portions of the **intergalaxy.com** domain, which, in many cases, results in client requests being resolved in less time.

You can implement zone delegation by using the **New Delegation Wizard** in the DNS console. You can run this wizard by right-clicking the zone that you want to delegate and clicking **New Delegation** on the shortcut menu. When implementing zone delegation, you need to provide the name of the DNS server that will host the delegated zones. You can have the same DNS server host all of the zones or different DNS servers host the parent zone and delegated zones. When an external DNS query is received for a delegated zone, it is first sent to the DNS server hosting the parent zone. This zone contains a **name service record** for the

Table 6-4   Delegated DNS zones

Zone types	Server name	Function
intergalaxy.com	planets.intergalaxy.com	Divides the work of administering between separate authorities
	constellations.intergalaxy.com	Decreases the time required to resolve names by the DNS server
Sub-domain: sun.intergalaxy.com (not delegated)		Remains under direct administration of intergalaxy.com

Figure 6-18

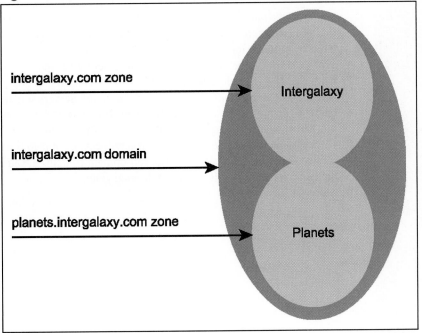

skill 6

Implementing Delegated DNS Zones (cont'd)

exam objective

Configure DNS zone options.

overview

name server of the delegated zone. This name service record acts as a pointer to the name server of the delegated zone and directs the query to the correct name server for resolution. For example, an external DNS query for the **planets.intergalaxy.com** sub-domain is first sent to the DNS server hosting the parent zone, the zone for the **intergalaxy.com** domain. This zone contains a name service record that points to the zone for the **planets.intergalaxy.com** domain, and the query is directed to this zone for resolution. In the case of a DNS query that originates within a zone, and the local DNS server is able to resolve the name to an IP address, then the server has no need to forward the query to a server in another zone.

how to

Create a DNS zone delegation on a DNS server for the sub-domain sales.mydomain.com.

1. Open the **DNS** console.
2. Right-click the zone you want to delegate (in this example it is called **mydomain.com**), and then click **New Delegation** on the shortcut menu (**Figure 6-19**). The first screen of the **New Delegation Wizard** opens. You will use this Wizard to delegate the selected zone to a DNS name server.
3. Click [Next >] to open the **Delegated Domain Name** screen (**Figure 6-20**). You use this screen to create a sub-domain, the authority for which will be delegated to a different zone.
4. In the **Delegated domain** text box, type the name of the sub-domain, for example, **sales.mydomain.com**, which will be created under mydomain.com and will delegate its authority to an existing resource in mydomain.com.
5. Click [Next >] to open the **Name Servers** screen. This screen enables you to specify the DNS name server that will host the delegated zone.
6. Click [Add...] to open the **New Resource Record** dialog box. In the **Server name** text box, type the name of the DNS server that will host the delegated zone. The server name that you enter here must already exist in the hierarchy of your DNS. You may also use the **Browse** button to locate the desired DNS server from the list of DNS servers available on your network. In the **IP address** text box, enter the IP address of the DNS server.
7. Click [OK] to close the New Resource Record dialog box and add the chosen DNS name server to the Name servers list on the Name Servers screen (**Figure 6-21**).
8. Click [Next >] to open the **Completing the New Delegation Wizard** screen, where you can view a summary of the settings you have selected.
9. Click [Finish] to close the Wizard. You will now be able to see the sub-domain that you created under the selected zone. The sub-domain contains a Name Server (NS) record for the name server that will host the delegated zone.
10. Close the DNS console.

Figure 6-19 Opening the New Delegation Wizard

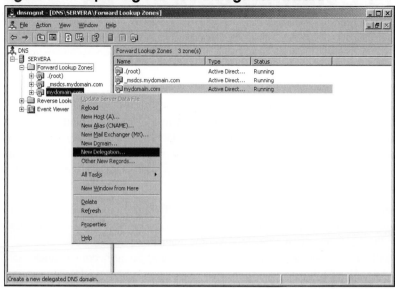

Figure 6-20 The Delegated Domain Name screen

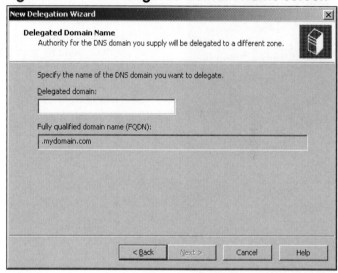

Figure 6-21 Name server selected for the delegated zone

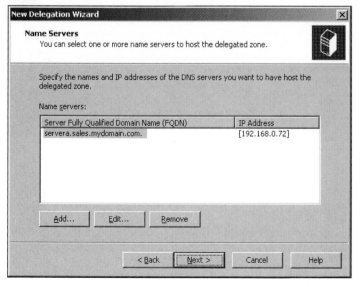

skill 7 | *Enabling Dynamic Updates for DNS Zones*

Configure DNS zone options.

DNS implementation in Windows Server 2003 supports dynamic updates of host name-to-IP address mappings in a DNS zone. Therefore, DNS in Windows Server 2003 is also an implementation of **Dynamic Domain Name System (DDNS)**. Enabling **dynamic updates** for zones allows resources on a network to register with the zone and update any future changes in their configuration dynamically.

Support for dynamic updates for zones in Windows Server 2003 helps make management of DNS easier compared to static implementations of DNS, which require you to perform activities such as adding, modifying, and removing resource records manually. Managing zones manually is feasible on a small network, but as the network grows, management becomes much more difficult. For large networks where you need to regularly update information related to network resources in the zone, implementing DDNS is highly beneficial.

Enable dynamic updates for a zone on a DNS server.

1. Open the **DNS** console.
2. Right-click the name of the zone that you want to configure, and then click **Properties** on the shortcut menu to open the **Properties** dialog box for the zone (**Figure 6-22**).
3. Click the **General** tab, if it is not already in view.
4. Click the **Dynamic updates** drop-down list box, and then click the **Secure only** option to select it (**Figure 6-23**). This setting ensures that the zone will not permit dynamic updates from untrusted sources.
5. Click OK to close the Properties dialog box.
6. Close the DNS console.

Figure 6-22 The Properties dialog box

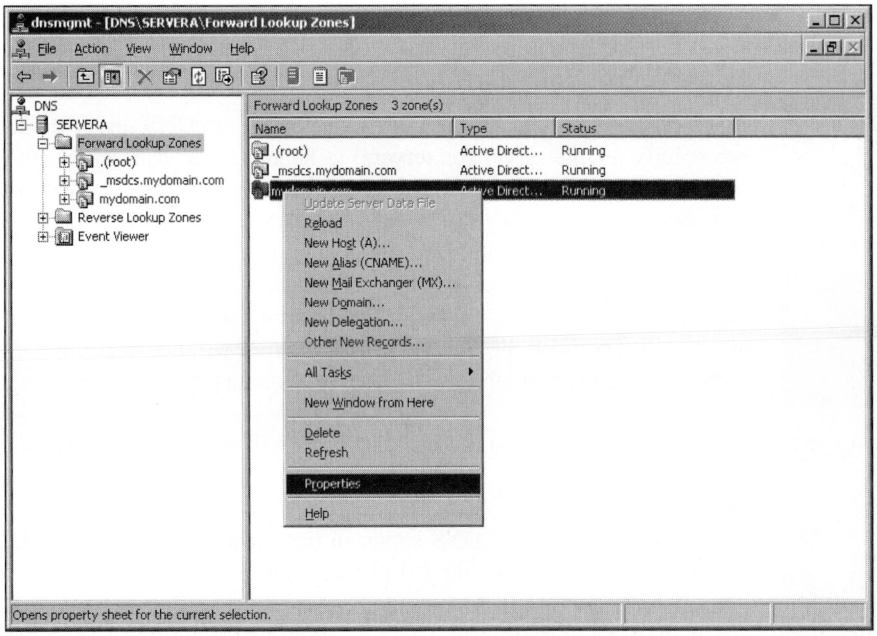

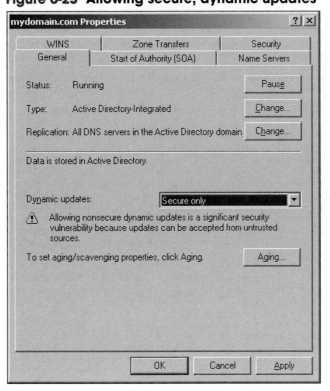

Figure 6-23 Allowing secure, dynamic updates

skill 8
Configuring DNS Forwarding

exam objective

Configure DNS forwarding.

overview

By configuring settings on the Forwarders tab of the DNS server Properties dialog box, you can specify a DNS server (or servers) to handle DNS requests that the local DNS server is either unable to resolve, or that you do not want the local DNS server to resolve. For example, you may not want to expose the internal DNS servers on your network to the dangers that exist on the Internet, such as hackers. Therefore, you can keep your internal DNS servers behind a firewall, inaccessible to the Internet, and have them forward all external DNS requests to a DNS server, a **forwarder**, that is outside the firewall and can communicate with other DNS servers on the Internet. The forwarder will not store any DNS information that is relevant to the internal DNS, so the Active Directory domain is protected from harm.

how to

Configure a forwarder on a DNS server that will service all requests made for hosts in other DNS domains.

1. Open the **DNS** console.
2. Right-click the local DNS server in the console tree, and then click **Properties** on the shortcut menu to open the **Properties** dialog box for the server.
3. Click the **Forwarders** tab in the Properties dialog box.
4. In the **DNS domain** list box, click **All other DNS domains (Figure 6-24)**.
5. Click in the **Selected domain's forwarder IP address** list box, and then type the IP address of the forwarder DNS server.
6. Click [Add...] to add the IP address of the forwarder to the address list.
7. Click [OK] to close the Properties dialog box.
8. Close the DNS console.

more

You can also use forwarders to forward DNS queries for a particular domain to another DNS server. To add a domain to the DNS domain list, click the **New** button on the Forwarders tab. The **New Forwarder** dialog box will open **(Figure 6-25)**. Type the domain for which you want DNS queries to be forwarded in the DNS domain text box, and then click OK. The domain you selected will now appear in the DNS domain list box on the Forwarders tab **(Figure 6-26)**, where you can select the domain and assign a forwarder to it.

By default, recursion on a Windows Server 2003 DNS server is enabled, which means that if the designated forwarder fails to resolve a DNS query, the local DNS server will then contact other name servers repeatedly until it finds one that can resolve the request for the original client. Recursion, therefore, can serve as a measure of fault tolerance. However, if the forwarder failed to resolve the query through no fault of its own, the local server will likely be unable to resolve the requested host name on its own. In this case, recursion merely delays the arrival of an additional error message. To eliminate this redundancy of failures, you can disable recursion by selecting the **Do not use recursion for this domain** check box near the bottom of the Forwarders tab. A DNS server that has forwarders configured and recursion disabled is sometimes known as a slave server because it is totally reliant on the forwarders to resolve DNS queries that are outside of its local zone.

Figure 6-24 The Forwarders tab

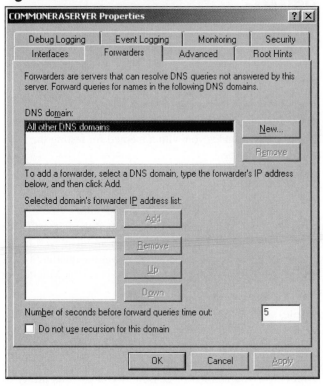

Figure 6-25 The New Forwarder dialog box

Figure 6-26 Adding a new forwarder domain

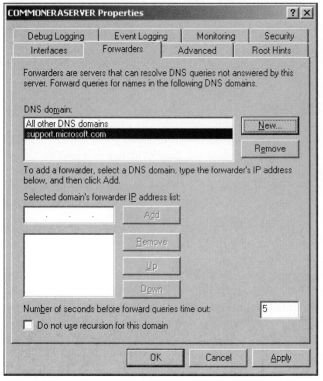

skill 9

Testing DNS Setup

Monitor DNS. Tools might include System Monitor, Event Viewer, Replication Monitor, and DNS debug logs.

overview

After you install and configure DNS, you need to test whether you have implemented DNS correctly on the network. The DNS console provides you with a method for testing the DNS setup, by allowing you to send two types of queries:

◆ Simple query: To test the active DNS server

◆ Recursive query: To test other DNS servers on the network from the active DNS server.

You can access the options to run these queries from the **Monitoring** tab of the Properties for your DNS server (**Figure 6-27**). The results of the query that you run are displayed in the dialog box. If the DNS server is implemented correctly and able to answer the queries, a **Pass** status property is listed in the appropriate column of the **Test results** box on the Monitoring tab. Otherwise, **a Failed** status appears.

In addition to using the DNS console, you can use certain diagnostic utilities to check the connectivity between two IP hosts on a TCP/IP network, or to check your DNS server for communication problems with other name servers. Two of these diagnostic utilities are Ping and Nslookup, both of which you can run from the command prompt:

◆ **PING (Packet Internet Groper)**: As you learned in Lesson 2, you use this utility to check the connectivity between two IP hosts on a TCP/IP network. You can use the IP address or the host name of the destination host to check for connectivity between the source host and the destination host. If you have implemented DNS, you can also use the FQDN of the destination host. The syntax for the PING command is: **ping <destination IP address> or <destination host>**

Using the Ping command sends an **Internet Control Message Protocol (ICMP) ECHO request** to the destination host. ICMP is used to check and report the status of the information that is transmitted over a TCP/IP network. If routing from the source to the destination is configured correctly and available, the destination host receives the ICMP packets sent by the source host. The destination host then returns the ICMP ECHO reply message to the original source host, if the routing back to the original host is configured correctly and available. If the number of ICMP packets returned is the same as the number of packets sent, then the network is properly routed from source to destination and back again. In addition, you can conclude that the network is up and running between the source and the destination, the destination is up and running in the eyes of the ICMP protocol, and the destination host has not filtered or blocked inbound Ping packets. The time values generated by Ping indicate degrees of network congestion. A mixed result of successful and dropped packets can also indicate congestion. If all packets are dropped, then you have evidence of a malfunction in the network, such as the destination host or a router being down, or a firewall blocking Ping packets. Using the Tracert utility will help you pinpoint the location of the problem.

To test your DNS setup using the Ping utility, ping the destination host using its IP address. Next, ping the destination host by using its FQDN. If the FQDN is resolved successfully to its associated IP address, then you know that your name resolution mechanism, DNS, is working correctly. However, a Ping request can still fail even when DNS is working, for various reasons (see above). For example, if the Ping command returns the message **Request timed out** and the number of packets received is 0, the source host has not been able to connect with the destination host (**Figure 6-28**). Note that this failure would not necessarily be due to a DNS problem. You can validate the server's name resolution mechanism by using Nslookup.

Figure 6-27 The Monitoring tab

COMMONERASERVER Properties
Interfaces
Forwarders
Advanced
Root Hints
Debug Logging
Event Logging
Monitoring
Security
To verify the configuration of the server, you can perform manual or automatic testing.
Select a test type:
A simple query against this DNS server
A recursive query to other DNS servers
To perform the test immediately, click Test Now.
Test Now
Perform automatic testing at the following interval:
Test interval:
1
minutes
Test results:
Date
Time
Simple Query
Recursive Q...
OK
Cancel
Apply

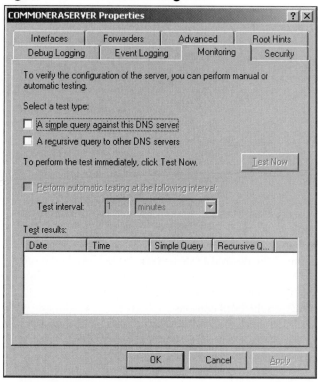

Figure 6-28 Using Ping

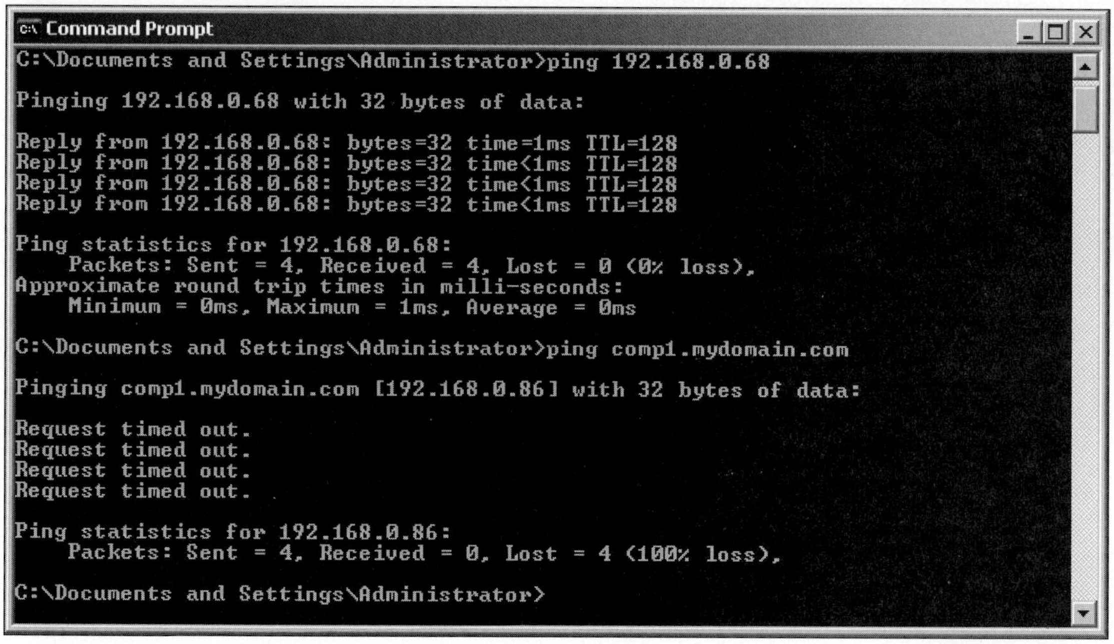

Command Prompt
C:\Documents and Settings\Administrator>ping 192.168.0.68
Pinging 192.168.0.68 with 32 bytes of data:
Reply from 192.168.0.68: bytes=32 time=1ms TTL=128
Reply from 192.168.0.68: bytes=32 time<1ms TTL=128
Reply from 192.168.0.68: bytes=32 time<1ms TTL=128
Reply from 192.168.0.68: bytes=32 time<1ms TTL=128
Ping statistics for 192.168.0.68:
Packets: Sent = 4, Received = 4, Lost = 0 (0% loss),
Approximate round trip times in milli-seconds:
Minimum = 0ms, Maximum = 1ms, Average = 0ms
C:\Documents and Settings\Administrator>ping comp1.mydomain.com
Pinging comp1.mydomain.com [192.168.0.86] with 32 bytes of data:
Request timed out.
Request timed out.
Request timed out.
Request timed out.
Ping statistics for 192.168.0.86:
Packets: Sent = 4, Received = 0, Lost = 4 (100% loss),
C:\Documents and Settings\Administrator>

skill 9

Testing DNS Setup *(cont'd)*

exam objective

Monitor DNS. Tools might include System Monitor, Event Viewer, Replication Monitor, and DNS debug logs.

overview

◆ **Nslookup**: This utility can be used to diagnose problems with DNS name servers on your network by making DNS queries to these DNS servers. The Nslookup utility has a simple (non-interactive) mode and an interactive mode. In the simple mode, you enter nslookup at the command prompt followed by the FQDN whose IP address you wish to find (**Figure 6-29**). To use the interactive Nslookup mode, which enables you to use a number of troubleshooting and look-up functions, type **nslookup** at the command prompt and press **[Enter]**. This will return the Nslookup command prompt, from which you can run various functions (enter ? to view the available functions).

You can verify a DNS server's ability to resolve host names by typing the host name of any network host at the Nslookup command prompt. If the IP address of the desired host is returned, DNS is working properly. By default Nslookup uses the DNS server of the local computer, but you can use Nslookup to check other DNS servers by typing **server <host name of the desired DNS server>** at the Nslookup prompt.

how to

Test the setup of a DNS server.
1. Open the DNS console.
2. Right-click the name of the DNS server in the console tree, and then click **Properties** to open the **Properties** dialog box for the DNS server.
3. Click the **Monitoring** tab.
4. Select the **A simple query against this DNS server** check box (**Figure 6-30**). In this test, the resolver on the DNS server computer will send a simple query, also known as an iterative query, to the name server on the same computer.
5. Click [Test Now] to send the simple query to the DNS server. The result of the query appears in the **Test results** box (**Figure 6-31**). If **Pass** appears in the **Simple Query** column of the Test results box, DNS is working properly; if **Failed** appears, DNS is not working properly.
6. Click [OK] to close the Properties dialog box of the DNS server and return to the DNS console.
7. Close the DNS console.

Figure 6-29 Using Nslookup

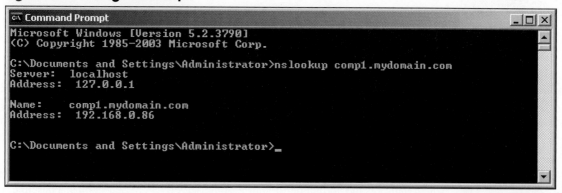

Figure 6-30 Testing DNS with a simple query

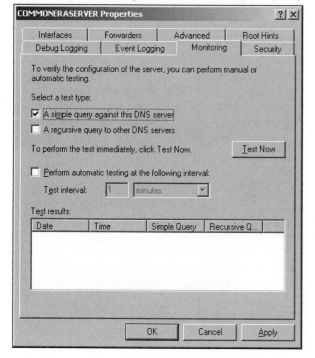

Figure 6-31 Test results

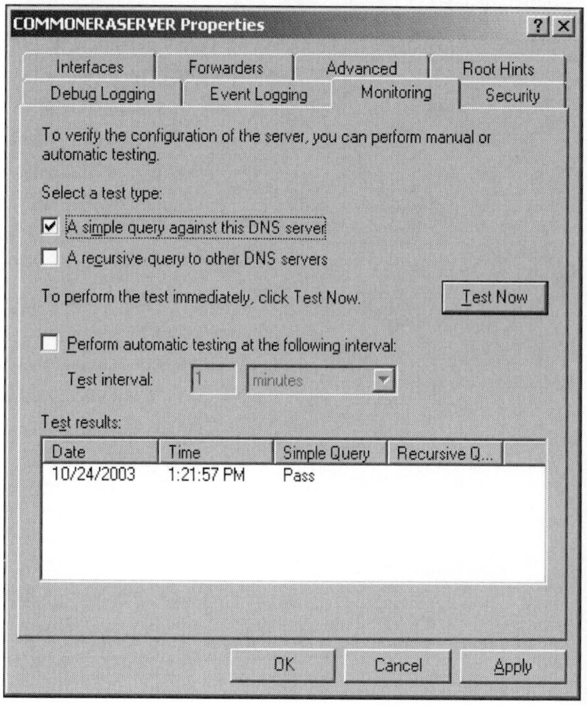

skill10 *Monitoring DNS Server Performance*

exam objective

Monitor DNS. Tools might include System Monitor, Event Viewer, Replication Monitor, and DNS debug logs.

overview

An important task that you need to perform once you have implemented and tested DNS is monitoring the performance of the DNS server. Monitoring the performance of a DNS server is a preventive measure for avoiding future problems related to name resolution. Monitoring the DNS server also provides you with performance data that you can use to diagnose problems and optimize performance.

Soon after you implement DNS, you need to establish a **baseline** for your DNS performance, which indicates the normal performance of the server. After you establish a baseline, you can compare it with the performance data that you collect over time to determine performance trends. If there is degradation in the performance of your DNS, the performance data that you collect helps you to identify bottlenecks that are affecting the performance of the DNS server. You should update the baseline regularly to reflect any changes in the DNS setup or other factors that may affect DNS performance.

To monitor different aspects of DNS, Windows Server 2003 provides you with different types of DNS server performance counters. **Table 6-5** describes these performance counter types. You use the **Performance** console tools, **System Monitor** and **Performance Logs**, to collect and analyze data based on these counters. The System Monitor tool depicts data collected by performance counters in the form of graphs, bar charts, and text reports. You use Performance Logs to maintain records of data collected by performance counters and to set alerts, which can be used to initiate actions such as sending a message and/or executing a program when a particular condition is true. If you want to monitor and analyze data collected using performance counters for a short period, use System Monitor. If you wish to collect and analyze data over a longer period, Performance Logs are a better choice.

how to

Monitor the performance of a DNS server.

1. Click <button>Start</button>, point to **Administrative Tools**, and then click **Performance** to open the Performance console **(Figure 6-32)**. The left pane of the window lists the two performance tools that are available in the console, **System Monitor** and **Performance Logs and Alerts**. System Monitor is selected by default. In the right pane, System Monitor immediately begins charting values for the default counters in real time. The default counters, which you can see at the bottom of the right pane, are **Pages/sec, Avg. Disk Queue Length**, and **% Processor Time**. Actual values for the counter that is selected appear between the graphical display and the list of active counters.

2. Click <button>+</button> on the Performance console toolbar above the graphical display area to open the **Add Counters** dialog box.

3. Click DNS in the **Performance object** list box **(Figure 6-33)**. The performance counters related to **DNS** display in the **Select counters from list** box.

4. Select the counter that you want to monitor in the Select counters from list box; for example, **Total Query Received**. You can get details about the counter that you select by clicking <button>Explain</button>.

5. Click <button>Add...</button> to add the selected performance counter to the list of performance counters that are being monitored. If you want to add more counters from the Add Counters dialog box, you may do so.

6. Click <button>Close</button> to close the Add Counters dialog box. You will now see the counter you selected in the list of active counters near the bottom of the Performance console. The counters are color-coded so that you can identify them in the graphical display. You can change the format of the display from a line graph to a bar graph (histogram) by clicking <button>Test Now</button>.

7. Close the Performance console.

tip

The Performance console toolbar also contains a Delete button, which you can use to delete a counter that you have selected in the list of active counters near the bottom of the Performance console.

Figure 6-32 The Performance console

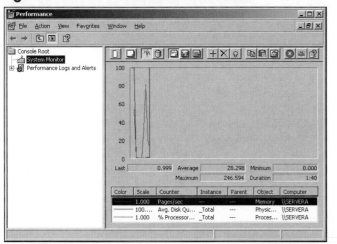

Figure 6-33 The Add Counters dialog box

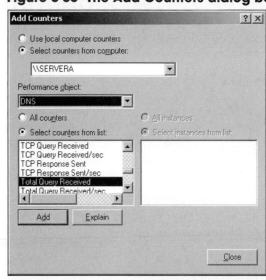

Table 6-5   DNS server performance counters

Counter type	Counter name	Description
All zone transfer (AXFR)	AXFR Request Received AXFR Request Sent AXFR Response Received AXFR Success Received AXFR Success Sent	Tracks the number of full zone transfer requests and responses processed by the DNS server.
Incremental Zone transfer (IXFR)	IXFR Request Received IXFR Request Sent IXFR Response Received IXFR Success Received IXFR Success Sent IXFR TCP Success Received IXFR UDP Success Received	Tracks the number of incremental zone transfer requests and responses by the DNS server.
Zone transfer	Zone Transfer Failure Zone Transfer Request Received Zone Transfer SOA Request Sent Zone Transfer Success	Tracks the number of requests and responses processed by the DNS server during the process of copying the DNS database between DNS servers.
DNS server memory	Caching Memory Database Node Memory Nbtstat Memory Record Flow Memory	Tracks the amount of memory used by the DNS server.
Dynamic update	Dynamic Update NoOperation Dynamic Update NoOperation/sec Dynamic Update Queued Dynamic Update Received Dynamic Update Received/sec Dynamic Update Rejected Dynamic Update TimeOuts Dynamic Update Written to Database Dynamic Update Written to Database/sec	Tracks the requests and responses processed by the DNS server during dynamic updating of DNS.
Secure dynamic update	Secure Update Failure Secure Update Received Secure Update Received/sec	Tracks the number of secure dynamic updates sent and received by the DNS server.

Monitoring DNS Server Performance
(cont'd)

exam objective

Monitor DNS. Tools might include System Monitor, Event Viewer, Replication Monitor, and DNS debug logs.

more

Monitoring the performance of a DNS server is not limited to the Performance console. You can also use the following Windows Server 2003 features to keep your DNS server running efficiently:

◆ **Event Viewer**: In Lesson 4, you used Event Viewer to monitor the DHCP Server service. You can likewise use Event Viewer to keep tabs on your DNS server. You can access the DNS Events log either from the main Event Viewer console or from the DNS console. In the DNS console, right-click **DNS Events** under the **Event Viewer** node and click **Properties** to open the **DNS Events Properties** dialog box. The DNS Events Properties dialog box contains a **General** tab and a **Filter** tab. On the General tab, you can control settings such as the file name of the DNS Events log, its storage location, and maximum size. On the Filter tab, you can control the content of the DNS Events log file by using filter parameters such as event ID, event source, event type, event date, and so on.

◆ **DNS debug log**: As mentioned earlier in this lesson, the Properties dialog box for a DNS server contains a **Debug Logging** tab. The options on this tab enable you to keep a log of the packets that a DNS server sends and receives. You can filter which packets are logged by criteria including:
  • Packet direction (outgoing and/or incoming)
  • Transport protocol (UDP and/or TCP)
  • Packet contents (queries/transfers, updates, and/or notifications)
  • Packet type (request or response)

You can access the DNS debug log file in Windows Explorer by navigating to **%system-root%\WINDOWS\system32\Dns\Dns.log**. The file is compiled in Rich Text Format (RTF) so you should view it with an application that can handle RTF properly such as WordPad. You must stop the DNS Server service in order to view the debug log, and you should not leave debugging active unless you are troubleshooting because it can tax your system's resources.

◆ **Replication Monitor**: Replication Monitor enables you to monitor the replication of DNS activity in Active Directory-integrated zones. In order to use Replication Monitor, you must install Windows Support Tools from your Windows Server 2003 CD-ROM. Once installed, you can access Replication Monitor by entering **replmon** in the Run dialog box. Among the duties that Replication Monitor can perform are the following:
  • Identifies a domain controller that has failed to replicate DNS data
  • Forces the replication of DNS data
  • Logs the success and failure rates of replication nodes
  • Checks the operational standing of domain controllers responsible for replication across forests
  • Displays a graphical representation of DNS replication topology

Table 6-5   DNS server performance counters (cont'd)

Counter type	Counter name	Description
Notification	Notify Sent Notify Received	Tracks the number of notifies sent by the master DNS server and the number of notifies received by the secondary DNS server.
Recursion	Recursive Queries Recursive Queries/sec Recursive Query Failure Recursive Query Failure/sec Recursive TimeOuts Recursive TimeOuts/sec	Tracks data related to recursive queries used by a DNS server.
TCP	TCP Message Memory TCP Query Received TCP Query Received/sec TCP Response Sent TCP Response Sent/sec	Tracks the number of requests and responses processed by the DNS server using TCP.
UDP	UDP Message Memory UDP Query Received UDP Query Received/sec UDP Response Sent UDP Response Sent/sec	Tracks the number of requests and responses processed by the DNS server using UDP.
Total	Total Query Received Total Query Received/sec Total Response Set Total Response Set/sec	Tracks the total number of requests and responses processed by the DNS.
WINS lookup	WINS Lookup Received WINS Lookup Received/sec WINS Response Sent WINS Response Sent/sec WINS Reverse Lookup Received WINS Reverse Lookup Received/sec WINS Reverse Response Sent WINS Reverse Response Sent/sec	Tracks the requests and responses sent to the WINS server by the DNS server when DNS is used for WINS lookup.

Summary

- You can manage and configure a DNS server by using the DNS console and by manually editing the DNS files available in the %systemroot%\WINDOWS\system32\dns folder.
- Forward lookup zones are used to resolve host names to IP addresses, and reverse lookup zones are used to resolve IP addresses to host names.
- These zones can be any of the following types: Active Directory-integrated, standard primary, standard secondary, or stub.
- To resolve an IP address to a host name, DNS uses the in-addr.arpa domain, which is a special domain that supports reverse lookups.
- The database file for an in-addr.arpa zone, also called the reverse lookup file, contains PTR records, which are resource records that associate an IP address with a host name in the in-addr.arpa domain.
- Caching-only name servers use caching to store information collected during the process of resolving client queries. Information stored on a caching-only server is subject to a Time-to-Live (TTL) attribute.
- Caching is a method of storing frequently-needed information in memory, enabling you to access the information quickly when required.
- In order to implement DNS on client computers, you need to configure DNS using the TCP/IP Properties dialog box.

- Zone delegation is the process of dividing a large single zone into smaller zones that are responsible for managing a portion of the DNS namespace for which the original zone was responsible.
- The parent zone of the delegated zone contains a name service record for the name server of the delegated zone. This name service record acts as a pointer to the name server of the delegated zone and directs the query to the correct name server for resolution.
- DNS implementation in Windows Server 2003 supports dynamic updates of host name-to-IP address mappings.
- Dynamic updates allow hosts on the network to register with the DNS database and update any future changes in their configurations dynamically.
- The DNS console provides you with a method of testing the DNS setup by sending a DNS query to the DNS server.
- Command-line utilities such as Ping and Nslookup can also be used to help you test your DNS setup.
- The Performance console provides two tools for monitoring DNS server performance: System Monitor and Performance Logs and Alerts.
- Event Viewer, DNS debug logging, and Replication Monitor can also help you monitor the performance of a DNS server.

Key Terms

Active Directory-integrated zone
Baseline
Caching
Caching-only name server
Delegated zones
Dynamic Domain Name System
(DDNS)

Dynamic updates
Forwarder
Forward lookup zone
in-addr.arpa domain
in-addr.arpa zone
Name service record
Reverse lookup file

Reverse lookup zone
Standard primary zone
Standard secondary zone
Stub zone
Zone delegation

Test Yourself

1. Which command-line utility enables you to manage a DNS server?
   a. Ping
   b. Nslookup
   c. Dnsmgmt
   d. Dnscmd

2. Which of the following types of zones would you create if you wanted to maintain a read-only copy of the zone database of an existing zone?
   a. Active Directory-integrated
   b. Standard secondary
   c. Standard primary
   d. Reverse lookup

3. When resolving an IP address to its corresponding host name, the client queries the DNS server for a _____ record for that IP address.
   a. NS
   b. SOA
   c. PTR
   d. A

4. Which of the following DNS servers does not participate in the process of zone transfers?
   a. Caching-only name server
   b. Primary name server
   c. Secondary name server

5. When you implement a caching-only DNS server for the first time, the cache of the server is empty.
   a. True
   b. False

6. To implement DNS on a client computer, you need to configure a DNS server by using the _____ dialog box.
   a. Set Aging/Scavenging Properties
   b. New Resource Record
   c. DNS server Properties
   d. TCP/IP Properties

7. Which record in the parent zone acts as a pointer to the name server of a delegated zone?
   a. Pointer
   b. Name service
   c. Start of Authority
   d. Canonical name

8. Which of the following utilities do you use to check the connectivity between two IP hosts on a TCP/IP network?
   a. Ping
   b. Nslookup
   c. System Monitor
   d. Debug Logging

9. You use the System Monitor tool in the Performance console to set alerts.
   a. True
   b. False

10. The System Monitor uses _____ to enable you to monitor the performance of a DNS server.
    a. Alerts
    b. Counters
    c. Resource records
    d. Zones

11. You can protect your DNS servers from exposure to the dangers of the Internet by configuring:
    a. Root zones
    b. Root hints
    c. Forwarders
    d. Reverse lookup zones

Projects: On Your Own

1. Create a standard primary forward lookup zone named miami.intercity.com and a Host record for a computer named Computer1 with the IP address 112.13.2.67. Also, create a reverse lookup zone for the network ID 112.13.2 on your DNS server.
   a. Open the **DNS console**.
   b. Initiate the **New Zone Wizard** from the **Forward Lookup Zone** container.
   c. Create a standard primary zone named **miami.intercity.com**.
   d. Open the **New Host** dialog box and create a resource record of the type Host with the name **Computer1** and the IP address **112.13.2.67**.
   e. Initiate the New Zone Wizard from the **Reverse Lookup Zone** container.
   f. Create a reverse lookup zone for the network ID **112.13.2.**

2. Configure the miami.intercity.com zone for dynamic updates and test your DNS server.
   a. Open the **Properties** dialog box for the miami.intercity.com zone.
   b. On the **General** tab, set the option to allow secure dynamic updates.
   c. Close the Properties dialog for the miami.intercity.com zone.
   d. Open the Properties dialog box for your DNS server.
   e. Go to the **Monitoring** tab.
   f. Manually test a simple query against your DNS server.

3. Monitor the performance of your DNS server.
   a. Open the **Performance** console.
   b. Add the following counters to the **System Monitor**: **Caching Memory**, **Total Query Received**, and **Total Response Sent**.

Problem Solving Scenarios

1. You are a Network Administrator at a financial services company. Some of the clients running Windows NT 4.0 on your LAN are having trouble registering DNS Host (A) records. All of the computers running Windows 2000 or later are not having any such problem. Furthermore, there have been several complaints regarding an application that requires IP addresses to be resolved to their respective computer names. This application uses the same DNS server as the Windows NT 4.0 computers, and coincidentally is installed on one of the Windows NT 4.0 computers. The application is mission critical and thus the problem requires immediate attention and resolution. Prepare a document that describes a plan for solving this problem in the most effective way.

2. You administer your company's DNS infrastructure. Recently, a new department was created that needs to use the DNS service. However, the configuration of this department will be static and, as such, all IP addresses and computer names will be predetermined. Your DNS server hosts two zones: one is an Active Directory-integrated zone and the other is a standard primary zone. The new department has been handed down Windows NT 4.0 computers. The Sales department, which is now using Windows XP Professional clients, has been complaining about slow response times for name resolution. Prepare a presentation explaining what conclusion can be drawn from the facts presented and how you would resolve the situation.

Implementing and Managing WINS

In order for client computers to communicate with each other on a NetBIOS-based network, the NetBIOS names of each of the clients must be known. These names are a part of the identification process for computers on a network. Along with the NetBIOS names, client computers using the TCP/IP protocol need to know the IP addresses of other computers in order to identify them on the network. Therefore, to communicate with a computer on a NetBIOS-based network using TCP/IP as a network protocol, you need a service that resolves NetBIOS computer names to the IP addresses of the computers. Such services are called naming services. Windows Internet Naming Service (WINS) is a naming service that resolves NetBIOS names to the IP addresses of computers on a TCP/IP-based network. If you happen to work with a network from which older operating systems have been phased out, you may not require the WINS service at all. However, many networks still contain computers running versions of Windows such as Windows 98, Windows NT, and Windows Me that make WINS necessary.

To begin the implementation of WINS, you need to install the service on a Windows Server 2003 computer, which will enable the computer to function as a WINS server. In addition to configuring a WINS server on the network, you will need to enable the clients on the network to use the WINS server for NetBIOS name resolutions. Once configured to access the WINS server, the client computers will function as WINS clients.

WINS clients automatically register their NetBIOS names and IP addresses with their configured WINS server. However, for clients that do not register their NetBIOS names and IP addresses automatically, you can register the information manually by creating static mapping entries for each client in the WINS server's database.

Additionally, Windows Server 2003 enables you to configure a DNS server to query the WINS databases for name resolution if the DNS server is unable to resolve a host name-to-IP address query using its own database. Windows Server 2003 also enables you to configure WINS replication partners to make sure that the entries on multiple WINS servers are consistent and current. Finally, Windows Server 2003 provides a variety of tools for managing, monitoring, and troubleshooting problems that you might encounter while implementing the WINS service.

Goals

In this lesson, you will learn about the WINS service and how to install and configure a WINS server. In addition, you will learn how to install and configure a WINS client to access a WINS server. You will also learn to register a static mapping for a computer and configure a DNS server to perform WINS lookup. Finally, you will learn about administering, monitoring, replicating, and troubleshooting the WINS service.

Lesson 7   Implementing and Managing WINS

Skill	Exam 70-291 Objective
1. Introducing WINS	Basic knowledge
2. Installing WINS on a Windows Server 2003 Computer	Basic knowledge
3. Configuring WINS Clients	Basic knowledge
4. Registering WINS Clients with Static Mapping	Basic knowledge
5. Configuring the DNS Service to Perform WINS Lookups	Manage DNS zone settings.
6. Administering WINS	Basic knowledge
7. Monitoring WINS	Basic knowledge
8. Replicating WINS Databases	Basic knowledge
9. Troubleshooting WINS Configuration Problems	Basic knowledge

Requirements

To complete this lesson, you will need administrative rights on two Windows Server 2003 computers, one with DNS installed, and a Windows XP Professional client computer, connected on a network.

skill 1   *Introducing WINS*

exam objective   Basic knowledge

overview

Before the proliferation of the Internet, organizations generally used the NetBIOS Extended User Interface (NetBEUI) protocol to establish communications between computers on a network. NetBEUI does not support routing, and is used to transfer data over a pre-defined route that cannot be changed. Therefore, NetBEUI is best suited for small networks having limited resources. The NetBEUI protocol implements the NetBIOS naming scheme, which uses NetBIOS names to identify and communicate with computers on a network (**Figure 7-1**). With the arrival of the Internet in the public domain, organizations started using the TCP/IP protocol, which uses IP addresses to identify and communicate with computers on the network. NetBEUI has been phased out to such a degree that you will not find support for it in a default installation of Windows Server 2003. However, while hosting TCP/IP networks, some organizations continued to use legacy applications and operating systems that required the resolution of NetBIOS names to IP addresses for communication. Microsoft's **Windows Internet Naming Service (WINS)** helps accomplish the task of resolving NetBIOS names to IP addresses on a TCP/IP network.

To begin the implementation of WINS, you need to install the service on a Windows Server 2003 computer, which will enable the computer to function as a **WINS server**. A WINS server is a NetBIOS Name Server (NBNS), which is server software dedicated to resolving NetBIOS names to IP addresses. An NBNS contains a database file that can accept dynamic NetBIOS name-to-IP address registrations and answer queries for NetBIOS name resolutions. As an NBNS, a WINS server hosts a **WINS database** for registration and resolution of client NetBIOS name-to-IP address queries.

After installing a WINS server, you need to configure WINS clients to use the WINS server for NetBIOS name resolution. To configure a WINS client, you assign the client the IP address of the WINS server to which the client can send its name resolution queries. This direct querying of a WINS server is preferable to using broadcasts to resolve NetBIOS names because it reduces network traffic.

A WINS client uses two processes during the implementation of WINS:
◆ **Dynamic registration:** The process of registering the NetBIOS name-to-IP address mappings of WINS clients on a WINS server starts with the **name registration request** (**Figure 7-2**). During the initial steps of a WINS client's boot process, the client sends a name registration request to the WINS server. Upon receiving the name registration request, the WINS server checks its database for an existing entry with the same name as the name in the request. If no matching record exists in the WINS database, the WINS server registers the NetBIOS name. After registering the NetBIOS name, the WINS server sends a **positive name registration response** that includes the Time-to-Live (TTL) for the registered name. Before the TTL for a registered name expires, the WINS client needs to renew its name with the WINS server. To renew its name, the client needs to send a **name refresh request** to the WINS server, asking to refresh the TTL for the name. When a WINS client no longer requires a registered name (i.e., during client shutdown), it sends a **name release message** to the WINS server to release the name.

Figure 7-1 The NetBEUI protocol and NetBIOS

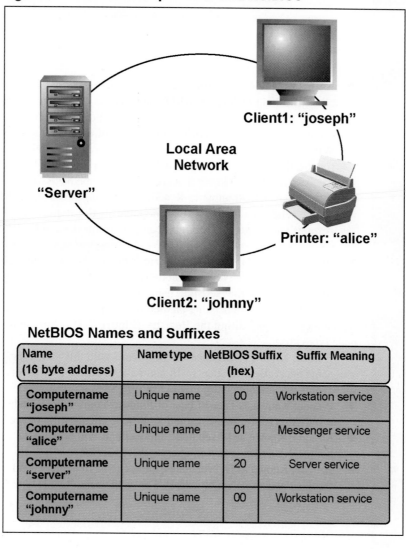

NetBIOS Names and Suffixes

Name (16 byte address)	Name type	NetBIOS Suffix (hex)	Suffix Meaning
Computername "joseph"	Unique name	00	Workstation service
Computername "alice"	Unique name	01	Messenger service
Computername "server"	Unique name	20	Server service
Computername "johnny"	Unique name	00	Workstation service

Figure 7-2 NetBIOS name registration process

NetBIOS Name Registration, Renewal, and Release

Name Registration	WINS client requests the use of a NetBIOS name on the network
Name Renewal	WINS client sends a NetBIOS name refresh request to a WINS server
Name Release	WINS client notifies the WINS server that it is no longer using its registered NetBIOS name

skill 1

Introducing WINS (cont'd)

exam objective   Basic knowledge

overview

◆ **NetBIOS Name Resolution:** The process of resolving NetBIOS names begins with the client checking its local NetBIOS name cache for a matching entry. If that action is not successful in resolving the desired name, the process continues with WINS and the client sending a request for NetBIOS name resolution, called the **name query request**, to a WINS server **(Figure 7-3)**. Through this request, the WINS client asks the WINS server for the IP address of a requested NetBIOS computer. The WINS server searches its database for the IP address that corresponds to the NetBIOS name of the computer. If the requested NetBIOS name-to-IP address mapping exists in the WINS database, the WINS server sends a name response message to the requesting WINS client. The **name response message** contains the IP address of the desired NetBIOS computer.

more

NetBIOS name resolution can be performed in one of four methods. The methods a client will use is defined by their NetBIOS node type. In all cases, clients will attempt to resolve a NetBIOS name using the NetBIOS name cache first. Then a client will use alternate methods (WINS or broadcast), depending on their node type. You can modify a client's NetBIOS node type either through editing the Registry **(Figure 7-4)** or through DHCP options. The four node types are:

◆ B-node: Known as Broadcast node, clients with this node type will simply broadcast the name query. B-node clients will not make use of WINS. This is the default node type for clients that are not configured to use WINS.

◆ P-node: Known as Peer-to-Peer or Point-to-Point node, P-node clients will simply query a WINS server for name resolution. P-node clients will not use broadcasts.

◆ M-node: Known as Mixed node, these clients will broadcast name queries, and if they do not receive a response, will query a WINS server.

◆ H-node: Known as Hybrid nodes, these clients first query a WINS server, and if unable to resolve the query, then broadcast. This is the default node type for WINS enabled clients.

Figure 7-3 NetBIOS name resolution process using WINS

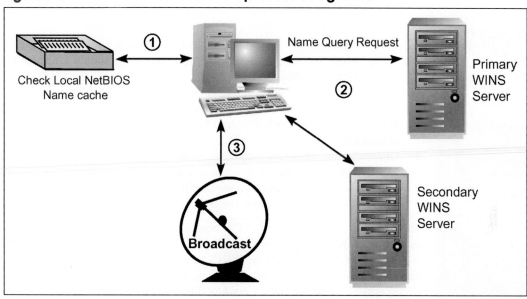

Figure 7-4 Changing the node type in the Registry

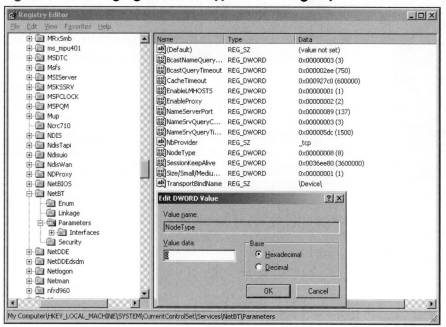

skill 2

Installing WINS on a Windows Server 2003 Computer

exam objective

Basic knowledge

overview

To enable a Windows Server 2003 computer to function as a WINS server, you need to install the WINS service. Before installing WINS, you should consider the following recommendations from Microsoft:

◆ Your network should contain one WINS server and a backup server for every 10,000 WINS clients in order to service name registrations and name queries effectively. A WINS server can typically register 1500 names and field 4500 name queries in the space of a minute.

◆ Disable logging of database changes, as this makes name registrations faster. You can set options in the Properties dialog box of a WINS server to disable detailed event logging for the server. As long as you have specified a backup directory for the WINS database, disabling logging does not put you at risk of losing the database in the event of a crash.

Besides these recommendations, you need to make sure that the computer on which you install the WINS service meets certain configuration requirements. On a TCP/IP-based network, you can only install the WINS service on a Windows NT Server, Windows 2000 Server, or Windows Server 2003 computer. Additionally, you must configure the computer with a static IP address, subnet mask, default gateway, and other TCP/IP parameters. To install the WINS service, you can use either the Windows Components Wizard or the Manage Your Server window.

caution

Since log files contain information about the events that occur on a WINS server, information about the last database updates will be lost if logging is disabled and the system crashes.

how to

Install the WINS service on a Windows Server 2003 computer.

1. Click **Start**, point to **Control Panel**, and click **Add or Remove Programs** to open the **Add or Remove Programs** window.
2. Click the **Add/Remove Windows Components** button on the left side of the window to start the **Windows Components Wizard**.
3. On the **Windows Components** screen (**Figure 7-5**), scroll down the **Components** list, and then double-click **Networking Services** to open the **Networking Services** dialog box.
4. Click the **Windows Internet Name Service (WINS)** check box to select the WINS service for installation (**Figure 7-6**), and then click ▢ OK to close the Networking Services dialog box.
5. Click ▢ Next> to open the **Configuring Components** screen. The Wizard will take a few moments to configure the services you have selected. If prompted, insert your Windows Server 2003 installation CD-ROM to proceed with the installation.
6. When the Wizard has finished configuring the WINS service, the **Completing the Windows Components Wizard** screen will open. Click ▢ Finish to close the Wizard.
7. Close the Add or Remove Programs window.

tip

To begin the process of installing WINS from the Manage Your Server window, click Add or remove a role.

Figure 7-5 The Windows Components screen

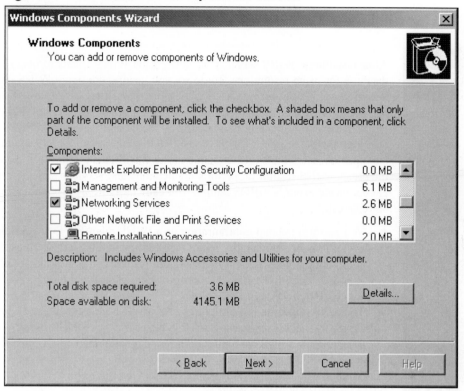

Figure 7-6 The Networking Services dialog box

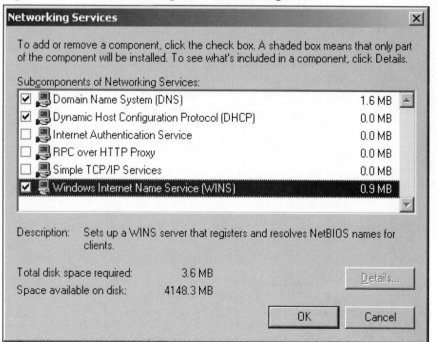

skill 3

Configuring WINS Clients

exam objective

Basic knowledge

overview

After installing a WINS server, you must enable WINS clients to query the WINS server's database for name resolutions. To do so, you need to configure WINS clients to access the WINS server. Configuring a WINS client to access the WINS server allows the client to register its NetBIOS name-to-IP address mapping in the WINS database. After you configure the WINS client, the client can attempt to locate another WINS client on the network by querying the WINS server with the NetBIOS name of the WINS client. The server then attempts to resolve the NetBIOS name of the WINS client to the IP address, as requested by the client. WINS resolution permits applications and services running on WINS clients to communicate using NetBIOS names. You can configure a WINS client both manually and automatically:

◆ You perform manual configuration of a WINS client (in this example, a Windows XP Professional computer) by using the **Advanced TCP/IP Settings** dialog box. If you configure the WINS client manually, the values that you provide will take precedence over the values that a DHCP server provides. Manual configuration of WINS is required for non-DHCP clients.

◆ You perform automatic configuration of a WINS client by using Dynamic Host Control Protocol (DHCP) services. If a WINS client is also a DHCP client, you can configure it to receive the WINS configuration information automatically from a DHCP server.

how to

Configure a Windows XP Professional WINS client to use a Windows Server 2003 WINS server for NetBIOS name resolution.

1. Log on to the Windows XP Professional client computer as an **Administrator**.
2. Click ⟦*Start*⟧, right-click **My Network Places**, and then click **Properties** on the shortcut menu to open the **Network Connections** window.
3. Right-click the **Local Area Connection** icon, and then click **Properties** on the shortcut menu to open the **Local Area Connection Properties** dialog box.
4. On the **General** tab, select **Internet Protocol (TCP/IP)** in the **This connection uses the following items** list box (**Figure 7-7**). Then, click ⟦Properties⟧ to open the **Internet Protocol (TCP/IP) Properties** dialog box.
5. On the **General** tab of the Internet Protocol (TCP/IP) Properties dialog box, click ⟦Advanced...⟧ to open the **Advanced TCP/IP Settings** dialog box. Then, click the **WINS** tab (**Figure 7-8**).
6. On the WINS tab, click ⟦Add...⟧ to open the **TCP/IP WINS Server** dialog box (**Figure 7-9**).
7. Type the IP address of the desired WINS server in the **WINS server** entry field, and then click ⟦Add⟧. The WINS server you have selected is added to the **WINS addresses, in order of use** list box on the WINS tab. This is the WINS server that the client will query for NetBIOS name resolution.
8. Click ⟦OK⟧ to close the Advanced TCP/IP Settings dialog box.
9. Click ⟦OK⟧ to close the Internet Protocol (TCP/IP) Properties dialog box.
10. Click ⟦OK⟧ to close the Local Area Connection Properties dialog box.
11. Close the Network Connections window.

**Figure 7-7 The Local Area Connection
Properties dialog box**

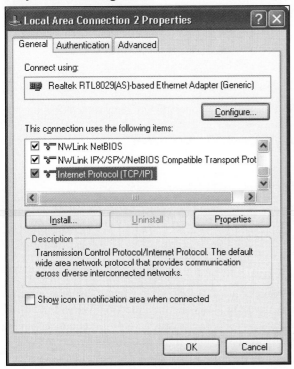

Figure 7-8 The WINS tab

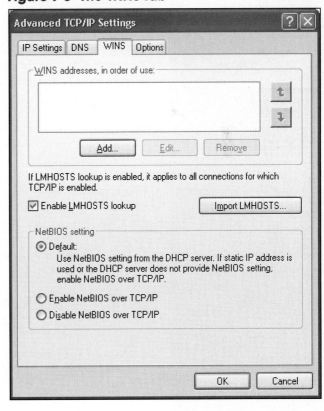

Figure 7-9 The TCP/IP WINS Server dialog box

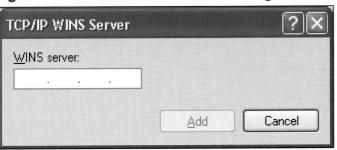

skill 3 | *Configuring WINS Clients* *(cont'd)*

exam objective   Basic knowledge

more

You can configure clients running any of the following operating systems as WINS clients:

◆ Windows Server 2003
◆ Windows 2000 Server, Advanced Server, and Datacenter Server
◆ Windows 2000 Professional
◆ Windows XP Professional
◆ Windows NT 3.5 and later versions
◆ Windows 95 and Windows 98
◆ Windows for Workgroups 3.11 running Microsoft TCP/IP-32
◆ Microsoft Network Client 3.0 for MS-DOS
◆ LAN Manager 2.2c for MS-DOS

Non-WINS clients can indirectly use the WINS server for NetBIOS name resolution if you configure a WINS proxy agent on your network. A **WINS proxy agent** listens for name request broadcasts by non-WINS clients. These requests are forwarded to a WINS server and either an appropriate IP address or a negative response is returned to the requesting client through the WINS proxy agent. To configure a Windows Server 2003 computer as a WINS proxy agent, you need to edit the Registry. To edit the Registry, open the **Run** dialog box and enter **regedt32** to open the **Registry Editor**. Next, navigate to the following folder so that you can add a value for the proxy agent:

HKEY_LOCAL_MACHINE\SYSTEM\CurrentControlSet\Services\NetBT\Parameters

After selecting this folder (**Figure 7-10**), find the entry in the right pane of the Registry Editor named **EnableProxy**. Double-click the EnableProxy entry to open the **Edit DWORD Value** dialog box. Change the value in the **Value data** text box to **1 (Figure 7-11)**. Click OK to close the Edit DWORD Value dialog box. This enables the WINS proxy agent.

WINS proxy agents cannot register names for non-WINS clients. To register a non-WINS client in the WINS database, you must use static mappings, as discussed in the next skill.

Figure 7-10 The Registry Editor

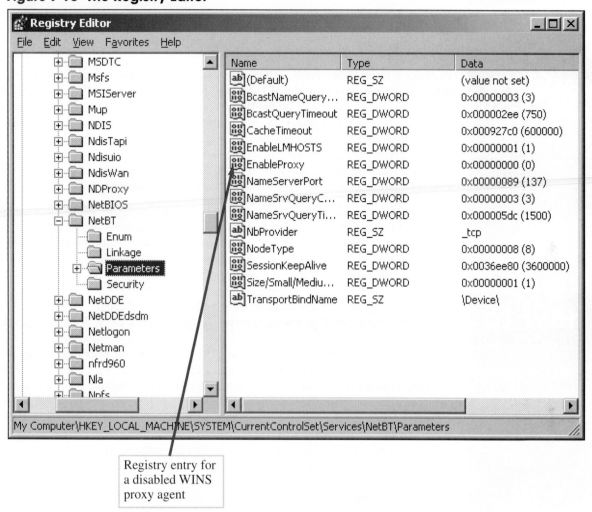

Registry entry for
a disabled WINS
proxy agent

Figure 7-11 The Edit DWORD Value dialog box

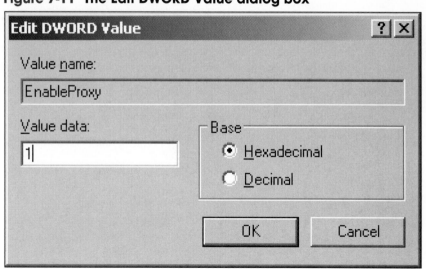

skill 4

Registering WINS Clients with Static Mapping

exam objective

Basic knowledge

overview

In addition to resolving the NetBIOS names of WINS clients, you might need to resolve remote computer names of non-WINS client resources. For example, computers running operating systems other than Windows may not be able to register their computer names directly with your WINS server. In such a situation, you can add the computer name-to-IP address mappings for these computers to your WINS server database by creating static mapping entries for them. A **static mapping entry** is a name resolution entry that you enter in the WINS database manually. Therefore, you use static mapping to create name resolution entries for any computer that does not create such entries automatically.

Windows Server 2003 enables you to create different types of static mapping entries depending on the client computer. For example, to create a static mapping entry to map a NetBIOS name to an IP address, you need to create a **Unique static mapping entry** in the WINS database. To create a static mapping entry for a group of computers, you need to create a **Group static mapping entry** in the WINS server database.

how to

Register a client with a WINS database using a Unique static mapping.

1. Click ![Start], point to **Administrative Tools**, and then click **WINS** to open **WINS** console.
2. Click the plus symbol next to the name of your WINS server to expand the server node. Then, click the **Active Registrations** folder. Every WINS server has an **Active Registrations** folder and a **Replication Partners** folder. The Active Registrations folder displays a list of computers and group names that are registered in the WINS database of the server. The Replication Partners folder lists the replication partners that are configured for the server.
3. Click **Action** on the Menu bar, and then click **New Static Mapping** to open the **New Static Mapping** dialog box (**Figure 7-12**). Here, you can create static mapping entries for clients that do not create mapping entries automatically.
4. In the **Computer name** text box, type the NetBIOS name of the computer that you want to configure with the WINS server. If the computer uses a NetBIOS scope identifier, type the identifier in the **NetBIOS Scope (optional)** text box.
5. In the IP address text box, type the IP address of the client that you are registering manually.
6. Click OK to close the New Static Mapping dialog box and add the static mapping entry to the WINS database.
7. To view mapping entries in the Active Registrations folder, click **Action**, and then click **Display Records**. When the Display Records dialog box opens, click Find Now . You will see the static mapping entry you just created listed in the Active Registrations folder (**Figure 7-13**).
8. Close the WINS console.

tip

You can use the WINS console for a variety of tasks including starting and stopping the WINS service and compacting the WINS database.

tip

A NetBIOS scope identifier allows you to differentiate among different logical NetBIOS networks that co-exist on the same physical network.

tip

To create more than one static mapping entry, click Apply after you create the first entry instead of clicking OK.

more

The WINS service enables you to add a variety of static WINS mapping types: Unique, Group, Domain Name, Internet Group, and Multihomed. **Table 7-1** describes these types.

Figure 7-12 The New Static Mapping dialog box

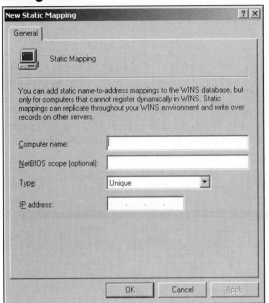

Figure 7-13 Active registrations

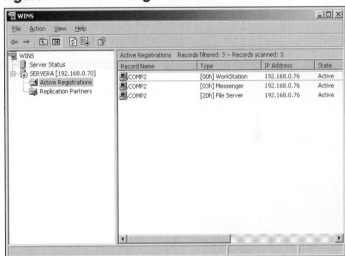

Table 7-1	Static WINS mapping types
Type	**Description**
Unique	To create a static mapping entry for each IP address, you need to select the Unique mapping type from the Type drop-down list in the New Static Mapping dialog box.
Group	The Group mapping type, also referred to as the normal group, is used to add mapping entries for a group of clients to a workgroup on your network. When creating Group type mapping entries, the IP addresses of each member group are not stored in the WINS database. Instead, you need to enter the computer name and IP address of each group member while adding the members to the group. If this mapping type is used, the IP address for the member computer is resolved through local subnet broadcasts.
Domain Name	For environments with domains running Windows NT Server 4.0 and earlier versions, the process of locating domain controllers involves the resolution of the Windows <Domain> name. This name is registered for use by the domain controllers within each domain and can contain up to 25 IP addresses. The first IP address is always for the primary domain controller (PDC). The additional (up to 24) IP addresses are for backup domain controllers (BDCs). Because this name is treated as a domain group by WINS, each member of the group (a domain controller) must renew its name individually in WINS, or else its IP address entry in the list is released and can be overwritten eventually.
Internet Group	This mapping type represents user-defined groups of resources, such as printers, for convenient browsing and access. Additionally, a dynamic member of an Internet Group does not replace a static member that is added using WINS Manager.
Multihomed	The Multihomed mapping type is used to register a unique name for a computer that has multiple network cards each having a single address, or on rare occasions, a single network card with more than one IP address.

skill 5

Configuring the DNS Service to Perform WINS Lookups

exam objective

Manage DNS zone settings.

overview

Windows Server 2003 uses DNS (Domain Name System) as its primary method of name resolution. WINS is generally used for backward compatibility in resolving NetBIOS names for applications and services running down-level clients, such as Windows 95 and Windows 98 computers. However, if a DNS server on a network is not able to resolve the NetBIOS name for a down-level client, the DNS server can be configured to query the WINS server with a NetBIOS name resolution request. In other words, the DNS server can be configured to perform WINS lookups.

When a DNS client sends a request for name resolution of a NetBIOS resource to a DNS server, the DNS server attempts to resolve the host name to an IP address from the data stored in its zones. Zones are the administrative units of DNS that help in effective management of DNS domains. If the DNS server is unable to resolve the host name to an IP address and the DNS server is configured to query a WINS server, the DNS server queries the WINS server with the host name portion of the fully qualified domain name (FQDN). The WINS server then attempts to match the host with a mapping entry in its database. If the resolution is successful, the WINS server returns the IP address to the DNS server. By using this type of resolution, the DNS server functions as a proxy agent for the DNS client and queries the WINS database. You configure a DNS server to perform WINS lookups using the Properties dialog box of a DNS zone, which you can access from the DNS console.

how to

Configure a DNS server, authoritative for a particular zone, to perform WINS lookups on a WINS server.

1. Click ![Start], point to **Administrative Tools**, and then click **DNS** to open **DNS** console.
2. Click the plus symbol next to the name of the DNS server in the console tree to expand the server node.
3. Click the **Forward Lookup Zones** folder in the console tree to select it. Then, right-click the name of the zone for which you want to configure WINS lookups in the details pane, and click **Properties** on the shortcut menu to open the **Properties** dialog box for the zone **(Figure 7-14)**.
4. Click the **WINS** tab, and the select the **Use WINS forward lookup** check box to enable WINS forward lookups by the DNS server **(Figure 7-15)**. If you do not want to replicate WINS-specific resource record data to other DNS servers during zone transfers, select the **Do not replicate this record** check box. Selecting this option can be useful in preventing zone update failures or zone data errors when you are using a combination of Microsoft and other DNS servers in your network to load the zone.
5. Type the IP address of the WINS server that the DNS server will use for WINS lookups in the **IP address** text box.
6. Click ![Add] to add the WINS server whose IP address you specified to the **IP address** list box. You may add more than one WINS server for the DNS server to use.
7. Click ![OK] to close the Properties dialog box.
8. Close the DNS console.

Figure 7-14 Configuring a DNS server for WINS lookup

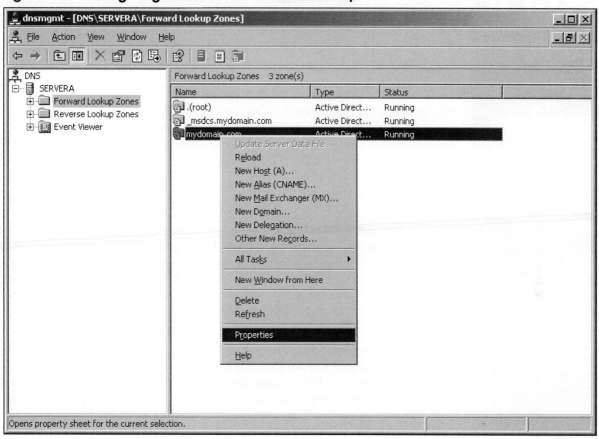

Figure 7-15 The WINS tab

Enter the IP address of the WINS server that the DNS server will use for lookups

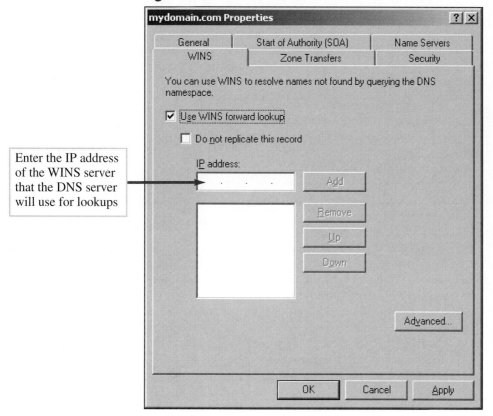

skill 6

Administering WINS

exam objective

Basic knowledge

overview

After installing and configuring the WINS service, you can use the WINS console to perform administrative tasks such as compacting the WINS database, checking entries in a WINS database for consistency, backing up and restoring the database, and backing up the WINS registry settings (**Figure 7-16**).

The size of a WINS database grows as entries are added. However, when a WINS server releases an entry, the server does not release the space that was used by the entry. Therefore, to recover the now unused disk space in the WINS database, you need to compact a WINS database periodically. The WINS service performs an operation, known as **online compaction**, as a dynamic background process to compact the WINS database automatically during idle time. However, online compaction does not recover the space used by released entries as significantly as **offline compaction**, so the database grows slowly. Therefore, you need to perform offline compaction (after stopping the WINS service) from time to time to recover the disk space that was previously used by released entries. You can compact a WINS database offline by using the **Jetpack** command.

In addition to compacting a WINS database, you can also check for consistency of entries across WINS databases. Checking the consistency of entries ensures that updated mapping entries are available to all WINS servers. During a consistency check, a WINS server verifies its database and compares its entries with entries on other WINS servers. All records of the other WINS servers are compared with records in the local database. If a record in the local database is identical to the corresponding record of the other WINS server, the timestamp of the local record is updated. If the record in the other database has a higher version ID, the record is added to the local database, and the existing local record is stamped for deletion.

The WINS console provides features that enable you to back up and restore the WINS database. If you specify a backup folder for the database, WINS performs complete database backups every three hours, using the specified folder. If you do not specify a folder, the default storage location is **%systemroot%\WINDOWS\system32\wins**. Actual backups of the WINS database are stored in this folder in a file named **Wins.mdb**. You can later restore the database from the directory where it was backed up by using the **Restore Database** command on the **Action** menu in the WINS console.

As part of managing your WINS server, you will also need to backup the WINS server's registry settings. You can use these settings later to rebuild the WINS server. The WINS server's Registry settings are saved in the **HKEY_LOCAL_MACHINE\SYSTEM\CurrentControlSet \Services\WINS** folder.

tip

These other WINS servers are replication partners of the WINS server being checked.

how to

Administer a WINS server by performing a consistency check and backing up the WINS database hosted by the server.
1. Open the WINS console.
2. Right-click the WINS server in the console tree, and then click **Verify Database Consistency** on the shortcut menu. A message box appears, informing you that a WINS database consistency check is both processor and network-intensive and asking if you want to continue (**Figure 7-17**).
3. Click [Yes] to proceed with the consistency check. A warning box appears, informing you that the request for a consistency check has been queued on the server.
4. Click [OK] to close the message box.
5. To configure a WINS backup directory, right-click the WINS server in the console tree, and then click **Properties** to open the **Properties** dialog box for the WINS server.

tip

The most effective way to repair a corrupt WINS database is to restore a good copy of the database that you have backed up previously.

Figure 7-16 Administering WINS

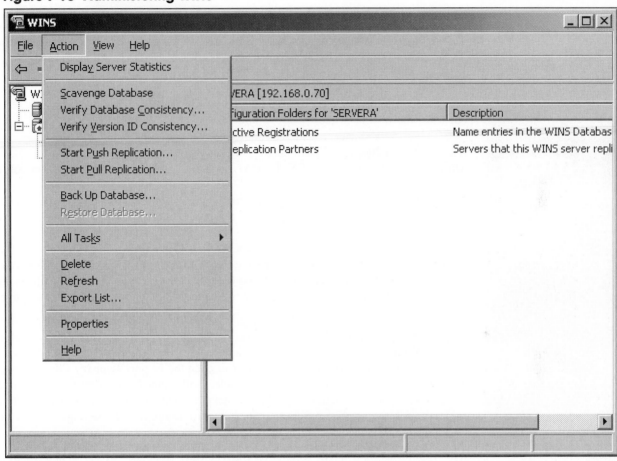

Figure 7-17 Verify Database Consistency message box

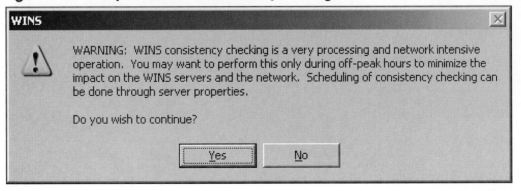

skill 6

Administering WINS *(cont'd)*

exam objective

Basic knowledge

how to

6. If you want the WINS backup file to be stored in the default location, leave the **Default backup path** text box on the **General** tab blank. Otherwise, you can enter a new default backup path **(Figure 7-18)**. You can also select the **Back up database during server shutdown** check box to initiate a backup of the database whenever you shut down the server.
7. Click [OK] to close the Properties dialog box.
8. Close the WINS console.

more

Windows Server 2003 stores all of the Registry entries related to a WINS server's operation in two important subkeys of **HKEY_LOCAL_MACHINE\SYSTEM\CurrentControlSet\ Services\WINS**:

◆ **Parameters:** All of the WINS server's configuration options are stored in the Parameters subkey. These server options include the renewal, extinction, and verify intervals, as well as the setting that defines whether WINS performs a backup on shutdown.

◆ **Partners:** The other important subkey of WINS is the Partners subkey, in which you will find information about the server's current replication partners. Within the Partners subkey, you'll see push and pull subkeys for each of the server's replication partners; you set update counts and time intervals for replication within these push and pull subkeys.

You can back up these WINS registry settings using the Registry Editor. In the Registry Editor window, navigate to the **HKEY_LOCAL_MACHINE\SYSTEM\CurrentControlSet\ Services\WINS** folder and select it (or the Parameters or Partners folders individually). Click **File** on the Menu bar, and then click **Export** to open the **Export Registry File** dialog box **(Figure 7-19)**. The dialog box enables you to select a file name for the Registry settings and a folder in which to save them (the dialog box defaults to the My Documents folder, but you may very well want to choose a different location). To restore Registry settings that you have saved, open the File menu and click the **Import** command.

While administering a WINS server, you can also start, stop, pause, resume, and restart the WINS service. To access the commands for these operations, open the **Action** menu in the WINS console and point to **All Tasks**.

Figure 7-18 Specifying a default backup path

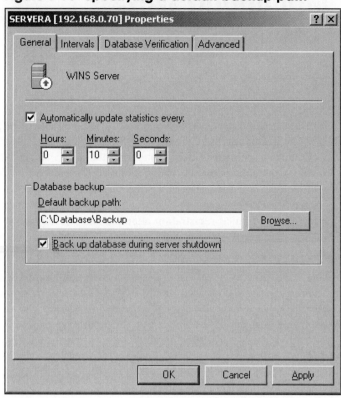

Figure 7-19 The Export Registry File dialog box

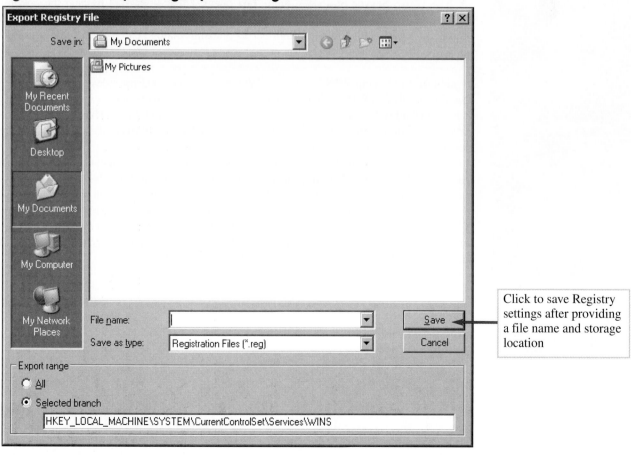

Click to save Registry settings after providing a file name and storage location

skill 7

Monitoring WINS

exam objective

Basic knowledge

overview

To use and administer the WINS service effectively, you need to monitor its performance. Consider a situation in which the WINS clients on your company's network are not able to communicate with each other. Monitoring the WINS server will enable you to determine if the break in communications is due to the performance of the WINS server, or to a problem with the network. You can monitor the performance of the WINS server through the **WINS Server Statistics** dialog box. The dialog box displays information such as the number of successful and failed registration attempts and the number of successful and failed WINS queries made to the server. Such statistical information enables you to narrow down the source of a problem and administer the WINS service accordingly.

The WINS Server Statistics dialog box also contains two buttons: **Reset** and **Refresh**. Clicking the Reset button sets the **Statistics last cleared** time to the current time and sets all counters to zero. After clearing all previously gathered statistics, the dialog box then begins displaying new statistics starting from the point of reset. The Refresh button updates the statistics that are displayed so that they are most current, without resetting the Statistics last cleared time.

how to

View WINS statistical information.
1. Open the **WINS** console.
2. Click the name of the WINS server in the console tree to select the server, open the **Action** menu, and then click **Display Server Statistics (Figure 7-20)**. Alternatively, you can right-click the server and then click **Display Server Statistics** on the shortcut menu.
3. The **WINS Server Statistics** dialog box opens. Click [Reset] to clear the previous statistics and begin recording statistical information from the current time (**Figure 7-21**).
4. Click [Close] to close the WINS Server Statistics dialog box.
5. Close the WINS console.

more

In addition to viewing WINS statistics, Windows Server 2003 provides tools for viewing specific records in a WINS database. You can search the database to view specific records by using the **Display Records** dialog box (**Figure 7-22**). To search the database, first select the server in the console tree. Then, right-click the **Active Registrations** folder and click **Display Records** on the shortcut menu to open the Display Records dialog box. The dialog box contains three tabs, each of which allows you to filter the records in the database by different criteria. On the **Record Mapping** tab, you can search for mapping records based on computer name or IP address. You do not need to know the entire computer name in order to use it as a search criterion. The **Record Owners** tab enables you to display records based on which WINS server has registered the records in the WINS database. On the **Record Types** tab, you can search for records according to their NetBIOS name types, such as records from a domain controller or a RAS (Remote Access Service) server.

caution

Searching for records on a WINS server can be a resource-intensive and time-consuming process.

Figure 7-20 Displaying server statistics

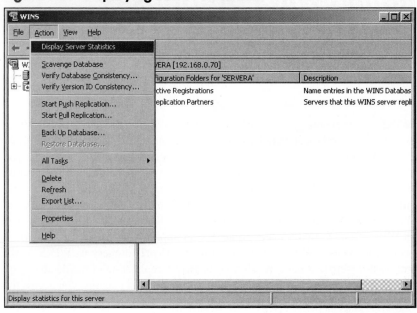

Figure 7-21 The WINS Server Statistics dialog box

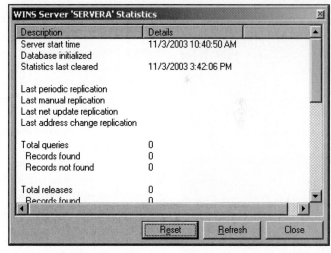

Figure 7-22 The Display Records dialog box—Record Mapping tab

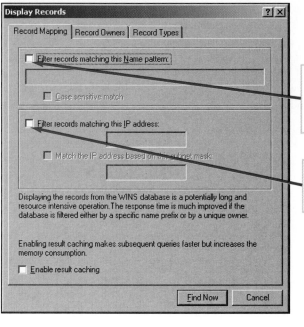

Select this check box to search for mapping records by computer name

Select this check box to search for mapping records by IP address

skill 8

Replicating WINS Databases

exam objective

Basic knowledge

overview

Monitoring a WINS server enables you to view data related to the performance of the WINS service. However, to ensure efficient NetBIOS name resolution, you need to deploy multiple WINS servers. To maintain consistency among the multiple WINS servers on a network, you need to implement a method by which the servers can share information with each other. **WINS replication** is the method of sharing information among WINS servers on a network. Replication enables a WINS server to resolve NetBIOS names of computers that are registered with another WINS server. The following scenario illustrates this concept: Host1 is registered with WINSserver1. Host1 needs to access an application or service located on Host2, which is registered with WINSserver2. In order for Host1 to query its WINS server and receive a successful NetBIOS name resolution for Host2, replication of the databases on the two WINS servers would need to take place. To replicate WINS databases, you access the **New Replication Partner** dialog box from the WINS console.

During the process of WINS database replication, entries are either pushed to or pulled from the WINS server's configured replication partner. A **push partner** is a WINS server that sends replication data to its partner after a specific number of changes. For instance, if the interval for push replication was set to 5, the push partner would push replication data every time five or more changes occurred. A **pull partner** is a WINS server that requests to receive changes from its partner after a specific period of time has elapsed. For example, if the pull interval was set to 5, the pull partner would attempt to retrieve changes every five minutes, regardless of whether any changes have actually occurred **(Figure 7-23)**. Due to the scheduled nature of pull partners, they are advised for WAN connections. However, pull replication does not function if the other side is not set to push, making pull-pull replication relationships impossible. For instance, in order for Server A to pull from Server B, Server B must be configured to push to Server A. To accomplish an effective pull-pull relationship, you must configure each server to be a push-pull partner of the other server. Then you set the pull interval to the time period you require (60, for instance, to have the servers pull every hour), and the push interval to 0. Setting the push interval to 0 effectively disables pushing of replication data, except when the other side requests to pull.

When configuring WINS replication, you should be aware of the replication topology you are creating. There are really only two useful topologies for effective WINS replication: mesh and star. The mesh topology is typically used when there are a small number of WINS servers and convergence time (the time required for all WINS databases to include the same information) is critical, but bandwidth use is not a major concern. With a mesh topology, every server is configured to replicate with every other server. For instance, if you had three servers, A, B, and C, A would replicate with B and C, B would replicate with A and C, and C would replicate with A and B.

In a star topology (also known as a Hub and Spoke), one server acts as a central "hub," while the other servers are configured as "spokes." The hub server will have a replication partnership with all WINS servers, but each spoke will only have a partnership with the hub server. This topology has the advantage of being both highly scalable and bandwidth friendly. However, the downside is that convergence takes twice as long as with a mesh, and your hub server effectively becomes a single point of failure.

Figure 7-23 WINS replication

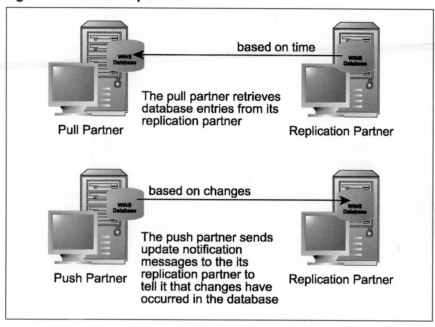

skill 8

Replicating WINS Databases (cont'd)

exam objective

Basic knowledge

overview

You can use the following configuration methods to initiate the replication of a WINS database:

◆ Configure the WINS service to start replication at system startup. This enables a WINS server to pull or push database entries automatically each time WINS is started.

◆ Configure the WINS service to start replication at a specific interval (e.g., every three hours, every five hours, every eight hours).

◆ Configure the WINS service to start replication when a WINS server performs a specific number of registrations and modifications to its WINS database. When the specified number of modifications is reached, the WINS server informs its pull partners; the pull partners then request the new entries.

◆ Use the WINS console to force replication now rather than wait for it to occur according to configuration settings.

how to

Configure a WINS pull replication partner for a WINS server and set the pull replication interval to one hour.

1. Open the **WINS** console.
2. Click the plus symbol next to the name of the WINS server in the console tree to expand the server node. Then, right-click the **Replication Partners** folder under the server and click **New Replication Partner (Figure 7-24)**.
3. The **New Replication Partner** dialog box opens (**Figure 7-25**). Type the IP address of the replication partner you wish to configure in the **WINS server** text box.
4. Click ⬚ OK ⬚ to close the dialog box.
5. Click the Replication Partners folder in the console tree to display its contents in the details pane. The name and IP address of the replication partner now appear in the Replication Partners folder (**Figure 7-26**).
6. Right-click the replication partner server in the details pane, and then click **Properties** to open the **Properties** dialog box for the replication partner.
7. Click the **Advanced** tab. Here, you can specify the replication settings for the replication partner.
8. Click the down arrow in the **Replication partner type** box, and then click **Pull** to select a partner type.
9. In the **Replication interval** section of the tab, select the default Hours value and type **1** to replace it. Similarly set the Minutes value to **0** (**Figure 7-27**).
10. Click ⬚ OK ⬚ to close the Properties dialog box.

tip

With the Use persistent connection for replication check box selected, the WINS server will not disconnect from replication partners once replication is complete. This will allow the server to begin sending records to partners for replication without having to establish a connection every time.

Figure 7-24 Configuring a replication partner

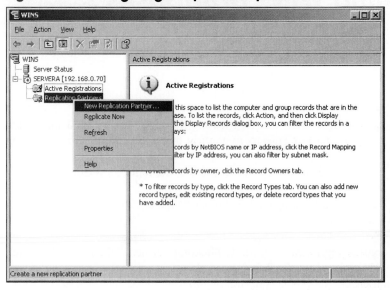

Figure 7-25 The New Replication Partner dialog box

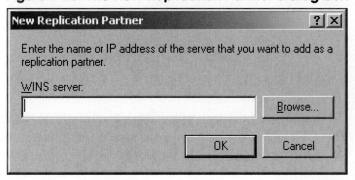

Figure 7-26 Added replication partner

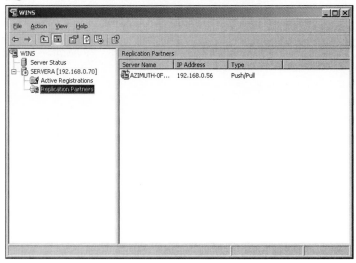

Figure 7-27 Configuring replication partner properties

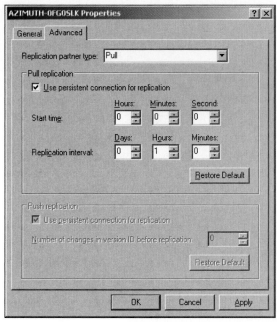

skill 8

Replicating WINS Databases (cont'd)

exam objective

Basic knowledge

how to

11. To force replication, right-click the **Replication Partners** folder, and then click **Replicate Now**. A warning box appears to confirm that you want to start replication (**Figure 7-28**).
12. Click [Yes]. A message box opens indicating that the replication request has been queued.
13. Click [OK] to close the message box and replicate the database.
14. Close the WINS console.

more

To enable partner configuring, right-click the Replication Partners folder, and then click Properties. On the Advanced tab of the Properties dialog box, select the Enable automatic partner configuration check box and specify the required multicast intervals in the corresponding text boxes.

An additional feature of WINS is the ability to automatically configure replication partners. By enabling automatic partner configuration, WINS attempts to locate and configure replication with all other WINS servers using multicasts. WINS servers use the multicast IP address 224.0.1.24 to find other WINS servers. However, automatic partner configuration will only function if the routers between the WINS servers support the forwarding of multicasts. If your network routers do not support multicasting, and you cannot configure the routers to forward multicast traffic to the multicast IP address, the WINS server finds only the WINS servers on its subnet. You must then configure partners manually.

Additionally, due to the inefficiency of the automatic partner relationship, automatic partner configuration is not recommended for replication between more than 3 WINS servers, nor is it recommended for replication over WAN links. Automatic partner configuration configures all detected WINS servers in a push/pull partnership with push replication at 2-hour intervals with all other WINS servers, effectively creating a mesh topology.

Figure 7-28 WINS replication confirmation box

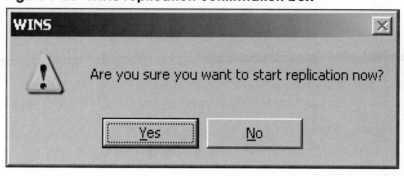

skill 9

Troubleshooting WINS Configuration Problems

exam objective

Basic knowledge

overview

While implementing WINS for name resolution on a network, you might encounter problems such as failed name resolution queries. Windows Server 2003 provides a number of methods, including Event Viewer, to help you identify the cause of such problems and troubleshoot them.

In order to troubleshoot name resolution problems effectively, you first need to identify the causes of the problems. You should make a determination as to whether a problem has occurred due to an error on the WINS client, on the WINS server, or on the network itself. **Table 7-2** lists common client-related WINS problems, and **Table 7-3** lists common server-related WINS problems. For example, to identify whether a WINS client is correctly configured to its WINS server, or servers, verify the WINS settings on the **WINS** tab of the **Advanced TCP/IP Settings** dialog box. You can also run ipconfig /all from the command prompt on a Windows 2000 or Windows XP client, and check whether NetBIOS is disabled. On the server, enable detailed event logging and verify that the server is configured to update static mappings dynamically.

how to

Enable detailed event logging on a WINS server.
1. Open the WINS console.
2. Right-click the name of the WINS server in the console tree, and then click **Properties** to open the **Properties** dialog box for the WINSserver.
3. Click the **Advanced** tab.
4. Select the **Log detailed events to Windows event log** check box. Note the warning below the check box that detailed event logging should only be enabled when you are actually troubleshooting because it can degrade server performance.
5. Click ▭ OK ▭ to close the Properties dialog box.
6. Close the DNS console.

more

To update static mappings dynamically, right-click the **Replication Partners** folder for the WINS server, and then click **Properties** to open the **Replication Partners Properties** dialog box. On the **General** tab, select the **Overwrite unique static mappings at this server (migrate on)** check box to instruct the WINS server to overwrite old name mappings dynamically with new name mappings.

Table 7-2   Client-related problems

Cause	Description	Solution
Incorrect WINS client configuration	An incorrect WINS server IP address on a WINS client causes client-related problems.	Check the configuration and correct it by adding the correct address of the WINS server.
Disable NetBIOS	If NetBIOS is disabled on the network adapter of a WINS client, it cannot communicate with another host on the network by using NetBIOS.	Check whether a user has disabled NetBIOS accidentally and enable NetBIOS on the client.
Interruption in connectivity	Interruption in connectivity between a WINS client and server can cause client-related problems. To identify connectivity problems, ping the WINS server IP address (see Lessons 2 and 6 for details on using Ping to determine network problems). If you do not get a response, you need to correct the client or the network.	Check the configuration of the WINS server and the TCP/IP settings.
Multiple secondary WINS servers configured on a computer	If there are many secondary servers and a name resolution entry is not available on the primary WINS server, the WINS service needs to check the secondary servers for name resolution. Therefore, a failed query error message will be delayed while the secondary servers are checked.	It is recommend that you do not configure a large number of secondary WINS servers. Generally, a primary server and one secondary server on each subnet is sufficient.

Table 7-3   Server-related problems

Cause	Description	Solution
WINS database problems	Corruption of the WINS database caused by improper shutdown of your computer can cause server-related problems. You can identify such problems from the Event Log.	In order to view the problems in the Event Log, you need to enable detailed event logging. If necessary, you can restore the WINS database from a backup copy.
Static mapping problems	If you upgraded a non-WINS client to a WINS client, the static mapping for the client is not upgraded automatically. This can cause name resolution problems.	Set up the WINS server to update static mapping information dynamically.
Improper functioning of the services of Windows Server 2003	If your Windows Server 2003 computer has inadequate memory, certain services, such as the WINS service, might not start during the boot process.	In such a situation, you can check the Services applet and the WINS console to determine whether the WINS service has started.
Network utilization	If your WINS server is located on a network segment that sees a large amount of network traffic, queries to your server may time out and name resolution will fail.	Run a protocol analyzer, such as Network Monitor, to assess the percentage of network utilization.

Summary

- A WINS server is a NetBIOS Name Server (NBNS), which is used to resolve NetBIOS names to IP addresses.
- The process of resolving NetBIOS names using WINS involves a client sending a request for NetBIOS name resolution directly to the WINS server, and the WINS server sending the IP address of the requested NetBIOS name back to the client. The following processes are involved in the dynamic registration of a WINS client and the implementation of WINS server NetBIOS name resolution:
    - Name registration request.
    - Positive name registration response.
    - Name refresh request.
    - Name release message.
    - Name query request.
    - Name response message.
- To support NetBIOS name resolution on your network, you need to install a WINS server using either the Windows Components Wizard or the Manage Your Server window.
- After installing a WINS server, client computers must be configured to use a WINS server to register their NetBIOS names and query for NetBIOS name-to-IP address name resolutions. A WINS proxy agent can be used to help non-WINS clients with name resolution for resources on the network.
- If certain clients are unable to register their IP addresses with the WINS server dynamically, you can manually add static mappings for these clients to the WINS database. There are a variety of static WINS mapping types: Unique, Group, Domain name, Internet group, and Multihomed.
- To enable name resolution interoperability between previous Microsoft operating systems and Windows Server 2003, you can configure the Windows Server 2003 DNS server to query a WINS server for names of computers that cannot dynamically register with the Windows Server 2003 DNS service.
- After installing the WINS server and configuring WINS clients to use a WINS server for NetBIOS name resolution, you need to administer the WINS service to ensure optimum performance. You can perform the following administrative tasks on the WINS service:
    - Compacting a WINS database.
    - Checking for consistency of entries in a WINS database.
    - Backing up and restoring a WINS database.
    - Backing up WINS Registry settings.

- To ensure effective administration of the WINS service, you need to monitor its performance. Windows Server 2003 provides tools for viewing a variety of statistical information about the WINS server; also provided are tools to easily search and view specific records in the WINS database.
- To ensure fault tolerance and efficient NetBIOS name resolution, you need to deploy multiple WINS servers. To maintain consistency among multiple WINS servers on a network, you need to replicate the WINS databases. To replicate database entries, you configure each WINS server as a push, pull, or push/pull partner with another WINS server.
    - A push partner is a WINS server that sends replication data to its partner after a specific number of changes.
    - A pull partner is a WINS server that requests to receive changes from its partner after a specific period of time has elapsed.
- While implementing the WINS service, you might encounter problems that require troubleshooting. The first step is to identify whether the problem occurred due to an error on the WINS client, on the WINS server, or on the network itself. Client-related problems may occur for the following reasons:
    - Incorrect WINS server IP address or configuration of the WINS DHCP scope option.
    - Interruption in connectivity between a WINS client and server.
    - Multiple secondary WINS servers are installed on the network, leading to increased network traffic and delayed failed query responses.
    - NetBIOS is disabled.
- Server-related problems may occur for the following reasons:
    - Corruption of the WINS database, possibly caused by improper shutdown.
    - Incorrect static mapping entries.
    - Improper functioning of the WINS services.
    - Over-utilization of network bandwidth.

Key Terms

Group static mapping entry
Name query request
Name refresh request
Name registration request
Name release message
Name response message
Offline compaction
Online compaction

Positive name registration response
Pull partner
Push partner
Static mapping entry
Unique static mapping entry
Windows Internet Naming Service
  (WINS)
WINS client

WINS database
WINS proxy agent
WINS replication
WINS server

Test Yourself

1. Which of the following messages is sent by a WINS client to create a NetBIOS name-to-IP address mapping entry on a WINS server?
a. Name registration response
b. Name refresh request
c. Name query request
d. Name registration request

2. To configure a WINS client running Windows XP Professional to access a WINS server for name resolution, you use the:
a. Windows Components Wizard
b. Advanced TCP/IP Settings dialog box
c. Services applet
d. WINS console

3. In order to create a NetBIOS name-to-IP address mapping for a client that does not register itself dynamically with the WINS server, you need to:
a. Create a static mapping entry.
b. Configure a proxy agent.
c. Configure a DNS server to perform WINS lookups.
d. Use the Registry Editor.

4. Which of the following static mapping types enables you to register a name for a computer that has more than one IP address?
a. Unique
b. Multihomed
c. Group
d. Domain name

5. Which of the following statements is true about interoperability between DNS and WINS?
a. Windows Server 2003 DNS servers can be configured to query WINS server databases for the NetBIOS names of the down-level clients that have registered with a WINS server.
b. Windows Server 2003 DNS clients can query a WINS server directly to access information from a WINS database.

c. To query a WINS server, a DNS server uses the entire FQDN being resolved.
d. To configure a DNS server to perform WINS lookups, you need to use the WINS console.

6. You notice that the size of your WINS database is growing. To reduce the size of the database, you need to:
a. Perform online compaction.
b. Set pull replication options.
c. Perform offline compaction.
d. Set push replication options.

7. To compact a WINS database offline, you use the:
a. WINS console
b. Services applet
c. Ipconfig /all command
d. Jetpack utility

8. Which of the following dialog boxes enables you to view the records registered by a WINS server?
a. WINS Server Statistics
b. Display Records
c. Properties
d. New Replication Partner

9. A WINS client named AQUARIUS is registered with a WINS server whose IP address is 192.168.1.2. AQUARIUS needs to access an application on another WINS client, LIBRA, which is registered with another WINS server whose IP address is 192.168.3.2. To enable NetBIOS name resolution of LIBRA by AQUARIUS, you need to:
a. Configure a WINS proxy agent.
b. Replicate the databases of the two WINS servers with each other.
c. Create a static mapping entry for the client registered on the WINS server 192.168.3.2.
d. Configure a DNS server on the client with the IP address 192.168.3.0 to perform WINS lookups on the WINS server with the address 192.168.1.2.

... of the following statements about replication in
... INS service is true?
   a. ... ou need to perform manual replication with all of
      ...he WINS servers on a network.
   b. You need to configure a replication partner as both a
      push and pull partner.
   c. You can configure a pull replication partner to send
      database information to replication partners.
   d. You can configure the WINS service to start
      replication at system startup.

11. Interruption in connectivity occurs between a WINS
    client and its configured WINS server. To begin
    troubleshooting the problem, you should:

   a. Ping the IP address of the WINS server from the
      client.
   b. Enable NetBIOS on the client.
   c. Check the number of secondary WINS servers for the
      client.
   d. Check the IP address of the WINS server.

12. Logging of detailed WINS events to the Windows event
    log should only be enabled when you are:
   a. Registering a WINS client.
   b. Replicating the WINS database.
   c. Troubleshooting.
   d. Installing the WINS service.

Projects: On Your Own

1. Configure a Windows XP Professional WINS client to
   use a WINS server with the IP address 192.168.0.2.
   a. Log on to the client as an **Administrator**.
   b. Open the **Advanced TCP/IP Settings** dialog box.
   c. Select the **WINS** tab.
   d. Configure the WINS server address **192.168.0.2** for
      the client.
2. Configure a DNS server to perform WINS lookups on a
   WINS server. Do not replicate WINS-specific resource
   record data to other DNS servers during zone transfers.
   a. Open the **DNS** console on the WINS server.
   b. Open the **Properties** dialog box for the zone for
      which you want to configure WINS lookups.
   c. Go to the **WINS** tab.
   d. Enable WINS forward lookups on a WINS server
      available on the network.

   e. Set options to avoid replicating WINS-specific
      resource record data to other DNS servers during
      zone transfers.
3. Check a WINS database for consistency.
   a. Open the **WINS** console.
   b. Execute the **Verify Database Consistency** command
      on the selected WINS server.
   c. Confirm that you want to run the consistency check.
4. Configure a replication partner for a WINS server.
   a. From the WINS console, open the **New Replication
      Partner** dialog box.
   b. Enter the **IP address** of the replication partner.
   c. Configure the replication partner as a **push** partner.
   d. Set the replication interval to **45** minutes.

Problem Solving Scenarios

1. You are a Network Administrator in charge of a
   network that includes a group of Windows NT 4.0
   and Windows 95 systems in the domain. Currently,
   all of them are set up to perform name resolution via
   the DNS service installed on a Windows Server 2003
   computer. A few systems, however, are having name
   resolution problems. Generally speaking, all of the
   clients running older versions of Windows are
   experiencing lengthy delays when it comes to name
   resolution. Prepare a document describing the steps
   necessary to eliminate this problem permanently.

2. You are trying to reduce the broadcast traffic in your
   existing network. You set up a WINS infrastructure to

address this problem, but there has been little
improvement. Your network is currently split into
three segments via a Cisco router that has been
configured to stop all broadcast-based messages. The
last segment in your network contains a Windows NT
4.0 computer that holds a critical shared directory.
Your network needs frequent access to this directory,
but due to name resolution problems, clients usually
connect to it using the IP address of the NT 4.0
computer. This, however, is not only inefficient, but
also conflicts with company security policies.
Prepare a document describing the actions you will
take to resolve the issue.

8

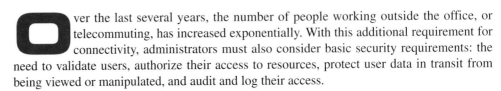

Implementing Remote Access

O ver the last several years, the number of people working outside the office, or telecommuting, has increased exponentially. With this additional requirement for connectivity, administrators must also consider basic security requirements: the need to validate users, authorize their access to resources, protect user data in transit from being viewed or manipulated, and audit and log their access.

As you saw in Lesson 3, Windows Server 2003 supports dial-up and VPN access methods for remote users through the implementation of Routing and Remote Access Service (RRAS). These methods utilize authentication protocols that are negotiated during the connection process. To be authenticated, the user provides a set of credentials that may be sent in either plain text or encrypted depending upon the authentication protocol used.

After a remote user has completed the authentication process, a well-designed remote access solution must determine if the actual connection is allowed. This is known as authorizing the connection. Windows Server 2003 uses information in the user account's dial-in properties as well as remote access policy settings to determine if the connection will be allowed or denied. This topic will be introduced in this lesson and explored in depth in Lesson 9.

In addition to authenticating and authorizing remote users, protecting data that is sent between the user and the company's private network is also critical. This data can include anything from e-mail correspondence to documents containing critical corporate strategies. Data protection can be accomplished by encrypting data using virtual private network protocols. Point-to-Point Tunneling Protocol (PPTP) with Microsoft's Point-to-Point Encryption (MPPE) protocol or Layer 2 Tunneling Protocol (L2TP), which incorporates Internet Protocol Security (IPSec), can be used to create secure tunnels over a public network such as the Internet. Data sent through these tunnels is encrypted.

When the number of remote access servers increases, you must consider how to incorporate remote access policies distributed across multiple servers. If policies on each remote access server are managed separately, it is conceivable that a user could be denied when connecting to one server, yet allowed access when connecting to another. Microsoft provides Internet Authentication Service (IAS) as a solution for centralizing your remote access policies as well as providing logging and accounting services for your enterprise.

Goals

In this lesson, you will learn about risks to network security when implementing remote access. You will become familiar with the authentication/encryption protocols used by Windows Server 2003 when implementing dial-up and VPN client access methods. You will also learn how remote access policies and a user account's dial-in properties can be used to control the authorization process.

Lesson 8 Implementing Remote Access	
Skill	**Exam 70-291 Objective**
1. Identifying Common Remote Access Security Risks	Configure Routing and Remote Access user authentication.
2. Implementing Authentication Methods	Configure Routing and Remote Access user authentication. Manage remote access.
3. Implementing Authentication Protocols	Configure Routing and Remote Access user authentication. Manage remote access. Configure remote access authentication protocols.
4. Configuring Encryption Protocols	Configure Routing and Remote Access user authentication. Manage remote access. Manage devices and ports. Implement secure access between private networks. Diagnose and resolve issues related to remote access VPNs. Troubleshoot Routing and Remote Access routing. Troubleshoot router-to-router VPNs.
5. Managing Devices and Ports	Configure Routing and Remote Access user authentication. Manage remote access. Manage devices and ports.
6. Introducing Remote Access Policies	Configure Routing and Remote Access user authentication. Manage remote access. Configure Routing and Remote Access policies to permit or deny access.

Requirements

To complete this lesson, you will need administrative rights on a Windows Server 2003 computer configured as a remote access server.

skill 1

Identifying Common Remote Access Security Risks

exam objective

Configure Routing and Remote Access user authentication.

overview

Whether you implement dial-up or virtual private networks as your remote access solution, you must consider the risks introduced into your network. The risks that must be addressed fall into three main categories (**Figure 8-1**):

◆ Authentication of remote users.
◆ Authorization of remote users.
◆ Protection of data while in transit between the remote user and the remote access server.

Authentication of Remote Users: **Authentication** is the process of verifying the credentials used during the connection attempt. With so many remote users connecting into the network, it is physically impossible to verify each one. If a weak authentication method is used, malicious hackers can obtain user names and passwords to penetrate the corporate network.

Windows Server 2003 uses authentication protocols to send a user's credentials safely to the remote access server when a connection is attempted. There are several protocols from which to choose. When selecting protocols for authentication, consider using the Microsoft Challenge Handshake Authentication Protocol (MS-CHAP) version 2 or Extensible Authentication Protocol (EAP) to provide the strongest security.

Authorization of Remote Users: After a user has been authenticated, they must still be authorized. **Authorization** is the process of verifying that the connection attempt is allowed. This is accomplished by checking the user account's dial-in properties as well as matching the connection to a remote access policy. Remote access policies can be used to restrict access to certain users, groups, times, or specific client configurations.

Routing and Remote Access also offers additional security by providing caller ID and call-back features. The caller ID specifies a number the remote user must call in from. If the user does not call in from that number, the connection is refused. The callback feature can also be used to secure the remote connection by disconnecting the user and then calling him or her back at a predefined number. This occurs after the authentication and authorization of the connection attempt has been made.

Protection of Data While In Transit: Information that is transmitted between the corporate network and a remote user may contain sensitive data. If a malicious hacker captures the information in transit by using a "sniffer program," the hacker could possibly view confidential information, modify it, or even, in some cases, corrupt the information.

Where data confidentiality is critical, the remote access server can be configured to require encryption. Once configured, it will deny any attempts to connect that are not encrypted. If your remote solution utilizes dial-up connections, the data can be encrypted between the remote access client and server by using the **Microsoft Point-to-Point Encryption (MPPE)** protocol. If you implement a virtual private network, there are two protocols available for encryption depending upon the tunneling protocol used: MPPE is used with the Point-to-Point Tunneling Protocol and **Internet Protocol Security (IPSec)** is used with Layer Two Tunneling Protocol (L2TP).

tip

Some telephone exchanges do not support caller ID. In those cases, consider using the callback feature to improve security.

Figure 8-1 Protecting remote access connections

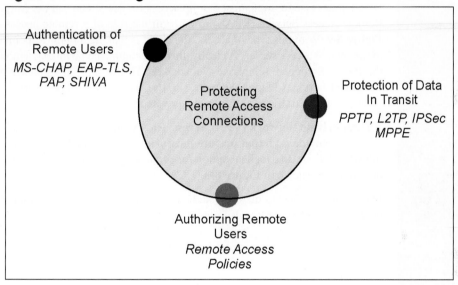

skill 2

Implementing Authentication Methods

exam objective

Configure Routing and Remote Access user authentication. Manage remote access.

overview

Remote clients connect to the private network via a **network access server**. This server can be configured as a router to perform the role of a gateway that provides users with access to their company's private network. It can also be configured to only provide users with access to resources on the network access server itself. There are two access methods that can be used to connect remote users.

Dial-Up Access: To implement dial-up access for users, you can use Microsoft's Routing and Remote Access Service (RRAS) to perform the role of a remote access server as shown in **Figure 8-2**. With this type of access, the client is making a point-to-point connection directly to the remote access server. Typically, this is accomplished by using a modem to connect over the Public Switched Telephone Network (PSTN) or an ISDN adapter to connect over the Integrated Services Digital Network (ISDN). The remote access server then functions as a gateway to pass traffic to and from the private network.

Virtual Private Network (VPN) Access: RRAS can also be configured to function as a VPN server to provide a **virtual private network (VPN) tunnel** for protection of data while in transit. VPNs are an excellent option for connecting remote users, branch offices, and vendors or partners as shown in **Figure 8-3**.

In each of these access methods, authentication protocols can be implemented to validate the user and encryption protocols to protect data while in transit.

Figure 8-2 Dial-up access

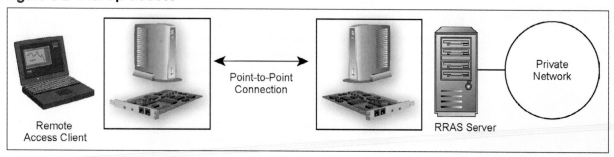

Figure 8-3 Virtual Private Network (VPN) access

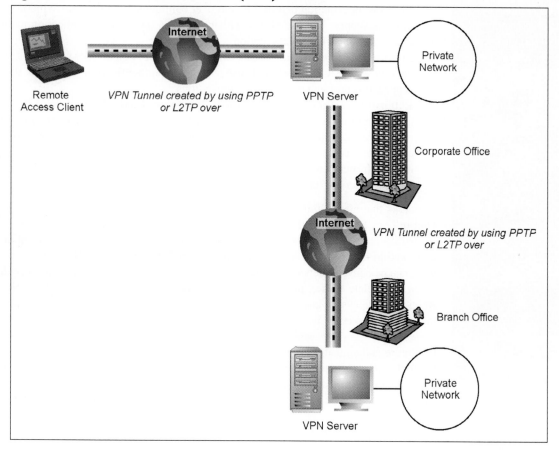

skill 3

Implementing Authentication Protocols

exam objective

Configure Routing and Remote Access user authentication. Manage remote access. Configure remote access authentication protocols.

overview

Both dial-up and Virtual Private Network (VPN) access methods take advantage of authentication protocols to validate users who perform remote connections to your private network. When a user makes a connection attempt to the remote access server, an authentication protocol is used to send the user's credentials to the server. The server typically forwards them to a domain controller to validate the user. When implementing authentication protocols, select the most secure protocol that is supported by the remote access server and remote clients.

The following authentication protocols are used by Routing and Remote Access and must be configured on both the remote client and the remote access server:

- **Password Authentication Protocol (PAP):** When using this protocol, the user name and password are requested by the remote access server and are sent by the remote client in plain text. This should only be used if clients cannot support any other protocol.
- **Shiva Password Authentication Protocol (SPAP):** Used with SHIVA remote access products. SPAP does not support encryption of the connection. SPAP authentication information is hashed, making it encrypted.
- **Microsoft Challenge Handshake Authentication Protocol (MS-CHAP) v1:** Encrypts password information before it is sent over communication link. All Windows operating systems support MS-CHAP v1, which utilizes a one-way authentication method. MS-CHAP v1 supports data encryption.
- **Microsoft Challenge Handshake Authentication Protocol (MS-CHAP) v2:** Enhanced version of MS-CHAP v1 that utilizes mutual authentication. Windows 95 does not support this protocol over dial-up connections.
- **Extensible Authentication Protocol-Transport Layer Security (EAP-TLS):** This authentication scheme is based on EAP, which provides an open architecture to incorporate additional authentication schemes as they are developed. EAP-TLS is a certificate-based authentication scheme that uses mutual authentication. It is commonly used with smart-card implementations. This authentication protocol is only supported by Windows Server 2003, Windows XP, and Windows 2000.

Networks that have multiple remote access servers will often use a Remote Authentication Dial-in User Service (RADIUS) server to provide centralized authentication. For example, many ISPs use a RADIUS server so that users from geographically disparate locations will all be routed to the RADIUS server for authentication. Having a RADIUS server on your network can be convenient because when you change a password, it is immediately updated, and when you delete a user, the user will be immediately locked out from the entire system. Replication delays, or any other holdups, are not a factor because the new authentication data takes effect immediately.

tip

Authentication itself does not guarantee you will be connected. You must also be authorized via your dial-up user properties and/or remote access policies as well.

tip

In order for Windows 9x, Me, and NT4 to support MS-CHAP v2, they will need the latest Dial-Up Networking upgrade.

how to

Configure authentication protocol settings on a Windows Server 2003 remote access server. (Note that Routing and Remote Access must be enabled and configured to perform this Skill. RRAS was configured for LAN and demand-dial routing in Lesson 3, Skill 6.)

1. Open the **Routing and Remote Access** console, right-click the server name, and click **Properties**.
2. Click the **Security** tab, and then click [Authentication Methods...].
3. Select the check boxes for the authentication methods you want to use **(Figure 8-4)**.

Configure authentication protocol settings on a Windows XP remote access client.

1. Right-click the dial-up connection and click **Properties**.
2. Click the **Security** tab and then the **Advanced (custom settings)** option button.
3. Click [Settings...] **(Figure 8-5)**. The **Advanced Security Settings** dialog box opens. From here you can configure or modify the existing authentication protocol settings.

Figure 9-4 Selecting the authentication protocols for a server

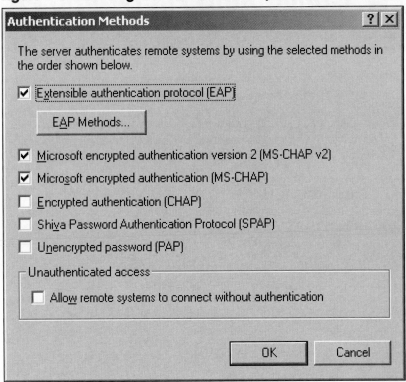

Figure 9-5 Selecting the authentication protocols for a client

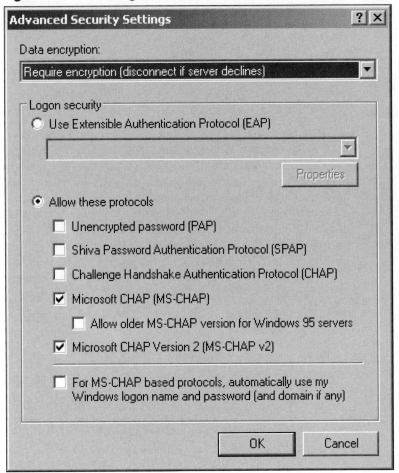

skill 4

Configuring Encryption Protocols

Configure Routing and Remote Access user authentication. Manage remote access. Manage devices and ports. Implement secure access between private networks. Diagnose and resolve issues related to remote access VPNs. Troubleshoot Routing and Remote Access routing. Troubleshoot router-to-router VPNs.

overview

tip

By default, RRAS is configured with 5 PPTP and 5 L2TP ports. Each port enables a single remote connection.

tip

When using PPTP, you can only encrypt data if you use MS-CHAP (v1 or v2) and EAP-TLS as the authentication protocol. L2TP is not dependent upon a specific authentication protocol.

tip

If both the VPN client and VPN server are running Windows Server 2003, a pre-shared key can be used in place of certificates, but it is not considered a very secure option.

Encryption should always be used when there is any chance that data transmitted may be accessible to unauthorized users. Windows Server 2003 provides data confidentiality by using encryption protocols.

When dial-up connections are used, the Routing and Remote Access Service (RRAS) implements the Microsoft Point-to-Point Encryption (MPPE) protocol to protect the data. For virtual private network (VPN) connections, RRAS uses Point-to-Point Tunneling Protocol (PPTP) with MPPE or Layer 2 Tunneling Protocol (L2TP) with Internet Protocol Security (IPSec) to protect the data.

Point-to-Point Tunneling Protocol (PPTP): PPTP uses the Microsoft Point-to-Point Encryption protocol to protect data in transit. Although this protocol is not considered as secure as an implementation of L2TP/IPSec, it can be a reasonably secure option if you implement it with a strong authentication protocol such as MS-CHAP v2. PPTP does not require the use of digital certificates so a Public Key Infrastructure (PKI) is not required.

Although PPTP ensures that the data in the packet cannot be viewed, it does not actually protect the packet against modification. This basically means that PPTP provides *confidentiality* but cannot ensure the *integrity* of the data itself. PPTP also does not implement any mechanisms that ensure the data was actually sent by an authorized person.

PPTP works by encapsulating **Point-to-Point Protocol (PPP)** packets in Internet Protocol (IP), Internetwork Packet Exchange (IPX), or NetBEUI packets to send them over the Internet. MPPE, as discussed earlier, encrypts the PPP frame before it is encapsulated (**Figure 8-6**).

Layer 2 Tunneling Protocol (L2TP)/IPSec: Unlike PPTP, which supports authentication of the user only, L2TP/IPSec requires that the *computers* involved mutually authenticate themselves to each other. The computer portion of the authentication process is performed *before* the user is actually authenticated.

L2TP supports the use of digital certificates, pre-shared keys, or Kerberos for mutual authentication purposes. Digital certificates provide a more secure option because they are stored in a format that cannot be modified, and are also issued by a Certification Authority (CA) that you trust. Unlike certificates, **pre-shared keys** are essentially large passwords, and are not considered a very secure option. Consider using pre-shared keys if you want to set up a test network that uses L2TP/IPSec. This will eliminate the need to set up a Public Key Infrastructure. Kerberos is the native authentication protocol in Windows Server 2003, and it provides perhaps the easiest method of securing VPN connections in a domain environment. Kerberos provides for mutual authentication, anti-replay, and non repudiation, just like certificates. However, Kerberos can only be used when both computers involved in the L2TP tunnel are members of the same forest. L2TP uses Internet Protocol Security (IPSec) to encrypt the PPP packets.

Figure 8-6 PPTP encapsulation process

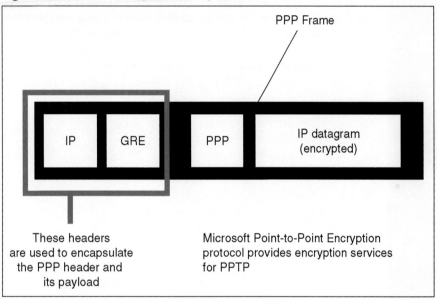

skill 4

Configuring Encryption Protocols
(cont'd)

exam objective

Configure Routing and Remote Access user authentication. Manage remote access. Manage devices and ports. Implement secure access between private networks. Diagnose and resolve issues related to remote access VPNs. Troubleshoot Routing and Remote Access routing. Troubleshoot router-to-router VPNs.

overview

tip

Since IPSec encryption is very processor intensive, consider offloading the workload from the processor to an IPSec-enabled network adapter.

L2TP/IPSec is supported natively by Windows 2000, Windows XP, and Windows Server 2003. If you are running previous versions such as Windows 9x, Windows Me, or Windows NT Workstation 4.0, there is a L2TP/IPSec VPN client (Mls2tp.exe) that is available from Microsoft's Web site.

L2TP/IPSec connections provide data confidentiality, and data integrity as well as proof that an authorized individual sent the message. This makes L2TP/IPSec a more secure choice when compared to PPTP. **Figure 8-7** provides an example of an L2TP/IPSec packet.

Both Microsoft Point-to-Point Encryption (MPPE) and IPSec can be configured by selecting the Encryption tab in the profile settings for the appropriate remote access policy **(Figure 8-8)**. If you are using Windows Server 2003, Windows XP, or Windows 2000 with the high encryption pack, consider using the **Strongest encryption** setting which uses 128-bit encryption keys; otherwise, adjust the setting to support older operating systems.

Figure 8-7 L2TP/IPSec packet encapsulation

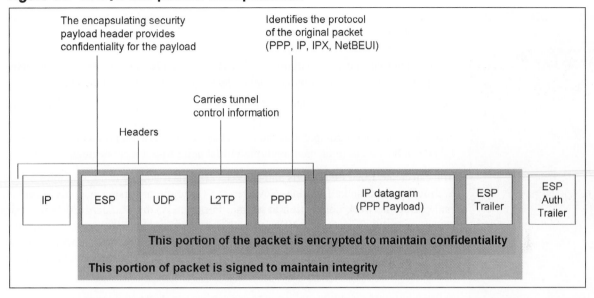

Figure 8-8 Configuring encryption settings on a remote access policy

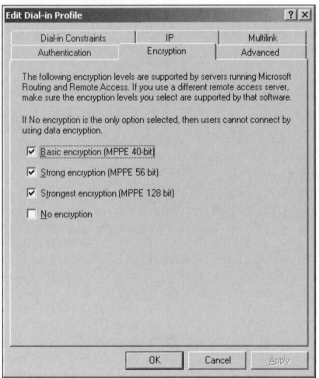

skill 5

Managing Devices and Ports

exam objective

Configure Routing and Remote Access user authentication. Manage remote access. Manage devices and ports.

overview

Ports and devices must be configured on the Routing and Remote Access Service server. Each port provides a communication channel to the server for a single remote user.

Devices come in two forms: physical or virtual. Physical devices such as a modem provide a single communication port. A **modem pool** can be used to increase the number of ports available for incoming/outgoing connections. Virtual private network protocols such as PPTP and L2TP can be used to implement multiple virtual point-to-point connections to the server.

You can create 1,000 PPTP ports and 1,000 LT2P ports if you are using Windows Server 2003 Web Edition or Standard Edition. However, the Web Edition version can only accept one virtual private network connection at a time. Fortunately, the Standard Edition version can accept up to 1,000 concurrent VPN connections. If more than 1,000 remote users attempt to connect at one time, their connections will be blocked until the total number of connections drops below 1,000. The Windows Server 2003 Enterprise and Datacenter versions can support an unlimited number of concurrent connections.

When configuring Routing and Remote Access Service, you should only configure the appropriate number of devices and ports that are necessary to support your remote access solution. If you are not using a specific device, disable it to increase the security on the remote access server. If your security policy only allows 20 users to connect to the corporate network through the remote access server, modify the number of ports to reflect the actual usage requirements instead of leaving multiple ports open by default.

how to

Configure Port properties on a Windows Server 2003 Routing and Remote Access Service server.

1. Click **Start**, point to **Administrative Tools**, and then click **Routing and Remote Access**.
2. In the left pane of the Routing and Remote Access console, right-click **Ports** and click **Properties** on the menu.
3. Select the appropriate device, for instance, WAN Miniport (L2TP) and click **Configure...**.

more

Within the **Configure Device** dialog box, you can configure the port for inbound only, inbound and outbound, or demand-dial routing connections (outbound only), as well as configure the appropriate number of ports as determined by your security policy for remote access connections (**Figures 8-9 and 8-10**).

The **Phone number for this device** option represents the phone number for the remote access server when a modem is used. The phone number is also used as the Called Station ID attribute in a remote access policy. It is also used when Bandwidth Allocation Protocol (BAP) connections are used. When a BAP-enabled client requests an additional connection, this number is returned to the client and is used to initiate a second connection. This technique provides additional bandwidth when it is needed by combining two or more circuits into a single circuit with a much higher level of data throughput.

Figure 8-9 WAN Miniport (PPTP) device cannot be set to 0 ports

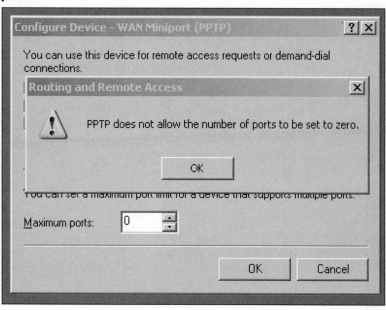

Figure 8-10 Disabling the WAN Miniport (PPTP) device

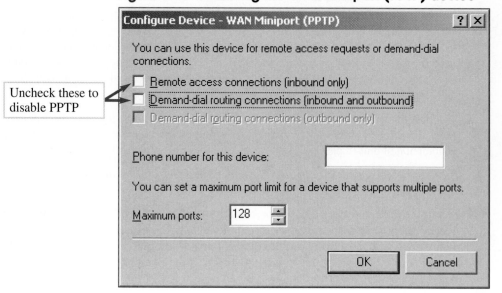

skill 6

Introducing Remote Access Policies

exam objective

Configure Routing and Remote Access user authentication. Manage remote access. Configure Routing and Remote Access policies to permit or deny access.

overview

tip

A default installation of Windows Server 2003 results in the domain being installed at the Windows 2000 mixed mode. The Control access through Remote Access Policy option is only available if you convert it to Windows 2000 native mode or Windows Server 2003 mode.

At the beginning of this lesson, we discussed the concept of authorization. After a remote user has provided his credentials and passed the authentication process, he still must be authorized to complete the connection attempt. Authorization involves checking the user account's dial-in properties as well as the first remote access policy that matches the incoming connection.

A user account's dial-in remote access permission is configured by accessing the Dial-in tab in the **User Account Properties** dialog box. This can be accessed via the Active Directory Users and Computers console if the user has a domain account or via the Local Users and Groups console if the user account is stored on a standalone server. As **Figure 8-11** shows, there are three possible remote access permissions: Allow access, Deny access, and Control access through Remote Access Policy.

A remote access policy consists of conditions, permissions, and profile settings (**Figure 8-12**).

Remote access policy conditions are composed of attributes that are compared against the incoming connection attempts. In order for the policy to apply, all conditions set in the policy must match. If a policy condition sets the Day-And-Time-Restrictions attribute to allow access between 8:00 AM and 5:00 PM Monday–Friday, and also sets the Windows-Groups attribute to include the Remote User global security group, then in order for the policy to be applied, both conditions must match the connection. Otherwise, the policy is ignored and the connection is checked against the next policy in the list.

tip

Since remote access policies are tried in the order they are listed, move policies that are more specific to the top of the list.

Once an incoming connection matches all conditions specified in the remote access policy, permissions are checked. The permissions set in the policy itself will be processed if the dial-in property setting for the user's account is set to **Control access through Remote Access Policy**. Otherwise, these permissions set in the policy itself are ignored.

The profile settings can be accessed by clicking the **Edit Profile** button, which is found on the Settings tab of the Properties dialog box for the policy. Profile settings are applied after a connection is authorized and can be used to control how long a user's connection can remain idle before it is disconnected, maximum connection time before disconnect, authentication methods, encryption levels, input/output filters to control traffic received and sent, as well as how multi-link connections are handled (**Figure 8-13**).

Now that you have a better idea of the components that make up a remote access policy, let's take a closer look at how they work together to authorize an incoming connection based on a combination of dial-in permissions, remote access permissions, and profile settings.

tip

A user's dial-in remote access permission is configured by accessing the Dial-in tab in the user account's Properties dialog box as shown in Figure 8-11.

The following examples assume the incoming connection matches all conditions of a remote access policy that has been configured on the remote access server.

Example #1: If the user's Dial-in permission is set to **Control access through Remote Access Policy**, then the permission set on the matching remote access policy is applied. If the permission setting is **Grant remote access permission**, the profile settings will also be checked and applied to the incoming connection. If the permission setting is **Deny remote access permission**, the profile settings are not processed and the connection is denied.

Example #2: If the user's Dial-in permission is set to **Allow access**, then the permission set on the matching remote access policy is ignored. The profile settings will be checked and applied to the incoming connection.

Figure 8-11 Dial-In tab in User Properties dialog box

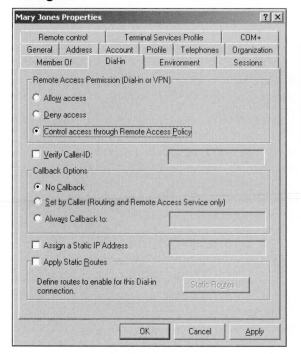

Figure 8-12 Remote access policy components

Deny/grant remote access permissions, and edit profile

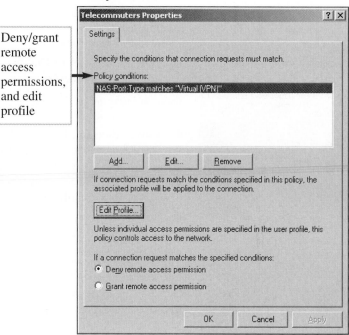

Figure 8-13 Profile settings

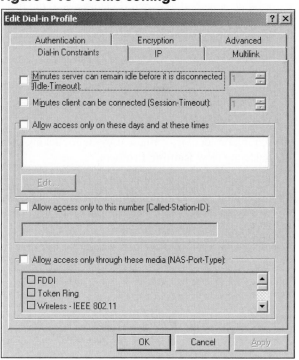

skill 6

Introducing Remote Access Policies
(cont'd)

exam objective

Configure Routing and Remote Access user authentication. Manage remote access. Configure Routing and Remote Access policies to permit or deny access.

overview

Example #3: If the user's Dial-in permission is set to **Deny access**, then the permission set on the matching remote access policy is ignored. The profile settings will also be ignored.

There are two default remote access policies when you enable and configure Routing and Remote Access Service on a demand-dial router or when you install IAS:

◆ **Connections to Microsoft Routing and Remote Access server**. This is the first policy listed and configured to match every incoming connection. If a RADIUS server reads the policy, non-Microsoft vendors may allow network access.

◆ **Connections to other access servers**. This policy is configured to match all incoming connections regardless of the type of network access server.

Be careful about deleting remote access policies. If there are no policies present, the connection will be refused even if the user's Dial-in permission is set to **Allow access**.

After setting up the user account's dial-in properties and configuring remote access policies, the user still may not be able to access resources on the internal network. In order for remote users to gain access to resources behind the remote access server, the server must be configured as a router. This is accomplished on the General tab of the remote access server properties. Click the **Router** option and select either **Local area network (LAN) routing only** or **LAN and demand-dial routing (Figure 8-14)**. Your choice depends upon how your internal routing structure is configured. If the system is not configured as a router, remote users are limited to connecting to the remote access server only.

In addition, you must configure the following on the IP tab of the remote access server Properties dialog box to provide access to the internal network after configuring the computer to perform routing functions:

◆ Provide a method to assign IP addresses to the incoming clients that places them on the same logical network as the internal network **(Figure 8-15)**.

◆ Enable IP routing on the IP tab to allow the server to forward packets between its interfaces.

◆ Enable broadcast name resolution for clients that want to use My Network Places to browse if a WINS server is not configured for the client.

◆ Add the appropriate routing protocol to exchange route information with neighboring routers if necessary.

The routing protocol is configured by right-clicking the General node, under IP Routing and then selecting **New Routing Protocol**.

If you choose to use a remote DHCP server to assign IP addresses to RRAS clients, be aware that, by default, clients will only receive an IP address and subnet mask. In other words, the clients will not receive any DHCP options, and therefore, may not be able to access resources properly. In order to give the RRAS clients DHCP options, you must also configure and enable the DHCP relay agent protocol on the RRAS server.

Figure 8-14 Configuring a RRAS server as a router

Router option selected →

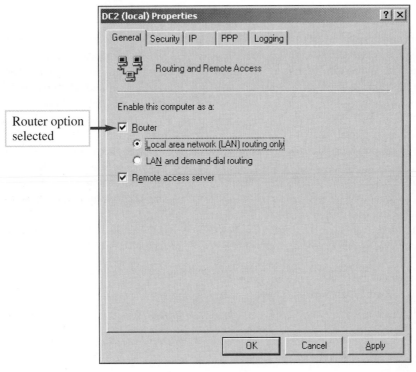

Figure 8-15 IP tab

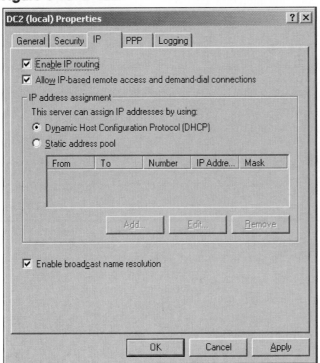

Summary

◆ There are two remote access methods: Dial-Up and Virtual Private Networks (VPNs).

◆ In each of these access methods, authentication protocols can be implemented to validate the user and encryption protocols to protect data while in transit.

◆ When a user makes a connection attempt to the remote access server, an authentication protocol is used to send her credentials to the server.

◆ RRAS supports PAP, SPAP, MS-CHAP v1 and v2, and EAP-TLS authentication protocols.

◆ Windows Server 2003 provides data confidentiality by using encryption protocols such as Microsoft Point-to-Point Encryption (MPPE) and Internet Protocol Security (IPSec).

◆ When using the Point-to-Point Tunneling Protocol (PPTP), MPPE is used to encrypt the data, Layer Two Tunneling Protocol (L2TP) utilizes the services of IPSec for encryption.

◆ L2TP/IPSec requires the use of pre-shared keys or digital certificates for mutual authentication. Digital certificates provide a more secure option.

◆ Ports provide a communication channel to the server. Each supports a single remote user.

◆ Windows Server 2003, Web Edition only supports one VPN connection at a time, whereas Windows 2003 Server Standard Edition allows up to 1,000 concurrent connections to the server. The Windows Server 2003, Enterprise and Datacenter versions can support an unlimited number of concurrent connections.

◆ A remote access policy consists of conditions, permissions, and profile settings. If an incoming connection matches all conditions of the policy, the permission settings on the policy will be checked. These permissions settings will only apply if the user account's dial-in property is set to Control access through Remote Access Policy.

◆ If there are no policies present, the connection will be refused. You must leave the default remote access policies in place.

Key Terms

Authentication

Authorization

Extensible Authentication Protocol-Transport Layer Security (EAP-TLS)

Internet Protocol Security (IPSec)

Layer Two Tunneling Protocol (L2TP)

Microsoft Challenge Handshake Authentication Protocol (MS-CHAP) v1

Microsoft Challenge Handshake Authentication Protocol (MS-CHAP) v2

Microsoft Point-to-Point Encryption (MPPE)

Modem Pool

Network access server

Password Authentication Protocol (PAP)

Point-to-Point Protocol (PPP)

Point-to-Point Tunneling Protocol (PPTP)

Pre-shared Key

Shiva Password Authentication Protocol (SPAP)

Virtual private network (VPN) tunnel

Test Yourself

1. Which encryption protocol is used to encrypt information when using PPTP?
   a. PPP
   b. IPSec
   c. MPPE
   d. L2TP
   e. TCP/IP

2. Which authentication protocol will pass a user's name and password in plain text?
   a. MSCHAP-v2
   b. MSCHAP-v2
   c. EAP-TLS
   d. PAP

3. When using PPTP, you can only encrypt data if you use which authentication protocols? (Choose all that apply.)
   a. MS-CHAP v1
   b. MS-CHAP v2
   c. EAP-TLS
   d. PAP
   e. SPAP

4. Which virtual private network protocol requires the computers involved to mutually authenticate themselves?
   a. PPTP
   b. L2TP
   c. PPP
   d. TCP/IP

5. When implementing L2TP/IPSec in your virtual private network, which of the following statements are accurate? (Choose all that apply.)
   a. Pre-shared keys are more secure than certificates.
   b. Certificates are more secure then pre-shared keys.
   c. Pre-shared keys can be viewed on the local computer.
   d. Certificates require a CA that you trust.

6. Mary would like to disable PPTP on her VPN server. What two steps are required for her to accomplish this?
   a. Set the PPTP maximum port setting to 0 ports.
   b. Clear the Remote Access connections (inbound only) check box.
   c. Clear the Demand-dial routing connections (inbound and outbound) check box.
   d. You cannot disable PPTP on a VPN server. It must always be enabled.

7. Fred's dial-in property is set to Control access through Remote Access Policy, and the permission setting on the policy is Deny remote access permission. Which of the following are correct answers? (Choose all that apply.)
   a. The profile settings in the policy will be applied to Fred's connection.
   b. The permission settings on the policy will deny him access.
   c. The profile settings in the policy will not be ignored.
   d. The connection will be allowed.

8. James's dial-in properties are set to Allow access. Mary, the Network Administrator, has accidentally deleted all remote access policies on the only RRAS server in the company. Which of the following is true?
   a. James will still be able to connect because he is not affected by remote access policies anyway.
   b. James will not be able to connect.
   c. James could still connect but might be disconnected based on restrictions in the profile of an existing policy.
   d. None of the above are true.

Projects: On Your Own

The following projects require a Windows Server 2003 configured as a domain controller set at the Windows Server 2003 domain functional level and a Windows XP Professional computer. The server needs two network cards. One will function as the Internet interface and should be assigned 192.168.50.1/24. The other interface should be assigned 10.10.10.10/8 in its IP configuration. The network card that functions as the Internet interface must be connected to the Windows XP Professional computer using a hub or cross-over cable. The network interface on the Windows XP Professional computer should be assigned 192.168.50.2/24.

1. Set up a Remote Access VPN Server on a Windows Server 2003 computer.
   a. Open the **Routing and Remote Access** console
   b. In the console, locate the servername(local), right-click and select **Configure and Enable Routing and Remote Access**.
   c. Click **Next** at the **Welcome** screen and then select **Remote access (dial-up or VPN)** for the configuration. Click **Next**.
   d. Select **VPN** and click **Next**.
   e. For the VPN connection, select the network card that is connected to the Windows XP Professional computer and click **Next**. This will function as the Internet interface.

   f. For IP address assignment, select **From a specific range of addresses** and click **Next**.
   g. Click **New** to add a range of addresses. Enter the **Start IP address** as 10.10.10.20 and the **End IP address** as 10.10.10.30 and click **OK**, then **Next**.
   h. Select **No** in the prompt to configure a RADIUS server. Click **Finish** and then **OK** in the prompt for a DHCP relay agent.
   i. Access the **Administrator** account in the **Active Directory Users and Computers** console and make sure the Dial-in properties for the Administrator account is set to **Allow Access**. Click **OK**.

2. Set up a VPN client to connect to the VPN Server.
   a. Click **Start**, then **Settings**, then **Network Connections**.
   b. Select **File**, then **New Connection**.
   c. In the **Location Information** text box, enter your area code and click **OK**. Click **Cancel** in the **Phone and Modem** options. Click **Next** to continue configuring the connection.
   d. In the **Network Connection Type** dialog box, select **Connect to the network at my workplace**. Click **Next**.
   e. Select **Virtual Private Network connection** in the **Network Connection** dialog box. Click **Next**.

f. For the connection name, enter **MyVPNServer** and click **Next**.

g. In the **VPN Server Selection** dialog box, enter the IP address for the VPN server. This will be the Internet interface you set up on the VPN server earlier. It is **192.168.50.1**. Click **Next**.

h. For the **Connection Availability** setting, select **Anyone's use** and click **Next**. Click **Finish** to complete the wizard.

i. In the **Connect MyVPNServer** dialog box, enter **Administrator** and the password you used on the Windows Server 2003 computer for the Administrator account. Click **Connect**. You should now connect to the VPN server.

3. Once you have the VPN client and server set up, create a remote access policy that has the following parameters and place it at the top of the Remote Access Policies list:

Conditions: Windows-Groups matches YourDomain-Name\Domain Users

Permission: Grant remote access permission

Profile Setting: Minutes server can remain idle before it is disconnected (Idle-Timeout), 1 minute.

Use the examples in **Skill 6** to see how the combination of dial-in permissions, remote access permissions, and profile settings function.

Problem Solving Scenarios

1. You would like to control users' remote access by using remote access policies. When you view the account properties for one of the users, you notice that the Control access through group policy option is dimmed. Explain why this option is not available.

2. You have configured a remote access policy that allows users in the Sales group to connect between the hours of 8:00 AM–5:00 PM (Monday-Friday). Your company currently has three remote access servers that are used to handle incoming connections. Lately, you have discovered that users in the Sales group are connecting on Saturday and Sunday. What could be causing this problem and what should be done to address it?

3. William has set up 1,000 PPTP ports on a VPN server that was installed using Windows Server 2003, Standard Edition. Lately, users have indicated their connections are being blocked. After waiting a few minutes and then attempting to connect again, they are successful. What could be causing the problem and how would you solve it?

LESSON

9

Managing Remote Access

Remote access policies are perhaps the most complicated component of RRAS for the administrator new to Windows 2000 and Windows Server 2003. Remote access policies are highly flexible and powerful, but this power and flexibility also increase their complexity.

In this lesson, you will learn about remote access policies from the ground up. The lesson begins by reviewing the basic dial-in properties of user accounts, as user account dial-in properties can control certain aspects of the dial-in session regardless of the remote access policy.

Next, you will examine the policy application process, walking through the application order and the order in which each policy component is analyzed and applied. You will look at policy conditions and profiles in detail, listing and defining each option that can be modified in a remote access policy. After this examination, you will take a close look at the actual effects of several example policies, and discuss how to tailor remote access policies to achieve a particular goal. Finally, to complete our survey of remote access policies, you will investigate how to troubleshoot remote access policy issues, including how to determine if the remote access policy is, in fact, the cause of the difficulty.

When the number of remote access servers increases, you must consider how to incorporate remote access policies distributed across multiple servers. If the policies on each remote access server are managed separately, it is conceivable that a user could be allowed access when connecting to one server, yet denied access when connecting to another. The final two skills in this Lesson will introduce Internet Authentication Service (IAS), which is Microsoft's solution for centralizing your remote access policies, as well as for providing logging and accounting services for your enterprise.

Goals

In this lesson, we will thoroughly explore remote access policies. You will learn about remote access policy analysis, troubleshooting, and configuration.

Lesson 9 Managing Remote Access

Skill	Exam 70-291 Objective
1. Examining User Account Dial-in Properties	Manage Routing and Remote Access clients. Configure Routing and Remote Access policies to permit or deny access.
2. Understanding Policy Application	Manage Routing and Remote Access clients. Configure Routing and Remote Access policies to permit or deny access.
3. Configuring Conditions	Manage Routing and Remote Access clients. Configure Routing and Remote Access policies to permit or deny access.
4. Configuring Profile Settings	Manage Routing and Remote Access clients. Configure Routing and Remote Access policies to permit or deny access.
5. Analyzing Policy Application	Troubleshoot user access to remote access services. Diagnose and resolve issues relating to establishing a remote access connection.
6. Troubleshooting Remote Access	Troubleshoot user access to remote access services. Diagnose and resolve issues relating to establishing a remote access connection.
7. Configuring Internet Authentication Service (IAS)	Configure Routing and Remote Access user authentication. Configure Internet Authentication Service (IAS) to provide authentication for Routing and Remote Access clients.
8. Monitoring Remote Access	Troubleshoot user access to remote access services. Diagnose and resolve issues relating to establishing a remote access connection. Diagnose and resolve user access to resources beyond the remote access server. Monitor network protocol security. Tools might include IP Security Monitor Microsoft Management Console (MMC) snap-in and Kerberos support tools. Troubleshoot network protocol security. Tools might include IP Security Monitor MMC snap-in, Event Viewer, and Network Monitor.

Requirements

To complete this lesson, you will need administrative rights on two Windows Server 2003 computers.

skill 1

Examining User Account Dial-in Properties

exam objective

Manage Routing and Remote Access clients. Configure Routing and Remote Access policies to permit or deny access.

overview

As mentioned in Lesson 8, a user account's dial-in properties are the first method used to control remote access permission. Only after the user account's properties have been examined is the remote access policy examined. In addition, there are several settings controlled by the user account that cannot be set in a remote access policy. For instance, callback settings are only available in the user account's properties. For this reason, it is important to understand user dial-in properties before considering remote access policies in greater detail.

The **Dial-in** tab in the user account's properties contains five settings to control the remote access user (**Figure 9-1**):

◆ **Remote Access Permission:** This setting is primary in determining whether the user account is allowed to connect. If set to **Allow access**, the user account is allowed entry unless the account does not match the conditions of any remote access policies, or it cannot support the settings offered in the profile of the remote access policy. If set to **Deny access**, the user account is not allowed to connect, regardless of the policy settings. If set to **Control access through Remote Access Policy**, the user account is allowed access only if the permissions defined on its matching remote access policy are set to allow access.

◆ **Verify Caller-ID:** This setting ensures that the user calls from a specific number to connect to the remote access server. In order for this setting to function correctly, the RAS server's phone line and modem must support caller ID.

◆ **Callback Options:** Allows you to specify whether or not to make use of callback features and, if so, the type of callback to use. If you select **Set by Caller**, the caller is prompted to enter a phone number for the RRAS server to call back directly after successfully logging on. This setting does not significantly improve security. However, it is useful when traveling users must dial-in long distance from hotel rooms, as the long distance charges can be charged to the company phone line, rather than the hotel line. If you select **Always Callback to** and enter a valid number, after connecting and logging in, the RRAS server will disconnect the call and immediately call the user back at the specified number. This is a major security improvement, but it requires significant configuration effort.

◆ **Assign a Static IP Address:** This is the only method available for assigning a static IP address to a remote access client without using a remote access policy or manually configuring the client. Reservations in DHCP will not function correctly over RRAS connections. If you need to ensure that a client always receives the same IP address, you can either enter that IP address here, define a specific remote access policy for that client, or manually configure the IP properties on the client machine.

◆ **Apply Static Routes:** Allows you to configure one or more static routes to be added to the routing table on the RRAS server when this connection is established. This setting is typically configured only for user accounts that are used as the authentication entity for demand-dial routing connections.

Most of these settings are optional; in most cases, the only mandatory setting is the dial-in permission setting for the user account. We will examine how this setting affects the user in the next skill.

tip

In a Windows 2000 mixed mode or a Windows NT domain, the Control access through remote access policy setting is not available.

Figure 9-1 The Dial-in tab on the Properties dialog box for a user account

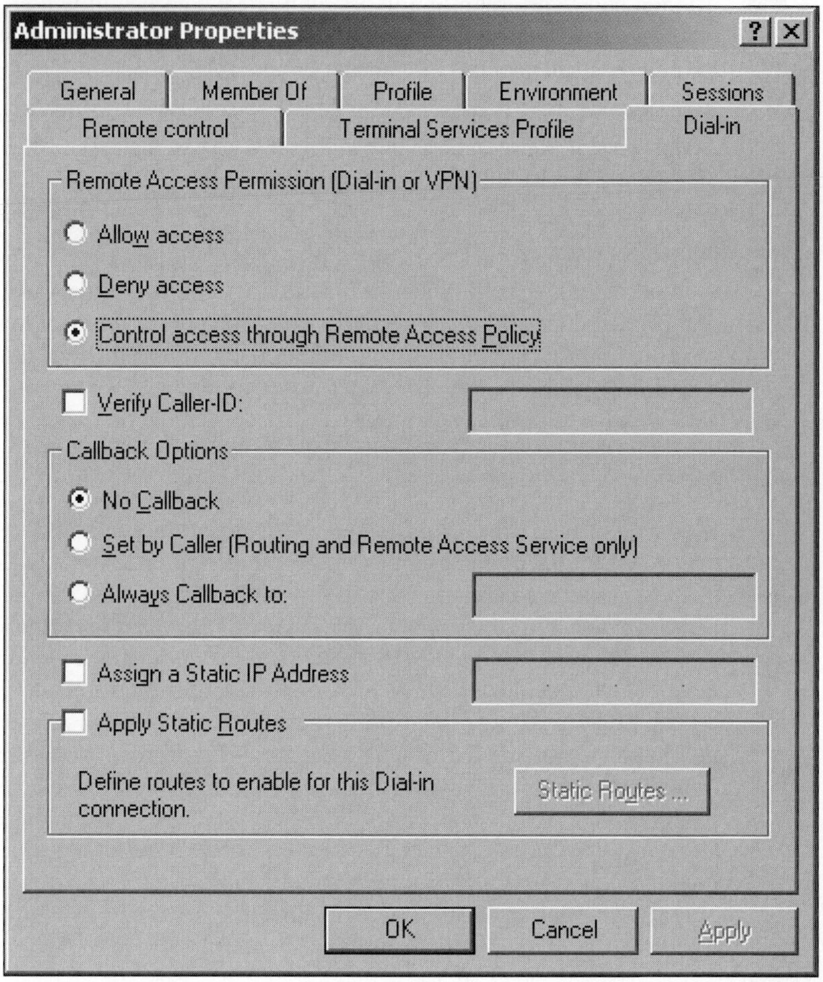

skill 2

Understanding Policy Application

exam objective

Manage Routing and Remote Access clients. Configure Routing and Remote Access policies to permit or deny access.

overview

The key to remote access policy design and troubleshooting is the ability to accurately predict whom a policy, or group of policies, will affect, and how it will affect them. Therefore, in order to create, manage, and troubleshoot remote access policies, an understanding of the way the policy actually applies is mandatory.

In the last lesson, we discussed the basic components of a policy and the purposes of those components. It is also important to understand how each of the components is applied and the order in which they are applied. To do this, we will use the simple flowchart shown in **Figure 9-2**.

Walking through the flowchart, you can see that the first thing to happen in all cases is that the user successfully logs in. After that, the RRAS server will begin looking at the conditions section of each policy in order, from the top of the policy list to the bottom. When the RRAS server detects that a user meets all of the conditions in a single policy, it stops looking at the rest of the conditions, even if a better match for the user is in a policy further down the list. This is called the first match rule, and it means that the first set of conditions to match, prevails. For this reason, more specific policies should be placed towards the top of the policy list.

If a condition match is found, RRAS then examines the permissions settings in the **Properties** dialog box for the user account on the **Dial-in** tab. It is important to realize that RRAS goes directly from the conditions in the policy to the user account's properties, rather than to the permissions section of the remote access policy. If the Dial-in permission for the user account is set to **Allow access**, the RRAS server *skips* the permissions section of the policy and goes directly to the profile. Similarly, if the Dial-in permission for the user account is set to **Deny access**, the RRAS server simply drops the connection, with no further processing. Only when the Dial-in permission for the user account is set to **Control access through Remote Access Policy** does RRAS actually use the permissions section of the remote access policy. While it may seem like a confusing way of doing things, dial-in permissions are handled this way to allow for versatility. Administrators who are used to controlling access through user account properties can operate on the same principles they are used to, because selecting **Allow access** in the user's **Dial-in** permissions will allow the user access using the default policies, while any other user account setting will deny the user access.

After the user matches the conditions for a policy, and the permissions for that user allow access, he still may not gain access. This is because the profile of a remote access policy stipulates various settings with which the client must comply. If the client does not match the rules set forth in the profile, the client is disconnected. For example, if you specify in the profile that the only allowed authentication protocols are EAP and MS-CHAPv2, then a user running Windows 95 would never be allowed access, regardless of permissions settings, since Windows 95 does not support these authentication protocols.

While policy application may seem somewhat complex at this point, it is important that you spend some time examining the provided flowchart and understand what occurs at each juncture. Understanding policy application is mandatory for any RRAS administrator. In addition, RRAS policy application and troubleshooting are important topics on the 70-291 exam.

tip

Conditions are simply for matching. Conditions do not restrict access. The profile restricts access.

caution

If the user does not match the conditions of at least one policy, access will be denied regardless of permissions settings. For this reason, deleting all of your policies will result in all users being denied access.

Figure 9-2 Policy application flowchart

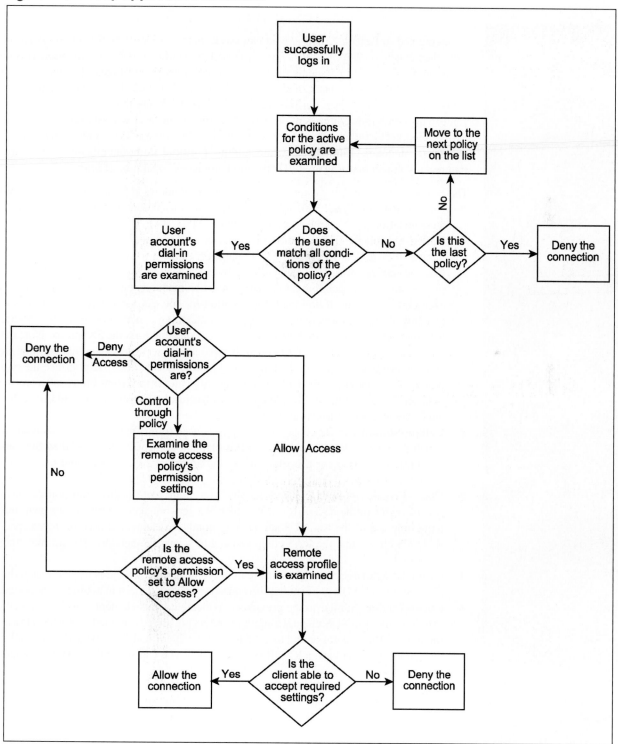

skill 3

Configuring Conditions

exam objective

Manage Routing and Remote Access clients. Configure Routing and Remote Access policies to permit or deny access.

overview

As mentioned in Lesson 8, and as you can see from the previous skill, conditions are little more than matching agents. They are used to match a specific policy to a given user. This is an important point, as many students (and administrators) get the mistaken idea that conditions are used to define restrictions. Conditions, however, simply match. They cannot restrict unless there is only a single policy. For this reason, you want to ensure that when creating a policy, you use the conditions component properly. This important facet will be examined further in Skill 5. First, let's examine the different components that you can use to create your condition statement in detail. Remember, when adding multiple components into a conditions statement, you will be using an *AND* operation, not an *OR* operation (**Figure 9-3**).

The components for creating a condition statement in Windows 2003 Server are (**Figure 9-4**):

♦ **Authentication-Type:** This condition element is used to match users by the type of authentication protocol they are using, such as MS-CHAPv1 or PAP (**Figure 9-5**).

♦ **Called-Station-Id:** This condition element is used to match users based on the phone number they dialed. In order for this condition element to function, the server's phone line and modem must be capable of receiving the Called-Station-Id information, or the phone number for each line on the server must be manually entered in the properties for each port. When specifying the Called-Station-Id, you can use patterns to define blocks of numbers that are acceptable using pattern matching syntax. For example, 555.555.* would match all phone numbers in the 555 area code that used the 555 prefix. Note that a period is required instead of a hyphen to separate the sections of the number. For more complicated use of pattern matching, see Windows Server 2003 Help, or use the online product documentation available at the following site: **http://www.microsoft.com/technet/treeview/default.asp?url=/technet/prodtechnol/windowsserver2003/proddocs/-entserver/sag_ias_patternmatch.asp**

♦ **Calling-Station-Id:** This condition element is used to match users by the number from which they are calling. The syntax of this element is identical to the Called-Station-Id. In addition, in order for this element to function correctly, the line and modem must support caller ID.

♦ **Client-Friendly-Name:** Contrary to what you might expect, this condition defines the friendly name of the RADIUS client (which is a network access server on its own) that is requesting use of the RADIUS server. This condition element is used to match specific RADIUS clients that the RAS client is using to access the network. Pattern matching is supported.

♦ **Client-IP-Address:** Similar to the previous element, this element is used to match the IP address of the RADIUS client that is requesting access. Pattern matching is supported.

♦ **Client-Vendor:** Similar to the previous two elements, this element is used to match the vendor of the RADIUS client. Common vendors are already defined in RRAS. However, for vendors that are not on the list, the RADIUS vendor code may be added manually. If the vendor does not have a RADIUS vendor code, you can select the RADIUS Standard vendor code.

♦ **Day-and-Time-Restrictions:** This element is used to match the user based on the day of the week and time of day he attempts to connect. The time is relative to the system time of the server.

Figure 9-3 Multiple condition elements are ANDed together

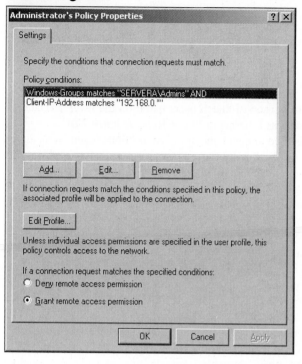

Figure 9-4 The Select Attribute dialog box

This is where you select the components for a condition statement

Figure 9-5 The Authentication-Type dialog box

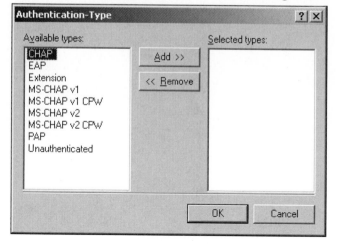

skill 3

Configuring Conditions *(cont'd)*

exam objective

Manage Routing and Remote Access clients. Configure Routing and Remote Access policies to permit or deny access.

overview

♦ **Framed-Protocol:** This element is used to match users based on the layer 2 (Datalink layer) protocol they are using, such as Ethernet or Frame Relay **(Figure 9-6)**.

♦ **NAS-Identifier:** This element is used to match incoming connections based on the name of the network access server used to make the connection. Typically used only in RADIUS implementations. Pattern matching is supported.

♦ **NAS-IP-Address:** This element is used to match incoming connections based on the IP address of the network access server used. Typically used only in RADIUS implementations. Pattern matching is supported.

♦ **NAS-Port-Type:** This element is used to match incoming connections based on the media type in use. Valid media types include Ethernet, asynchronous (such as POTS), and ISDN. Typically used only in RADIUS implementations.

♦ **Service-Type:** This element is used to match incoming connections based on the RADIUS service class being requested. For example, PPP connections are the Framed service type **(Figure 9-7)**.

♦ **Tunnel-Type:** This element is used to match incoming connections based on the VPN tunneling technology used (L2TP or PPTP) **(Figure 9-8)**.

♦ **Windows-Groups:** Probably the most commonly used condition element, this element matches incoming connections based on the user's group membership.

Figure 9-6 The Framed-Protocol dialog box

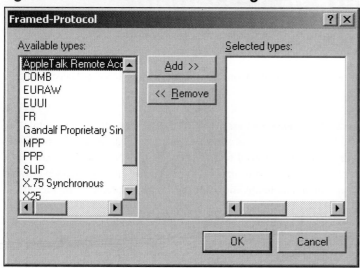

Figure 9-7 The Service-Type dialog box

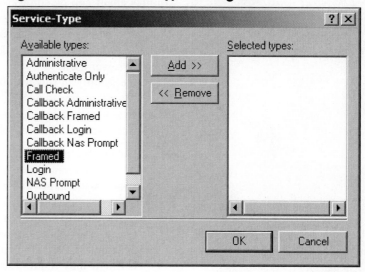

Figure 9-8 The Tunnel-Type dialog box

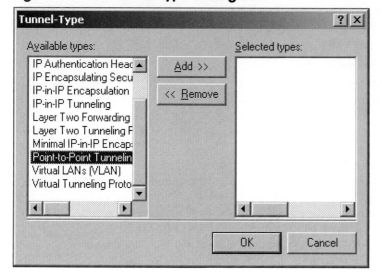

skill 4

Configuring Profile Settings

exam objective

Manage Routing and Remote Access clients. Configure Routing and Remote Access policies to permit or deny access.

overview

As mentioned previously, condition elements are used to match a specific policy, while the profile is used to restrict which remote access settings are supported. When the profile is applied, the settings in the profile are offered to the client. With some settings, the offer simply means that the user has the ability to utilize the remote access feature. However, with other settings, such as encryption and authentication settings, non-compliance with the setting results in the client being disconnected. In order to better understand the effects of the profile on remote access connections, let's examine the different profile settings in detail.

When you open a profile, the first tab you will see is the **Dial-in Constraints** tab (**Figure 9-9**). On this page, you can define any needed restrictions for the dial-in properties for this policy. The settings on this tab are:

◆ **Minutes server can remain idle before it is disconnected (Idle-Timeout):** This is how long any session to which the policy applies can remain connected without any activity.
◆ **Minutes client can be connected (Session-Timeout):** This is the total time that any session to which the policy applies can remain connected, regardless of activity.
◆ **Allow access only on these days and at these times:** This setting forces a session to disconnect if the session is outside of the specified range. The time of day clock is relative to the server itself.
◆ **Allow access only to this number (Called-Station-ID):** This setting can be used to disconnect any session to which the policy applies that did not call the number entered.
◆ **Allow access only through these media (NAS-Port-Type):** This setting is used to define which types of media are allowed for the policy.

The next available tab is the **IP** tab (**Figure 9-10**). This tab is used to define the IP properties associated with the connections to which this profile applies. The settings on this tab are:

◆ **IP Address Assignment (Framed-IP-Address):** This setting is used to define how clients affected by this policy receive an IP address.
  • If **Server must supply an IP address** is selected, the server must issue the clients IP addresses, either from a poll of addresses defined in RRAS, or through a poll of addresses leased from a DHCP server.
  • If **Client may request an IP address** is selected, the client can use a statically entered IP address.
  • If **Server settings determine IP address assignment** is selected, the settings configured for the entire server will be used.
  • Finally, the **Assign a static IP address** setting will configure a matching client to use the defined static IP.
◆ **IP filters:** This section is used to create incoming and outgoing IP packet filters that only apply to the matching connections.

The next tab is the **Multilink** tab (**Figure 9-11**), which defines the settings applied to multilink connections for this policy. The settings available for this tab are:

◆ **Multilink settings:** These settings define whether or not to allow multilink connections. You can also choose to limit the number of ports available for any single multilink session.
◆ **Bandwidth Allocation Protocol (BAP) settings**
  • **Percentage of capacity:** Defines the threshold level for reducing the number of ports assigned to a given multilink session. When the session's bandwidth falls and remains below this level after a configured period of time (specified in the next setting), a single port will be removed from the session.
  • **Period of time:** Defines the threshold unit of time that must elapse before a single port is removed from the multilink session.

tip

If the Multilink tab is not available, ensure that the **Dynamic bandwidth control using BAP and BACP** checkbox is enabled in the PPP tab of the server properties dialog.

Figure 9-9 Dial-in constraints tab

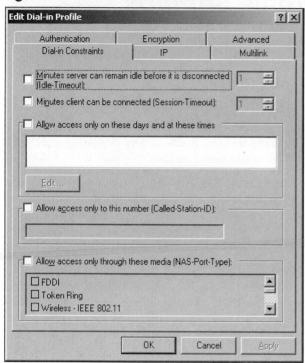

Figure 9-10 IP tab

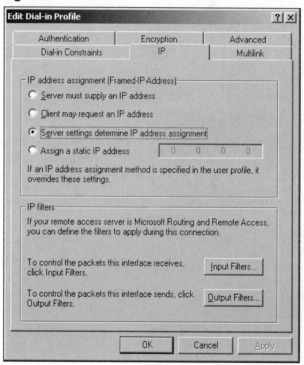

Figure 9-11 Multilink tab

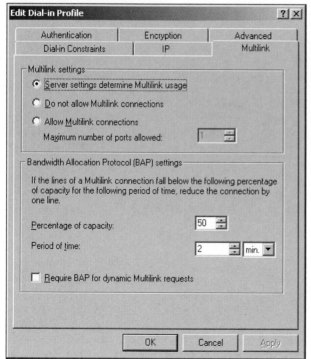

skill 4

Configuring Profile Settings (cont'd)

exam objective

Manage Routing and Remote Access clients. Configure Routing and Remote Access policies to permit or deny access.

overview

- **Require BAP for dynamic Multilink requests:** When enabled, specifies that all sessions which can dynamically increase bandwidth by requesting more ports must also allow the bandwidth to be reduced by removing ports through BAP.

The next tab is the **Authentication** tab **(Figure 9-12)**, which defines the authentication methods allowed by this policy. Each authentication method can be selected or deselected independently of the others. If all authentication methods are chosen, the server will negotiate authentication with the client, beginning with the strongest method and ending with the weakest. Note that while you can choose to allow unauthenticated access, doing so is a great security risk.

The next tab is the **Encryption** tab **(Figure 9-13)**. This tab defines MPPE encryption levels (IPSec encryption levels are defined by the IPSec policy configured on the machine) for the connection. If multiple encryption levels are selected, the client and server will negotiate the encryption level, choosing the highest level that is supported by both parties. If a compatible encryption level cannot be negotiated, then the connection will be terminated. Be aware that the authentication protocols selected in the authentication tab have an effect upon the available encryption levels. Only MS-CHAPv1 or higher authentication protocols are capable of using data encryption.

The final tab is the **Advanced** tab **(Figure 9-14)**. The Advanced tab defines special settings to be returned from RADIUS servers to RADIUS clients. This section of the remote access policy is unused unless you are using RADIUS authentication.

Figure 9-12 Authentication tab

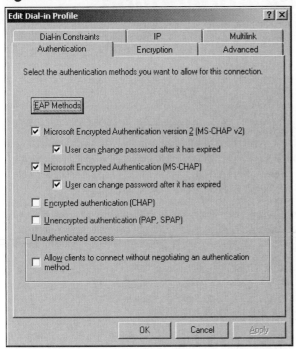

Figure 9-13 Encryption tab

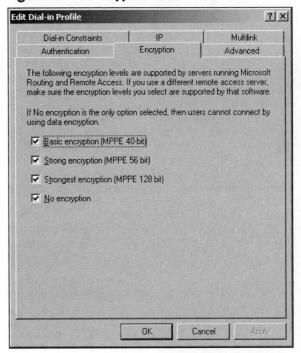

Figure 9-14 Advanced tab

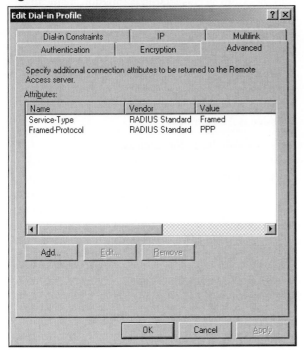

skill 5

Analyzing Policy Application

exam objective

Troubleshoot user access to remote access services. Diagnose and resolve issues relating to establishing a remote access connection.

overview

The ability to analyze policy application is probably the most important skill a good RRAS administrator can have. Without understanding how a group of policies will be applied, and to whom they will be applied, you cannot effectively create and manage remote access policies. In addition, policy application is an important topic on Exam 70-291, so you should make sure that you have a firm grasp of this topic before attempting the exam.

Analyzing policy application requires a firm grasp of both the order in which policy elements are examined, as well as a solid understanding of the individual policy elements themselves. If you have any difficulty following this skill, review Skills 2-4 until you are certain you understand the underlying concepts. With that said, let's walk through some example policies in order to fully understand the implications of the policy order and settings.

In the policy configuration shown in **Table 9-1**, the only policy that will apply is the first one, **Allow access if dial-in permission is allowed**. This is simply because the conditions set for the first policy will automatically apply to all sessions, so policy processing will stop at the first policy to match. This is a simple lesson in why you will always want to set more specific policies higher in the evaluation order. Now, the secondary effects of this policy configuration are not so easy to see, unless you were paying close attention in Skill 2. Most people assume that since everyone matches the first policy in the list, and since the permissions on that policy are set to deny access, that everyone would be denied access. This is not the case. Remember from the flowchart in Skill 2 that the only time the permissions setting in the policy is used is when the user account's dial-in permissions are set to **Control access through remote access policy**. Therefore, if the user account's dial-in permissions are set to **Allow access**, then this policy will allow the user access, and the permissions setting in the policy itself will be ignored.

The policies shown in **Table 9-1** appear to have the following goals:
◆ Allow administrators access, no matter what time of day or day of week.
◆ Deny guests access at all times.
◆ Allow any other user access who has the **Allow access** Dial-in permission at any time.
◆ Deny all other access.

So, how do you modify the policy list to accomplish these goals? Actually, all you have to do is correctly order the policies. If you changed the order, all of your goals would be achieved, as follows:
◆ First: Allow Administrators access
◆ Second: Prevent Guest access
◆ Third: Allow access if Dial-in permission is Allow access

With this order, anyone who is a member of the Administrators group will match the first policy, and be allowed access (as long as the Dial-in permissions on their user account are not set to Deny access). Anyone who is not a member of the Administrators group will be compared to the next policy, which will match only those users who are members of the Guests group. Users who match the second policy will be denied access, unless the Dial-in permissions on their user account are configured to Allow access. All other users will be compared to the final policy, which will only allow users whose Dial-in permission is set to Allow access. All other users will be denied.

In truth, it doesn't really matter whether the Allow Administrators access policy or the Prevent Guest access policy is applied first, the effect will be the same either way in this case.

Table 9-1   Policy Example 1

Policy Name	Conditions	Permissions	Profile
Allow access if dial-in permission is allowed	Day and Time restrictions: Anytime	Deny access	Default settings
Allow Administrators access	Windows Groups: Administrators	Allow access	Default settings
Prevent Guest access	Windows Groups: Guests	Deny access	Default settings

skill 5

Analyzing Policy Application *(Cont'd)*

exam objective

Troubleshoot user access to remote access services. Diagnose and resolve issues relating to establishing a remote access connection.

overview

Let's examine a slightly more complex example this time. In this scenario, you have been given the task of creating a set of policies that achieves the following goals:

◆ Administrators should be allowed access at all times, but should always be required to use High Encryption.

◆ All members of the Temporary global group should be allowed access during working hours only.

◆ All other users should be allowed access as long as their user account is not configured to deny access.

An example of the policy settings a typical administrator might create to accomplish these goals is shown in **Table 9-2**. Unfortunately, this configuration will not accomplish those goals. The reason for this is simple: *Conditions do not restrict (profiles restrict)*. In this example, the goal for temporary users to be allowed access only during working hours *will not* be achieved because the hours are specified in the conditions. This means that if the users in the Temporary group do not call during those hours, they will not be automatically denied. Instead, they will never match the second policy, and *will* match the third policy, which would allow their account as long as their account was not specifically denied access, regardless of the time or day they are calling. The correct policy settings required to accomplish these goals are shown in **Table 9-3**. Notice that the restrictions on the time of day have been moved from the conditions column to the profile column. Remember, conditions are used to match, profiles are used to restrict.

Table 9-2　Policy Example 2

Policy Name	Conditions	Permissions	Profile
Policy 1	Windows Groups: Administrators	Allow access	Encryption: Strongest only
Policy 2	Windows Groups: Temporary Day and Time restrictions: Mon 0800-1700, Tues 0800-1700, Wed 0800-1700, Thur 0800-1700, Fri 0800-1700	Allow access	Default settings
Policy 3	Day and Time restrictions: Anytime	Allow access	Default settings

Table 9-3　Policy Example 3

Policy Name	Conditions	Permissions	Profile
Policy 1	Windows Groups: Administrators	Allow access	Encryption: Strongest only
Policy 2	Windows Groups: Temporary	Allow access	Day and Time restrictions: Mon 0800-1700, Tues 0800-1700, Wed 0800-1700, Thur 0800-1700, Fri 0800-1700
Policy 3	Day and Time restrictions: Anytime	Allow access	Default settings

skill 6

Troubleshooting Remote Access

exam objective

Troubleshoot user access to remote access services. Diagnose and resolve issues relating to establishing a remote access connection.

overview

Troubleshooting remote connections can require skills in several areas, depending on the problem you are experiencing. Be aware that in many cases, your problem may not even involve your policy settings. Failure to complete the handshaking process with a modem connection, for instance, could mean that the modem is defective, the line is noisy, or the connection settings (bit rate, parity bits, echo, etc.) are incorrect. Always troubleshoot problems from the lowest layer and work your way up **(Figure 9-15)**.

Similarly, if you establish the connection properly, but cannot access resources, your problem most likely lies with RRAS configuration or the configuration of your IP services. In this case, check your IP configuration first, and then examine your RRAS settings to ensure that other settings (such as IP filters) are not the cause of the problem.

In general, problems with remote access policies will lead to one of two situations:
◆ Connections are denied when they should be allowed
◆ Connections are allowed when they should be denied

In most cases, these problems are easily remedied by analyzing the application of your remote access policies (as examined in the previous skill), and correcting any problems you find.

However, there are some cases in which your connection may be correctly allowed, but you still experience errors. For example, you may find that you cannot communicate with any servers on a particular network after connecting, even though your IP configuration is correct. In this case, examine your IP filters in the applied remote access policy and modify them as necessary. Similarly, if you cannot communicate using a particular protocol, ensure that the ports for that protocol are not denied in your IP filters.

Another common problem is the failure of the server to drop links when bandwidth is not being used on a multilink connection. In this case, examine the relevant remote access policy settings in the profile component under the Multilink tab, and ensure that BAP is correctly configured.

In all cases, a thorough analysis of the remote access policy order and settings will generally pinpoint the problem. Remember to eliminate all other common RRAS difficulties before examining the policy itself.

Figure 9-15 Remote access troubleshooting process

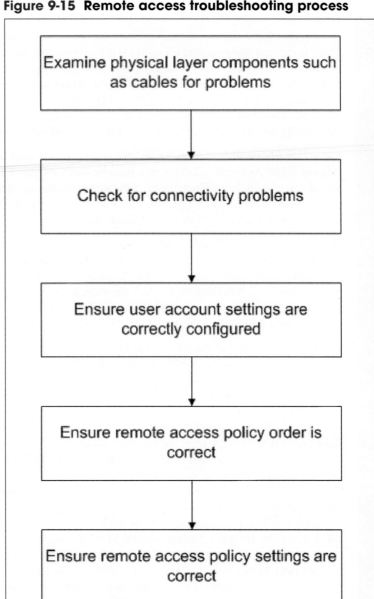

skill 7

Configuring Internet Authentication Service (IAS)

exam objective

Configure Routing and Remote Access user authentication. Configure Internet Authentication Service (IAS) to provide authentication for Routing and Remote Access clients.

overview

Remote access policies are stored locally on the remote access server where they are created. This can produce some unexpected results if the same remote access policy is not configured on all remote access servers. If you set up a remote access policy on Server A that restricts access to the network on weekends but on Server B you did not include the same policy, it is possible that remote users connecting to Server B would be allowed access on weekends. In cases where you have more than one remote access server, rather than managing policies on each server individually, take advantage of Microsoft's **Internet Authentication Service (IAS)**.

Using IAS, Microsoft introduces the ability to configure a RADIUS server or a RADIUS proxy **(Figure 9-16)**. As noted in Lesson 8, a **Remote Authentication Dial-In Service (RADIUS) server** can provide centralized remote authentication, authorization, and accounting capabilities for incoming connections. Although the Internet Authentication Service can be installed on a separate computer, it is not unusual to find it configured on a network access server as well.

When implementing a RADIUS server, remote clients can connect to multiple remote access servers that function as RADIUS clients. These **RADIUS clients** are configured to send the requests to a RADIUS server running IAS by using the RADIUS protocol. The RADIUS server will then contact a domain controller for validation, and then check remote access policies for a match to the incoming connection. Once the user is validated and authorized, the information is returned to the RADIUS client. The RADIUS client then provides access to the remote client.

IAS can also be used in the role of a **RADIUS proxy** that forwards the authentication and accounting requests to other RADIUS servers. RADIUS servers can be placed in server groups. These groups are typically organized based on remote access policies for a domain, forest, or organization. The following demonstrates the process for configuring a RADIUS (IAS) server and a RADIUS client.

how to

Configure a RADIUS server to run Internet Authentication Service (IAS).
1. To install IAS, click **Add or Remove Programs** in the Control Panel.
2. Click **Add/Remove Windows Components**.
3. In the **Windows Components Wizard**, double-click **Networking Services**.
4. In the **Networking Services** dialog box, select the **Internet Authentication Service**, click ⬛ OK ⬛, and then click ⬛ Next > ⬛.
5. Launch the **Internet Authentication Service** console from the **Administrative Tools** menu (click **Start**, point to **Administrative Tools**, click **Internet Authentication Service**). In order for the IAS server to authenticate users, it must be registered in Active Directory. This allows it to read the dial-in attributes of user accounts in the domain. It also adds the IAS computer into the RRAS and IAS servers domain local group in the domain for which the IAS server is a member.
6. Right-click the **Internet Authentication Service**, and click **Register Server in Active Directory (Figure 9-17)**. Click **OK** on the **Server registered** dialog box.
   Next, specify RADIUS clients that will forward requests to IAS.
7. Right-click the **RADIUS Clients** folder in the Internet Authentication Service console and select **New RADIUS Client**.
8. In the **New RADIUS Client** dialog box, enter the friendly name and IP address or DNS name for the RADIUS client and then click ⬛ Verify ⬛ **(Figure 9-18)**.
9. In the **Verify Client** dialog box, click ⬛ Resolve ⬛, then ⬛ OK ⬛, and then ⬛ Next > ⬛.
10. In the **Additional information** dialog box, leave the **Client-Vendor** setting as **RADIUS Standard**. For the **Shared secret**, enter a strong password, and then confirm it **(Figure 9-19)**. Click ⬛ Finish ⬛ to close the dialog box.

Figure 9-16 RADIUS Configurations

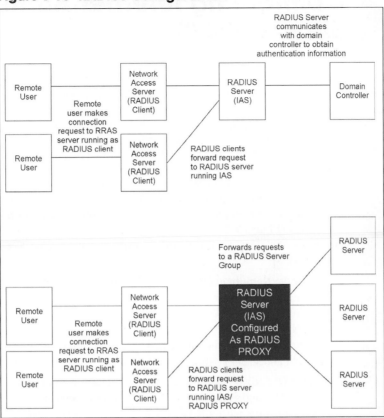

Figure 9-17 Register Server in Active Directory

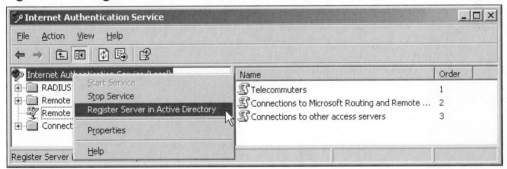

Figure 9-18 Verify RADIUS Client

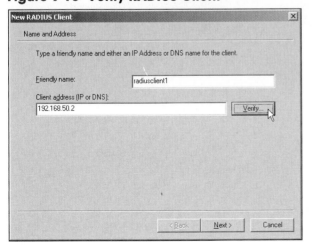

Figure 9-19 Entering Shared Secret—server

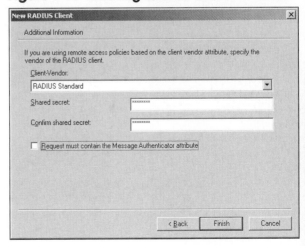

skill 7

Configuring Internet Authentication Service (IAS) *(cont'd)*

exam objective

Configure Routing and Remote Access user authentication. Configure Internet Authentication Service (IAS) to provide authentication for Routing and Remote Access clients.

how to

Configure a RADIUS client.

The following assumes you do not have Routing and Remote Access Service enabled on the computer that will function as a RADIUS client. If you have followed the skills in this book in order, first right-click the server name and click **Disable Routing and Remote Access**.

1. Launch the **Routing and Remote Access** console via the **Administrative Tools** menu.
2. Right-click the server name and then click **Configure and Enable Routing and Remote Access (Figure 9-20)**.
3. In the **Welcome to the Routing and Remote Access Server Setup Wizard**, click [Next >] .
4. Select the **Remote access (dial-up or VPN)** option and then click [Next >] .
5. On the **Remote Access** screen, select **VPN** or **Dial-up** depending upon the configuration required in your network **(Figure 9-21)**. In our example, we will configure the server as a VPN server.
6. On the **Network Selection** screen, select the network interface that is connected to the Internet and select [Next >] .
7. On the **IP address assignment** screen, select **Automatically** and click [Next >] .
8. On the **Managing Multiple Remote Access Servers** screen, select **Yes, set up this server to work with a RADIUS server**. Click [Next >] .
9. On the **RADIUS Server Selection** screen, enter the primary RADIUS server to use and the shared secret you used in Step 10 of the RADIUS server setup **(Figure 9-22)**, and click [Next >] .
10. Click [Finish] after reviewing the configuration summary.
11. Click [OK] for the message regarding the setup of the DHCP Relay agent.

After Routing and Remote Access has initialized, you should see a green arrow next to the name of the server indicating the service is now running and can service remote clients.

Figure 9-20 Configure and Enable RRAS

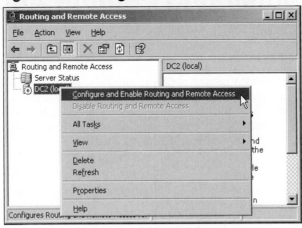

Figure 9-21 Selecting Server Role

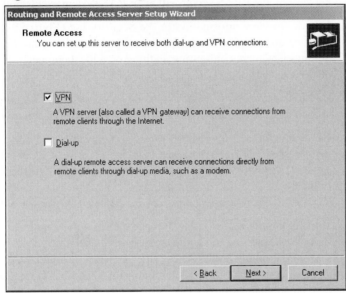

Figure 9-22 Entering Shared Secret—client

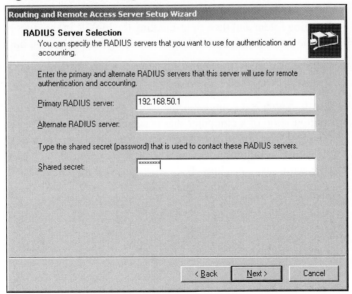

skill 8 | *Monitoring Remote Access*

Troubleshoot user access to remote access services. Diagnose and resolve issues relating to establishing a remote access connection. Diagnose and resolve user access to resources beyond the remote access server. Monitor network protocol security. Tools might include IP Security Monitor Microsoft Management Console (MMC) snap-in and Kerberos support tools. Troubleshoot network protocol security. Tools might include IP Security Monitor MMC snap-in, Event Viewer, and Network Monitor.

overview

After implementing your remote access solution, you must continue to monitor the server(s) for potential problems. Windows Server 2003 provides several tools and logs that can provide information to an administrator.

Event Viewer: **Event Viewer** provides information about events that have occurred on the remote access server. This information is stored in application, security, and system event logs. When event logging is configured on the remote access server (as discussed in the next paragraph), the RRAS server will enter RAS system events in the system log specifically.

In order to view information in the Security log (**Figure 9-23**), you may need to enable auditing and logging of specific security events. This can be done via the Local Security Settings if you are configuring auditing on a local computer. If you are configuring auditing on domain controllers, you can enable it by accessing the Domain Controller Security Policy.

Routing and Remote Access servers support event logging, local authentication and accounting logging, and RADIUS-based authentication and accounting logging.

Event logging records remote access server warnings, errors, and other information in the system event log. To enable event logging, select the server name in the Routing and Remote Access console, right-click and select **Properties**. On the **Logging** tab of the server's Properties dialog box, select the event types you want to log (**Figure 9-24**). Information recorded in the system event log can be reviewed by using **Event Viewer**.

To track remote access usage and authentication attempts on a server running Routing and Remote Access, you should review the information stored in the **%systemroot%\ System32\Logfiles** folder. These files are saved in Internet Authentication Service (IAS) or database-compatible format; therefore, any database program can read the file directly. Each time an authentication attempt is made, the information is stored in this log indicating the remote access policy that accepted or rejected the connection. In order to use this type of logging, you will need to enable Windows Authentication as the Authentication provider or Windows Accounting as the Accounting provider in the server's properties. Once these have been enabled, you can configure what you want to log by selecting the **Remote Access Logging** folder and then right-clicking the log file in the right pane to configure its properties. On the **Settings** tab of the Properties dialog box, select the information you want to log.

If you are using a Remote Authentication Dial-In User Service (RADIUS) server, the logs will be stored on the IAS server.

Netsh: **Netsh** is a command-line utility that will allow you to display or modify the network configuration of a computer that is currently running. When used on a remote access server, the **netsh ras diagnostics show logs** command can be used to dump information regarding the server's configuration into a diagnostic report. This includes tracing logs (modem logs, connection manager logs, IP Security logs), Remote Access Event logs, as well as Security Event Logs as shown in **Figure 9-25**.

Figure 9-23 Security Log Contents

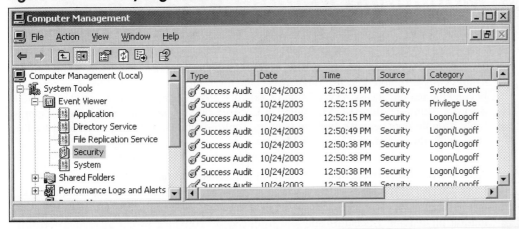

Figure 9-24 Selecting Event Types to Log

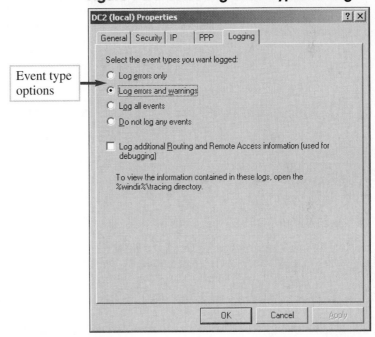

Figure 9-25 Diagnostic Report Using Netsh command

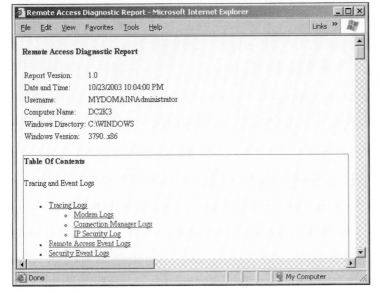

skill 8

Monitoring Remote Access (cont'd)

exam objective

Troubleshoot user access to remote access services. Diagnose and resolve issues relating to establishing a remote access connection. Diagnose and resolve user access to resources beyond the remote access server. Monitor network protocol security. Tools might include IP Security Monitor Microsoft Management Console (MMC) snap-in and Kerberos support tools. Troubleshoot network protocol security. Tools might include IP Security Monitor MMC snap-in, Event Viewer, and Network Monitor.

overview

Network Monitor: If you are experiencing problems with remote connectivity or want to monitor a specific connection to the server, you can use **Network Monitor** to capture packets that are sent between the remote access client and the server **(Figure 9-26)**. For more information on reading trace information produced by Network Monitor, read Microsoft's Knowledge Base Article 169292, **The Basics of Reading TCP/IP Traces**, available at http://support.microsoft.com.

IPSec Monitor Snap-in: The IPSec Monitor snap-in is another tool that can be used to monitor whether or not your communications are secured. This is done by viewing active security associations (SA). An SA is a set of parameters that define the services and mechanisms (authentication protocols, encryption protocols, etc.) used between the two computers. SA confirms whether your secured communications are successful **(Figure 9-27)**.

Using Event Viewer, Netsh, Network Monitor, and the IPSec Monitor snap-in is covered in further detail in Lesson 11.

Figure 9-26 Network Monitor

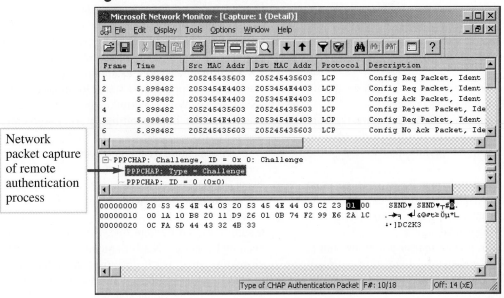

Network packet capture of remote authentication process

Figure 9-27 IPSec Monitor

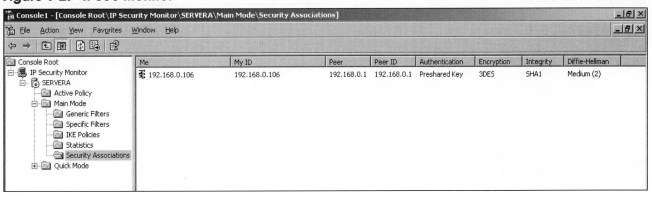

Summary

- The Dial-in properties for a user account are the first method for controlling a user's remote access permissions.
- There are several settings controlled by the user account that cannot be set in a remote access policy.
- The key to remote access policy design and troubleshooting is the ability to accurately predict whom a policy, or group of policies, will affect, and how it will affect them.
- Conditions are simply for matching. Conditions do not restrict access. The profile restricts access.
- It is important to realize that RRAS goes directly from the conditions in the policy to the user account properties, instead of to the permissions section of the remote access policy.
- If the user does not match the conditions of at least one policy, access will be denied, regardless of permissions settings. For this reason, deleting all of your policies will result in all users being denied access.
- Only when the Dial-in permission for a user account is set to Control access through Remote Access Policy does RRAS actually use the permissions section of the remote access policy.
- If the client cannot match any of the rules set forth in the profile, the client is disconnected.

- When there are multiple components to a conditions statement, they are applied as an AND operation, not an OR operation.
- Be aware that in many cases, your connection problem may not involve your policy settings.
- In all cases, a thorough analysis of the remote access policy order and settings will generally pinpoint the problem. Remember to eliminate all other common RRAS difficulties before examining the policy itself.
- Remote access policies are stored locally on each remote access server. When multiple remote access servers are used, consider implementing Internet Authentication Service (IAS).
- After implementing your remote access solution, you must continue to monitor the server(s) for potential problems. Event Viewer can be used to monitor application, security, and system event logs. Netsh can be used to display information regarding a server's configuration. This includes tracing logs and Remote Access Event logs, as well as Security Event logs. Network Monitor can be used to track incoming connections by analyzing the traffic and providing information regarding communications to the RRAS Server. The IPSec Monitor snap-in can be used to provide information on security associations, as well as remote policies that affect the server.

Key Terms

Event logging
Event Viewer
Internet Authentication Service (IAS)

Netsh
Network Monitor
RADIUS client

RADIUS proxy
RADIUS server

Test Yourself

1. Which of the following most correctly describes the purpose of the conditions component of a remote access policy?
   a. Used to restrict access.
   b. Offers settings to client machines.
   c. Allows or denies access.
   d. Determines which policy applies to the client.

2. Which of the following would most likely be a remote access policy-related problem?
   a. Failure to complete the modem handshake.
   b. Inability to ping any server by name, while being able to ping by IP address.
   c. Low baud rates for a modem connection.
   d. Being denied or allowed access improperly.

3. Remote access policies can be used to do which of the following? (Choose all that apply.)
  a. Define which users are allowed access.
  b. Define how many lines are available for multilink connections.
  c. Define the maximum transfer rate for modem connections.
  d. Define the desktop settings for remote access clients.
  e. Define IPSec encryption levels.

4. BAP is used to do which of the following?
  a. Define the maximum transfer speed on a POTS connection.
  b. Create tunnels using PPP and MPPE.
  c. Statically bond ISDN lines.
  d. Dynamically release connections in a multilink session.

5. Identify the correct statement.
  a. Remote access permissions are only examined if the user's dial-in permission is set to Control access through Remote Access Policy.
  b. Remote access policies do not apply to multilink sessions.
  c. Callback is configured using remote access policies.
  d. Remote access permissions apply regardless of the dial-in permissions.

6. A day and time restriction of Mon 0800-1700 set in the conditions section of the remote access policy will have which effect? (Choose all that apply.)
  a. Connections occurring at 10PM on Monday will match the condition.
  b. Connections will only be allowed on Monday.
  c. Connections occurring between 8AM and 5PM on Monday will match the condition.
  d. Connections occurring on Tuesday at 2PM will not match the condition.

7. Which of the following settings are available in a remote access profile? (Choose all that apply.)
  a. Maximum bps
  b. Idle timeout
  c. Maximum session time
  d. DNS server search order

8. Which of the following statements are correct about a remote access condition? (Choose all that apply.)
  a. Multiple conditions are combined with OR statements.
  b. Conditions are used to determine which policy applies.
  c. You may only apply one condition per profile.
  d. All condition statements must evaluate to true in order for a policy to apply.

Problem Solving Scenarios

1. You are working as an administrator with the London branch of Spearhead Consultants. You must create a set of remote access policies to achieve the following goals:

  ◆ All users should be allowed access between 7AM and 6PM, Monday through Friday, London local time.
  ◆ Guest accounts should never be allowed access.
  ◆ All accounts should be required to use MSCHAPv1 or higher.
  ◆ Administrator accounts should be required to use encryption.
  ◆ All accounts except administrator accounts should be limited to a maximum session time of 20 minutes.
  ◆ All accounts except administrator accounts must be denied unless they dial into the 555-555-1212 line.

10

Implementing and Managing Certificate Services

APublic Key Infrastructure (PKI) consists of protocols, standards, and technologies that provide both authentication and encryption services. To utilize Windows Server 2003 in your PKI solution, you must understand the core components involved in verifying and authenticating entities. These include:

◆ Public/private keys
◆ Digital certificates
◆ Certification Authorities

By using Microsoft Windows Server 2003 Certificate Services, you can implement your own Public Key Infrastructure which will allow you to strengthen authentication by utilizing smart cards, protect data in transit by using the services of Internet Protocol Security (IPSec), or even protect data stored on local hard drives using Encrypting File System (EFS).

Computers, users, and services use certificates as a way of identifying themselves on the network. Certificates are digital credentials that are issued by a Certification Authority, which vouches for their validity. The information contained in each certificate is dictated by the X.509 certificate standard.

By installing Certificate Services on a Windows Server 2003 computer, you can configure your own Certification Authority. In addition to issuing certificates, CAs also manage the certificates to maintain the integrity of the PKI. Some networks will have only one CA, while others will have multiple CAs configured in what is known as a certification hierarchy. Certificate Services are managed by using the Certification Authority tool which can be added into a Microsoft Management Console or accessed via the Start-Administrative Tools menus.

Certificates can be obtained by using the Microsoft Certificate Services Web Enrollment Support pages or by using the Certification Request Wizard.

Now, let's take a closer look at each of these components and how to use them to implement a Public Key Infrastructure (PKI).

Goals

In this lesson, you will learn about the various components of a PKI. You will learn how to set up both a Standalone and an Enterprise Certification Authority, and, once your CA has been installed, how to use both the certificate enrollment Web pages and the Certificate Request Wizard to request and install certificates. You will also learn how to renew and revoke a certificate. The lesson concludes with an overview of the Encrypting File System (EFS).

Lesson 10   Implementing and Managing Certificate Services

Skill	Exam 70-291 Objective
1. Introducing the Public Key Infrastructure	Basic knowledge
2. Introducing the Core Components of a Public Key Infrastructure	Basic knowledge
3. Implementing a Standalone Certificate Authority	Basic knowledge
4. Using Web Enrollment Services for Certificate Enrollment	Basic knowledge
5. Viewing Certificates	Basic knowledge
6. Implementing an Enterprise CA	Basic knowledge
7. Using the Certificate Request Wizard for Certificate Enrollment	Basic knowledge
8. Renewing a Certificate	Basic knowledge
9. Revoking a Certificate	Basic knowledge
10. Introducing the Encrypting File System	Basic knowledge

Requirements

To complete the skills in this lesson, you will need administrative rights on a Windows Server 2003 computer with Internet Information Services and Internet Explorer installed and a connection to the Internet available.

skill 1

Introducing the Public Key Infrastructure

overview

Public Key Infrastructure (PKI) is a set of services that supports the use of cryptography. **Cryptography** is the art of hiding information while it is stored or in transit. In today's high-tech world of computers, cryptography deals with converting clear text into cipher text through a process called **encrypting** and then converting it back into clear text in a process known as **decrypting**.

Public key cryptography, used in PKI implementations, is an encryption method for securing data transmissions over networks that are not trusted, such as the Internet. Before reviewing how it works, let's consider its predecessor: secret key cryptography.

Secret key cryptography, also known as symmetric cryptography, involves sharing a private or secret key between the two individuals involved in a communication session. This single key both encrypts and decrypts information. In order for a user to share encrypted information with others, he must distribute the secret key to those individuals. If any one of them loses or makes the secret key available to someone outside of the group, the security of the data is compromised. The same key both encrypts and decrypts information! As you might imagine, key management is a serious problem when symmetric cryptography is used.

Public key cryptography solves the key management problem by using a pair of keys: one **public key** and one **private key**. The public key is mathematically related to the private key; therefore, when either of the keys is used to encrypt a message, the other key can be used to decrypt it. When using a key pair, only the owner has possession of the private key. **Figure 10-1** compares secret key and public key cryptography. In the public key example, the public key is used to *encrypt* messages; the private key to *decrypt*.

In addition to encrypting/decrypting information, key pairs can also be used to authenticate and verify the entity that sent the data. This is known as public key authentication.

In **public key authentication**, the public key is used to *decrypt* the digital signature in a message where the private key has been used to create a digital signature that binds the sender's identity to the actual data that is sent. In other words, only someone with the private key could have created the digital signature, which provides assurance that the information comes from someone you trust.

Just as we trust the information on a driver's license because it is issued by a known authority such as the Department of Motor Vehicles (DMV) or a passport because it is issued by a government agency, the entire public key cryptography system is also founded on a certain level of trust. In this situation, we must trust the entities that issue the key pairs, which are known as **Certification Authorities (CAs) (Figure 10-2)**.

To obtain a pair of keys, the CA must be contacted and you must present some form of proof of identity. What you are required to provide for proof is entirely up to the issuing CA. In some cases, this may just be your e-mail address, but in others, it could be a passport, a driver's license, or even a meeting with a representative of the company that has the CA. As you can see, identification verification can vary widely from one situation to another.

Figure 10-1 Secret versus public key cryptography

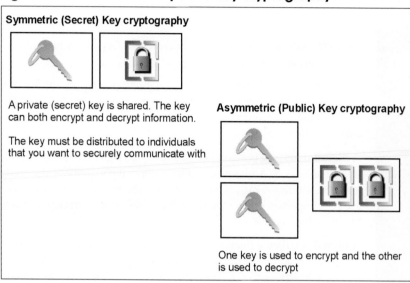

Symmetric (Secret) Key cryptography

A private (secret) key is shared. The key can both encrypt and decrypt information.

The key must be distributed to individuals that you want to securely communicate with

Asymmetric (Public) Key cryptography

One key is used to encrypt and the other is used to decrypt

Figure 10-2 Certificate analogy

Department of
Motor Vehicles (DMV)
CERTIFICATION AUTHORITY

Server running Certificate
Services
CERTIFICATION AUTHORITY

Driver's License

Digital Certificate

skill 2
Introducing the Core Components of a Public Key Infrastructure

exam objective

Basic knowledge

overview

Public/private keys, digital certificates, and Certification Authorities (CAs) are all core components of a PKI.

Earlier you learned how public key cryptography solves the key management problem by using a pair of keys: one public key and one private key. Although these keys can be used to encrypt and decrypt information, they can also be used to provide digital signing and authentication capabilities as well.

A **digital signature** is much like a handwritten signature in that it holds the same legal authority in most cases. A digital signature ensures the identity of the entity that sent the message and makes sure the message has not been altered while in transit. As you can imagine, these are very important services in many business-related transactions such as signing contracts or buying/selling online.

A **digital certificate** (usually referred to simply as a certificate) verifies the identity of a user, computer, or service. It matches the user/computer/service with its public and private key pair. As we indicated earlier, a good analogy for a digital certificate is a driver's license. Just as a driver's license verifies the identity of the holder and the privileges and rights the driver has, a digital certificate gives its holder rights and permissions to conduct trusted communications.

A Certification Authority (CA) issues digital certificates and verifies the information submitted before approving the release of the certificate. In other words, a CA vouches for the authenticity of the public keys that belong to users, computers, and/or other CAs. The level of verification performed is dependent upon the security requirements of the organization, as well as what the certificate will be used for. As we indicated earlier, this can include anything from submitting a valid e-mail address to requiring an extensive background check.

You can use **Certificate Services** in Windows Server 2003 to host your own CA hierarchy. There are two types of CAs: **Enterprise CAs** and **Standalone CAs**. **Table 10-1** provides characteristics of each type.

For each category, a Root CA or Subordinate CA is implemented. A **Root CA** signs its own certificate during the installation process and is considered the point of trust for a PKI hierarchy. A Root CA can issue certificates to computers and users but is designed to issue certificates only to other CAs, known as Subordinate CAs. **Subordinate CAs** issue certificates to users and computers.

Table 10-1   Standalone versus Enterprise Certification Authorities

Standalone Certification Authority	Enterprise Certification Authority
Can be removed from the network and placed in a secure physical location.	Cannot be removed from the network due to its dependency upon Active Directory.
When a small number of certificates are required, the manual approval process required is manageable.	Provides for auto-enrollment and approval of certificate requests by using information stored in Active Directory. No manual intervention is required.
Clients cannot take advantage of Active Directory.	Clients can take advantage of integration with Active Directory.
Certificate enrollment is only accessible via the Microsoft Certificate Services Web Enrollment Support pages.	Certificate enrollment can be handled via the Web Enrollment Support pages or using the Certificates snap-in via a Microsoft Management Console (MMC).
Users must manually enter information to identify to identity themselves when requesting a certificate.	User's information is automatically retrieved from Active Directory and entered, regardless of method used to enroll.
Certificates are manually approved or denied.	Certificates are approved manually, or automatically through Active Directory.
Can be installed on domain controller, member server, or standalone server. (Note: Microsoft recommends not installing a CA on a domain controller due to security reasons.)	Can be installed on domain controller or member server. Since it is registered as a resource in the forest, it must not be installed on a standalone server. (Note: Microsoft recommends not installing a CA on a domain controller due to security reasons.)

skill 3

Implementing a Standalone Certificate Authority

exam objective

Basic knowledge

overview

The following example demonstrates the steps involved in setting up a **Standalone Root CA**. This is the top-level CA in a CA hierarchy and may or may not be a member of a domain. Standalone Root CAs can be disconnected from the network to provide a higher level of security for the PKI. This CA can be used to issue certificates to users, computers, and services but, due to security reasons, should only issue certificates to Subordinate CAs. Subordinate CAs can obtain their certificate from the offline Standalone Root CA by saving their request to a floppy disk and then using the Web Enrollment pages on the Standalone Root CA to submit their request. Once the request has been approved, the new certificate can be downloaded to the floppy disk and then installed on the Subordinate CA. Subordinate CAs are then configured to issue certificates to users, computers, and services.

When using a Standalone CA, users can only request certificates by using the Web Enrollment Support pages. This means users must enter more information to identify themselves to a Standalone CA as compared to an Enterprise CA. Enterprise CAs obtain their information directly from Active Directory.

The certificate request is then placed into a pending state until the Administrator for the CA can review it. Once the certificate request has been accepted, the certificate is issued to the user. The user must then access the CA through the Microsoft Certificate Services Web site to install the certificate on his or her local computer.

tip

Standalone CAs may or may not be members of the domain. A Standalone CA does not require Active Directory to function, but will use it, if it is present, to publish certificates and certificate revocation lists.

how to

Install a Standalone Root CA. (The following assumes that Internet Information Services has been installed on the computer that will run Certificate Services.)

1. Click **Start**, point to **Control Panel**, and click **Add or Remove Programs**.
2. Click **Add/Remove Windows Components** and check **Certificate Services (Figure 10-3)**. When prompted, click **Yes** in the message box that opens to inform you that you will not be able to change the computer name or domain membership.
3. Click **Next>** in the **Windows Components** dialog box.
4. Select **Stand-alone root CA** for the CA type (**Figure 10-4**).
5. Enter **Stand-alone Root CA** in the **Common name for this CA** text box and then click **Next>**. Note that the validity period, which indicates when the CA expires, will be left at its default.
6. Leave the default locations for the certificate database and certificate database log, and do not select the **Store configuration information in a shared folder** check box. Click **Next>** (**Figure 10-5**).
7. During the component configuration process, a message box will appear indicating that Certificate Services must temporarily stop Internet Information Services. Click **Yes** to continue.
8. Click **Yes** to enable Active Server Pages. Note that Active Server Pages are required to use the Web Enrollment Support pages. They provide a Web-based user interface to a CA.
9. Click **Finish** to close the **Windows Component Wizard**.
10. Click **Start**, point to **Administrative Tools**, and click **Certification Authority** to confirm the installation. You should see a green check mark next to the CA's name (**Figure 10-6**).

Figure 10-3 Installing Certificate Services

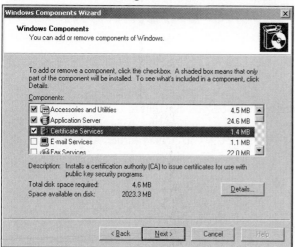

Figure 10-4 Configuring a Standalone Root CA

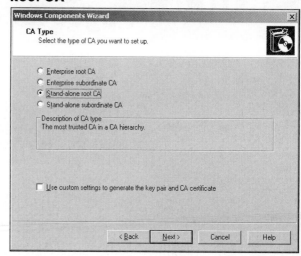

Figure 10-5 Default storage settings

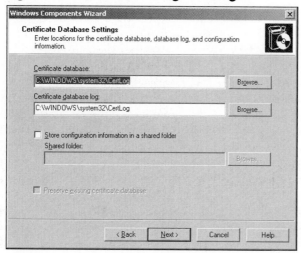

Figure 10-6 Confirming Certificate Services is running

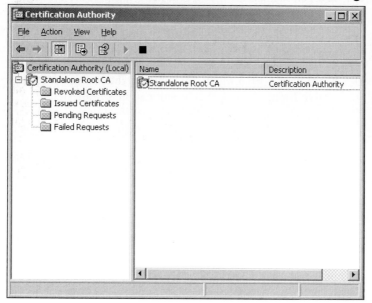

skill 4

Using Web Enrollment Support Pages for Certificate Enrollment

exam objective

Basic knowledge

overview

Once you have a Public Key Infrastructure in place, you can start to issue certificates. In the following exercise, you will learn how to request a certificate by using the Web Enrollment Support pages. You will use the Standalone Root CA you created earlier. As previously indicated, the Web Enrollment Support pages are the only way to request certificates from this type of CA.

The Microsoft Certificate Services Web Enrollment pages are located at **http://*servername*/certsrv**, where servername is the computer name of the computer that hosts the Certification Authority.

The Web Enrollment Support pages can be used to request certificates, check on the status of a recently submitted request, and retrieve the CA's certificate to place in your trusted root store. Certificates are stored locally in the Registry on the computer from which they were requested. This is known as a certificate store.

tip

By default, certificates can only be requested from a Standalone CA by using Web Enrollment Support pages. Enterprise CAs support Web Enrollment Support pages or the use of the Certification Request Wizard for obtaining certificates.

how to

Request a Web browser certificate from a Standalone CA using Web Enrollment Support pages.

1. Click [🏁 Start], point to **Programs**, and click **Internet Explorer** on a computer that can connect to the Microsoft Certificate Services Web site's Web Enrollment Support pages.
2. In the Address field, enter **http://*servername*/certsrv**. The servername is the name of the computer that you are running Certificate Services on. In this case, it is **dc2k3** (**Figure 10-7**).
3. Under the **Select a task** heading, click the **Request a certificate** link.
4. On the **Request a Certificate** page, select **Web Browser Certificate**.
5. In order to complete your certificate, you must manually enter your **Identifying Information (Figure 10-8)** and then click [Submit >].
6. A message box appears. Click [Yes] to request a certificate.
7. Upon submission of your request, you should see **Figure 10-9** indicating your certificate is now in a pending state awaiting approval by the CA's administrator. Click the **Home** link in the upper-right corner to return to the Certificate Services home page.

   The following steps are performed by the CA administrator on the CA from which you requested the certificate.

8. On the CA from which you requested the certificate, click [🏁 Start], point to **Administrative Tools**, and then click **Certification Authority**.
9. Click the "+" next to the name of the CA and click the **Pending Requests** folder. In the right pane, you should see the request for a certificate that was generated in Steps 1-7.
10. Right-click the certificate, select **All Tasks**, then click **Issue** to approve the certificate request (**Figure 10-10**). Note that before issuing the certificate, you would normally review the information submitted and approve or deny it based on your company's CA policies. Remember that by approving the certificate request, your CA is vouching for the user's identity based on the information submitted.
11. Click the **Issued Certificates** folder to confirm the certificate has been approved and issued.
12. On the computer you requested the certificate from, open Internet Explorer and return to the Microsoft Certificate Services Web site located at: **http://*servername*/certsrv**.

Figure 10-7 Accessing the Web Enrollment Web Page

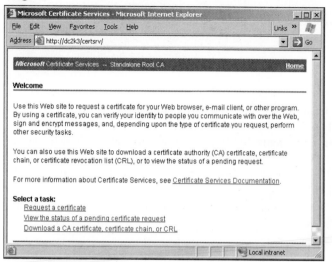

Figure 10-8 Entering Identifying Information to request certificate

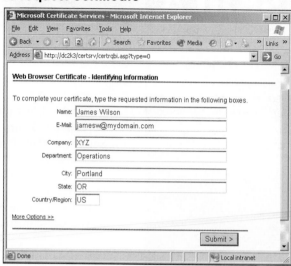

Figure 10-9 Certificate in pending status

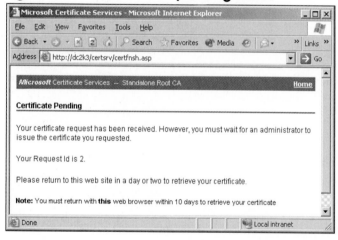

Figure 10-10 Approving the certificate request

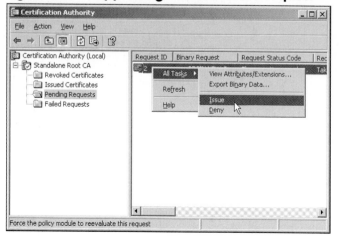

skill 4

Using Web Enrollment Support Pages for Certificate Enrollment *(cont'd)*

exam objective

Basic Knowledge

how to

13. Under the **Select a task** heading, click the **View the status of a pending certificate request** link (**Figure 10-11**).
14. Select the **Web Browser Certificate** link to view the status of the certificate you requested earlier.
15. On the **Certificate Issued** Web page, click **Install this certificate (Figure 10-12)**.
16. In the message box, click [Yes] when prompted if you want to add the certificate now. The message **Your new certificate has been successfully installed** is now displayed. Close Internet Explorer.

Figure 10-11 Checking on the status of certificate

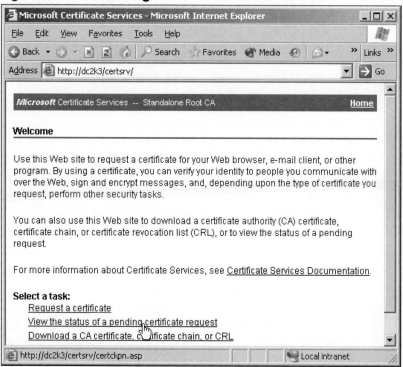

Figure 10-12 Installing the certificate

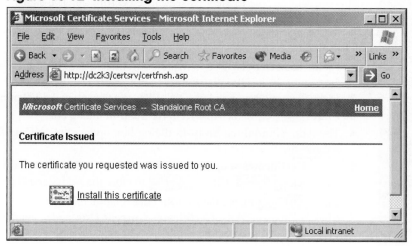

skill 5

Viewing Certificates

exam objective

Basic knowledge

overview

Now that you have completed the process for obtaining a digital certificate from a Certification Authority (CA), let's take a closer look at the certificate itself. A Certification Authority uses its private key to digitally sign the certificate that includes a public key. The digital signature binds the value of the public key to a user, computer, or service that holds the corresponding private key. Certificates are based on the **X.509 certificate standard**. This standard specifies the format and information contained within the certificate itself. Typically this includes the public key, and information about the person or entity to whom the certificate was issued, as well as information about the certificate and the CA that issued it.

Each certificate is broken down into three tabs: General, Details, and Certification Path.

The **General** tab provides information regarding whom the certificate was issued to, what CA issued it, and the period of time the certificate is valid (**Figure 10-13**).

The information on the **Details** tab provides details on the version of the certificate, its serial number, and the algorithm used to create the certificate (**Figure 10-14**). It also includes information on the CA that issued the certificate including its validity period. In the subject field, you will see to whom the certificate is issued. You will also see the type and length of the public key that is associated with the certificate. The enhanced key usage indicates what the certificate can be used for (e. g., client authentication, Encrypting File System, secure e-mail).

The **Certification Path** tab provides information on the path of certificates that lead to the trusted root (**Figure 10-15**). In our example we issued the certificates from a Root CA, so it is the only one that shows up in the path. If the certificate was issued by a Subordinate CA, it would show up in the path as well. If you click on the Standalone Root CA in the Certificate path, you will be able to view its self-signed certificate. The status of the certificate is also indicated on this tab.

how to

View a certificate.

1. On the computer you used to request a certificate in Skill 4, click [Start], click **Run**, and enter **mmc** in the **Run** dialog box.
2. In the Console Root window, click **File**, and then click **Add/Remove Snap-in**.
3. Click [Add...] in the **Add/Remove Snap-in** dialog box.
4. The **Add Standalone Snap-in** dialog box opens. Select **Certificates** and then click [Add].
5. In the **Certificates snap-in** dialog box, select the **My user account** option button, and then click [Finish]. Click [Close] to close the Add Standalone Snap-in dialog box.
6. Click [OK] to exit the Add/Remove Snap-in dialog box.
7. Click "+" to expand the **Certificates-Current User** node, and then click the "+" next to **Personal** to expand it.
8. Click the **Certificates** folder, right-click the name of the person to whom the certificate was issued (see Skill 4, Step 5), and click **Open** to view the certificate in the right pane (**Figure 10-16**). The certificate is the Web Browser certificate requested in Skill 4.

Figure 10-13 The General tab in the Certificate dialog box

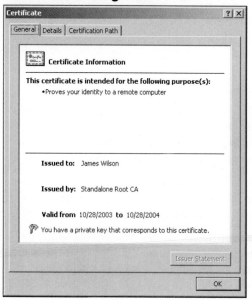

Figure 10-14 The Details tab

Figure 10-15 The Certification Path tab

Figure 10-16 Viewing a user's certificate

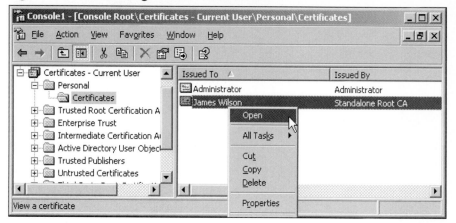

skill 6

Implementing an Enterprise CA

exam objective

Basic knowledge

overview

Both Standalone and Enterprise CAs self-sign their own digital certificates. Unlike Standalone CAs, an Enterprise CA requires that Active Directory be implemented on the network. You can use Enterprise CAs to take advantage of several features that Active Directory provides, such as smart card authentication and predefined certificate templates.

As you may have noticed when requesting a Web Browser certificate using the Standalone CA, you had to enter several pieces of information to identify yourself. An Enterprise CA uses information in Active Directory to automatically identify the requester.

Enterprise CAs use Group Policy to enter certificates in the trusted root store of all users/computers in the domain. To accomplish this on a Standalone CA, you would access the Web Enrollment Support pages to install the CA certificate chain manually. This allows you to trust certificates issued by that CA.

tip

Microsoft does not support the installation of Certificate Services on systems that are members of a server cluster.

how to

Install an Enterprise Root CA.

1. Click **Start**, point to **Control Panel**, and click **Add or Remove Programs**.
2. Click **Add/Remove Windows Components** and then select the **Certificate Services** check box. Click **Yes** in the message box that informs you that you will not be able to change the computer name or domain membership.
3. Click **Next >** in the **Windows Components** dialog box.
4. For the CA type, select **Enterprise root CA (Figure 10-17)** and then click **Next >**.
5. Enter Enterprise root CA in the **Common name for this CA** text box and then click **Next >**. Note that the validity period, which indicates when the CA expires, will be left at its default.
6. Leave the default locations for the certificate database and certificate database log, and do not select the **Store configuration information in a shared folder** check box. Click **Next >**.
7. Click **Yes** when you receive the message indicating Certificate Services must temporarily stop Internet Information Services.
8. Click **Finish** to close the **Windows Component Wizard**.
9. Click **Start**, point to **Administrative Tools**, and click **Certification Authority** to confirm the installation. You should see a green check mark next to the CA's name (**Figure 10-18**).

Figure 10-17 Configuring an Enterprise Root CA

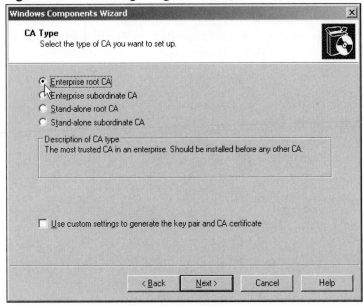

Figure 10-18 Confirming Certificate Services is running

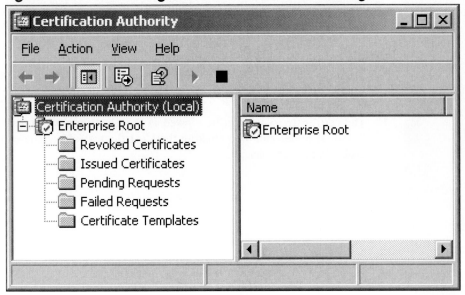

skill 7

Using the Certificate Request Wizard for Certificate Enrollment

exam objective

Basic knowledge

overview

To request a certificate from an Enterprise CA, you have two options: the Web Enrollment Support pages or the Certificate Request Wizard. Earlier in the lesson, you requested a certificate using the Web pages approach.

The Certificate Request Wizard is the preferred method when using Enterprise CAs in your organization. It can be accessed from the Certificates snap-in.

When using this tool, you will need to select the CA from which you want to request the certificate, and then select the appropriate certificate template based on your requirements.

tip

The Certificate Request Wizard only works with Enterprise Root and Enterprise Subordinate CAs.

how to

Use the Certificate Request Wizard.

1. Click [🏁 Start], click **Run**, and enter **mmc** in the **Run** dialog box.
2. In the Console Root window, click **File**, and then click **Add/Remove Snap-in**.
3. In the **Add/Remove Snap-in** dialog box, click [Add...].
4. Select the **Certificates** snap-in from the list and then click [Add].
5. In the **Certificates snap-in** dialog box, select the **My user account** option button, and then click [Finish]. Click [Close] to return to the Add/Remove Snap-in box.
6. Click [OK] to return to the console.
7. In the console, right-click the **Certificates** folder, point to **All Tasks**, and then click **Request New Certificate (Figure 10-19)**. This will launch the **Certificate Request Wizard**.
8. Click [Next>] on the **Certificate Request Wizard Welcome** screen.
9. For Certificate type, select **User (Figure 10-20)**, then click [Next>].
10. Enter a friendly name and a description for the certificate **(Figure 10-21)** and click [Next>].
11. Click [Finish] after reviewing the settings you have configured.
12. Since the user information is stored in Active Directory, the certificate does not go into pending state. Click [OK] in the message box indicating the certificate request was successful.
13. The certificate issued can be viewed in the **Certificates** snap-in by expanding the **Personal** folder and then clicking the **Certificates** folder. The certificate should be visible in the right pane.

tip

The User certificate template is used for encrypting files and securing e-mail as well as for client authentication purposes.

Figure 10-19 Requesting new certificate

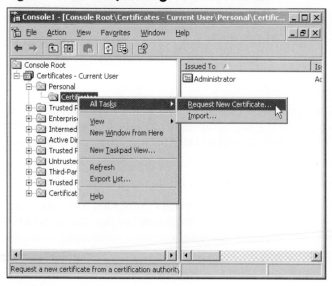

Figure 10-20 Selecting certificate type

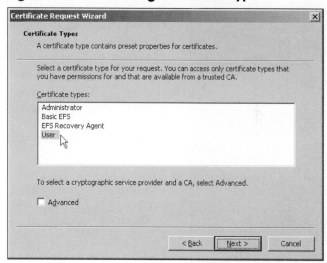

Figure 10-21 Entering friendly name for certificate

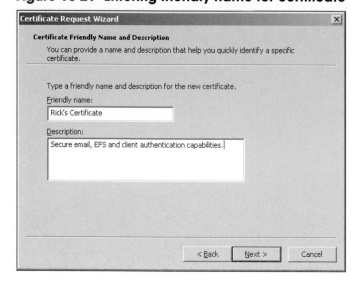

skill 8

Renewing a Certificate

exam objective

Basic knowledge

overview

If you review the User certificate you just issued, you will notice it has a validity period, which can be viewed on the General tab. If you used the default settings, this will be set to one year. Once the validity period expires, the user will no longer be able to use the certificate to validate his or her identity.

You can use the Certificates snap-in to renew a certificate before or after it becomes invalid.

In order to renew the certificate you will need to know which Certification Authority issued the certificate and whether or not you want a new public and private key pair. The longer a key pair is used, the more vulnerable it is to attack; therefore, Microsoft recommends that each time you renew a certificate you also renew the key sets.

tip

When a CA certificate is renewed, all certificates issued by the CA must also be renewed.

how to

Renew a certificate.
1. On the computer you used to request the certificate, click **Start**, click **Run**, and enter **mmc** in the **Run** dialog box.
2. In the Console Root, click **File**, and then click **Add/Remove Snap-in**.
3. Click **Add...** in the **Add/Remove Snap-in** dialog box, select **Certificates** in the **Add Standalone Snap-ins** dialog box, and then click **Add**.
4. In the **Certificates snap-in** dialog box, select the **My user account** option button, and then click **Finish**. Click **Close** to close the Add Standalone Snap-in dialog box.
5. Click **OK** to exit the Add/Remove Snap-in dialog box.
6. Click "+" to expand the **Certificates-Current User**, then click the "+" next to **Personal** to expand it.
7. Click the **Certificates** folder and select the certificate that you want to renew in the right pane.
8. Right-click the certificate, point to **All Tasks**, and then click **Renew Certificate with New Key (Figure 10-22)**.
9. Click **Next >** in the **Certificate Request Wizard Welcome** screen.
10. Select **Yes**, and accept the default values in the **Certificate Renewal** options box.
11. Click **OK** and then **Finish** after reviewing your settings.
12. When the message **The certificate request was successful** appears, click **OK** (Figure 10-23).

Figure 10-22 Renewing certificate with new key

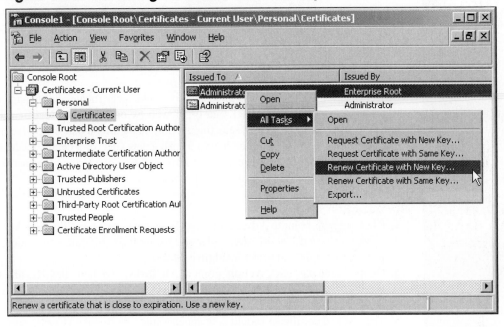

Figure 10-23 Certificate request approved

skill 9

Revoking a Certificate

exam objective

Basic knowledge

overview

As the administrator of a Public Key Infrastructure, it is critical that you maintain the integrity of your certificates. If a user leaves your organization or a private key is compromised, you must revoke the certificate. You may also find it necessary to revoke a certificate when it no longer aligns with your security policy. When certificates are revoked, they become part of a **Certificate Revocation List (CRL)**. Every Certification Authority will publish the CRL, by default, weekly.

The Certification Authority snap-in is used to revoke a certificate and manage the Certificate Revocation List (CRL). The CRL can be viewed by opening the **Certification Authority**, selecting **Revoked Certificates,** selecting **Action** on the Menu bar, then selecting **Properties**. Certificate Revocation Lists come in two forms: a new CRL or a delta CRL. A delta CRL is a small CRL that lists the certificates that have been revoked since the last full CRL. Both settings can be configured as shown in **Figure 10-24**.

tip

Certificates can also be revoked from a command line using **certutil—**revoke *SerialNumber* ReasonCode.

how to

tip

If you select Certificate Hold as the Reason code, you can unrevoke it later if you choose. This is the only code that will allow you to unrevoke the certificate later.

Revoke a certificate.
1. Click **Start**, point to **Administrative Tools**, and click **Certification Authority**.
2. Click the **Issued Certificates** folder and locate the certificate you want to revoke in the pane on the right and select it **(Figure 10-25)**.
3. On the Menu bar, click **Action**, point to **All Tasks**, and then click **Revoke Certificate**.
4. Enter the appropriate reason for revoking the certificate in the **Reason code** text box and then click [Yes] **(Figure 10-26)**.
5. The revoked certificate should now appear under the Revoked Certificates folder and will show up on the CRL the next time it is published.

Figure 10-24 CRL publication schedule configuration

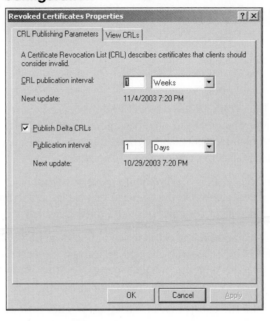

Figure 10-25 Locating the certificate to revoke

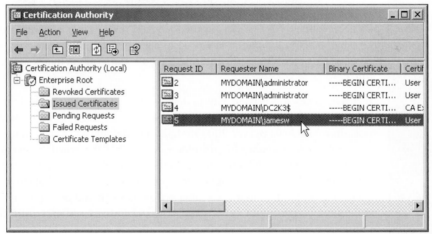

Figure 10-26 Reason code for revoking certificate

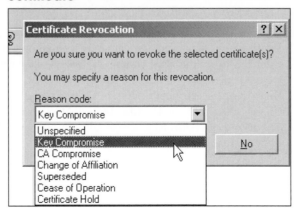

skill 10

Introducing the Encrypting File System

exam objective

Basic knowledge

overview

The **Encrypting File System (EFS)**, introduced with the release of Windows 2000, uses public key cryptography to store data more securely on NTFS volumes. The keys used to perform encryption/decryption are obtained from the certificate of the user, additional users who have been given access, and/or recovery agents.

Encrypting files is a very simple process. Right-click the file you want to encrypt and then select **Properties**. On the **General** tab, click the **Advanced** button and select the check box next to **Encrypt contents to secure data**. The file encryption bit has been set on the file.

At this point, EFS will check to see if there is an EFS certificate for the user who is encrypting the file. The EFS certificate and the private keys used in EFS can be issued by a Microsoft Certification Authority or a third-party CA if they are available; otherwise, the EFS certificate and private keys will be generated automatically.

Once the file encryption bit is set, a **file encryption key (FEK)** is generated for the file. The FEK is encrypted by using the user's public key, which corresponds to the user's EFS certificate. By encrypting the FEK, only the user who holds the matching private key can decrypt the file later. The FEK is also protected by using the public key of each user who has been authorized to decrypt the file and each recovery agent as well.

To decrypt files, the FEK has to be decrypted first. This is accomplished by using a priva e key that matches the public key used to encrypt the FEK. Decrypting files is a very simp.e process. Clear the **Encrypt contents to secure data** option that was set earlier to encrypt the file.

If a user loses his private key or leaves the company, you must be able to decrypt his information. Fortunately, a person who is designated as a **recovery agent** can accomplish this task. In a Windows Server 2003 domain, the default recovery policy assigns the recovery agent role to the domain administrator account when the first domain controller is configured. Other users can be added to this default policy as needed. Recovery agents have special certificates, which are associated with a private key that allows data to be decrypted. Recovery agent certificates and their associated private keys should be exported to portable media and stored in a safe location. After exporting, delete the certificate from the local computer to improve security.

When the recovery agent needs to decrypt information, he or she will restore the certificate/private key using the Certificates snap-in. Do not forget to delete the certificate after completing the recovery process.

tip

EFS does not protect data in transit, only on the local hard drive. Use IPSec to protect data in transit.

tip

Windows XP and Windows Server 2003 support storage of encrypted files on remote servers but the client and server must be in the same family forest.

tip

If you encrypt a parent folder, all files and folders added to it later will be encrypted as well.

how to

Export a certificate and delete the private key.
1. Create a Microsoft Management Console (MMC) that includes the **Certificates-Current User** snap-in. Make sure the snap-in is focused on **My user account**.
2. Click the "+" next to the **Personal** folder and select **Certificates**. In the right pane, locate the certificate that you want to export.
3. Right-click the certificate, point to **All Tasks**, and then click **Export (Figure 10-27)**.
4. Click Next > in the **Certificate Export Wizard Welcome** screen.
5. The **Export Private Key** screen appears. Select **Yes, export the private key**. Click Next > **(Figure 10-28)**.

Figure 10-27 Exporting a certificate

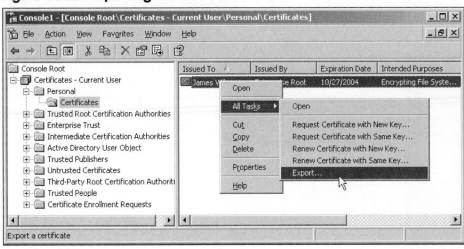

Figure 10-28 Exporting private key with certificate

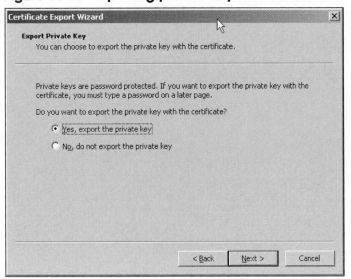

skill 10

Introducing the Encrypting File System (cont'd)

exam objective   Basic knowledge

how to

6. For the export file format, select **Include all certificates in the certification path if possible, enable strong protection, and delete the private key if the export is successful**. Click [Next >].

7. Enter a password to protect the private key **(Figure 10-29)**, then click [Next >].

8. Specify the name of the file you want to export, for instance JamesPrivateKey, and click [Next >]. Note that the file will be stored in the user's profile (c:\documents and settings\username\JamesPrivateKey.pfx) if you do not browse to a portable device such as a floppy. It is important to remember to move this to a secure location by moving it to a portable device such as a floppy disk, or preferably, a writable CD, and then protect the disc itself.

9. Click [Finish] after reviewing the summary and then click [OK].

Figure 10-29 Using a password to protect the private key

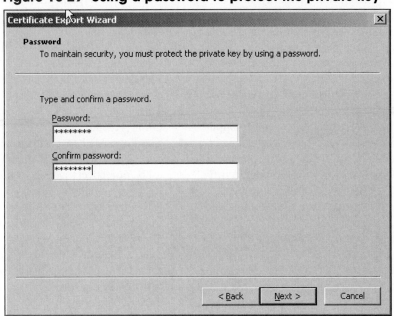

Summary

- A Public Key Infrastructure (PKI) is a set of services that supports the use of cryptography.
- Public key cryptography uses a pair of keys: one public key and one private key.
- Certificate Services allows a Windows Server 2003 computer to become a Certification Authority.
- Digital certificates are used to verify the identity of a user, computer, or service. They match the entity with their public and private key pair. Certificates are obtained by contacting a CA and presenting information to prove your identity.
- Root CAs (Enterprise or Standalone) self-sign their own certificates.
- A Root CA can issue certificates to users/computers/services, but it is recommended that they issue certificates only to other CAs for security purposes. Subordinate CAs (CAs that have received their certificates from another CA) should issue these certificates.
- Enterprise CAs require Active Directory, Standalone CAs do not.
- A Standalone Root CA can be removed from the network to improve PKI security.
- There are two options for requesting certificates from CAs. If a Standalone CA is used, you must use the Web Enrollment Support pages. If an Enterprise CA is used, use either the Web Enrollment Support pages or the Certificate Request Wizard.
- Certificates issued to a user/computer/service can be viewed by using the Certificates snap-in. The same snap-in can be used to renew a certificate after it has been issued or before it becomes invalid. This can occur when a CA that issued the certificate has had its certificate renewed due to compromise or a reinstallation.
- You may also have to revoke a certificate if an employee leaves the organization or if his private key is compromised. This can be done using the Certification Authority snap-in.
- Revoked certificates are added to the Certificate Revocation List (CRL).
- The Encrypting File System (EFS) also uses public key cryptography to protect files.
- Certificates for EFS can be issued automatically if no CA is present.
- The keys used to perform encryption/decryption are obtained from the certificate of the user, additional users, or recovery agents.
- Recovery agents can decrypt files after an employee leaves the company or if he or she loses the private key. This ensures no data can be lost due to encryption.
- The domain administrator is assigned the recovery agent role by default. Other users can be added as recovery agents if necessary. Always export the recovery agent certificates and private keys to removable media for increased security.

Key Terms

Certificate Revocation List
Certification Authorities (CAs)
Certificate Services
Cryptography
Decrypting
Digital certificate
Digital signature
Encrypting

Encrypting File System (EFS)
Enterprise CA
File encryption key (FEK)
Private key
Public key
Public key authentication
Public key cryptography
Public Key Infrastructure (PKI)

Recovery agent
Root CA
Secret key cryptography
Standalone CA
Standalone Root CA
Subordinate CA
X.509 certificate standard

Test Yourself

1. Which of the following can use certificates in a Public Key Infrastructure? (Choose all that apply.)
   a. Users
   b. Computers
   c. Services
   d. Domain controllers
   e. Windows 2003 Servers

2. In public key authentication, the public key is used to decrypt the _____ in a message.
   a. Digital Signature
   b. Private key
   c. EFS
   d. PKI

3. James has implemented a Standalone CA on his network. Which method(s) can be used to request a certificate? (Choose all that apply.)
   a. Certificate Request Wizard
   b. Web Enrollment Pages
   c. MMC
   d. Digital Signature
   e. SHIVA

4. Mary would like to set up a Root CA that can be taken offline to increase security for her PKI. Which of the following are true statements? (Choose all that apply.)
   a. A Standalone Root CA cannot be taken offline.
   b. A Standalone Root CA can be taken offline.
   c. An Enterprise Root CA can be taken offline.
   d. An Enterprise Root CA cannot be taken offline.

5. You have implemented a Standalone CA on your network to issue Web Browser certificates to users. Which method(s) below will provide them with a way to request their certificates? (Choose all that apply.)
   a. http://servername/certsrv
   b. Web Enrollment Pages
   c. Certificate Request Wizard
   d. MMC

6. Which of the following standards dictates the format and syntax of a digital certificate?
   a. X.508
   b. X.509
   c. X.502
   d. X.510

7. Which statements below are true regarding Certificate Revocation Lists (CRL)? (Choose all that apply.)
   a. CRLs list the certificates that have been revoked.
   b. A delta CRL is a small CRL that lists certificates revoked since the last full CRL.
   c. A CRL publication interval is set to one week by default.
   d. A delta CRL publication interval is set to one week by default.

8. When using EFS, which statements are true regarding issuing certificates? (Choose all that apply.)
   a. EFS certificates can be issued automatically.
   b. EFS certificates can be issued by a CA.
   c. EFS certificates can be issued by a third-party CA.
   d. None of the above.

Projects: On Your Own

The following projects require a Windows XP Professional computer and a Windows Server 2003 domain controller. Join the Windows XP Professional computer to the domain. Create a domain user account for Mary Jones. Add Mary Jones' domain user account as a member of the local Power Users group on the Windows XP Professional computer to allow her to share the Sales folder.

1. Encrypt folder/files using EFS.
   a. Log on to the domain as **Mary Jones**.
   b. Create a folder name **Sales** and share it. Add a text file to the folder named **finances.txt**.
   c. Next, right-click the **Sales** folder and select **Properties** and then **Advanced**.
   d. Check the appropriate box to encrypt the folder and its contents and then click **OK**.
   e. Click **OK** and then select **Apply changes to this folder, subfolders, and files** in the Confirm Attribute Changes dialog box. Click OK. Log off.

   f. Log on using the Domain Administrator's account.
   g. Test access to the file named **finances.txt**. You should receive an **Access Denied** message because the file was en-crypted under Mary's account.
   h. Right-click the **finances.txt** file and select Properties. Click the **Advanced** button and attempt to uncheck the **Encrypt contents to secure data** check box. Select **OK**.
   i. Click **OK** to close the **finances.txt Properties** dialog box. You should receive an **Access Denied** message because you do not have rights to decrypt the file, even though you are logged on under the Domain Administrator account which is the EFS Recovery Agent for the domain.

2. Assume that Mary is no longer with the company and you need to gain access to the encrypted file **finances.txt**. Use the Recovery Agent's certificate to recover Mary's encrypted information. To accomplish this, you need to back up the **Sales** folder to a share

that is located on the domain controller named **FilesToRecover**. The domain controller is where the EFS Recovery Agent's certificate and private key are stored.

a. Log on the domain controller with the Administrator account.

b. Create a folder and name it **FilesToRecover**. You will use this folder as the restore point for Mary's **Sales** folder. Share the **FilesToRecover** folder so that **Everyone** has **Full Control**.

c. Create another folder named **EfsRecoveredFiles** on the domain controller as well.

d. Log on under the Domain Administrators account on the Windows XP Professional computer and back up the **Sales** folder to the **FilesToRecover** folder on the domain controller.

1. Launch the **Backup** tool which is located in the **System Tools** folder.

2. Select **Back up files and settings** and locate the **Sales** folder on Mary's computer.

3. In the **Items to Back Up**, select the **Sales** folder. This will automatically include the **finances.txt** file as well.

4. Save the backup to the **FilesToRecover** folder, the restore point, on the domain controller and name it **MarysEfsfiles**.

e. On the domain controller, use the **Backup** tool to restore the Sales folder to the **EfsRecoveredFiles** folder.

f. After the restore process has completed, access the **finances.txt** file, which is now located in the **EfsRecoveredFiles** folder and decrypt it.

g. The file is now decrypted and can be made available to the appropriate personnel.

Problem Solving Scenarios

1. Troy Jones has just taken over responsibility for administering a Windows Server 2003 network that uses EFS. Within a few minutes of arriving at his desk, he receives a phone call from his new boss who notifies him that the Human Resources Manager has fired an employee. Unfortunately, they have discovered that the employee encrypted some files before walking out the door. The files are extremely important and must be accessible to the Human Resources Manager. Can the files be recovered? If so, who will be able to decrypt them?

2. XYZ, Inc. would like you to create a CA hierarchy for its PKI. XYZ would like to be able to remove the server that performs the Root CA role to make the PKI more secure. Two other CAs will remain online to issue certificates to users/computers/services on the network. Mark, the CFO, indicates Enterprise CAs would be the most efficient because they automatically enroll and issue certificates. William, the IT Manager, indicates Standalone CAs should be used. Who is correct and what type of hierarchy should be set up to meet the company's objectives?

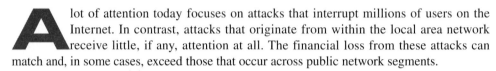

LESSON

11

Implementing and Managing IP Security

A lot of attention today focuses on attacks that interrupt millions of users on the Internet. In contrast, attacks that originate from within the local area network receive little, if any, attention at all. The financial loss from these attacks can match and, in some cases, exceed those that occur across public network segments.

As a network administrator, you are probably well aware of the mechanisms available for protecting resources on the network. These range from simply placing resources such as printers, hubs, switches, and servers in secure locations so that only selected individuals can physically access them to protecting data using NTFS and Microsoft's Encrypting File System (EFS).

Although these approaches will increase security of resources, they still represent only one component of your overall security plan. Information must be protected while it is in transit. If not, an attacker may be able to modify file contents or impersonate another computer to gain confidential information. Passwords that are in transit between two computers must also be protected.

In the security industry, three terms used frequently when it comes to protecting information are authentication, confidentiality, and integrity.

- Authentication is the process of verifying that an entity is who or what it claims to be.
- Confidentiality is the process of ensuring that data is safe from being intercepted, viewed, or copied while in transit.
- Integrity is the process of ensuring that data received is accurate and complete.

This lesson focuses on one of the security features available within Windows Server 2003 that can provide those capabilities: IPSec.

The lesson concludes with a discussion of how to further secure your computers by using security templates. By using either predefined templates or creating your own custom templates, you can establish a baseline of security for Windows 2000 computers on your network.

Goals

In this lesson, you will learn about the fundamentals of IPSec and how IPSec can be used to secure traffic as it transits within or between local networks. You will learn how to assign IPSec policies using Local Computer Policy as well as Group Policy. You will also learn how to create custom IPSec policies and then use monitoring tools to test your policies. The lesson concludes with a discussion of security templates and how they can be used to establish a baseline for computers on your network.

Lesson 11   Implementing and Managing IP Security

Skill	Exam 70-291 Objective
1. Introducing Internet Protocol Security (IPSec)	Monitor network protocol security. Tools might include the IP Security Monitor Microsoft Management Console (MMC) snap-in and Kerberos support tools.
2. Examining IPSec Fundamentals	Monitor network protocol security. Tools might include the IP Security Monitor Microsoft Management Console (MMC) snap-in and Kerberos support tools.
3. Implementing IPSec	Monitor network protocol security. Tools might include the IP Security Monitor Microsoft Management Console (MMC) snap-in and Kerberos support tools.
4. Assigning Default IPSec Policies Using the Local Computer Policy	Monitor network protocol security. Tools might include the IP Security Monitor Microsoft Management Console (MMC) snap-in and Kerberos support tools.
5. Assigning Default IPSec Policies Using Group Policy	Monitor network protocol security. Tools might include the IP Security Monitor Microsoft Management Console (MMC) snap-in and Kerberos support tools.
6. Configuring Components of an IPSec Policy	Monitor network protocol security. Tools might include the IP Security Monitor Microsoft Management Console (MMC) snap-in and Kerberos support tools.
7. Creating a Custom IPSec Policy	Monitor network protocol security. Tools might include the IP Security Monitor Microsoft Management Console (MMC) snap-in and Kerberos support tools.
8. Monitoring IPSec Sessions	Monitor network protocol security. Tools might include the IP Security Monitor Microsoft Management Console (MMC) snap-in and Kerberos support tools.
9. Troubleshooting IPSec Communications	Troubleshoot network protocol security. Tools might include the IP Security Monitor MMC snap-in, Event Viewer, and Network Monitor.
10. Working with Security Templates	Implement secure network administration procedures. Implement security baseline settings and audit security settings by using security templates. Implement the principle of least privilege.

Requirements

To complete this lesson, you will need administrative rights on a Windows XP Professional computer and a Windows Server 2003 computer. Some procedures will require that Active Directory be installed on the server.

skill 1

Introducing Internet Protocol Security (IPSec)

exam objective

Monitor network protocol security. Tools might include the IP Security Monitor Microsoft Management Console (MMC) snap-in and Kerberos support tools.

overview

Companies are expanding by placing branch offices in cities closer to their customer base, employees are telecommuting or traveling outside the office more, and the use of intranets to distribute information is becoming the norm rather than the exception. The traffic generated in these situations uses the Internet Protocol (IP).

Internet Protocol Security (IPSec), an extension to the Internet Protocol (IP), is a suite of network layer protocols. These protocols provide a method for ensuring authentication, confidentiality, and integrity of data in IP-based communications. **Authentication** is the process of verifying an entity is who it claims to be. **Confidentiality** implies the data in transit is safe from being intercepted, viewed, or copied. **Integrity** implies the data in a received message is accurate and complete. IPSec also protects against replay attacks **(Figure 11-1)**. In a **replay attack**, an attacker uses a protocol analyzer to capture packets as they move across the network. Once he has the packets on his computer, the attacker can extract the packets that contain authentication codes and digital signatures. Once extracted, they can be placed back on the network; that is why the term *replay* is used. At this point, the attacker is able to gain access to the target computer.

IPSec protects IP and higher layer protocols by using security policies to secure user communications within a local area network and/or between sites. The policies can be created using the IP Security Policies snap-in from within a Microsoft Management Console (MMC). Each policy includes one or more rules that contain filters. These filters determine whether or not the packets need to be encrypted, digitally signed or, in some cases, both.

Since IPSec packets travel across the network inside IP packets, the entire process is transparent to applications and users. Devices (routers/switches) between the two computers do not require any modifications to pass the IPSec packets.

Although firewalls and routers can protect against many external threats, they do not address threats against network resources that originate from inside the network. IPSec can protect against both. IPSec allows an administrator to encrypt communications between all computers in the network or between specific computers within a domain.

Figure 11-1　IPSec benefits

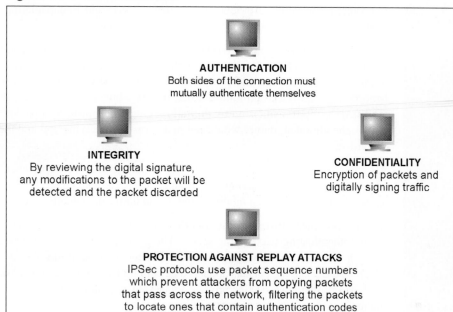

AUTHENTICATION
Both sides of the connection must
mutually authenticate themselves

INTEGRITY
By reviewing the digital signature,
any modifications to the packet will be
detected and the packet discarded

CONFIDENTIALITY
Encryption of packets and
digitally signing traffic

PROTECTION AGAINST REPLAY ATTACKS
IPSec protocols use packet sequence numbers
which prevent attackers from copying packets
that pass across the network, filtering the packets
to locate ones that contain authentication codes
and/or digital signatures, and then placing them
back on the network (replaying) in an attempt
to gain the desired access

skill 2

Examining IPSec Fundamentals

exam objective

Monitor network protocol security. Tools might include the IP Security Monitor Microsoft Management Console (MMC) snap-in and Kerberos support tools.

overview

To understand how IPSec works, you must understand the underlying protocols that it uses to protect information: Authentication Header (AH) and Encapsulating Security Payload (ESP).

The **Authentication Header (AH)** protocol ensures authentication and message integrity for transmitted packets. It can identify the sender (i.e., authentication) and ensure the data in the packet is accurate and complete (integrity). AH will not encrypt the data to keep it from being read (i.e., maintain confidentiality), but will ensure that the data cannot be modified during transmission by digitally signing the traffic. If a packet were modified in transit, the digital signature would not match on the receiving end and the packet would be discarded.

AH can also protect against replay attacks by adding sequencing numbers into each packet, which are read on the receiving end. If an attacker attempted a replay attack, AH would recognize the packet had been modified and would notify the intended recipient.

AH also provides **mutual authentication**. Traditional network authentication involves the client authenticating itself to the server. The assumption is that the server is trusted on the network. This may not always be the case if someone is **spoofing** the identity of the server, which would make the packets appear to be coming from a trusted host. Microsoft introduced **Kerberos** in Windows 2000 to provide a means to authenticate both ends of a communication channel before sensitive data is transmitted.

As we mentioned earlier, the AH protocol does not ensure that data in transit is safe from being intercepted, viewed, or being copied (confidentiality). Fortunately, the **Encapsulating Security Payload (ESP)** protocol can encrypt the actual application data that is included within the IP packet itself. In general, encryption is not used for the IP Header itself unless IPSec tunnel mode is used. ESP provides authentication, integrity, and anti-replay services as well. You might be wondering why AH would ever be used if ESP can perform the same services. The biggest difference between the two is that ESP protects only the TCP/UDP header (not the IP Header) and the actual application data from being inspected. AH protects the entire packet from modification. You can combine both protocols when implementing an IPSec security association.

Examples of both Authentication Header packet and Encapsulating Security Payload packet contents can be seen in **Figure 11-2** and **Figure 11-3**.

IPSec provides two modes for the Authentication Header and Encapsulating Security Payload protocols to operate with: transport mode and tunnel mode.

Transport mode: If your security design dictates that traffic must be secure over the entire path between the client and server, use **transport mode** (the default mode for IPSec). When transport mode is used, IPSec can use AH, ESP, or both to protect the data while it is in transit between the two computers.

Use transport mode in your security plan when you want to ensure the data is protected over the *entire path* between the source and destination computer. Only the computers that need to communicate with each other using IPSec should have their policy configured.

tip

Kerberos was created by the Massachusetts Institute of Technology in the 1980s. The current version, Kerberos version 5, is discussed in RFC 1510.

tip

Using IPSec in tunnel mode is not recommended for remote access VPNs. Use L2TP/IPSec or PPTP for remote access connections.

Figure 11-2 Authentication header packet contents

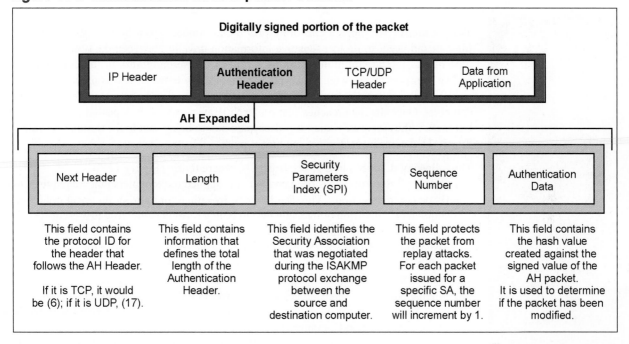

Figure 11-3 Encapsulating Security Payload packet contents

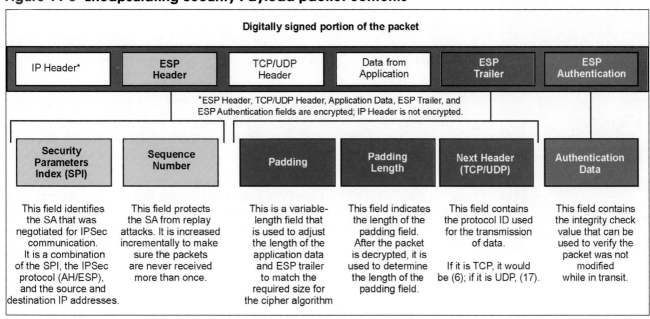

skill 2

Examining IPSec Fundamentals
(cont'd)

exam objective

Monitor network protocol security. Tools might include the IP Security Monitor Microsoft Management Console (MMC) snap-in and Kerberos support tools.

overview

Tunnel mode: You have a corporate office that connects to a branch office through the Internet and needs to protect sensitive information traveling between the two locations. This type of end-to-end communication uses routers as the endpoints in the communication. Unlike transport mode, which encrypts communication between two computers as it is sent on the local network, in **tunnel mode** data is sent unencrypted to the router closest to the computer. Once the data reaches that router, it is encrypted as it is passed across the public Internet. At the corporate router, it is decrypted before being sent to the destination computer. **Figure 11-4** compares transport and tunnel mode.

The following describes how IPSec is used to secure traffic (**Figure 11-5**):

1. Once an IPSec Policy has been created, it is applied to computers that are required to use IPSec communications. This can be done by either configuring the local policy on the computers in question or by using Group Policy if Active Directory is present. The IPSec policy defines how the IPSec driver will process traffic. It also defines the **security association (SA)** which controls the type of encryption to be used for specific types of traffic. The SA defines the authentication method (Kerberos, certificates, pre-shared keys) to use.
2. When Computer A sends a packet to Computer B, the IPSec driver on Computer A will intercept the packet and compare the destination IP address and protocol with the IPSec filters configured on Computer A.
3. If there is a matching IPSec filter, the IPSec driver on Computer A will send the packet to the Internet Key Exchange (IKE) module to begin the negotiation process with Computer B to establish a security association (SA). This is a two-phase process, which is discussed later in this lesson.
4. The IPSec driver on Computer A will then apply the appropriate level of encryption, as well as the algorithm to ensure data integrity, send it to the network adapter, and then on to Computer B.
5. When the packet is received on Computer B, it is passed to the IPSec driver where it is decrypted, checked for data integrity and passed to the appropriate application.

As indicated earlier, this is all transparent to the applications being used. IPSec encrypts the information after it leaves the application on Computer A and before it reaches the application on Computer B.

In step 3, we indicated that the Internet Key Exchange (IKE) begins a negotiation process to establish a security association. This actually occurs in two phases: Main Mode and Quick Mode.

During the Main Mode phase, Computers A and B go through the process of authenticating each other using IKE. The authentication methods available include Kerberos, certificates, and/or pre-shared keys. Once the Main Mode phase has been completed, a Main Mode security association is created. Note that Main Mode must complete before moving to the second phase of negotiations, Quick Mode.

In the second phase of negotiations, also known as the Quick Mode phase, the security protocols are established. During this phase, the computers must agree on the security protocols to use, either Authentication Header, Encapsulating Security Payload, or both. The protocols used depend upon the settings of the IPSec policy used. Once the security protocols are agreed, the security association is sent by IKE to the IPSec driver for processing.

tip

IKE is also known as ISAKMP (Internet Security Association and Key Management Protocol) or ISAKMP/Oakley (Oakley is a protocol by which two authenticated parties can agree on secure and secret keying material).

Figure 11-4 Transport/Tunnel Modes

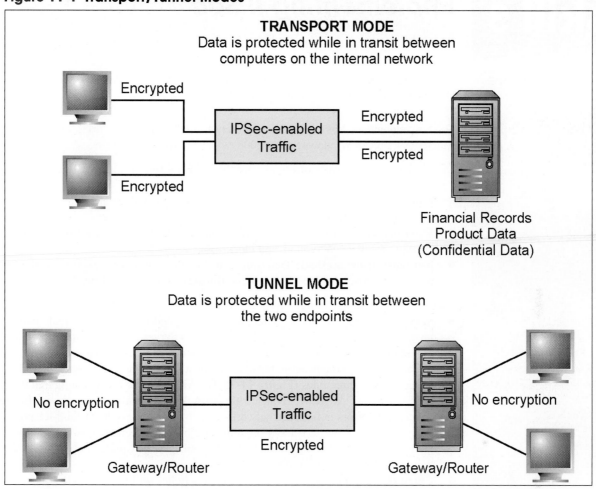

Figure 11-5 IPSec communication process

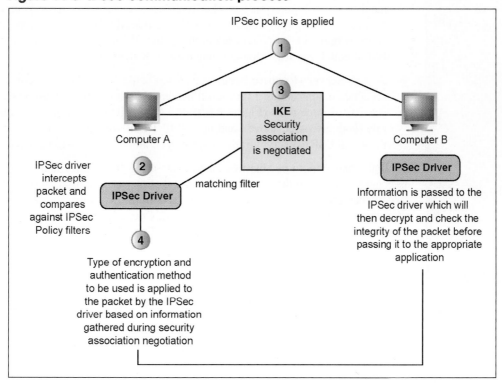

skill 3

Implementing IPSec

Monitor network protocol security. Tools might include the IP Security Monitor Microsoft Management Console (MMC) snap-in and Kerberos support tools.

overview

IPSec is implemented by either creating a custom IPSec policy or using one of the default policies available in Windows Server 2003.

Each IPSec policy consists of one or more rules. Each rule is composed of a filter, a filter action, and an authentication method.

◆ **Filter:** Identifies the type of traffic that the filter action will be applied to. Filters include protocols, ports, IP addresses, and DNS names.

◆ **Filter action:** Identifies what to do if the filter matches. Available actions include do not encrypt, negotiate encryption, and block.

◆ **Authentication method:** Determines the method used to authenticate the entities involved. Methods include Kerberos, certificates, or pre-shared keys.

There are three policies configured for IPSec by default (**Figure 11-6**).

◆ **Server (Request Security):** This policy is assigned to servers or clients that will be involved in communications with both Windows Server 2003 computers and computers running down-level operating systems. The client will attempt to use IPSec; if it cannot initiate IPSec communication, then communication will continue unencrypted. This policy consists of three rules (**Figure 11-7**). The All IP Traffic rule is configured to request ESP traffic, the All ICMP Traffic rule permits ICMP traffic which is used to report connectivity errors in IP-based networks, and the third rule is the Default Response rule. When this rule is used, trust is implemented by using Kerberos as the authentication method. The computer configured with this policy will request Encapsulating Security Payload (ESP) for all IP traffic.

◆ **Client (Respond Only):** Computers using this policy will never initiate a request to use IPSec for data transmissions but will enter a negotiation with Internet Key Exchange when requested to do so by another computer. This means that if a computer tries to access a system that does not use IPSec, it will not insist on using it either. On the other hand, if the computer on the other end does request IPSec, then your computer will support it. This policy consists of only one rule, the Default Response rule discussed above (**Figure 11-8**). When used in this policy, the hosts will respond to requests to use ESP if both hosts are in domains that trust each other.

◆ **Secure Server (Require Security):** When using this policy, the computer will only accept communications if they are IPSec-enabled. It can be used on servers or clients. It consists of three rules (**Figure 11-9**): the All ICMP Traffic rule, the Default Response rule (both discussed above), and the All IP Traffic rule, which differs in that it *requires* the use of ESP to encrypt traffic; otherwise, communication will not occur.

For both computers to be able to communicate using IPSec, they must establish a security association. Earlier in the lesson you learned that the security association (SA) controls the type of encryption to be used for specific types of traffic, as well as the authentication method (Kerberos, certificates, pre-shared keys) to use. If Computer A is configured with a policy that uses certificates as the authentication method and Computer B is configured with a policy that requires Kerberos, the two will not be able to agree; therefore, they will not be able to negotiate a security association.

tip

A computer can only have one active IPSec policy applied at any given time.

tip

A rule can use more than one authentication method. Pre-shared keys are considered the most insecure.

tip

All default IPSec policies use Kerberos authentication as their preferred method of authentication. If the computers involved are in different Active Directory forests, certificates must be used.

Figure 11-6 Default IPSec Policies

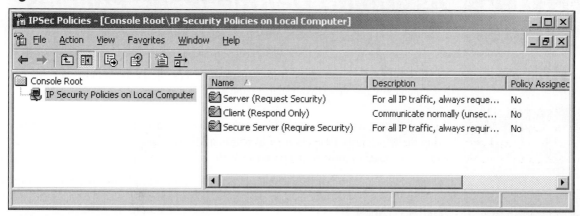

Figure 11-7 Server (Request Security) policy

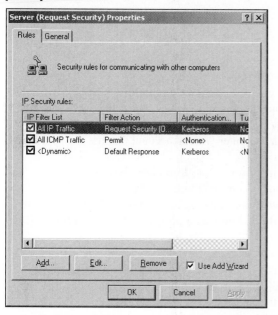

Figure 11-8 Client (Respond Only) policy

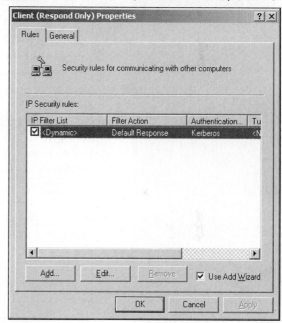

Figure 11-9 Secure Server (Require Security) policy

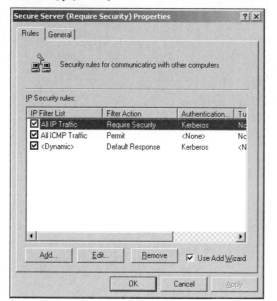

Exam 70-291

skill 4

Assigning Default IPSec Policies Using the Local Computer Policy

exam objective

Monitor network protocol security. Tools might include the IP Security Monitor Microsoft Management Console (MMC) snap-in and Kerberos support tools.

overview

To configure a system to use IPSec, you will need to assign a policy. This can be done by using the IP Security Policies snap-in within a Microsoft Management Console. This snap-in can also be used to un-assign a policy as well.

By using the IP Security Policies snap-in, you can manage IP Security policies on the local computer the console is running on, centrally with Active Directory, or on a remote computer **(Figure 11-10)**.

how to

Assign the default IPSec policy Secure Server (Require Security) to a Windows Server 2003 computer using the Local Computer policy.

tip

In order to complete these steps, you will require a Windows XP Professional computer and a Windows Server 2003 computer. Optionally, you can use two Windows Server 2003 computers.

1. Create a folder on the Windows Server 2003 computer and name it **Sales**. Add a text file named **salesfigures.txt** to the folder.
2. Share the folder so that **Everyone** has **Full Control**.
3. Test connectivity to the share from the Windows XP Professional client computer by clicking **Start**, selecting **Run** and typing **\\server\sales** in the **Run** dialog box. (Replace server with your actual computer's name.) You must have access to this share before continuing.
4. Log on to the Windows Server 2003 computer with an account that has the appropriate credentials to perform the task.
5. Click [*Start*], click **Run**, and then enter **mmc** in the **Run** dialog box.
6. Click **File**, and then click **Add/Remove Snap-in (Figure 11-11)**.
7. Click [Add...] in the **Add/Remove Snap-in** dialog box and select **IP Security Policy Management** in the **Add Standalone Snap-in** dialog box **(Figure 11-12)**. Click [Add].
8. Select **Local Computer** when prompted for the computer this snap-in will manage. Click [Finish], then click [Close], and then click [OK] to return to your console.
9. Select **IP Security Policies on Local Computer** in the left pane of the console to make the default IPSec policies visible in the right pane **(Figure 11-13)**.
10. Right-click the **Secure Server (Require Security)** policy and select **Assign (Figure 11-14)** to assign this policy to the computer. Under the **Policy Assigned** column, you should now see **Yes**. This indicates the policy has been assigned.
11. Test access again to the shared folder you created before starting this procedure. You should not be able to access the Sales folder because the client computer does not have IPSec policies assigned. The Windows Server 2003 computer requires IPSec in order to communicate. For both computers to be able to communicate using IPSec, they must establish a security association.

Figure 11-10 Managing IPSec policy options

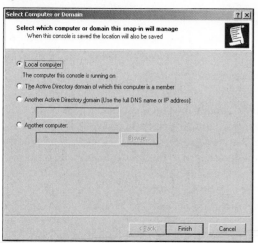

Figure 11-11 Adding snap-ins to a MMC

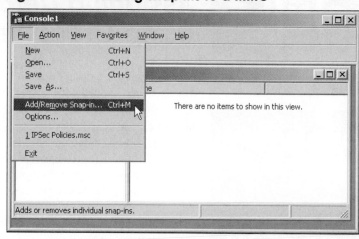

Figure 11-12 Selecting the IP Security Policy Management snap-in

Figure 11-13 Selecting IP Security Policies to make default policies visible

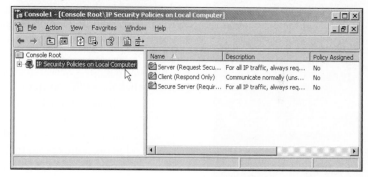

Figure 11-14 Assigning the Secure Server (Require Security) policy

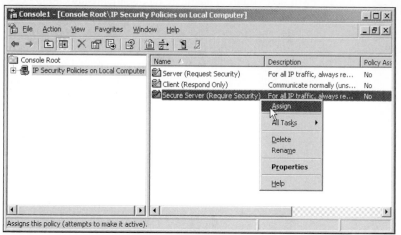

skill 5

Assigning Default IPSec Policies Using Group Policy

exam objective

Monitor network protocol security. Tools might include the IP Security Monitor Microsoft Management Console (MMC) snap-in and Kerberos support tools.

overview

In Skill 4, you learned how to configure an IPSec policy on a local computer. This works well if the number of computers on your network is small and you do not have access to Active Directory. In situations where you have an Active Directory-based network, you can use Group Policy to configure multiple computers to use a specific IPSec policy. This is accomplished by using the Active Directory Users and Computers console.

how to

Assign the default IPSec policy Secure Server (Require Security) to a Windows Server 2003 computer using Group Policy.

tip

In order to complete these steps, you will need a Windows 2000 Professional or Windows XP Professional computer, and a Windows Server 2003 computer running Active Directory.

tip

When applying Group Policy to selected systems/users, it is always a good idea to group them into their own OU to streamline administration of policy.

1. Create a folder on the Windows Server 2003 computer and name it **Sales**. Add a text file named **salesfigures.txt** to the folder.
2. Share the folder so that **Everyone** has **Full Control**.
3. Test connectivity to the share from the Windows XP Professional computer by clicking **Start**, clicking **Run** and typing **\\server\sales** in the **Run** dialog box. (Replace **server** with your actual computer's name.) You must have access to this share before continuing with the exercise.
4. Open the **Active Directory Users and Computers** console on the Windows Server 2003 domain controller.
5. Right-click your domain name, point to **New**, and then click **Organizational Unit**.
6. Enter **IPSec Systems** as the name for the organizational unit and click [OK] (**Figure 11-15**).
7. Move the Windows Server 2003 computer into this organizational unit (**Figure 11-16**).
8. Right-click the **IPSec Systems** OU and select **Properties**.
9. Select the **Group Policy** tab in the **IPSec Systems Properties** dialog box and then click [New] to create a new Group Policy.
10. Enter the name **Secure Server Require Security Policy** (**Figure 11-17**) and then click [Edit] to open the Group Policy for editing.
11. In the **Group Policy Object Editor** console, expand **Computer Configuration**, **Windows Settings**, and **Security Settings** and then click **IP Security Policies on Active Directory (Figure 11-18)**.
12. In the details pane, right-click **Secure Server (Require Security)** and select **Assign**. Under the **Policy Assigned** column, you should now see **Yes (Figure 11-19)**. This indicates the policy has been assigned.
13. Open a command prompt on the server computer, type **gpupdate /force** and press **[Enter]** so that the policy will be updated to reflect the latest change on the server. This step will save you from having to reboot after using Group Policy to apply IPSec security.
14. Close the command prompt window.
15. Click **File**, and then click **Exit** to close the Group Policy Object Editor console. Then click [OK] to close the IPSec Systems Properties dialog box.
16. Test access again to the shared folder you created in Step 2. You should not be able to access the Sales folder because the Windows XP Professional computer does not have IPSec policies assigned. The Windows Server 2003 computer requires IPSec in order to communicate. For both computers to be able to communicate using IPSec, they must establish a security association.

Figure 11-15 Creating an Organizational Unit

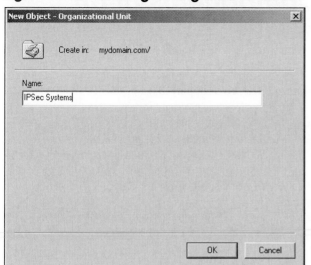

Figure 11-16 Moving the Windows Server 2003 computer into the OU

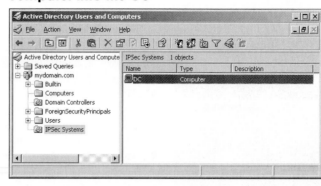

Figure 11-17 Creating New Group Policy

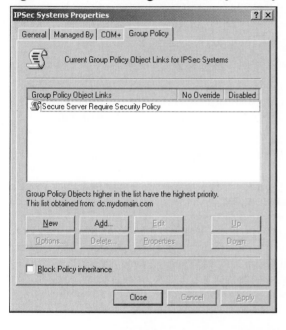

Figure 11-18 Accessing IP Security Policies settings

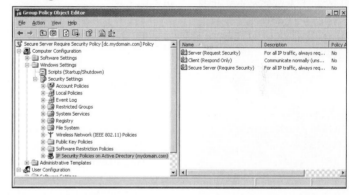

Figure 11-19 Assigning the Secure Server (Require Security) Policy

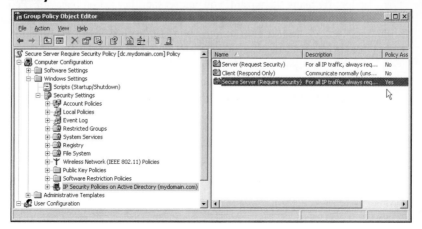

skill 6
Configuring Components of an IPSec Policy

exam objective

Monitor network protocol security. Tools might include the IP Security Monitor Microsoft Management Console (MMC) snap-in and Kerberos support tools.

overview

If necessary, an administrator can configure custom IPSec policies to fit the security needs of his or her company. The elements that must be configured in an IPSec policy include the following:

♦ **IP Security Policy Name**: A unique name for the policy. An optional description of the policy can also be provided.

♦ **Default Response Rule**: This rule is used when no other rule applies to the connection. Note that this rule allows insecure communications.

♦ **Default Response Rule Authentication Method**: Identifies the authentication method for the security rule. During the initial setup, you will only be able to choose one method. You can add additional authentication methods by editing the rule after completing the wizard. Options here include Kerberos V5 protocol, certificates, and a pre-shared key.

♦ **IP Filter List**: Defines which traffic will be secured with this rule. There are two default filters which can be used (All ICMP traffic, All IP traffic) or you can create your own filters.

♦ **Filter Action**: Lists the security actions that will occur if the traffic matches the IP filter (Permit, Block, or Negotiate Security). The first method listed will always take precedence. If the action you specify first in the list cannot take place, the next filter action will be tried.

When a packet arrives or exits an interface of a computer configured with an IPSec policy, the IPSec Policy Agent will apply the assigned filter action. If the computer has multiple network cards, the policy will apply to all of them.

The **IPSec Policy Agent** is a service that starts automatically when the computer starts. It will retrieve the IPSec Policy that is assigned to the computer and send it to the IPSec driver.

There are three default filter actions available **(Figure 11-20)**.

• **Permit**: Allows unsecured IP packets to pass through the computer without using IPSec protection.

• **Request Security (Optional)**: Computers with this setting will accept unsecured communication but will request that clients establish trust and security methods. If a client does not respond to this request, unsecured communication will be allowed.

• **Require Security**: Computers with this setting will accept unsecured communication initially but will always require that clients establish trust and security methods. This means that the server will accept an unsecured communication and respond with a request for a security association (SA) to define the encryption and authentication protocols to be used. Unsecured communications are not allowed with non-IPSec-aware computers.

If the default filter actions do not match your needs, you can add a new filter action via the Filter Action tab. Click [Add...] on the **Filter Action** tab of the **New Rule Properties** dialog box **(Figure 11-21)** and then follow the IP Security Filter Action Wizard to specify the new filter action. By using the wizard, you can set the filter action behavior (Permit, Block, or Negotiate Security), determine how you want the computer to respond to clients that do not support IPSec, and specify whether data is protected by using integrity (Authentication Header), confidentiality (Encapsulating Security Payload), or the integrity/encryption algorithm.

♦ **Connection Type**: This setting indicates where the policy is active. There are three options: All network connections, Local Area Network (LAN), and Remote Access.

♦ **Tunnel Setting**: This setting determines whether the traffic uses a tunnel. There are two options: **This rule does not specify an IPSec tunnel**, which means you are operating in transport mode (discussed earlier), and **The tunnel endpoint is specified by this IP address**.

♦ **Authentication Methods**: These settings determine how you establish trust between the computers involved. Options here include Kerberos V5, certificates, and/or a pre-shared key.

Figure 11-20 Default Filter Actions

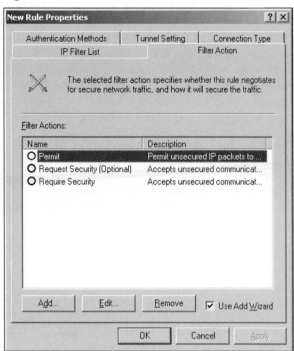

**Figure 11-21 Launching the IP Security
Filter Action Wizard**

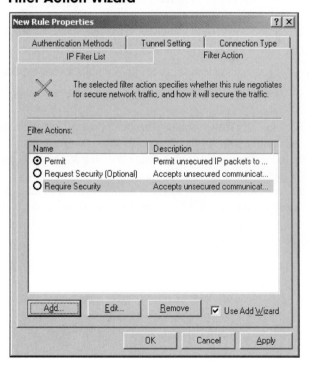

skill 7 | *Creating a Custom IPSec Policy*

exam objective

Monitor network protocol security. Tools might include the IP Security Monitor Microsoft Management Console (MMC) snap-in and Kerberos support tools.

overview

As indicated earlier, there may be situations where the default policies do not meet your security needs. When those situations occur, you will need to create a custom IPSec policy to enforce your unique security requirements. Consider the following: Mary would like to use Telnet to connect to a Windows Server 2003 domain controller from her Windows XP Professional computer. Because Telnet transmits information in clear text, anyone who captures the traffic will be able to see her password.

You can create a custom IPSec policy to protect the Telnet traffic that Mary generates. This will require that you create a custom policy on both the Windows Server 2003 computer and a Windows XP Professional computer. You will also need to create a shared folder on the Windows XP Professional computer named **Secure Telnet Policy**. This will be used when you export the policy you create on the Windows Server 2003 computer.

how to

Configure a custom IPSec policy to encrypt Telnet traffic on a Windows Server 2003 computer configured as a domain controller.

1. Create a Microsoft Management Console (MMC) that includes the **IP Security Policy Management** snap-in and the **Computer Management** snap-in. Focus the snap-ins on the local computer.
2. Click [OK] in the **Add/Remove Snap-in** dialog box to return to the console. Save the console by clicking **File** and then **Save** and typing **IPSec Tools** as the console name.
3. Expand **Computer Management (Local)**, **Services and Applications**, and select **Service**. In the right pane, right-click **Telnet** and select **Properties**. Set the **Startup type** to **Automatic**, click [Start], and then [OK].
4. Right-click **IP Security Policy Management** in the left pane and select **Create IP Security Policy (Figure 11-22)**. Click [Next >] in the **Welcome to the IP Security Policy Wizard** screen.
5. Enter **Secure Telnet** as the IP Security Policy Name and click [Next >].
6. Clear the **Activate the default response rule** check box **(Figure 11-23)** and click [Next >]. Leave the default authentication method of **Active Directory default (Kerberos V5 protocol)**, click [Next >] and then [Finish] to complete the IP Security Policy Wizard.
7. Select the **Rules** tab, and then click [Add...] to create a new rule. Click [Next >] to continue through the IP Security Rule Wizard.
8. In the **Tunnel Endpoint** dialog box, select **This rule does not specify a tunnel** and click [Next >] **(Figure 11-24)**.
9. To ensure that this policy remains active no matter which interface the Telnet traffic arrives on, select **All network connections** in the **Network type** dialog box and click [Next >].
10. In the **IP Filter List** dialog box **(Figure 11-25)**, click [Add...]. In the **IP Filter list**, provide a name for the new filter and then click [Add...] to launch the **IP Filter Wizard**.
11. Click [Next >] at the **Welcome** screen and enter a description for the filter. Click [Next >].
12. Select **A specific IP Address** on the **IP Traffic Source** screen and enter the IP address for the Windows XP Professional computer **(Figure 11-26)**. Click [Next >] to continue.

Figure 11-22 Creating a new IPSec Policy

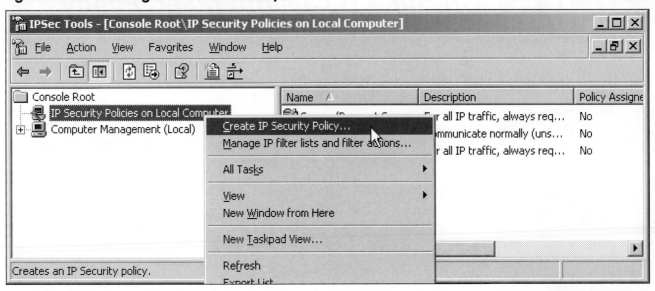

Figure 11-23 Clearing the default response

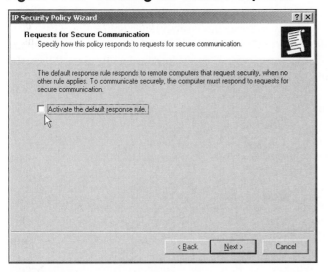

Figure 11-24 Configuring Tunnel Mode settings

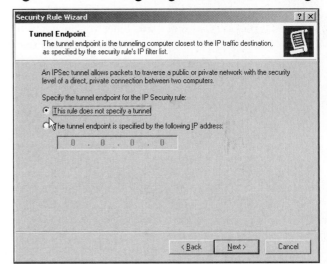

Figure 11-25 Creating a new IP Filter

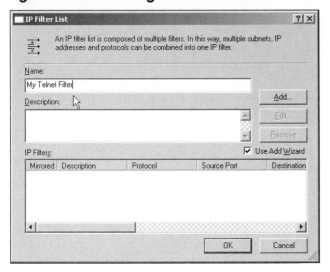

Figure 11-26 Specifying the IP Traffic Source

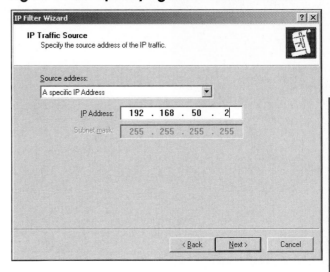

Creating a Custom IPSec Policy
(cont'd)

Monitor network protocol security. Tools might include the IP Security Monitor Microsoft Management Console (MMC) snap-in and Kerberos support tools.

13. Select **A specific IP Address** in the **Destination address** list box on the **IP Traffic Destination** screen and enter the IP address for the Windows Server 2003 computer (**Figure 11-27**). Click [Next >] to continue.

14. On the **IP Protocol Type** screen, select **TCP** as the protocol type and click [Next >] to continue.

15. On the **IP Protocol Port** screen, select the **To this port** option button and enter **23** (**Figure 11-28**). This is the well-known port used by Telnet. Click [Next >] and then [Finish] to complete the IP Filter Wizard.

16. Make sure the **My Telnet Filter** is selected in the IP filter list and then click [Next >].

17. Select **Require Security in the Filter Action** and then click [Next >].

18. In the **Authentication Method**, select **Active Directory default (Kerberos V5 protocol)** and click [Next >] and then [Finish] to complete the setup. Click [OK] to close the rule's **Properties** dialog box.

19. Click [OK] to close the **Secure Telnet Rule Properties** dialog box.

20. Since you are not using Group Policy to create this custom IPSec policy, you will need to export the Secure Telnet policy from the Windows Server 2003 computer and then import it into the Windows XP Professional computer. This can be done by selecting **IP Security Policies on Local Computer**, clicking **All Tasks**, and then clicking **Export Policies** (**Figure 11-29**).

21. Save the file as **Secure Telnet** in the **Secure Telnet Policy** folder that you created previously and shared on the Windows XP Professional computer.

22. Click **IP Security Policies on Local Computer** on the Windows Server 2003 computer and locate the **Secure Telnet** policy you created earlier. Right-click the policy and select **Assign (Figure 11-30)**.

23. To assign the policy on the Windows XP Professional computer, you will need to open the IP Security Policies snap-in from a Microsoft Management console on that computer.

24. Right-click **IP Security Policies on Local Computer**, select **All Tasks**, and then click **Import Policies (Figure 11-31)**.

25. Locate the policy that was exported to the **Secure Telnet Policy** folder and select **Open**.

26. To install the policies on the Windows XP Professional computer, right-click the **Secure Telnet** policy in the right pane and select **Assign (Figure 11-32)**.

Figure 11-27 Specifying the IP Traffic Destination

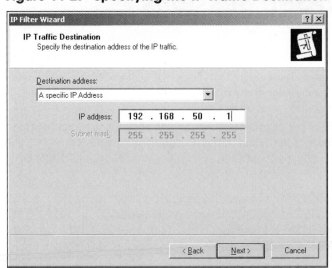

Figure 11-28 Configuring Telnet port information

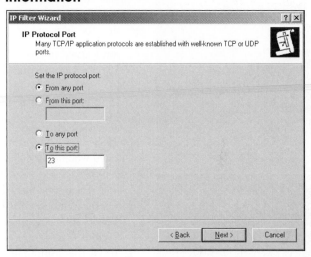

Figure 11-29 Exporting the policy

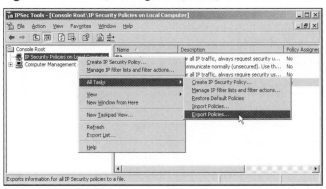

Figure 11-30 Assigning the policy on the Windows Server 2003 computer

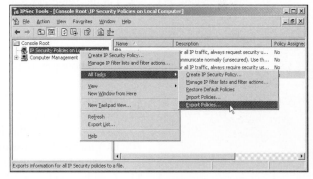

Figure 11-31 Importing the policy on the Windows XP Professional computer

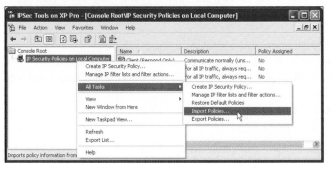

Figure 11-32 Assigning the policy on the Windows XP Professional computer

skill 8

Monitoring IPSec Sessions

exam objective

Monitor network protocol security. Tools might include the IP Security Monitor Microsoft Management Console (MMC) snap-in and Kerberos support tools.

overview

Now that you have set up an IPSec policy and assigned it to both of your computers, you need to make sure it is working to protect the Telnet traffic. In order to accomplish this task, you need to actually monitor the connections. Microsoft provides both Netsh and IP Security Monitor for these purposes.

As you learned in Lesson 9, Netsh is a command line tool that is native to Windows Server 2003. It can be run from a batch file or from the command prompt. Although it can be used to create a policy, the focus in this lesson is how it can be used for monitoring IPSec sessions. Any information that is available in the IP Security Monitor snap-in is also available using this tool.

The **IP Security Monitor** provides information on which IPSec policy is active on the computer and whether a secure association has been established.

tip

IP Security Monitor in Windows Server 2003 cannot be used to monitor sessions on Windows 2000 systems. Use netdiag or ipsecmon.

how to

Monitor IPSec sessions using Netsh and IP Security Monitor.

1. On the Windows XP Professional computer, launch a Telnet session with the Windows Server 2003 computer by clicking ⊞ Start, clicking **Run** and typing **cmd** in the **Run** dialog box.
2. From the command shell, type **telnet 192.168.50.1** (enter the IP address you have configured for the Windows Server 2003 computer), and press **[Enter]**.
3. Select **yes** when prompted by the Telnet software that you are about to send your password information to a remote computer on the Internet.
4. When the **Welcome to Microsoft Telnet Server** screen appears, minimize it.
5. On the Windows Server 2003 computer, click ⊞ Start, **Run**, and type **cmd** to access a command shell.
6. From the command prompt, type **netsh** and press **[Enter]** to start the utility.
7. Next, enter **ipsec static** after the netsh> prompt and press **[Enter]**.
8. Type **show policy all normal** after the netsh ipsec static> prompt and press **[Enter]** to see all policies on the server. As you can see, the Secure Telnet policy is shown as being assigned (**Figure 11-33**).
9. Next, type **dynamic** at the netsh ipsec static> prompt and press **[Enter]** to enter dynamic mode and set the diagnostic value and the log interval as shown in **Figure 11-34**.
10. By running the **show mmsas all** command you can view the information associated with the current security association.
11. Type **bye** and press **[Enter],** then close the command shell by typing **exit** and pressing **[Enter]**.

The same information can be viewed by using **IP Security Monitor** from the Windows XP Professional computer.

12. Add the **IP Security Monitor** snap-in to a Microsoft Management Console.
13. Locate the name of the Windows XP Professional computer under IP Security Monitor and then expand the **Main Mode** folder. Select the **Security Associations** folder and then right-click the entry in the details pane and select **Properties (Figure 11-35)**.
14. You can now view the information regarding the session that is currently active (**Figure 11-36**). Notice that Kerberos is used for authentication as we saw in the netsh output. We can also see the algorithms used for encryption and integrity (3DES, SHA1).

tip

Netsh commands can be found in the Windows Server 2003 Help and Support Center.

Figure 11-33 Viewing the Assigned Policies using Netsh

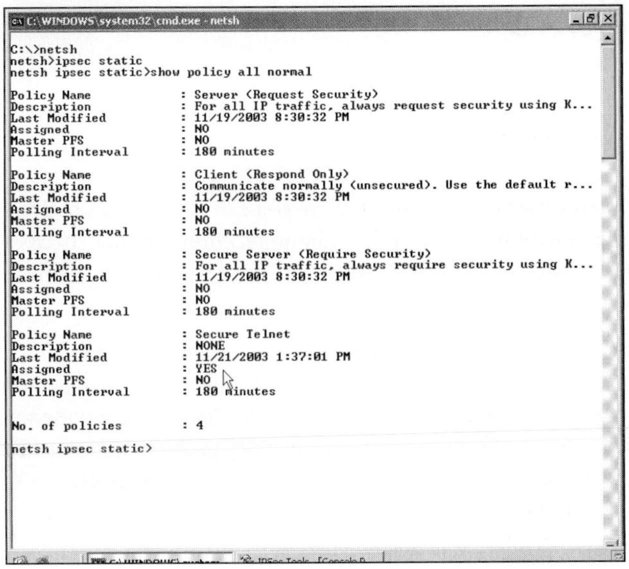

Figure 11-34 Viewing the Active Security Association

Figure 11-35 Accessing session details

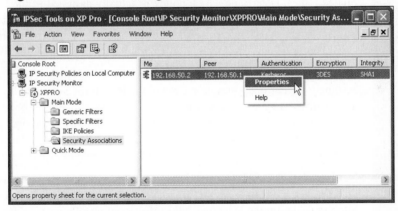

Figure 11-36 Security Association information

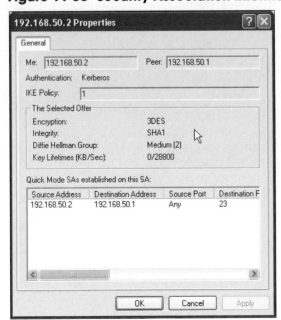

skill 9

Troubleshooting IPSec Communications

exam objective

Troubleshoot network protocol security. Tools might include the IP Security Monitor MMC snap-in, Event Viewer, and Network Monitor.

overview

Using the default IPSec policies is pretty straightforward but, as you can see, custom policies can sometimes be very complex. In situations where IPSec communications are not successful, you will need to put your troubleshooting skills to work. There are several tools available to assist in troubleshooting IPSec-related problems.

When experiencing a problem with IPSec, you should first determine if it is related to IPSec or if it is a basic connectivity problem. The quickest way to make this determination is to stop the IPSec Policy Agent (IPSEC Services) service on both of the computers and then attempt to ping. If you do not get a response, then you have a basic connectivity problem that must be addressed. Check your TCP/IP configuration settings, cables, and hub/switch, then attempt to ping the other system again. Once you have basic connectivity, you can then start the IPSec Policy Agent service. If your policies are still not working, you are now troubleshooting an IPSec Policy issue.

Once basic connectivity has been established, you will need to turn your attention to IPSec related issues. Determine which policy is actually assigned to the computers involved. This can be done by using the **IP Security Policy Management snap-in**. Netsh can also provide information by using the **ipsec static** and **show gpoassignedpolicy** commands (**Figure 11-37**). These commands can be run only on Windows Server 2003.

If your IPSec policies are being distributed by using Group Policy and the computer is not assigning the correct policy, you can use the **Resultant Set of Policy (RSOP)** snap-in from a Microsoft Management Console to see which Group Policy object is responsible. When policies are assigned at different levels (site, domain, organizational unit), some settings may conflict and produce unexpected results. The Resultant Set of Policy snap-in can help you determine the policies that have been applied to the computer as well as their precedence.

Netdiag.exe (Network Connectivity Tester) is another tool that can be run from a command line to see the active IPSec policy applied to the computer (**Figure 11-38**). It is available in the Support folder on the Windows XP Professional installation CD. It is not installed as part of the normal operating system installation process.

Event Viewer can also provide information to assist you in troubleshooting IPSec communication problems. In general, look for events in the system log that are generated by the IPSec Policy Agent or IPSec Driver. Security association details can be seen in the security log. In order to review these types of events in the security log, you will need to make sure auditing is enabled.

Security association information presented in the event log can provide insight into exactly where the IPSec communication is failing. **Figure 11-39** shows a successful IKE Quick Mode security association. This indicates the two computers have already completed the Main Mode security association and agreed upon the authentication method to use. The information in **Figure 11-39** demonstrates they have also agreed upon the security protocols to use to establish a secure channel. With a basic understanding of the two phases previously discussed in the lesson, you can begin to identify the area of the configuration that may need to be reviewed if communication is failing. Note that the details of the existing policies (authentication modes/encryption settings) can be obtained by using **netsh ipsec static>show all** (**Figure 11-40**) or by using the IP Security Policy Management snap-in.

tip

Ipseccmd is a command line alternative to the IP Security Policies snap-in.

tip

Netdiag.exe can also be used to test the network driver, protocol driver, and the send and receive capabilities of your computer.

Figure 11-37 Using the Netsh command

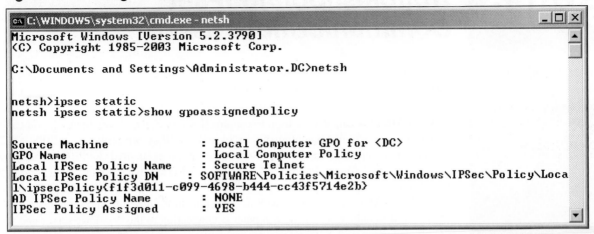

Figure 11-38 Using the Netdiag command

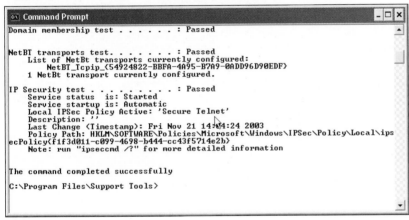

Figure 11-39 Viewing Security Log

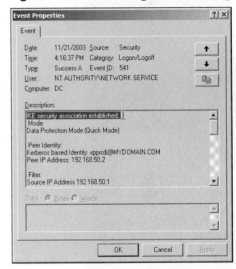

Figure 11-40 Reviewing policy details using Netsh

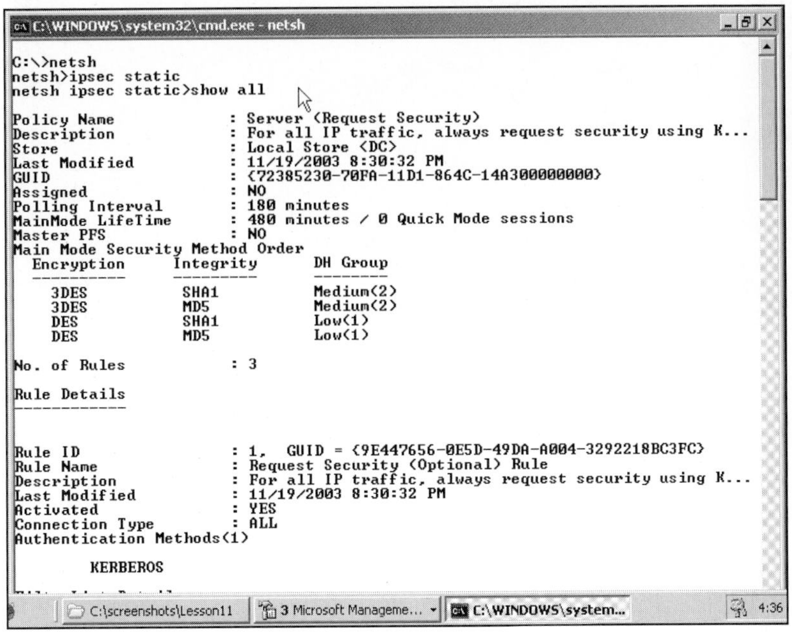

skill 9

Troubleshooting IPSec Communications (cont'd)

exam objective

Troubleshoot network protocol security. Tools might include the IP Security Monitor MMC snap-in, Event Viewer, and Network Monitor.

overview

Network Monitor can also be used to capture IPSec packets. Using this tool, you can see if the packets are actually reaching the server and that they are protected by IPSec **(Figure 11-41)**. This capture was made when the computer named XPPRO (Windows XP Professional) was connecting to the Windows server (DC) using Telnet. Notice the protocol being used is Encapsulating Security Payload (ESP). As you may recall from earlier in the lesson, ESP provides encryption as well as authentication, integrity, and replay services. This captured traffic indicates that the computer is connecting to the Windows server and the data is encrypted using ESP. Secured packets may also display an Authentication Header as part of the TCP, ICMP, or UDP packets. IPSec packets may appear in Network Monitor as ISAKMP or ESP.

Figure 11-41 Using Network Monitor to capture IPSec traffic

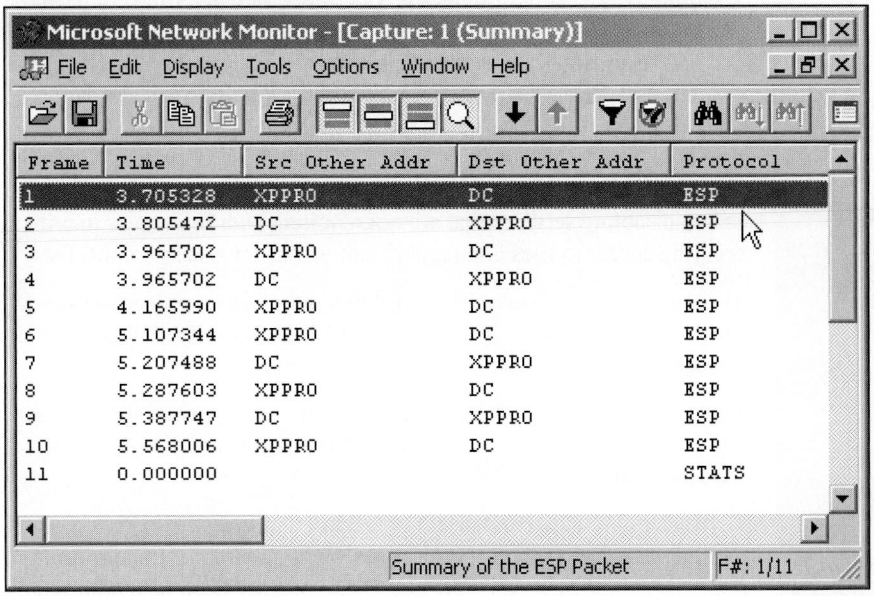

skill 10

Working With Security Templates

exam objective

Implement secure network administration procedures. Implement security baseline settings and audit security settings by using security templates. Implement the principle of least privilege.

overview

Windows Server 2003 provides a wide range of capabilities that can enhance the security of your network. The primary goal when dealing with security in your network is the concept that Microsoft refers to as "*the principle of least privilege.*" This means that when assigning permission and access to resources on your network, you should never give users more access than they need to perform their jobs. When a user's job function changes, his or her security privileges should also change to accommodate new job responsibilities. There are a variety of ways to adhere to this principle, such as restricting users from groups that have administrative scope, disabling services that are not required, auditing access to critical resources, as well as securing access to files and registry settings using access control lists.

Through the use of **security templates**, administrators can set a wide range of global and local security settings. Settings controlled by security policies include NTFS permissions, registry permissions, and service configuration.

Every network consists of several components: users, groups, services, protocols, and computers. Each of these components has its own security settings to configure to ensure they are protected.

As you might imagine, this can be a very daunting task for even the most experienced network administrator. In nearly all cases, you will have to make configuration changes across more than one computer on the network. It can quickly become a very large project as the number of computers increases.

Windows Server 2003 provides the **Security Templates snap-in** tool to organize all of your security parameters into one location, which makes security administration more efficient.

Another tool, the **Security and Configuration Analysis snap-in**, is used to analyze existing security settings and apply templates. By using either predefined templates or creating your own custom templates, you can establish a baseline of security for computers on your network.

To utilize security templates effectively, you need to have a thorough understanding of the components that make up the template itself. Each security template consists of categories that can be configured by using the Security Templates snap-in. These categories are shown in **Table 11-1**.

When creating templates, you have several options. One option is to use the Security Templates snap-in and create a new template. Another option is to use one of the predefined templates and modify it to fit your needs.

Windows Server 2003 has several predefined templates, which are shown in **Figure 11-42**. Use the Windows Server 2003 Help and Support Center to learn more about the characteristics of each of these templates.

The following exercise demonstrates how the Security Templates snap-in and the Security Configuration and Analysis tool can be used to create a custom template that will disable the Telnet service and only allow members of the Domain Admins group Full Control over the service. The custom template also remove any users from the Power Users group when the policy is applied, create a message that appears at logon indicating that only authorized users are allowed to access the corporate network, and not display the name of the user who last logged on to the computer. The following steps will be performed on a Windows XP Professional computer that is a member of a domain.

tip

Security templates are stored in the %systemroot%\ Security\Templates folder.

tip

Templates can also be used to analyze your system for potential security policy violations.

tip

To read more information about how to use templates to provide security for your computer systems, read the "Windows Server 2003 Security Guide" on Microsoft's Web site.

Table 11-1   *Security Template Components*

Categories	Description of Category
Account Policies	These settings apply to user accounts. (Examples: minimum password lengths, password history, account lockout options, lifetimes for Ticket Granting Tickets (TGT), Service Tickets)
Local Policies	These settings define configurations that only apply to the computer on which the security template is applied. (Examples: events to be audited, and user rights, such as the ability to change system time, add workstations to domain, backup files and directories, shut down system)
Event Log	These settings define configurations that allow you to manage the event logs. (Examples: minimum/maximum log sizes, retention periods, shut down system when security log is full)
Restricted Groups	The users/groups added to this section of the template can be used to control group membership. It does not keep an administrator from adding users/groups through the normal utilities, but once the policy is refreshed, the group membership setting in this section of the template will override any changes made elsewhere.
File System	These settings allow you to configure security permissions for files and folders.
Registry	These settings allow you to control access to existing registry keys.
System Services	These settings allow you to change the startup settings of services (automatic, disabled, manual) as well as determine who can perform these tasks on a specific service.

Figure 11-42 Windows Server 2003 predefined templates

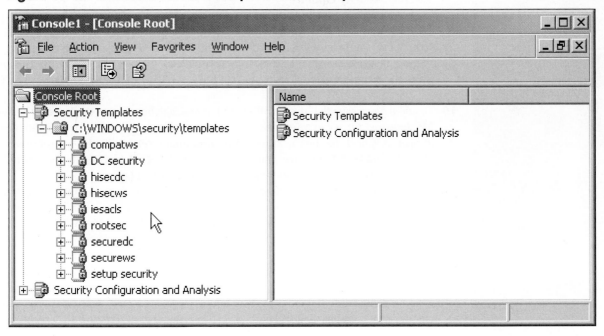

skill 10

Working With Security Templates
(cont'd)

exam objective

Implement secure network administration procedures. Implement security baseline settings and audit security settings by using security templates. Implement the principle of least privilege.

how to

Create a custom Security Template.

1. Create a Microsoft Management Console that includes the **Security Templates** snap-in and the **Security Configuration and Analysis** snap-in **(Figure 11-43)**. Save the console as **XP Security Template**.
2. To keep your custom security templates separate from the predefined templates already on the computer, right-click **Security Templates** and select **New Template Search Path (Figure 11-44)**.
3. In the **Browse For Folder** dialog box, browse to a location on your hard drive and create a new folder on your C: drive named **CustomTemplates**. Click [OK].
4. Next, right-click the **C:\CustomTemplates** folder and select **New Template (Figure 11-45)**. For the template name, enter **SecureXP**. Information in the **Description** field is optional but should be completed with information that will identify the purpose of the template. Click [OK] to finish.
5. First, disable the Telnet service and configure it so that only the Domain Admins group can stop, start, or pause the service. To accomplish this, you will need to select the **System Services** folder and then locate the Telnet service in the right pane. Right-click **Telnet** and select **Properties** from the menu.
6. In the **Telnet Properties** dialog box, click the box next to **Define this policy setting in the template** and then select **Disabled**. Next, click [Edit Security...] and configure it as shown in **Figure 11-46**. Click [OK] to return to the Telnet Properties dialog box. Click [OK] to close the Telnet Properties box.
7. Next, you will configure the policy **not** to display the name of the user who last logged on to the computer, and to include a warning message that states that only authorized users allowed to log on to this computer. This is done by expanding **Local Policies** and then selecting **Security Options**.
8. Locate the **Interactive logon: Do not display last user name** policy in the right pane, check the box next to **Define this policy setting in the template** and select **Enabled**.
9. Next, locate the **Interactive logon: Message title for users attempting to log on** policy in the right pane and double-click to open it. Check the box next to **Define this policy setting in the template** and type **WARNING: AUTHORIZED USERS ONLY**. Click [OK].
10. To add the message that users will see in the message box, locate the **Interactive logon: Message text for users attempting to logon on** policy in the right pane and double-click to open it. Check the box next to **Define this policy setting in the template** and type **Only Authorized Users are allowed to access the XYZ Corporate Network**. Click [OK]. These template settings are shown in **Figure 11-47**.
11. The last part of the policy ensures that when the policy is applied to the computer, any members of the Power Users group will be removed. To accomplish this task, right-click **Restricted Groups** and select **Add Group** as shown in **Figure 11-48**. To add the group, you can either enter its name or use the **Browse** function. Type **Power Users**.
12. In the **Power Users Properties** dialog box, you will notice that the default setting is **This group should contain no members (Figure 11-49)**. That is exactly the setting you want. If a user were to be added to this group, the next time the policy was applied, the user would automatically be removed. If you look closely, you will notice that you can also identify which groups the Powers Users can be a member of. For now, accept the defaults to accomplish your security goal. Click [OK]. The Power Users group should not show in the right pane.
13. To save the template, right-click **SecureXP** and select **Save**.

Figure 11-43 MMC with Security Template and SCA snap-in added

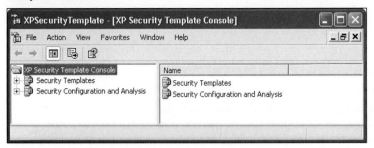

Figure 11-44 Creating New Template Search Path

Figure 11-45 Creating a new template

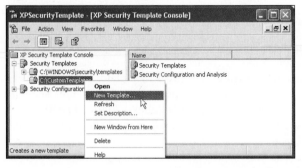

Figure 11-46 Disabling Telnet/Providing Full Control for Domain Admins

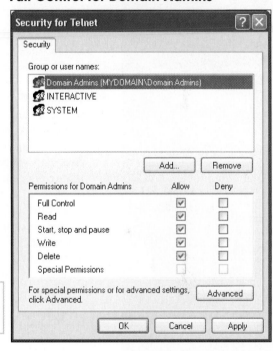

Figure 11-47 Adding warning message to users

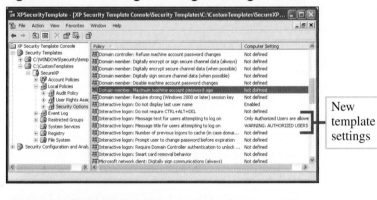

Figure 11-48 Adding Power Users to Restricted Groups

Figure 11-49 Default settings for Restricted Groups

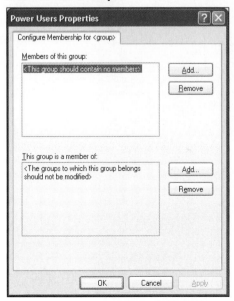

skill10

Working With Security Templates
(cont'd)

Implement secure network administration procedures. Implement security baseline settings and audit security settings by using security templates. Implement the principle of least privilege.

how to

Once you have configured the template the way you want, you can use the Security Configuration and Analysis (SCA) snap-in, secedit, or import it into the Local Security Policy on the computer to apply it to the computer. **Secedit** is a command line equivalent of the SCA. If you want to apply it to multiple computers, you can import the template into Security settings, which is an extension of Group Policy.

In the next part of the exercise, you will use the SCA snap-in tool to first compare the template changes against the current security settings on your Windows XP Professional computer, and then apply the template to the computer.

Use the Security Configuration and Analysis snap-in to apply the template.

1. Using the XP Security Template you created earlier, right-click the **Security Configuration and Analysis** snap-in and select **Open Database (Figure 11-50)**.
2. Create a name for the database. To maintain consistency, name it the same as your template **SecureXP** and select **Open**.
3. Next, import the SecureXP template you created earlier into the new database you just created. Navigate to the **C:\CustomTemplates** folder and select the **SecureXP** template **(Figure 11-51)**. Note that the **Clear this database before importing** option seen in the figure is used to specify that any stored templates in the analysis database will be overwritten by the imported template. Since this is the first and only template you have created, there are no other templates in the database; therefore, you will leave this option unchecked. Click [Open].
4. To compare the computer's current security settings against the setting in our database, right-click **Security Configuration and Analysis** and select **Analyze Computer Now**. Accept the defaults for the error log file path and select [OK].
5. Once the analysis is complete, you will see the report under the **Security Configuration and Analysis** folder **(Figure 11-52)**. The red "x" next to the policy settings in the right pane indicates the security values in the database and on the machine do not match. A green check would indicate the settings on the local computer match those in the database.
6. After reviewing the analysis, apply the template to the Windows XP Professional computer. Right-click the **Security Configuration and Analysis** folder and select **Configure Computer Now**. Select the default path for the error log file path and select [OK].
7. After the process has been completed, save your console template and exit. Log off the computer and then log back on to test the template.

tip

To analyze security, you will need to be logged on as an administrator or use an account that is a member of the Administrators group.

Figure 11-50 Opening database

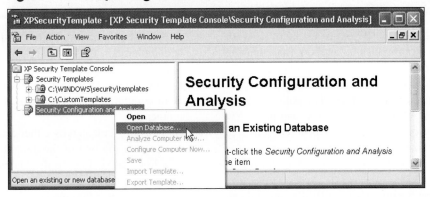

Figure 11-51 Importing SecureXP template into database

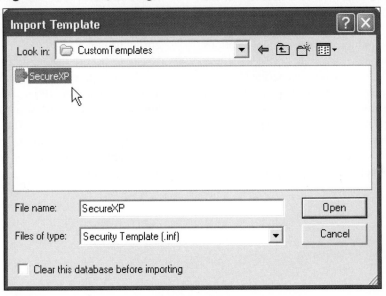

Figure 11-52 Results of analysis

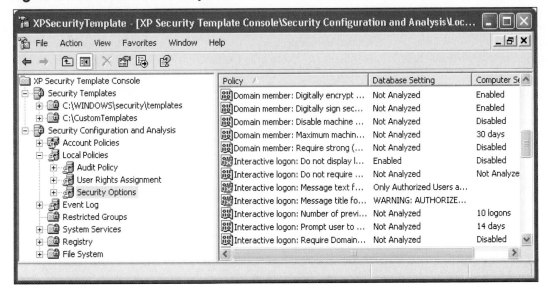

Summary

- Internet Protocol Security (IPSec) is a suite of network layer protocols. It provides a method for ensuring authentication, confidentiality, and integrity of data.
- IPSec protects Internet Protocol (IP) and higher layer protocols by using security policies. The policies can be created by using the IP Security Policies snap-in.
- The Authentication Header (AH) protocol ensures authentication and message integrity for trans mitted packets. AH protocol does not ensure data confidentiality.
- The Encapsulating Security Payload (ESP) protocol can encrypt the actual data in the packet. It also provides authentication, integrity, replay services, and confidentiality.
- IPSec transport mode ensures traffic is secure over the entire path between the client and server. It is the default mode for IPSec.
- Unlike transport mode, which encrypts communications between two computers as it was sent on the local network, in tunnel mode, data is sent unencrypted to the router closest to the computer. Once it reaches that router, it is encrypted as it is passed across the public Internet. At the corporate router, it is decrypted before being sent to the destination computer.
- The Internet Key Exchange (IKE) establishes a security association (SA) between two computers. This is done in two phases: Main Mode phase and Quick Mode phase.
- SAs control the type of encryption to be used for specific types of traffic. They also define authentication methods. Both computers must establish an SA in order to communicate.
- IPSec is implemented by either creating a custom IPSec policy or using one of the default policies available in Windows 2003. Each policy consists of one or more rules. Each rule is composed of a filter, a filter action, and an authentication method.
- There are three default policies: Server (Request Security), Client (Respond Only), and Secure Server (Require Security).
- IPSec policies can be assigned using the Local Computer Policy or Group Policy. The IP Security Policy Management snap-in or Netsh can be used to create the policy.
- Netsh, IP Security Monitor, the Resultant Set of Policy, Netdiag.exe, Event Viewer, and Network Monitor can be used to troubleshoot IPSec connections.
- Security templates allow administrators to set a wide range of security settings. They are configured using the Security Templates snap-in. The Security Configuration and Analysis snap-in is used to analyze the system and apply the template.

Key Terms

Authentication
Authentication Header (AH)
Authentication method
Client (Respond Only)
Confidentiality
Encapsulating Security Payload (ESP)
Filter
Filter action
Integrity
Internet Protocol Security (IPSec)

IPSec Policy Agent
IP Security Monitor
Kerberos
Main Mode
Mutual authentication
Netdiag.exe (Network Connectivity Tester)
Replay attack
Resultant Set of Policy (RSoP) snap-in
Secedit

Secure Server (Require Security)
Security association (SA)
Security template
Security Configuration and Analysis
Security Template snap-in
Server (Request Security)
Spoofing
Transport mode
Tunnel mode

Test Yourself

1. Which of the following terms is used to describe the process of verifying that an entity is who or what it claims to be?
   a. Confidentiality
   b. Authentication
   c. Integrity
   d. Security
   e. Encryption

2. Which statements are true regarding IPSec? (Choose all that apply.)
   a. IPSec protects Internet Protocol and higher layer protocols.
   b. IPSec is implemented by using policies.
   c. IPSec packets travel across the network inside of IP packets.
   d. IPSec can protect traffic between networks and within a network.

3. Which of the following are correct statements regarding the Authentication Header protocol used in IPSec? (Choose all that apply.)
   a. Authentication Header protocol ensures authentication and message integrity.
   b. Authentication Header protocol can maintain confidentiality.
   c. Authentication Header protocol can protect against replay attacks.
   d. Authentication Header protocol does not provide mutual authentication capabilities.

4. Which of the following statements are true regarding security associations? (Choose all that apply.)
   a. SAs control the type of encryption to be used for specific types of traffic.
   b. SAs define the authentication method used (Kerberos, certificates, pre-shared keys).
   c. Quick Mode SAs are established after the authentication method is agreed upon.
   d. Main Mode SAs are established after computers agree on the security protocols to use.

5. Which of the following are true statements regarding rules in an IPSec policy? (Choose all that apply.)
   a. The filter action identifies the type of traffic the filter will be applied to.
   b. The filter identifies what to do if the filter action matches.
   c. An IPSec policy can consist of one or more authentication methods.
   d. Kerberos, certificates, and pre-shared keys are examples of encryption protocols.

6. Which if the following are true statements regarding the default IPSec policies? (Choose all that apply.)
   a. Computers configured with the Client (Respond Only) policy will initiate a request to use IPSec.
   b. Computers configured with the Client (Respond Only) policy will never initiate a request to use IPSec.
   c. A computer using the Secure Server (Request Security) policy will use IPSec to encrypt communications or allow communication to occur unencrypted if necessary.
   d. None of the policies listed above are default IPSec policies.

7. Mary has set up IPSec policies on two computers in her domain. Unfortunately, they are unable to communicate. Which of the following tools can be used to troubleshoot her IPSec communication problem? (Choose all that apply.)
   a. IP Security Monitor
   b. Netsh
   c. Event Viewer
   d. Network Monitor

8. You have just created a new security template using the Security Templates snap-in. Which area in the template would you need to configure in order to turn on auditing?
   a. Restricted Groups
   b. Event Log
   c. Local Policies
   d. Account Policies

Projects: On Your Own

The following projects require a Windows XP Professional computer and a Windows Server 2003 domain controller. Join the Windows XP Professional computer to the domain. The Windows Server 2003 computer will be configured to use the Secure Server (Require Security) policy and the Windows XP Professional will be configured to use the Client (Respond Only) policy. Once the policies are in place, you can use IP Security Monitor to view security associations to determine the authentication method used, as well as the security protocols established.

Before implementing the IPSec policies, make sure you can ping each computer by its IP address.

1. Assigning the IPSec Secure Server (Require Security) policy to a Windows Server 2003 domain controller.
   a. On the domain controller, create a Microsoft Management Console (MMC) and add the IP Security Monitor and IP Security Policy Management snap-in.
   b. Using IP Security Policies on Local Computer, assign the Secure Server (Require Security) IPSec policy to the domain controller.

2. On the Windows XP Professional computer, create a Microsoft Management Console that includes the same snap-in choices you set up on the domain controller.

   a. Using IP Security Policies on Local Computer, locate the Client (Respond Only) IPSec policy and assign it to the Windows XP Professional computer.
   b. If you have not logged onto the domain, log on using the Domain Administrator's account.

3. Using the IP Security Monitor on both computers, review the security association information on both computers under the Main and Quick Mode folders.
   a. Has a security association been established between the two computers?
   b. During the Main Mode phase, the computers will go through the process of authenticating each other using IKE. The authentication methods available can include Kerberos, certificates, and/or pre-shared keys. Can you identify the authentication method being used?
   c. During the Quick Mode phase, the security protocols are established. Can you identify the security protocols being used for this security association?

Problem Solving Scenarios

1. James has set up two Windows Server 2003 computers. In order to secure traffic between the two, he used the IP Security Policies snap-in within a Microsoft Management Console to create a custom IPSec policy and assign the policy to the two computers. The policy encrypts Telnet traffic between the two computers. Although he can send/receive Telnet data from both computers, he is not sure if the Telnet traffic is being encrypted. What options/tools are available to determine if the Telnet traffic is indeed encrypted?

2. Mary is responsible for trying to figure out why two computers on the network that have been configured to use IPSec are not encrypting traffic as they should. She is concerned that a conflict in one of the policies is causing the problem.

After looking at the problem more closely, she notices the company has configured policies at the site, domain, and organizational unit levels of its Active Directory hierarchy. What tool could she use to determine the policies that are actually being applied to the computer?

3. Ted, the new junior network administrator at XYZ, Inc., has been asked to use IP Security Monitor to monitor sessions on three Windows 2000 Server computers and two Windows Server 2003 computers on the network. After working with the tool for an hour, he calls to say he can monitor some of the servers but not all of them. Why is he experiencing the problem and what solutions would you recommend to solve his problem?

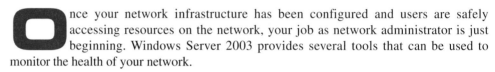

LESSON 12

Maintaining a Windows Server 2003 Network Infrastructure

Once your network infrastructure has been configured and users are safely accessing resources on the network, your job as network administrator is just beginning. Windows Server 2003 provides several tools that can be used to monitor the health of your network.

Task Manager, which has been around for some time, provides information regarding the processes and programs that are running on the computer. It provides a quick method for monitoring memory and processor utilization as well. In the Windows Server and Windows XP versions, a new feature has been added to monitor network performance. In this lesson, we will review some of the new information it provides.

Another tool that can be used to monitor the health of servers on your network is the Performance console. If you have worked with Windows NT, you will remember this as the Performance Monitor. The Performance console includes both the System Monitor utility and the Performance Logs and Alerts. Unlike Task Manager, which provides information regarding memory and processor utilization as it happens, these tools provide the administrator with the capability to monitor a wider range of information over a longer period of time. This information can then be viewed at the Administrator's convenience.

We will also revisit Network Monitor in this lesson. Earlier, we used this tool to capture IPSec traffic. In this lesson, we discuss the information you can view within Network Monitor and demonstrate the process for using it to capture traffic generated by the Ping utility.

This lesson will conclude with a brief discussion of services. Services are programs that are started when the computer boots and, in some cases, continue to run in the background. When these services fail to start, the administrator can configure options for addressing the problem.

Goals

In this lesson, you will learn about the new features of Task Manager and how it can be used to monitor network traffic. Next, you will learn how the Performance console, System Monitor, and the Performance Logs and Alert tool can be used to track information over longer periods of time and send alerts when parameters that have been configured are triggered. Microsoft's protocol analyzer, Network Monitor, will be discussed, along with how services can be managed on Windows Server 2003.

Lesson 12   Maintaining a Windows Server 2003 Network Infrastructure

Skill	Exam 70-291 Objective
1. Monitoring Network Traffic Using Task Manager	Monitor network traffic. Tools might include Network Monitor and System Monitor.
2. Monitoring Network Traffic Using System Monitor	Monitor network traffic. Tools might include Network Monitor and System Monitor.
3. Monitoring Network Traffic Using Performance Logs and Alerts	Monitor network traffic. Tools might include Network Monitor and System Monitor.
4. Monitoring Network Traffic Using Network Monitor	Monitor network traffic. Tools might include Network Monitor and System Monitor.
5. Troubleshooting Server Services	Troubleshoot server services. Diagnose and resolve issues related to service dependency. Use server recovery options to diagnose and resolve service-related issues.

Requirements

To complete this lesson, you will need administrative rights on a Windows Server 2003 computer and a Windows XP Professional computer.

skill 1

Monitoring Network Traffic Using Task Manager

Monitor network traffic. Tools might include Network Monitor and System Monitor.

overview

Windows Server 2003 provides several tools to assist you in monitoring network traffic. **Task Manager**, which has been around for some time, provides information regarding the processes and programs that are running on the computer. It provides a quick method for monitoring memory and processor utilization as well.

In the Windows Server 2003 and Windows XP versions, a new feature has been added to monitor network performance. The Networking tab provides a graphical view of network performance **(Figure 12-1)**. By reviewing the information, you can determine the amount of network bandwidth being utilized by your network adapter(s).

The bandwidth scale on the left of **Figure 12-1** represents the percentage of bandwidth used and adjusts automatically based on how much the link is being used. You can also determine if the network adapter is operational by looking under the **State** column. If you need to review additional counters to monitor network traffic, click **View** on the Menu bar and select **Columns**. The counters are shown in **Figure 12-2**.

As you can see, there are several counters that you can configure. If you see a high number in the **Nonunicasts/Interval** counter, for instance, the network interface on the computer is processing a lot of broadcast packets. In this situation, the problem may be a malfunctioning network adapter on another computer in the network. This could also occur if you have down-level operating systems on the network and have not provided a method such as WINS to resolve broadcast traffic for name resolution.

If you are trying to determine if the computer itself is a bottleneck for users on the network, review the **Link Speed** counter to make sure it is running at the maximum speed of the network. If the link speed is lower than expected (10 Mbps instead of 100 Mbps), you may have older hardware on the network that runs at a much slower speed, which causes the computer to fall back to the slower transmission rate to establish communications. Consider upgrading the network hardware to support the higher transmission rates.

For a more detailed explanation of each of the counters shown in **Figure 12-2**, go to **http://www.technet.com** and perform a search for **networking fields overview**.

Figure 12-1 Task Manager

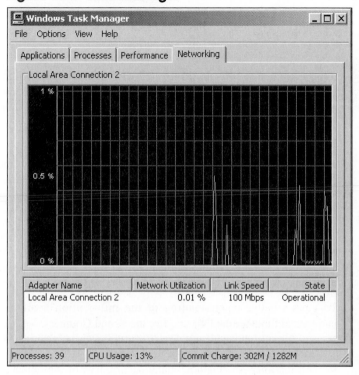

**Figure 12-2 Counters for networking fields
in the Task Manager**

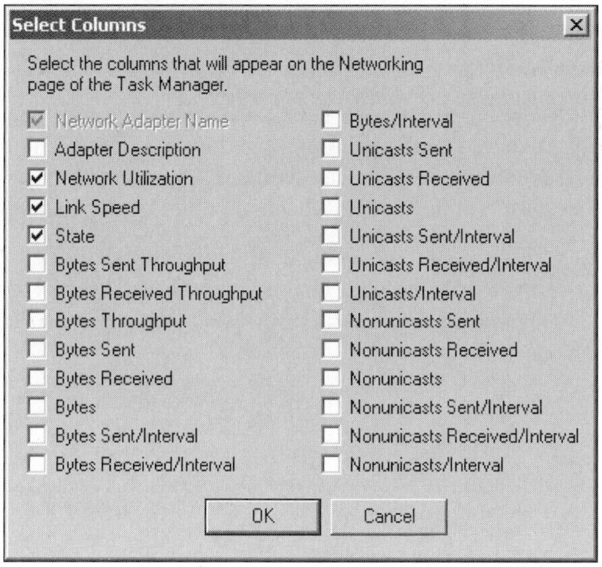

skill 2

Monitoring Network Traffic Using System Monitor

exam objective

Monitor network traffic. Tools might include Network Monitor and System Monitor.

overview

The Performance console (**Figure 12-3**) provides access to both System Monitor and the Performance Logs and Alerts tools. These tools can be used when a more thorough analysis needs to be done on the data collected, or an alert needs to be sent when critical system values are reached.

System Monitor provides real-time monitoring that can provide you with valuable insight as to how processes are progressing using the process, memory, and disk input/output counters on the server. This tool will also allow you to log network information over a period of time and export it to a file that can be opened in a spreadsheet program such as Excel. From there you can analyze the information further.

The **Performance Logs and Alerts** tool can be used to monitor how the system is performing over a period of time. It can also be configured to monitor critical system values and then send alerts to an event log, to an administrator, or run a particular program when the parameter has been exceeded.

To gain a better understanding of the information available in these tools, you must understand three terms: Objects, Instances, and Counters.

◆ An **object** represents any system component that can be measured, such as a processor, memory, disk volume, process, or thread.

◆ An **instance** reflects how many occurrences of the object are on the computer. If there were two processors in the computer, there would be two instances of the processor object.

◆ A **counter** represents a characteristic of an object that can be measured, such as the Average Disk Queue length, which indicates how many read/write requests, on average, are waiting to use the disk subsytem.

If you look closely at **Figure 12-3**, you will notice the System Monitor is selected and Windows Server 2003 includes three counters added by default. The **Pages/sec**, **Avg. Disk Queue Length**, and **%Processor Time**.

Each of these counters is represented by a different color in the graphic. High numbers in these counters might indicate bottlenecks in the memory subsystem, disk subsystem or, in some cases, not having a fast enough processor to handle the workload.

Since this section of the lesson deals with network traffic monitoring, there are a few counters that can provide you with insight as to how the server is performing on the network. The following section demonstrates how to add these counters and provides a brief explanation for each one.

tip

Performance monitor consumes resources, which may skew results. Remotely monitoring the server can reduce the load.

Figure 12-3 Performance console

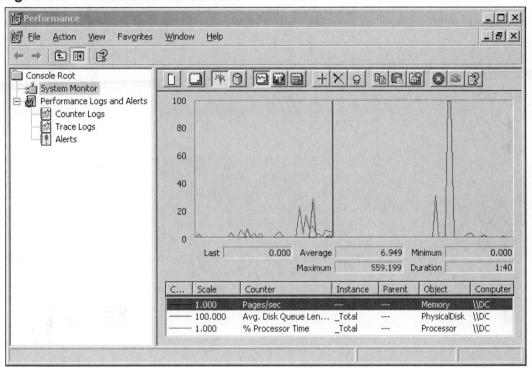

skill 2

Monitoring Network Traffic Using System Monitor (cont'd)

exam objective

Monitor network traffic. Tools might include Network Monitor and System Monitor.

how to

Monitor network traffic using System Monitor.

1. Click ⊞ **Start**, click **Run,** and type **perfmon** in the **Run** dialog box. Click ▢ OK ▢.
2. In System Monitor, click ⊞ on the toolbar (**Figure 12-4**).
3. In the **Add Counters** box, select the **Server** performance object and select the **Bytes Total/sec** counter. Click ▢ Add ▢ to add the counter as shown in **Figure 12-5**. The Bytes Total/sec counter for the Server object indicates just how busy the server really is. It records the number of bytes the server is sending and receiving. If you decide to add a second server to reduce the load on this server, you can use this counter to determine if the project was a success.
4. Select the **Server Sessions** counter for the **Server** performance object. Click ▢ Add ▢ to add the counter (**Figure 12-6**). The Server Sessions counter for the Server object indicates the number of connections users have with the server. If this counter is high, you may consider moving shares to other servers to reduce the load on this server. After you make the move, check this counter again to see if the load decreases.
5. Select the **Network Interface** performance object and then select the **Bytes Total/sec** counter. Click ▢ Add ▢ to add the counter (**Figure 12-7**). This counter indicates at how many bytes per second the server sends to or receives from any computer using the network interface to communicate with it. It does not show activity local to the server. By measuring the Bytes Total/sec with the Network Interface object, you can determine if your network adapter is performing at the speed you expect. For instance, if you have a 100 Mbps ethernet card and the network interface is sending and receiving at a much slower rate, the card may be malfunctioning.
6. Once you have added these counters, your System Monitor should look like **Figure 12-8**. To preserve the settings, save the console to your hard drive.
7. In this example, you are using **Graph view** mode. You can also use **Histogram view** by selecting ▣ or **Report view** by selecting ▣.

tip

You can click the Explain button for each counter to read more information about what the counter is monitoring.

tip

The Bytes Total/sec counter provides information on how fast the network adapter is sending and receiving data over the network. If you have a 100 Mbps network interface adapter and the results of this counter indicate the send/receive rate is much slower, check for problems with the adapter or the port configuration settings on switches on your network.

Figure 12-4 Adding Counters

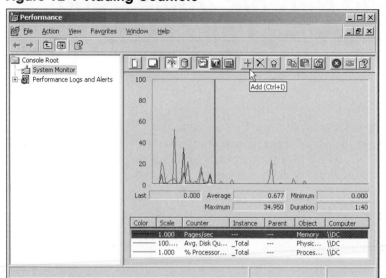

Figure 12-5 Adding the Bytes Total-/sec counter for the Server object

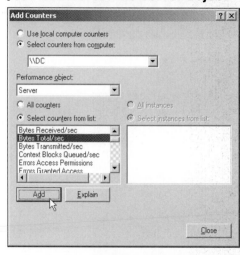

Figure 12-6 Adding the Server Session counter for the Server object

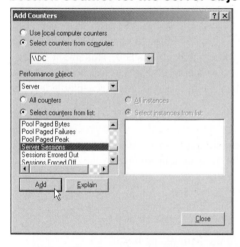

Figure 12-7 Adding the Bytes Total/sec counter for the Network Interface object

Figure 12-8 System Monitor with network-related counters added

Shows the rate, in incidents per second, at which bytes were sent and received on the network interface, including framing characters; Bytes Total/sec is the sum of the values of Bytes Received/sec and Bytes Sent/sec

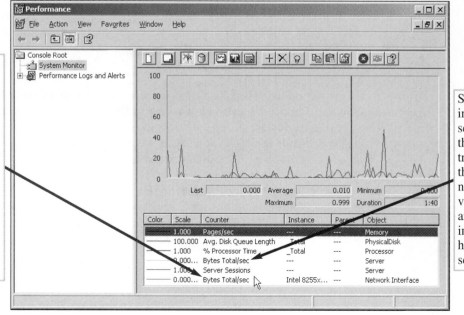

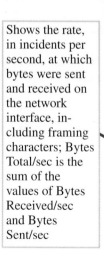

Shows the rate, in incidents per second, at which the server transmitted bytes through the network; this value provides an overall indication of how busy the server is

skill 3
Monitoring Network Traffic Using Performance Logs and Alerts

exam objective

Monitor network traffic. Tools might include Network Monitor and System Monitor.

overview

The Performance Logs and Alerts tool can be used to capture data that can be reviewed later. In other words, it allows the administrator to collect information over extended periods of time without having to sit and watch. The data can then be exported in comma-separated or tab-separated format. Later, it can be imported into a spreadsheet program for analysis.

Although graphs are useful when you need to monitor the system to see what is happening to it at that time, logs are better for long-term monitoring. How frequently you monitor differs with the situation. If you are looking for a specific problem, you may want to log activity frequently. If you are unsure of the problem and expect to have to watch it over time, you will log activity over a longer interval.

There are three types of logs used: Counter Logs, Trace Logs, and Alerts (**Figure 12-9**):
- **Counter logs** are used to collect information from counters that monitor how hardware is used, as well as system services.
- **Trace logs** are used to collect information on memory events, such as a page fault, or a resource event, such as disk input/output.
- **Alert logs** allow administrators to configure System Monitor to watch specific counters and then perform an action when a specific value has been reached. This might include running a program or sending an alert message to the administrator. Administrators can use alerts to inform them when processor utilization has reached an unacceptable level or when disk input/output becomes too high.

The following exercise demonstrates the process for creating an alert when processor utilization exceeds 80%. When monitoring in a real-world situation, spikes of 80% or more are very common in most processors and do not necessarily indicate a problem. On the other hand, if the processor exceeds 80% utilization a majority of the time, you should consider replacing it with a faster processor or add additional processors to the computer.

tip

If you expect to monitor a computer for more than 8 hours, set an interval of 300 seconds or more. 150 seconds is recommended for activity collected over a 4-hour time span.

how to

Set up an Alert Log.
1. Click 🏁**Start**, click **Run**, and type **perfmon** in the **Run** dialog box. Click [OK].
2. Right-click **Alerts** and select **New Alert Settings (Figure 12-10)**.
3. Enter a name for the new alert, such as Processor Alert, and click [OK].
4. In the **Processor Alert** dialog box, click [Add...] to add the **Processor** performance object and the **%Processor Time** counter. Leave the Instance setting at its default, _**Total** (**Figure 12-11**). Click [Add], then [Close].
5. In the **Alert when the value is** drop-down list box, select **Over**. In the **Limit** text box, type **80 (Figure 12-12)**.
6. On the **Action** tab, when the alert is triggered, select **Log an entry in the application event log** and **Send a network message to DC**. This is the Administrator's computer name (**Figure 12-13**).
7. On the **Schedule** tab, select **Start scan: Manually**. You could schedule this to start at a certain time/date but you will launch it manually in the next step. Click [OK] to close the Processor Alert box.
8. To start the log, right-click **Processor Alert** and select **Start (Figure 12-14)**.
9. Move the mouse around to generate processor activity or open a few files. When the processor reaches 80% utilization, you should see an alert message and an entry in the system event log (**Figures 12-15** and **12-16**).

tip

The Messenger service must be running in order for pop-up alert messages to appear on the computer's monitor screen.

Figure 12-9 Performance Logs and Alerts

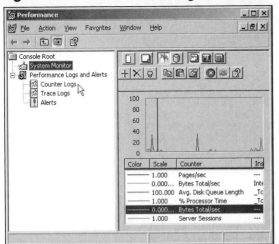

Figure 12-10 Configuring new alert

Figure 12-11 Adding Object, Counter, Instance

Figure 12-12 Setting Alert limit value

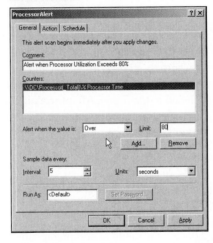

Figure 12-13 Configure actions

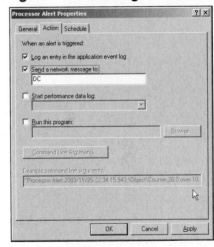

Figure 12-14 Starting Log

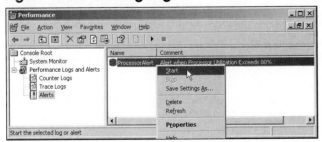

Figure 12-15 Pop up Alert message on computer

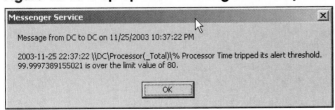

Figure 12-16 System Event Log entry

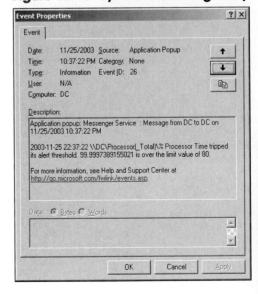

skill 4

Monitoring Network Traffic Using Network Monitor

exam objective

Monitor network traffic. Tools might include Network Monitor and System Monitor.

overview

Network Monitor, a protocol analyzer, allows you to view packets as they traverse the network and copies them into a buffer for viewing. The process of copying the frames to the buffer is known as data capture. In order to capture all packets, the network interface adapter is placed into promiscuous mode by Network Monitor. Once the monitoring process has finished, the network adapter is returned to normal operating mode. The version that comes with Windows Server 2003 can only capture packets to and from the computer running Network Monitor. The "full" version that comes with Microsoft Systems Management Server (SMS) can allow you to capture traffic from any of the devices on the network segment.

There are two components to Network Monitor: The Network Monitor Administration tool and the Network Monitor Agent.

Network Monitor is installed by using **Add/Remove Programs** and selecting **Network Monitor Tools** under the **Management And Monitoring Tools** option. If you install Network Monitor, the **Network Monitor Agent** is installed automatically on the same computer. You have to install the agent itself on any Windows XP, Windows 2000, or Windows Server 2003 computer you want to monitor.

Data travels around the network in a format known as a **frame**. Each frame contains both the source address where the frame originated and the destination address to which the frame is directed. Every frame contains information about the protocols used to send the information. Data is also included in the frame. All information in a frame is captured by Network Monitor and can be viewed in the Capture window. View **Figure 12-17** to become familiar with the panes in the window.

By analyzing information in the capture window, you can:
◆ Determine the MAC addresses used by computers.
◆ Determine the Globally Unique Identifier, which can be used to pre-stage Remote Installation Service clients.
◆ Determine port numbers being used by applications.
◆ Troubleshoot a wide range of communications problems that can occur on your network.

By using the function keys, you can start, stop, and view captures very easily. **[F10]** starts the capture process. **[F11]** is used to stop the capture, and **[F12]** is used to view the capture information.

In the process that follows, we will capture a very common type of frame used to troubleshoot basic network connectivity: an ICMP frame used in an echo request and echo reply process, more commonly known as a ping.

In order to perform the exercise that follows, you will need a Windows Server 2003 computer with Network Monitor installed and a Windows XP Professional computer. The server in this exercise is assigned 192.168.50.1/24 and the Windows XP Professional computer is assigned 192.168.50.2/24.

tip

Switches forward frames directly to the recipient computer; therefore, protocol analyzer functionality is reduced in those environments. Hubs, on the other hand, do not forward frames directly.

how to

Monitor network traffic using Network Monitor.
1. On the Windows XP Professional computer, execute the following command to continuously ping the Windows Server 2003 computer: **ping –t 192.168.50.1** (–t tells the computer to continuously ping until you stop the process).
2. On the Windows Server 2003 computer, click **Start**, point to **Administrative Tools**, and then click **Network Monitor**. If this is the first time you have run Network Monitor on the computer, you will be prompted to specify a network on which to capture data. Select **Local Area Connection (Figure 12-18)**. Click OK.

Figure 12-17 Capture window

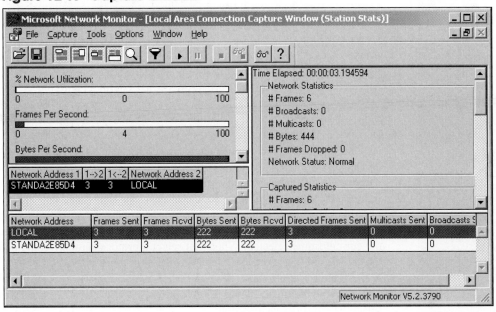

Figure 12-18 Select Local Area Connection

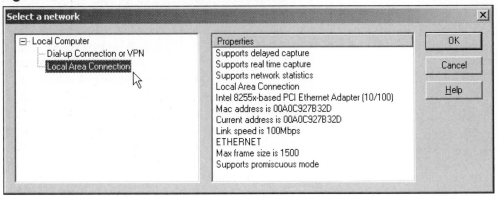

skill 4

Monitoring Network Traffic Using Network Monitor *(cont'd)*

Monitor network traffic. Tools might include Network Monitor and System Monitor.

how to

3. In the **Capture** window, either press **[F10]** to start the capture process or select **Capture-Start (Figure 12-19)**.

4. Wait for a few seconds, and then press **[F11]** to stop the capture process or select **Capture-Stop**.

5. To view the captured data, select **[F12]** or **Capture-Display Captured Data**. The frame viewer window will appear and display the frames you captured, in the order they were captured, from the Windows XP Professional computer pinging the Windows Server 2003 computer **(Figure 12-20)**. Since the computer located at 192.168.50.2 initiated the ping, we can see that it is listed as the source address in the first frame captured.

6. Before continuing, go back to the Windows XP Professional computer, and press **[Ctrl]+[C]** within the command shell to stop the ping process.

7. Now that you have captured network traffic, take a closer look at the contents of frame #1 **(Figure 12-20)** in the summary window by double-clicking the frame. Note that you can return to the summary view by double-clicking the frame again.

8. In **Figure 12-21**, you can see three panes. The top pane is known as the **Summary pane**. It lists the frames captured. The **Details pane** below it provides protocol information for the current frame selected. When you select a protocol in the Details pane, you can see the contents of that protocol in the **Hexadecimal pane** below.

9. In the Details pane, you can see that the protocols are listed from the lowest layer of the OSI model to the highest layer (FRAME, ETHERNET, IP, ICMP). To view the contents, select the **+** next to each section.

   a. The **FRAME** section provides information regarding the properties of the frame itself such as the time the frame was captured, its length, and the number of bytes of data in the frame itself.

   b. The **ETHERNET** section provides information on source and destination Media Access Control (MAC) addresses **(Figure 12-22)**. These are 48-bit addresses that are burnt into every network interface adapter by their manufacturer. Computers use the information to determine if the frame is for them. If it is, they will pull the frame from the wire and pass it to the computer for processing.

   c. The **IP** section provides information on the routing protocol used. In this case, it is the Internet Protocol (IP). By expanding this section, you can determine the version of IP used, as well as the source and destination IP addresses.

   d. The **ICMP** section provides information on the type of communication occurring. When using ping to contact another computer, you initiate an echo request packet. The other computer responds by sending an echo reply.

10. The capture can be saved and viewed later, if necessary. The process that Network Monitor uses to read, analyze, and describe the contents of a frame is known as **parsing**. These are dynamic link library (dll) files that are used to read the information sent by different protocols. In situations where a new protocol is required, you will need to add a parser for Network Monitor. This is done by adding the .dll file to the **%systemroot%\- system32\Netmon\Parsers** folder.

11. To complete the process, add an entry for the new parser and protocol into the Parser.ini file, which can be found in the Netmon folder.

Figure 12-19 Start capture

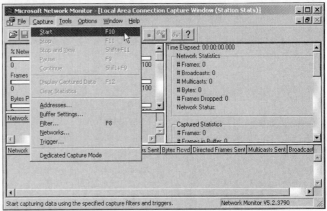

Figure 12-20 View capture

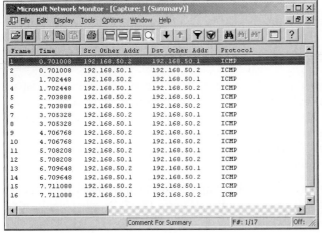

Figure 12-21 Frame details

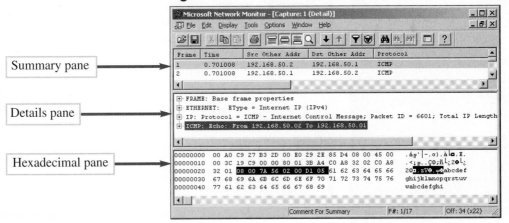

Figure 12-22 Ethernet layer details

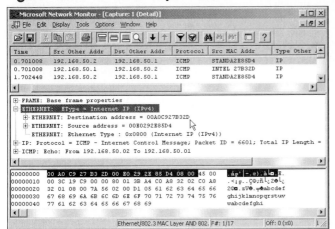

skill 5

Troubleshooting Server Services

exam objective

Troubleshoot server services. Diagnose and resolve issues related to service dependency. Use server recovery options to diagnose and resolve service-related issues.

overview

Depending on the range of components you choose when installing Windows Server 2003, several services are added. You can view these services by right-clicking **My Computer** and selecting **Manage**. **Figure 12-23** some of the services found on a Windows Server 2003 computer. **Services** are programs that are started when the computer boots and in some cases continue to run in the background.

The Services tab provides both an extended and standard view. When working in extended view, you can select a service in the right pane and see its description. You can start the service as well.

By double-clicking one of the services, the **Alerter service** in this example, you can see there are three possible Startup type settings: **Automatic**, **Manual**, or **Disabled** (**Figure 12-24**). By setting the service to Automatic, the service will automatically start when the computer is started. If you set the startup type to Manual, the service will only start if another process calls for it or if you open the Service Properties dialog box and start it manually. The Disabled option means that the service will not start even if a process calls it.

If you select the **Dependencies** tab in the Service Properties dialog box, you will see that the Alerter service depends upon the Workstation service (**Figure 12-25**). In other words, if the Workstation service does not start, neither will the Alerter service.

The Alerter service is not the only service that depends upon the Workstation service to start. In **Figure 12-26**, you can see that the Computer Browser, Distributed File System, Messenger, Net Logon, and Remote Procedure Call (RPC) Locator services all depend on it as well. As you can imagine, if the Workstation service did not start, your event logs would fill up with several error messages regarding services not starting. The upside to this is that by troubleshooting the problem with the Workstation service and resolving it, you will fix the other dependency errors.

If a service fails, you have four options to choose from in order to address the problem (**Figure 12-27**):
◆ Take No Action
◆ Restart the Service
◆ Run a Program
◆ Restart the Computer

These options can be configured differently for each time the failure occurs. In most cases, the first failure should be configured to restart the service. Subsequent failures can be configured to Run a Program or Restart the Computer.

For instance, if a service fails to start, and you select **Run a Program**, you can run an application or batch file that will alert you to the problem or launch another program to collect the status of services on the computer.

If you use the **Restart the Computer** option when a service fails to start, you can also send a message to computers on the network before the restart occurs. This provides them time to disconnect from any shared resources on the computer before it shuts down.

tip

If you set the computer to restart when a service fails, consider the impact it will have on applications and other computers who may be using services that are already running.

Figure 12-23 Services list

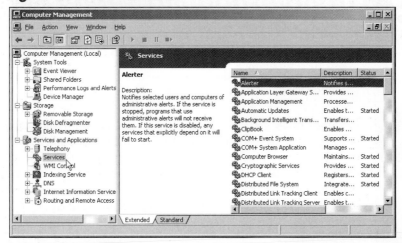

Figure 12-24 Possible Service Startup type settings

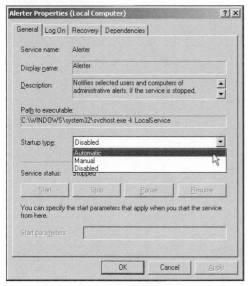

Figure 12-25 Alerter service depends upon Workstation service

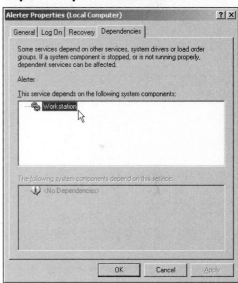

Figure 12-26 Other services that depend on the Workstation service

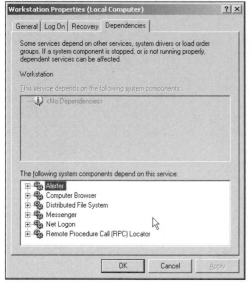

Figure 12-27 Options for addressing service failures

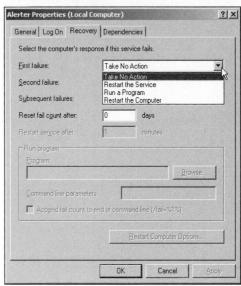

skill 5

Troubleshooting Server Services
(cont'd)

exam objective

Troubleshoot server services. Diagnose and resolve issues related to service dependency. Use service recovery options to diagnose and resolve service-related issues.

overview

In **Figure 12-28**, you can see that, for instance, the **ClipBook** service runs under the context of the Local System account. Most services use this account to control when they are started or stopped. If you install third party applications, you may need to configure an account specifically for them. There are a lot of data backup programs on the market that require you to set up a user account for them to function. In those cases, you will need to make sure the services that require the account are configured to use them.

When an account is used for a service, you will need to make sure it has the **Log on as a service** right. If you are using a domain-based account, this is configured under the Domain Controller Security Policy. This is accomplished by locating the local policies node and double-clicking the **User Rights Assignment**. Select **Log on as a service** as shown in **Figure 12-29**. If the account is on a standalone system, you can provide the right by using the Local Computer Policy. To access the policy, click 🏁 **Start**, click the **Run** command, and then enter **gpedit.msc**. Configure the policy as shown in **Figure 12-30**.

Figure 12-28 The Local System account

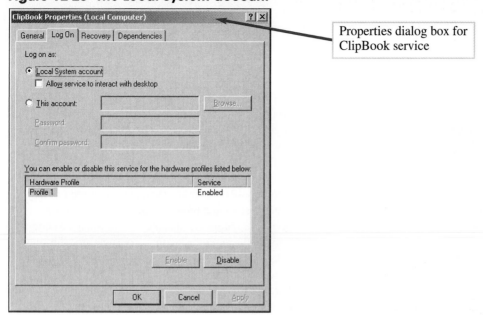

Properties dialog box for ClipBook service

Figure 12-29 Setting the Log on as a service right for domain user accounts

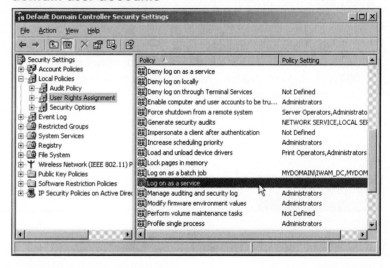

Figure 12-30 Setting the Log on as a service right for non-domain user accounts

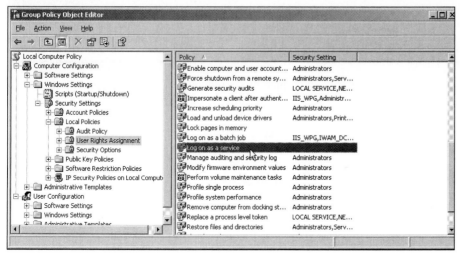

Summary

- Task Manager in Windows Server 2003 and Windows XP has a new feature that allows you to monitor network bandwidth usage. You can also determine if the adapter is operational.
- The Performance console provides both System Monitor and the Performance Logs and Alerts tool.
- System Monitor uses objects, instances, and counters to view your network over time. You can then export the file for later manipulation and analysis in a spreadsheet.
- Performance Logs and Alerts can be used to log information over extended periods or to alert you when critical values have been reached. You then can review this data later.
- The Server: Bytes Total/sec, Server Sessions, and Network Interface: Bytes Total/sec counters can be used to troubleshoot network-related problems.
- Counter logs, trace logs, and alert logs are used with the Performance Logs and Alerts tool.
- Network Monitor is used to view packets as they traverse the network and to copy them into a buffer for viewing. The copying process is known as data capture.
- To view frames, Network Monitor places the network adapter into promiscuous mode while capturing traffic.
- The basic version of Network Monitor in Windows Server 2003 only supports capturing traffic to and from the computer running the tool. The "full" version is found on Windows Systems Management Server.
- Switches forward frames directly to the recipient computer; therefore, functionality of protocol analyzers

such as Network Monitor, is reduced. Hubs, on the other hand do not forward frames directly.
- The Network Monitor agent must be installed on computers you want to monitor.
- The process that Network Monitor uses to read, analyze, and describe the contents of a frame is known as parsing. New protocols require you to add a new parser for Network Monitor. This is done by obtaining and adding the appropriate .dll file to the %systemroot%\system-32\Netmon\Parsers folder. You must also add an entry for the new parser and protocol into the parser.ini file.
- Services are programs that are started when the computer boots and, in some cases, continue to run in the background. Some services are dependent upon other services starting.
- There are three possible settings for managing the startup of services: Automatic, Manual, and Disabled.
- There are four actions that can be taken if a service fails to start: Take No Action, Restart the Service, Run a Program, or Restart the Computer.
- Most services run under the context of the Local System account. It is common for a third party application to require a special user account to be configured. This account must be given the Log On As A Service right. This setting is available under the Domain Controller Security Policy if you are using a domain user account, or under the Local Computer Policy if you are working on a standalone system.

Key Terms

Alert logs	Instance	Services
Counter	Object	System Monitor
Counter logs	Parsing	Task Manager
Frame	Performance Logs and Alerts	Trace logs

Test Yourself

1. Which of the following are true statements regarding Network Monitor in Windows Server 2003?
   a. It comes as part of the Windows Server 2003 operating system.
   b. It can capture traffic between any two systems on the network.
   c. It can capture traffic that is sent to and from the computer it is installed on.
   d. It places the network adapter in promiscuous mode when performing data capture.

2. Which of the following are correct regarding the use of counters, objects, and instances?
   a. An instance represents any system component that can be measured.
   b. An object represents any system component that can be measured.
   c. A processor is an example of an object.
   d. An instance reflects a characteristic of an object that can be measured.

3. The Average Disk Queue length is an example of:
   a. An instance
   b. A counter
   c. An object
   d. None of the above

4. Which are the default counters added to System Monitor when it is first started?
   a. Pages/sec
   b. Avg. Disk Queue Length
   c. %Processor Time
   d. %Idle Time

5. Which of the following are actions you can take if a service fails?
   a. Take No Action
   b. Restart the Service
   c. Run a Program
   d. Restart the Computer

6. Which of the following are true statements regarding using services in Windows Server 2003?
   a. Most services in Windows Server 2003 run under the context of the Local System account.
   b. Some third party applications may require that you set up a specific account for them to run under.
   c. The Log on as a service right can be configured under the Local Computer Policy for standalone systems.

   d. The Log on as a service right can be configured under the Domain Controller Security policy.

7. When using Microsoft's protocol analyzer, which statements are correct?
   a. You must have Network Monitor on a Windows Server 2003 system.
   b. You must have the Network Monitor agent installed on computers you want to monitor.
   c. You can monitor network traffic between any two computers on the network.
   d. You must manually set your network interface adapter to promiscuous mode.

8. The process that Network Monitor uses to read, analyze, and describe the contents of a frame is known as parsing. Which statements are true regarding parsing?
   a. Dynamic link libraries are used to read information sent by different protocols.
   b. New protocols may require that you add a parser for Network Monitor.
   c. Add new .dll files for the protocol into the %systemroot%\system32\Netmon\Parsers folder.
   d. Add an entry for the new parser and protocol into the parser.ini file.

Projects: On Your Own

1. Using the **Performance Logs and Alerts** tool, create an alert that triggers when the computer's processor utilization exceeds 70%.
   a. Start **Performance** monitor.
   b. Create a new alert setting. Name the alert **PingTest**.
   c. Add the appropriate object, counter, and instance.
   d. Set the alert to trigger when the processor reaches **70%** or greater utilization.
   e. Set the alert to log an entry in the application event log and then to send a network message to the Administrator's computer.
   f. Schedule the job to run manually.
   g. Start the job once it is set up, and then move the mouse to generate processor activity.
   h. Click **OK** in the pop-up message box. If you do not see one, make sure the **Messenger service** is running on the computer.
   i. Look in the application event log for an event that shows source as **SysmonLog**. The information in the event should indicate the counter **%Processor Time** has tripped its alert threshold.

2. Using **Network Monitor**, capture ping packets.
   a. Install **Network Monitor** on a Windows Server 2003 computer (Computer A).
   b. Install the **Network Monitor** agent on a Windows XP Professional computer. (Computer B)
   c. From Computer B, use the Ping command to continuously ping the IP address of Computer A.
   d. On Computer A, open Network Monitor and press **[F10]** to start the capture process.
   e. After about 10 seconds, press **[F11]** to stop the capture process.
   f. Return to the Computer B and terminate the continuous ping.
   g. To view the frames that you captured, press **[F12]**.
   h. Double-click the first frame in the summary window to view its contents in detail.
   i. Identify the source and destination Media Access Control addresses for each of the computers.
   j. Identify the source and destination IP addresses for each of the computers.
   k. Save the capture for viewing later.

Problem Solving Scenarios

1. William has just completed the setup of his small Windows Server 2003 test lab. In the lab, he has two Windows Server 2003 computers, and two Windows XP Professional computers. He has installed Network Monitor on one of the Windows Server 2003 computers and has also installed the Network Monitor Agent on all of the other computers. He is having trouble connecting to a shared folder on one of the Windows XP Professional computers from the other Windows XP Professional system. He would like to use the Network Monitor tool to observe the traffic between the two. Unfortunately, after several attempts, he is unsuccessful and has asked you for assistance. What advice can you give him to resolve his problem?

2. Your small network consists of five Windows XP Professional computers and one Windows Server 2003 computer that functions as a domain controller. These systems are connected by a hub. You have installed Network Monitor on the Windows Server 2003 computer that performs the domain controller function. You want to capture network traffic when a user logs on to the domain controller from one of the Windows XP Professional computers. What problems, if any, will you have?

Glossary

Active Directory-integrated zone A DNS zone that stores DNS information in Active Directory.

Address (A) record A resource record that associates a host name to the host's IP address.

Address Resolution Protocol (ARP) A protocol responsible for resolving IP addresses to hardware (MAC) addresses on the local subnet.

Alias A nickname for a computer name that is mapped to an IP address.

Alert logs A tool that allows Administrators to configure System Monitor to watch specific counters and then perform an action when a specific value has been reached.

AppleTalk LAN architecture built into Apple Macintosh computers and laser printers used to interact with the OSI model.

Application layer Located at the top of the TCP/IP protocol stack, the Application layer enables applications to access the services of the other layers and defines the protocols that applications must use to exchange data.

Application Program Interface (API) Generic code that permits application programmers to program application code to call functions such as network functions.

ANDing An operation that is performed by multiplying one binary number by another binary number resulting in the network address for a given IP address. ANDing is also referred to as the logical AND operation.

ARP cache A storage area that maintains a temporary record of mappings of IP addresses to hardware addresses.

ARP utility Utility used to display and modify the IP address-to-physical address (MAC address) translation tables used by the Address Resolution Protocol.

Audit logging The process by which a DHCP server maintains a record of its activities in a text file; serves as a troubleshooting tool.

Authentication The process of verifying that an entity is who or what it claims to be.

Authentication Header (AH) A protocol that ensures authentication and message integrity for transmitted packets.

Authentication Method Determines the method used to authenticate the entities involved.

Authorization The process that determines what the user is permitted to do on the system or network.

Automatic Private IP Addressing (APIPA) Feature of Windows Server 2003 that computers use to assign themselves an IP address automatically when a DHCP server is not available.

Baseline Data that represents the normal performance of a server such as a DNS server.

Bootstrap Protocol (BOOTP) A protocol that enables diskless clients to configure TCP/IP automatically and thereby obtain IP addresses.

Border Gateway Protocol (BGP) An exterior routing protocol used to exchange information between networks that are administered under different administrative authorities.

Broadcast A method of NetBIOS name resolution that sends requests simultaneously to all network hosts.

Caching A method of storing frequently used information in memory so that it can be accessed quickly when required.

Caching-only name server A DNS server that does not have its own local zone database file.

Certificate A digital document that is used for authentication and to secure information. It binds a public key to the user/computer/service that holds the private key.

Certificate Revocation List A document maintained and published by a CA. It lists revoked certificates.

Certification Authorities Entities that issue, manage, and vouch for the authenticity of the public keys they issue to users/computers/services. They also can vouch for other CAs.

Certification Services A Windows Server 2003 service that issues certificates for a particular CA. Installing this service allows a server to perform the role of a Certificate Authority in a Public Key Infrastructure.

Classless Inter-Domain Routing (CIDR) A method of subnetting that removes the requirement that all subnets be of equal size and provides an easy way of notating subnet masks. In CIDR, the class of address you are given does not necessarily denote the network section of an address.

Client (Respond Only) A default IPSec policy under which computers will never initiate a request to use IPSec for data transmission but will enter a negotiation with Internet Key Exchange when requested to do so by another computer.

Confidentiality The process of ensuring that data is safe from being intercepted, viewed, or copied while in transit.

Counter Represents a characteristic of an object that can be measured.

Counter logs A tool that is used to collect information from counters that monitor how hardware is used, as well as system services.

Cryptography The process of keeping information secure.

Default gateway A router that links networks and manages the information needed to do so, enabling client hosts to get data to or from a computer outside the local subnet. A client host identifies whatever router that is on its own subnet as its default gateway.

Delegated zones Zones created to manage portions of the chain of domains using contiguous names.

Demand-dial interface Helps a Windows Server 2003 computer establish a connection with a remote router on another network.

Demand-dial routing Cost-saving method of connecting to a remote network only for the time during which the connection is required.

DHCPAcknowledgment Message packet sent by the DHCP server to the client that verifies that the client can use the IP address that was offered.

DHCPDiscover Message packet that DHCP clients broadcast to locate a DHCP server on the network.

DHCPOffer Message packet the DHCP server sends to the DHCP client to offer an available IP address.

DHCPRequest Message packet sent by the DHCP client to the DHCP server to request use of the IP address that has been offered.

DHCP Relay Agent A routing protocol that makes it possible for DHCP clients to request an IP address from a DHCP server that is located on a remote subnet. Without a relay agent, broadcast packets cannot travel through routers.

Digital Signature Provides a way for an entity that sends a file, message, or other digital information to bind its identity to the information being sent.

DNS namespace The hierarchical arrangement of domains in DNS.

DNS server A server that maintains a DNS database for the purpose of resolving host names to IP addresses.

Domain name A name of an IP host such as prenhall.com that is used in place of an IP address.

Domain Name System (DNS) A naming system service that is used to locate IP-based computers by translating their fully qualified domain names into their associated IP addresses.

Dynamic Domain Name System (DDNS) DNS that supports dynamic updates of host name-to-IP address mappings.

Dynamic Host Configuration Protocol (DHCP) Service used to allocate IP addresses dynamically to network clients that are configured to obtain an address automatically.

Dynamic routing Method of routing used by routers to share their routing information on a network.

Dynamic updates Allow resources on a network to register with a zone and update any changes in their configurations dynamically.

Encapsulating Security Payload (ESP) Provides encryption, authentication, integrity, and anti-replay services.

Encrypting File System (EFS) A feature of Windows that allows users to encrypt files and folders that are stored on NTFS volumes through public key cryptography.

Enterprise CA A CA that is integrated with Active Directory and uses information stored there to identify users, computers, and services requesting certificates.

Event logging A feature that records remote access server warnings, errors, and other information in the system event log.

Event Viewer Maintains logs about program, security, and system events.

Exclusion An IP address that falls within the address range of a scope, but which the DHCP server may not lease to a client.

Exterior routing protocol A protocol, such as BGP (Border Gateway Protocol), used to exchange information between networks administered under different administrative authorities.

Filter Identifies the type of traffic that the filter action will be applied to. Filters include protocols, ports, IP addresses, DNS names.

Filter Action Identifies what to do if the filter matches.

Forward lookup zone A DNS zone that resolves host names to IP addresses.

Forwarder A DNS server outside of a firewall that can communicate with other DNS servers on the Internet enabling you to keep your internal DNS servers safe from harm behind the firewall.

Frame A logical grouping of information created at the Data link layer of the OSI model. It uses source/destination MAC addresses in the header.

Fully qualified domain name (FQDN) A method of naming a host using Internet naming conventions to fully identify the host, as in hostname.domain_name.

Globally Unique Identifier A unique number for the computer. It can be found in the BIOS, inside or outside of the computer case. Used by servers running the Remote Installation Service to control which clients it will service.

Group static mapping A type of static mapping used to create an entry for a group of computers.

Hop count The number of routers through which a data transmission must pass in order to reach its destination.

Host Any device on a network that is identified using an IP address.

Host ID The group of bits in the 32-bit IP address, distinct from the network bits and also known as the host address, that is used to identify individual network entities including servers, workstations, printers, routers, and gateways on a network.

Host name A name given to a host on a TCP/IP network in addition to the host's IP address.

Host name resolution A process, such as the TCP/IP utilities, DNS name resolution or WINS name resolution, that looks up the IP address of a host over a TCP/IP network by using a host name.

Hostname Utility used to display or set the host name of the local computer.

HOSTS file A text file available on the local computer that contains the static mappings of host names to IP addresses and is used by TCP/IP utilities to resolve host names to their IP addresses.

in-addr.arpa A special domain that contains nodes with names based on IP addresses to facilitate reverse lookups (finding a host name given an IP address).

in-addr.arpa zone The zone that is authoritative for the in-addr.arpa domain.

Infrared Data Association (IrDA) Protocol suite designed to provide line-of-sight wireless connectivity for devices such as a PDA or wireless mouse.

Instance Reflects how many occurrences of an object there are on the computer.

Integrity The process of ensuring that data received is accurate and complete.

Interior routing protocol A protocol, such as RIP (Routing Information Protocol), used to exchange routing information between routers administered under a common administrative authority.

Internet Assigned Numbers Authority (IANA) The organization that manages the root domain of the Internet. Web site: www.iana.org.

Internet Authentication Service (IAS) A service that enables you to configure a RADIUS server that can provide centralized remote authentication, authorization, and accounting capabilities for incoming connections instead of managing policies on individual servers.

Internet Control Message Protocol (ICMP) Protocol that supports packets containing error, control, and informational messages. The ping utility generates an ICMP Echo request.

Internet Group Management Protocol (IGMP) Protocol responsible for the management of IP multicasting, which is the transmission of an IP datagram to a set of hosts called the IP multicast group that is identified by a single IP multicast address.

Internet Key Exchange (IKE) A protocol that establishes the security associations between two entities.

Internet layer Layer in the DARPA model that is responsible for transferring packets between computers that are located on the same or different networks.

Internet Protocol (IP) A connectionless protocol that is responsible for the delivery of packets, including the process of fragmenting them and reassembling them at the destination.

Internet Protocol Security (IPSec) A suite of network-layer protocols that extends IP by providing authentication, confidentiality, and data integrity mechanisms for data in transit.

Internet Protocol version 4 (IPv4) The version of Internet Protocol that is generally installed by default during the installation of the Windows Server 2003 operating system.

Internet Protocol version 6 (IPv6) New version of Internet Protocol that has been developed to replace IPv4.

Intranet A private TCP/IP network within an organization.

IP Address Under IPv4, a 32-bit number divided into 4 octets separated by periods, used to identify a host on a TCP/IP network. An IP address has two parts: the network ID and the host ID. An IPv6 IP address has 128 bits.

IP Routing A technique that enables data transfer from one computer to another regardless of their physical locations or proximity.

IP Security Monitor A tool for testing whether IPSec communications are secure.

Ipconfig A command-line tool used to verify TCP/IP configuration settings.

IPSec Driver Uses the defined filters to determine which data packets are blocked, permitted, or secured.

IPSec Policy Agent (IPSec Services) Retrieves the appropriate IPSec policy and sends the information to the IPSec driver. The IPSec Policy Agent starts automatically at system startup. If no IPSec policies are assigned, it will wait for a policy to be assigned.

Iterative query A type of DNS query that calls a name server to reply with the data requested by a resolver or with a reference to another name server that would be able to answer the request of the resolver.

Jetpack A utility used to compact a WINS database.

Kerberos Used by IPSec for authentication.

Key Sequence of numbers created by an algorithm that is used to encrypt/decrypt information.

Layer Two Tunneling Protocol (L2TP) Protocol used to create a secure tunnel for virtual private networks.

LMHOSTS file A text file available on the local computer that contains the static mappings of NetBIOS names to IP addresses of computers and is used to resolve NetBIOS names to IP addresses.

Logical infrastructure Software components of a network including, but not limited to network protocols, IP addressing schemes, name resolution services, remote access services, routing, network address translation service, and security services.

Main Mode First phase of SA negotiation; involves authentication of entities.

Master name server See *Primary DNS server.*

Media Access Control Addresses Hardware addresses (48 bits) that are burned into network cards. They are used to uniquely identify the nodes on the network.

Member scopes The scopes included in a superscope.

Microsoft Certificate Services A service that enables Network Administrators to implement a Certificate Authority (CA) for issuing, renewing, managing, and revoking digital certificates.

Microsoft Challenge Handshake Authentication Protocol (MS-CHAP) v1 A protocol that encrypts password information before it is sent over a communication link, utilizing one-way authentication.

Microsoft Challenge Handshake Authentication Protocol (MS-CHAP) v2 An enhanced version of MS-CHAP v1 that utilizes mutual authentication.

Microsoft Management Console (MMC) A standard administrative interface for managing Windows Server 2003 and its applications.

Microsoft Point-to-Point Encryption A protocol used to secure remote access connections.

Modem Pool Consists of several modems integrated into a single card or several modems placed in an external chassis.

Multicast Address Dynamic Client Allocation Protocol (MADCAP) A standard introduced by the Internet Engineering Task Force (IETF) that defines the allocation of multicast addresses (see RFC 2730).

Multicast scope A group of Class D IP addresses that is used by a DHCP server to lease IP addresses to the multicast DHCP clients.

Multicasting The process of transmitting a message to a select group of recipients.

Mutual Authentication Authentication of both ends of a communication session.

Name query request A message sent by a WINS client to a WINS server requesting the IP address of a NetBIOS computer.

Name refresh request A message sent by a WINS client to a WINS server asking to refresh the TTL (Time-to-Live) of the NetBIOS name of the client.

Name registration request A message sent by a WINS client to a WINS server to register the NetBIOS name of the client.

Name release message A message sent by a WINS client to a WINS server when the client does not require the registered name any longer.

Name response message A message sent by a WINS server to a WINS client containing the IP address of the desired NetBIOS computer.

Name server A program that runs on a server computer that contains address information about network hosts.

Name server record A resource record that acts as a pointer to the name server of the delegated zone and directs the query to the correct name server for resolution.

NetBIOS An industry-standard interface between NetBIOS-based applications and TCP/IP protocols that is used for accessing NetBIOS services.

NetBIOS name A unique 16-byte name assigned to each NetBIOS resource on a network.

NetBIOS name cache A storage facility that stores information about recently resolved NetBIOS names.

NetBIOS name resolution The process of mapping a NetBIOS name to an IP address.

NetBIOS name server (NBNS) An application responsible for mapping NetBIOS names to IP addresses.

Netdiag Used to test the network driver, protocol driver, and the send and receive capabilities of your computer. It can also provide information on the IPSec policy that is currently active on the computer.

Netsh Command line utility that can be used to configure and monitor IPSec and perform DHCP and other administrative tasks from a command prompt.

Network access server Provides a dial-up or VPN entry point for remote access clients. Also known as a remote access server.

Network Address Translation (NAT) Routing protocol that exchanges information between routers and enables a LAN to use one set of IP addresses for internal traffic and another set of IP addresses for external traffic. NAT also allows multiple users to connect to the Internet through a single connection.

Network Bandwidth Bandwidth, measured in bits per second, is used to describe the amount of information that can be carried in a given amount of time. Also referred to as throughput.

Network ID The group of bits in an IP address also known as the network address that identify the network to which a computer belongs, as opposed to the Host ID bits, which identify the computer itself.

Network infrastructure Interconnected computers and the services required for communication between the computers.

Network Interface layer Layer in the DARPA model that is responsible for sending and receiving TCP/IP packets (and those of many other protocols) over network media.

Network Monitor Tool for capturing and monitoring packets.

NWLink Microsoft's 32-bit implementation of Novell NetWare's IPX/SPX protocol.

Object Represents any system component that can be measured.

Octet Any of the four 8-bit values used in an IP address.

Offline compaction A WINS server database process that you need to perform, after stopping the WINS service, to reduce the amount of disk space used by scavenged entries.

One-way authentication Authentication of only one end of the communication session. Typically the client is authenticated by the server.

Online compaction An automatic WINS server database compaction process that occurs in the background during idle time.

Open Shortest Path First (OSPF) Routing protocol that enables routers to exchange routing table information so that routers can find optimal routes for data transfer.

Open Systems Interconnection Model This 7-layer model serves as a reference for how messages are transmitted between two network devices.

Packet An individual unit in a communications stream, also known as a frame, datagram, or message depending on the context in which it is used.

Parsing The process that Network Monitor uses to read, analyze, and describe the contents of a frame.

Pathping Utility that combines the features of ping and tracert.

Performance Logs and Alerts A tool that allows an Administrator to capture data over an extended period of time for later review and analysis.

Physical infrastructure Hardware components of a network, including cables, network interface cards, hubs, and routers.

Ping (Packet Internet Groper) Used to test connectivity in IP-based networks.

Pointer (PTR) record A resource record in the reverse lookup file that associates an IP address with a host name in the in-addr.arpa domain.

Point-to-Point Protocol An industry standard protocol that is used to transport multiprotocol datagrams over point-to-point links. PPP is documented in RFC 1661.

Point-to-Point Tunneling Protocol (PPTP) TCP/IP protocol that provides an internal address configuration to the remote client; used in virtual private networks.

Positive name registration response A message sent by a WINS server to a WINS client indicating successful registration of the NetBIOS name of the client in the WINS database.

Pragmatic General Multicast (PGM) The reliable multicast protocol supported by Windows Server 2003 to transmit messages in a multicast data stream.

Pre-shared Key Used in IPSec communications for authentication.

Primary DNS server/Primary name server The name server that gets data for its zones from locally stored zone database files and is the main authority for its zones.

Promiscuous Mode Network interface cards operating in this mode accept all traffic regardless of the MAC address in the packet.

Protocol Predefined set of rules for sending information over a network. A protocol standardizes the content, format, timing, sequencing, and manner of error control of messages that are transmitted between devices on a network.

Protocol Analyzer A device that captures network traffic for analysis.

Public Key Infrastructure A set of services that supports the use of cryptography. Includes rules, policies, standards, and software that manage certificates and public/private keys in order to authenticate the validity of each party involved in a transaction.

Public/private keys Key pairs used to encrypt/decrypt information and verify digital signatures.

Pull partner A WINS server that pulls or requests replication of updated WINS database entries from other WINS servers at a configured interval.

Push partner A WINS server that notifies other WINS servers of the need to replicate their database entries at a configured interval.

Quick Mode Second phase of SA negotiations when security protocols are negotiated.

RADIUS client A remote access server to which remote clients can connect. RADIUS clients are configured to send requests to a RADIUS server running IAS.

RADIUS proxy A capability available through IAS that forwards authentication and accounting requests to other RADIUS servers.

RADIUS server With IAS installed, a RADIUS server can provide centralized remote authentication, authorization, and accounting capabilities for incoming connections.

Recovery Agent A person who has a public key certificate for the purpose of recovering user data that has been encrypted when EFS is implemented.

Recursive query A type of DNS query that calls a name server that assumes the full workload and responsibility for providing a complete answer to the query.

Remote Authentication Dial-In Service (RADIUS) A security authentication protocol used to authenticate and authorize dial-up and VPN connection users.

Remote Installation Service Used to provide images on demand for operating system installations.

Replay Attack An attack that is based on capturing packets and then resending them on the network.

Reservation Permits you to set aside a specific address in a scope for leasing by a particular DHCP client.

Resolver A host service that provides information about other network hosts to the client. The resolver initiates the search for an IP address once it is provided with the host name.

Resource record An entry in a DNS database that contains information about the resources in a DNS domain. Examples of resource records include name server (NS), start of authority (SOA), and alias (CNAME).

Resultant Set of Policy (RSoP) snap-in Tool used to simulate and test policy settings that are applied to computers or users using Group Policy.

Reverse lookup file A zone database file containing information that allows for finding a host name, given the IP address of the host.

Reverse lookup zone A zone that resolves IP addresses to host names.

RFC Refers to Request for Comments, the main technical documentation series maintained by the Internet Engineering Task Force

RIPv1 Distance vector routing protocol that provides information about the networks to which a router can connect and the distances to these networks.

RIPv2 Routing protocol that is an enhanced version of RIPv1 and provides the information about the subnet mask and broadcasts the routing information.

Root Certification Authority The most trusted CA in the PKI. It is at the top of the CA hierarchy and signs its own digital certificate. There is no higher level of certifying authority in the hierarchy. Typically used to issue certificates to subordinate CAs.

Root domain The domain at the top of the DNS namespace hierarchy.

Root name server The DNS server that has authority for the top-most domain in the DNS hierarchy.

Root zone The zone authoritative for the root domain.

Route Command used to modify the local routing table.

Router A network device used to transfer data between networks. You can use a router to connect LANs, as well as connecting a LAN to a WAN or to the Internet.

Routes Entries in a routing table that define the path to a network based on its IP address.

Routing The process of selecting the path by which a source computer transfers packets of data across networks to a destination computer.

Routing and Remote Access Service (RRAS) Multiprotocol routing service that enables routing of data traffic on IP, IPX, and AppleTalk networks, as well as providing remote access capabilities. You use RRAS to connect remote clients working from remote locations to a network.

Routing Information Protocol (RIP) Enables a router to exchange routing information with other routers to update them about changes in the network topology.

Routing table Table containing information records about networks and gateways known to the local host, including the host's own network. A routing table also specifies which gateway is to be used to forward packets to specific non-local networks.

Scope A pool of IP addresses and other related configuration parameters from which a DHCP server offers leases to its clients.

Secedit Command line equivalent of the Security Configuration and Analysis tool.

Secondary DNS server/Secondary name server A name server that contains a copy of the zone database file downloaded from the primary DNS server of a zone.

Second-level domain The level of domains under the top-level domains in the DNS namespace hierarchy.

Secret key cryptography A method of hiding information in transit that involves sharing a private or secret key between the two individuals involved in a communication session. Secret key cryptography is also known as symmetric cryptography.

Secure Server (Require Security) A default IPSec policy under which a computer will accept communications only if they are IPSec-enabled. The policy can be used on servers or clients.

Security Association Defines the encryption and authentication protocols used in the session.

Security Configuration and Analysis Tool used to analyze security settings and apply security templates.

Security template Allows administrators to set a wide range of security settings on computers.

Security Template snap-in Tool used to create and modify security template files.

Server (Request Security) A default IPSec policy that is assigned to servers or clients that will be involved in communications with both Windows Server 2003 computers and computers running down-level operating systems.

Services Programs that are started when the computer boots and, in some cases, continue to run in the background.

Spoofing Forging the source IP address of packets' addresses so it will appear as if they originated from a trusted host.

Standalone CA A CA that is not integrated with Active Directory. If Active Directory does exist, it can interact with a Standalone CA.

Standard primary zone A zone that stores DNS information in a text file.

Standard secondary zone A zone that maintains a read-only copy of the zone database, which is downloaded from the primary name server.

Start of Authority (SOA) The zone record that declares a server as authoritative for the zone and includes attributes such as the zone server name, contact name, refresh interval TTL values, and more.

Static mapping entry A non-dynamic name resolution entry in a WINS database.

Static routing Refers to hosts obtaining their data packet transmission paths using a manually built routing table.

Stub zone An abridged copy of a zone whose purpose is simply to maintain name server (NS) records for the name servers that resolve requests that are made in the master zone.

Sub-domain The level of domains under the second-level domains in the DNS namespace hierarchy.

Subnet mask 32-bit value that is used to distinguish the network ID and the host ID in an IP address. The network mask (or customized subnet mask) is used to make routing decisions. It distinguishes which bits of the 32-bit IP address are network bits: the "one-bits" in the subnet mask identify which of the 32 bits are network bits, and the "zero-bits" identify the host bits.

Subnetting Breaking a large network down into smaller, more manageable pieces.

Subordinate Certification Authority A CA that receives its certificate from a parent CA. Subordinate CAs provide certificates to users/computers/services on a network.

Superscopes Used to group and manage multiple scopes from one DHCP server.

System log A component of the Events Viewer that logs system events; enables you to obtain detailed information about related events that are recorded during DHCP audit logging.

System Monitor A tool that provides real-time monitoring that can provide you with valuable insight as to how processes are progressing using the process, memory, and disk input/output on the server.

Systems Management Server Provides application deployment, asset management, and monitoring services.

Task Manager A tool that provides information regarding the processes and programs that are running on the computer. Task Manager provides a quick method for monitoring memory and processor utilization as well.

TCP/IP filtering Method used to control the type of traffic that can enter a network based on port numbers.

Time-to-Live (TTL) The period of time for which information can be considered valid before it should be discarded.

Top-level domain The level of domains under the root domain in the DNS namespace hierarchy. Examples of top-level domains are .com, .net, .org, .ca, .uk, .au, and .biz.

Trace logs A tool that is used to collect information on memory events, such as a page fault, or resource events, such as disk input/output.

Tracert Utility used to search the route taken when data is transferred between communicating devices and to discover the point at which communication has failed. It displays the Fully Qualified Domain Name and IP address of each gateway along the route to a remote host.

Transmission Control Protocol (TCP) A network protocol that provides a one-to-one, stream-oriented, and reliable delivery of data between computers.

Transmission Control Protocol/Internet Protocol (TCP/IP) Protocol suite that enables computers to communicate with each other across a network. TCP/IP is the core set of protocols used by the Internet; can be used on both large and small networks to transfer data between computers using different operating systems and widely varying hardware platforms.

Transport layer Layer in the DARPA model that is responsible for establishing a connection between communicating devices and for transferring data.

Transport Mode The default mode for IPSec that protects the data over the entire path between two computers.

Tunnel Mode Under IPSec, a mode that protects data between two endpoints (typically routers/gateways). Traffic behind the routers/gateways remains unencrypted.

Unicast A packet that is sent to a specific computer.

Unique static mapping A static mapping type used to create a static mapping entry for each IP address.

User Datagram Protocol (UDP) Protocol that provides a one-to-one or one-to-many connectionless communications service. UDP is unreliable, as it does not guarantee the delivery of data.

Variable Length Subnet Masking (VLSM) A method of changing subnetting by removing the requirement that all subnets be of equal size. VLSM allows you to break an IP address up into its largest subnets and then subnet the subnets.

Virtual Private Network (VPN) A virtual network that can provide a secure connection between a user on an external network, such as the Internet, and an internal corporate network.

Virtual Private Network (VPN) tunnel A secure tunnel between two or more devices across a public network. Encryption and authentication protocols protect the data while in transit.

Windows Internet Name Service (WINS) Microsoft's implementation of a NetBIOS name server; used to translate NetBIOS names to IP addresses in order to locate a computer on a network.

WINS client A computer on the network that has been assigned the address of a WINS server to use for NetBIOS name resolutions.

WINS database The database used by WINS to resolve NetBIOS names to IP addresses.

WINS proxy agent A WINS client that allows non-WINS clients to participate in network communications.

WINS replication The method of sharing information among WINS servers on a network.

WINS server A server program that runs WINS for the purpose of resolving NetBIOS names to IP addresses.

X.509 certificate standards Standards that define the format and contents of a digital certificate. RFC 3647 discusses this standard in detail.

Zone An administrative unit of DNS that is responsible for a portion of the DNS namespace; contains information about domains within that portion.

Zone database file The database on a DNS server that contains information about a zone.

Zone delegation The process of dividing a large single zone into smaller zones, which are responsible for managing a portion of the DNS namespace for which the original zone was responsible.

Zone of authority The part of the DNS namespace for which a zone is responsible.

Zone transfer The process of transferring changes in the zone database file from the primary DNS server to the secondary DNS server.

Index

The Prentice Hall Certification Series features a building-block approach that organizes the material into a series of skills that students master one at a time. We adopted a two-page spread featuring a highly graphical approach with hundreds of screenshots that shows students how and why Windows Server 2003/Windows 2000/Windows XP works, rather than forcing them to memorize rote software procedures.

Windows Server 2003 Core Exam Texts

Exam 70-290: Microsoft Windows Server 2003: Managing and Maintaining Text: 0-13-144743-2 Project Lab Manual: 0-13-144974-5 Interactive Solution CD-ROM: 0-13-144974-5	**Exam 70-291:** Microsoft Windows Server 2003: Network Infrastructure: Implementing, Managing and Maintaining Text: 0-13-145600-8 Project Lab Manual: 0-13-145603-2 Interactive Solution CD-ROM: 0-13-145604-0
Exam 70-293: Microsoft Windows Server 2003: Network Infrastructure: Planning and Maintaining Text: 0-13-189306-8 Project Lab Manual: 0-13-189307-6 Interactive Solution CD-ROM: 0-13-189308-4	**Exam 70-294:** Microsoft Windows Server 2003: Active Directory Infrastructure: Planning, Implementing, and Maintaining Text: 0-13-189312-2 Project Lab Manual: 0-13-189314-9 Interactive Solution CD-ROM: ISBN TBD
Exam 70-297: Designing a Microsoft Windows Server 2003 Active Directory and Network Infrastructure Text: 0-13-189316-5 Project Lab Manual: 0-13-189320-3 Interactive Solution CD-ROM: ISBN TBD	**Exam 70-298:** Designing Security for a Microsoft Windows Server 2003 Network Text: 0-13-117670-6 Project Lab Manual: 0-13-146684-4 Interactive Solution CD-ROM: ISBN TBD

Value Pack Options Available

Series Features

The ONLY academic series developed by instructors for instructors that correlates to the MCSE and MCSA exam objectives.

4-color, 2-page layout
- Improves student retention through clear, easy-to-follow, step-by-step instructions.

Skills-Based Systematic Approach
- Uses integrated components: Main text, Project Lab Manual, Interactive Solution CD-ROM, and Web site with online quizzes.

Hands-on projects and problem-solving projects at the end of each lesson
- Help students better understand the material being taught.

Learning Aids
- Include Test Your Skills, On Your Own Projects, and Problem-Solving Cases at the end of each lesson.

Instructor's Resource CD
- PowerPoint slides containing all text graphics and lecture bullet points.
- Instructor's Manual that includes sample syllabus, teaching objectives, answers to exercises, and review questions.
- Test Bank with 40+ questions per lesson based on the text. Not generic MCSE questions.

Windows Server 2003 Enterprise 180 day evaluation software included in every text.

Project Lab Manuals

The Project Lab Manuals are designed as an additional tool that allow students to implement the concepts and practice the skills they have read about in the textbooks and CD-ROMs. With more hands-on projects and concept review, the Project Lab Manuals enable students to learn more about Windows 2003/2000/XP in real-world settings, practice the skills needed to prepare for the MCSE/MCSA exams, and prepare for a career as a network administrator.

The Project Lab Manual features:
- An overview of the task to be completed tied directly to the MCSA/MCSE Exam Objectives.
- 4-6 projects per lesson directly associated with the MCSA/MCSA Exam Objectives.
- Specific hardware requirements necessary to complete each lab.
- Step-by-step, hands-on instruction—it's like having an MCSE right by your side.
- Tips and Cautions elements designed to ease the learning process.
- Suggested completion times for each lab.

Interactive Solutions CD-ROMs

The Interactive Solutions CD-ROM was designed to directly support the Prentice Hall Certification Series texts by giving students a number of ways to enhance their studies.

The Interactive Solutions CD-ROM provides a simulated Windows 2003/2000/XP environment where students can learn and practice their skills without actually installing Windows 2003/2000/XP.

The learning modules are organized according to Microsoft knowledge domains and objectives. Conceptual overview sessions provide concise, animated descriptions of key networking concepts. Three types of interactive sessions (Play, Practice, and Assessment) provide students with hands-on experience with Windows Server 2003 and a realistic, challenging assessment environment.

Prentice Hall Certification Series for Windows 2000/Windows XP

Exam 70-210: Microsoft Windows 2000 Professional: Installing, Configuring, and Administering; Text: 0-13-142209-X; Lab Manual: 0-13-142257-X; Interactive Solutions CD-ROM: 0-13-142260-X

Exam 70-215: Microsoft Windows 2000 Server: Installing, Configuring, and Administering; Text: 0-13-142211-1; Lab Manual: 0-13-142281-2; Interactive Solutions CD-ROM: 0-13-142284-7

Exam 70-216: Microsoft Windows 2000 Network Infrastructure: Implementing and Administering; Text: 0-13-142210-3; Lab Manual: 0-13-142278-2; Interactive Solutions CD-ROM: 0-13-142277-4

Exam 70-217: Microsoft Windows 2000 Active Directory: Implementing and Administering; Text: 0-13-142208-1; Lab Manual: 0-13-142252-9; Interactive Solutions CD-ROM: 0-13-142254-5

Exam 70-218: Managing Microsoft Windows 2000 Network Environment; Text: 0-13-144744-0; Lab Manual: 0-13-144813-7; Interactive Solutions CD-ROM: 0-13-144812-9

Exam 70-270: Microsoft Windows XP Professional; Text: 0-13-144132-9; Lab Manual: 0-13-144450-6; Interactive Solutions CD-ROM: 0-13-144449-2

Test with Pearson VUE and Save 50%!

Get Certified Through the Microsoft Authorized Academic Testing Center (AATC) Program:

You invested in your future with the purchase of this textbook from Prentice Hall. Now, take the opportunity to get the recognition your skills deserve. Certification increases your credibility in the marketplace and is tangible evidence that you have what it takes to provide top-notch support to your employer.

Save 50% On Microsoft Exams!

Take advantage of this money-saving offer now. The cost of taking the exam is $60.00 with this offer.

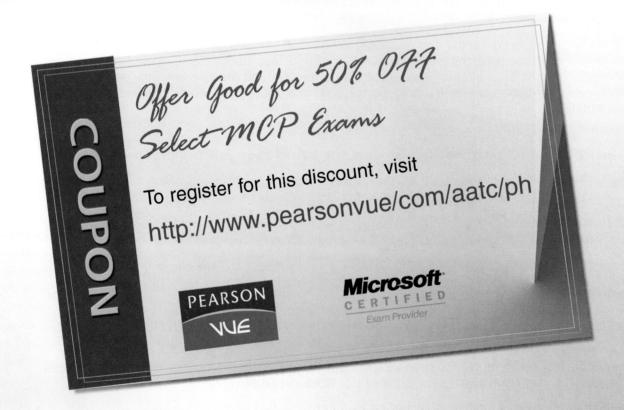

Offer Good for 50% Off Select MCP Exams

To register for this discount, visit
http://www.pearsonvue/com/aatc/ph

PEARSON VUE

Microsoft CERTIFIED
Exam Provider

COUPON

Select Microsoft exams, including the full suite of MCSA exams, are available at the discounted price to students and instructors who attend, or are employed by, academic institutions. Students and instructors can take advantage of this offer via the URL below.

MCSA on Microsoft Windows Server 2003 Certification Requirements for Students

Core Exams: Networking System (2 Exams Required)

72-290 Managing and Maintaining a Microsoft Windows Server 2003 Environment

72-291 Implementing, Managing, and Maintaining a Microsoft Windows Server 2003 Network Infrastructure

Core Exams: Client Operating System (1 Exam Required)

72-270 Installing, Configuring, and Administering Microsoft Windows XP Professional

72-210 Installing, Configuring, and Administering Microsoft Windows 2000 Professional

Elective Exams (1 Exam Required)

72-086 Implementing and Supporting Microsoft Systems Management Server 2.0

72-227 Installing, Configuring, and Administering Microsoft Internet Security and Acceleration (ISA) Server 2000, Enterprise Edition

72-228 Installing, Configuring, and Administering Microsoft SQL Server™ 2000 Enterprise Edition

72-284 Implementing and Managing Microsoft Exchange Server 2003

72-299 Implementing and Administering Security in a Microsoft Windows Server 2003 Network

Upgrade Exam for an MCSA on Windows 2000

An MCSA on Windows 2000 has the option to take Exam 70-292 instead of the two core network exams. No additional core or elective exams are required for an MCSA on Windows 2000 who passes Exam 70-292.

Upgrade Exam for an MCSA on Windows 2000 (1 Exam Required)

72-292 Managing and Maintaining a Microsoft Windows Server 2003 Environment for an MCSA Certified on Windows 2000

Offer also good on selected Windows 2000 exams.

For more information on Prentice Hall textbooks for MCSA and MCAD, visit www.prenhall.com/certification

Take advantage of this great offer! Go to www.pearsonvue.com/aatc/ph for complete details and to schedule a discounted exam at an AATC near you!